CRITICAL DIALOGUES IN SOUTHEAST ASIAN STUDIES

Charles Keyes, Vicente Rafael, and Laurie J. Sears, Series Editors

IMPERIAL BANDITS

OUTLAWS and REBELS in the CHINA-VIETNAM BORDERLANDS

Bradley Camp Davis

UNIVERSITY OF WASHINGTON PRESS
Seattle and London

Imperial Bandits is published with the assistance of a grant from the Charles and Jane Keyes Endowment for Books on Southeast Asia, established through the generosity of Charles and Jane Keyes.

This book was also supported by grants from the Association for Asian Studies First Book Subvention Program, and from the Office of the Provost and the Office for Equity and Diversity at Eastern Connecticut State University.

20 19 18 17 16 5 4 3 2 1

UNIVERSITY OF WASHINGTON PRESS
www.washington.edu/uwpress

LIBRARY OF CONGRESS CATALOGING-IN-PUBLICATION DATA
Names: Davis, Bradley Camp, author.
Title: Imperial bandits : outlaws and rebels in the China-Vietnam borderlands / Bradley Camp Davis.
Description: Seattle : University of Washington Press, [2017] | Series: Critical dialogues in Southeast Asian studies | Includes bibliographical references and index.
Identifiers: LCCN 2016011446 | ISBN 9780295742045 (hardcover) ISBN 9780295742052 (paperback)
Subjects: LCSH: Brigands and robbers—China—History—19th century. | Brigands and robbers—Vietnam—History—19th century. | Borderlands—China—History—19th century. | Borderlands—Vietnam—History—19th century. | Violence—Social aspects—China—History—19th century. | Violence—Social aspects—Vietnam—History—19th century.
Classification: LCC HV6453.C6 D39 2017 | DDC 364.109512/809034—dc23
LC record available at http://lccn.loc.gov/2016011446

The paper used in this publication is acid-free and meets the minimum requirements of American National Standard for Information Sciences—Permanence of Paper for Printed Library Materials, ANSI Z39.48–1984. ∞

Some elements of chapter 3 appeared in:

"Consular Optics: Rebels, Factions, and Commercial Interests in the China-Vietnam Borderlands, 1874–1879." *Cross-Currents: East Asian History and Culture Review* 11 (June 2014). https://cross-currents.berkeley.edu/e-journal/issue-11.

Some elements of chapter 4 appeared in:

"Black Flag Rumors and the Black River Basin: Powerbrokers and the State in the Tonkin-China Borderlands." *Journal of Vietnamese Studies* 6, no. 2 (June 2011): 16–41.

and

"Volatile Allies: Two Cases of Powerbrokers in the Vietnamese-Chinese Borderlands." In *China's Encounters on the South and Southwest: Reforging the Fiery Frontier Over Two Millennia*, edited by John Whitmore and James Anderson, 322–38. Leiden: Brill, 2014.

To Sam, Henry, and Alice
(Faster miles an hour)

CONTENTS

ACKNOWLEDGMENTS

THIS book resulted from a long period of research, reflection, writing, teaching, and revision. While I am grateful to the people and institutions named here, I should first thank my friends and family for their patience, support, and understanding.

Guidance and instruction from Kent Guy prepared me for extensive archival and textual research in Chinese sources, and his humane patience and sense of justice continue to inspire me. Christoph Giebel's enthusiasm for this borderlands project sustained me during the writing of the book. Without conversations with Laurie Sears, I would never have appreciated the importance of Jan Vansina's work on oral tradition, which forms a key part of this book. I also benefitted from conversations with Ray Jonas as he was finishing a project on Rimbaud in Africa, in which we noted amusing parallels between our two gun-dealers, although I doubt that Dupuis left a secret stash of angst-ridden poetry.

Thanks to support from the Fulbright-Hays Program, the Blakemore Foundation, and the Rondeau-Evans Fund, I was able to carry out research and language study in China, Vietnam, and France from 2004 to 2006. I would also like to thank the Ford Foundation for funding the Yao Script Project in Vietnam from 2007 to 2008, which afforded me chances, between administrative responsibilities, for further research.

In the People's Republic of China, the Southeast Asia Studies Office of the Guangxi Social Science Academy sponsored my research visa. Their assistance and wisdom was crucial to my archival and ethnographic research. Gu Xiaosong, who was head of the office, and Fan Honggui at the Minzu Xueyuan, who encouraged me to travel around Guangxi and Yunnan as widely as possible, advocated for my project, helped me with introduction letters for archives, and shared their vast knowledge in the spirit of intellectual comradeship. Above all, I thank Zhou Zhongjian, a retired historian of Cambodia who was my guide and walking companion in Nanning and introduced me to his extended Zhuang family in the village of Dashan.

In Vietnam, my work would have been impossible without the support of the Institute for Vietnamese Studies. Nguyễn Quang Ngọc, Đỗ Kiên, and the rest of the institute staff helped me navigate the bureaucratic requirements for ethnographic and archival work. Like so many others before me, I was honored to meet and receive the assistance of Phan Huy Lê, who later invited me to give a talk at the institute's anniversary celebration in Hanoi. The staffs at the Hán Nôm Institute, the Social Science Library in Hanoi, the National Library, and the First National Archives as well as the provincal libraries and museums in Thái Nguyên, Lào Cai, and Sơn La were helpful and professional. Trần Hữu Sơn, formerly the head of the Office of Culture and Information in Lào Cai and since my colleague in the Yao Script Project, generously shared his expertise in the Vietnamese uplands and aided me with finding avenues for fieldwork.

I reserve special thanks for the Hanoi office of the École française d'Extrême-Orient. Philippe Papin, Andrew Hardy, and Oliver Tessier welcomed me into their office as a colleague. With Philippe Le Failler, I found an intellectual companion who exemplifies the ideals of scholarly collaboration, sharing information and resources with like-minded researchers and constantly questioning the work we all do. Professor Papin and Professor Hardy share this trait, inviting me to present my work and participate in *séminaires* both in Paris and in Vietnam.

Whether at conferences, in workshops, or after some persuasion, many people have offered comments on earlier versions of this work. Talks at Yale, Harvard, Hong Kong University, Vietnam National University, Berkeley, and the University of Washington pushed my writing in new directions. Few have read my work as rigorously and attentively as Professor Hue-Tam Ho Tai; I owe her a debt of gratitude for years of comments and discussion, both in workshops and at her home in Cambridge. Erik Harms, David Biggs, Adriane Lentz-Smith, Christian Lentz, Duy Lap Nguyen, Chris Goscha, and Gerard Sasges have all offered candid and helpful comments on earlier versions of this work, as have Alexander Woodside, James Anderson, John Whitmore, Peter Zinoman, Peter Perdue, Charles Wheeler, Kate Baldanza, and Jeff Wasserstrom.

At the University of Washington Press, Lorri Hagman has maintained an interest in this project through delays and revisions. She has been an exemplary and understanding editor. Two anonymous reviewers provided insightful feedback that has helped me turn the original manuscript into a book. Of course, any shortcomings, errors, or blemishes are my own.

I would also like to thank those who financially supported the publication of this book. I was honored to receive an award from the Association for Asian

Studies. The Office of Equity and Diversity and the the Office of the Provost at Eastern Connecticut State University generously provided funds for the index.

Finally, I want to express my appreciation for my family. My parents, children, and my partner have been a source of support and, more importantly, confidence over the last few years. I could do very little without them, and I can only hope to do more for them.

NOTE ON LANGUAGE

THE material for this book includes sources in classical Chinese, contemporary Chinese, Vietnamese, and French. Where appropriate, I have included other languages throughout the text. When not clear from the context, linguistic origins for Chinese (C) and Vietnamese (V) terms are indicated. Chinese pronunciations are in standard Chinese (Mandarin) unless otherwise indicated. The glossaries and bibliography contain more complete information. For Chinese bibliographic sources I have used pinyin romanization. For the sake of accuracy, both traditional and simplified forms of written Chinese appear in the bibliography, which includes sources published before and after the advent of simplified written Chinese in the People's Republic of China.

IMPERIAL BANDITS

INTRODUCTION

Imperial Bandits, Cultures of Violence, and Oral Traditions

WE sat in a dirt-floor home at the end of a mountain road, drinking tea from small cups. As the late-morning sun rose above the green hilltops that overlooked the red-earth road, I asked our host, a Yao priest, if he had ever heard stories about the Black Flag Army. "Yes," he began, "I've heard my grandparents talk about the Black Flags, the Yellow Flags too."

> Earlier, these bandits came down to Vietnam from China, some on horseback and some on foot. They crossed the Red River into Lào Cai. I don't remember which year, but at some point the Black and Yellow Flags began abducting our people, taking our property [V: *cái của*] and our crops for themselves. People were so frightened that they ran deeper into the woods. No one dared resist out of fear that the entire community would be killed.
>
> I have heard several Yao elders tell it like this—when the bandit armies came, they wore uniforms and carried spears and swords. People had no idea who these people were, at least not at first. They appeared at the village and everyone scattered. Then came a loud blast, like a landmine; that was the signal for the raid to begin. After they took animals and rice, they took people, first the able-bodied men, then the women. They left the sick and the young.[1]

He paused and refilled our cups. "Those who could not escape had to work. The bandit leader would stand at the edge of the forest, shouting: 'Out of the woods! Everyone to work!' They forced people to work for them."

In his eightieth year, our host was the oldest person in the village, one of several Yao communities in Vietnam's Lào Cai Province, near the border with

Yunnan in China. As a small crowd gathered outside, he recounted stories of raids, abandoned settlements, pillage, rape, murder, and sexual slavery. The woods became a place of refuge for Yao people fleeing bandits. In this twenty-first-century retelling, the bandits, the Black and Yellow Flags, targeted property and people, threatening the prosperity and the very existence of the Yao community. The raids had a pattern: a blast signaled the arrival of the bandits, after which residents would hide, flee, or surrender their possessions (or themselves). The bandits took young men and women from the community, contributing to a demographic shift throughout China's and Vietnam's mountainous borderlands in the nineteenth century. The 1860s was a time of tremendous change in the uplands, a change we can glimpse in these stories.

Many of them come from the oral traditions of Yao communities. The term *Yao* likely once referred to exemption from corvée, the Chinese government's tax-in-labor instituted since at least the Tang dynasty (618–907).[2] *Yao* was used to describe populations known elsewhere as *Mien*, becoming an official ethnonym in China during the twentieth century.[3] In Vietnam, its Sino-Vietnamese equivalent, *Dao*, replaced the more derisive *Man* ("savage") as a referent for Mien speakers in the late 1970s.[4] While Mien speakers in Vietnam tend to refer to themselves as either *Mien* or *Mun*, they often use the term *Yao* for self-reference when conversing with people from outside their community. Interplay of ethnic terminology happens during conversations that mix Mien with the language of political power, which, in the mountainous area around Lào Cai, remains Vietnamese.

In the second half of the nineteenth century, uplands populations such as the Yao and the Hmong suffered the most from armed groups such as the Black Flags. Originally part of a regional rebellion in southern China, the Black Flags began operating in the mountains of northern Vietnam in the late 1860s. Led by their founder, Liu Yongfu, the Black Flags fought for territory and trade, engaging in a decades-long war against their rivals, the Yellow Flags. Between these two groups, borderlands communities of Yao, Hmong, Tai-speakers, and Vietnamese settlers endured raids, mass killings, assasinations, and kidnappings. For the imperial authorities of Vietnam and China, and for the French colonial regime after the 1880s, these armed mobile groups both aided and inhibited the establishment of sovereign political authority. They were imperial bandits who helped shape a culture of violence in the borderlands.

Elsewhere, in another mountainous district of northern Vietnam, an elder from a Tày community recounted the stories passed down by her family about the Black Flags.

> They [the Black Flags] came down from China. People here in Vietnam also called them *giặc Ngô*. The Black Flags beat the men and raped the women. After that, they would take the children and roast them over a spit. It was awful. They had this huge gun, an infantry rifle [*ống lính*]. It frightened everyone. When they arrived, all the rice was used to cook for them, along with the pigs and chickens. Throughout the village, people abandoned their homes [*bỏ nhà*] and fled to the forest to camp out. Life was hard there; people ran out of rice and resorted to eating roots and grass.

Fleeing homes and abandoning settlements for refuge at even higher elevations was a common tactic for evading these raids. When our Tày host described the Black Flags as "Ngô bandits" (*giặc Ngô*), she was referencing Wu Cong and Wu Yazhong, the father-son pair who led the southern Chinese bandit kingdom from which the Black and Yellow Flags were formed in the 1860s.[5] While *Ngô* is the Vietnamese pronunciation of the Chinese name Wu, the same term also refers more generally to China.

In the 1420s, Nguyễn Trãi's "Proclamation of Victory over the Ngô" announced the Lê dynasty's defeat of China's Ming dynasty (1368–1644), which had occupied Vietnam for two decades.[6] Stories of the Ngô from the nineteenth century remind us of the multiple meanings of words across times and settings, while also suggesting the deeper sense, within borderlands spaces, of unwelcome forces coming from the north.

Often grouped with the Nùng in contemporary ethnolinguistic terms, Tày communities speak a Tai language. While most Tai speakers in southern China are known as Zhuang, a term standardized during the 1950s, two Tai groups live in Vietnam. In the northwest, Thái communities have historical connections to *muăng* or "polities" that represent a certain arrangement of political and economic obligations. In the northeast, other communities of Tai speakers, such as the Tày, the Nùng, and Giáy (or Giấy) have longer histories of interaction with Chinese and Vietnamese imperial authorities, with many lineages traceable to uprisings from the ninth century.[7] Communities from each of these Tai groups related to imperial bandits in different ways, with the violence of raids echoing into the twenty-first century through their oral traditions.

Historically, speakers of Tày and Nùng, in the imperial Vietnamese gaze, were Thổ (C: Tu). A term that denoted indigeneity (literally, "dirt" or "soil"), Thổ conveyed a sense of coming directly from the earth. Particularly during the nineteenth century, most Thổ communities, including the Tày and Nùng but also the Giấy, practiced sedentary agriculture to a much greater extent than their neighbors. In the northeast, the relative affluence of Tai communities made them targets for raids; in one village, Tày elders recalled that the Black Flags and their rivals "wiped out the Kinh [Việt] for salt, wiped out the Thổ [Tày] for land." This statement illustrates the divisions between communities in the borderlands, divisions that sometimes fell along vertical lines and, at other times, reflected relations of production, whether to commerce or to agriculture.

These divisions were also political. When an elder member of a Tày community recounts stories about Thổ and Kinh communities or when a Yao priest explains tales of raids in the mountains, each of these storytellers uses an ethnic framework tied to contemporary Vietnam. During the mid-ninteenth century, raiding "the Kinh for salt" meant the Black Flags targeted communities that, in contemporary Vietnamese terms, would have been understood as ethnically Vietnamese. As in China, salt, both in terms of its extraction and its trade, was subject to an imperial monopoly in Vietnam. During the ninteenth century, only licensed merchants could deal salt, and these merchants, in mountainous areas of the northwest and northeast, tended to be Vietnamese.

At present, both China and Vietnam are countries with many officially defined ethnicities or nationalities (C: *minzu*; V: *dân tộc*). Although the majority populations in China and Vietnam are, respectively, ethnic Chinese (usually Han) and ethnic Vietnamese (Việt or Kinh), both countries each have over fifty other officially identified ethnic groups.[8] In different historical contexts, the connections between Vietnamese, Chinese, Yao, Tai, and other borderlands communities challenge the concept of a hierarchical political culture grounded in the putative centrality of Chinese civilization.

During the nineteenth century, few Kinh residents lived near the uplands areas populated by speakers of Tai, Yao, and Hmong languages. In the 1830s, the Vietnamese imperial authorities tried to change this by incentivizing settlements in uplands areas, encouraging many Kinh subjects into the mountains with tax breaks and promises of new lands to farm.[9] In the northwestern corner of the country, one Vietnamese official, Ngụy Khắc Tuấn, imposed strict demands on these new settlers, ordering them to register with the imperial administration.[10] At the same time, he pushed for further migration into the areas of Lai Châu, Điện Biên, and Tuần Giáo, all areas traditionally dominated by Tai-speaking communities. From the perspective of the Vietnamese authorities, a larger Kinh population would effectively increase the fiscal reach of the imperial state.[11]

During the twentieth century, a similar yet more intensive series of official efforts pushed Kinh people to uplands regions, particularly in northern Vietnam.[12] Many of these people settled in Lào Cai Province, where the Black Flags once conducted raids. Some, such as an older resident of Lào Cai whose family came from Nam Định, a city south of Hanoi in the Red River Delta, carried stories of the Black Flags with them.

> The Black Flag Army [*quân*]? My family is from Nam Định, so I say "the Black Flag bandits" [*giặc*]. My home village [*quê*] is still in Nam Định.
>
> When the Black Flag bandits came to the village, they beheaded many, many people, so the Kinh people fled, including three brothers from the Trần family. I don't know why, but they decided to run to Lào Cai and split the family into three: Trần, Lương, and Hà. After hiding in the woods for months and nearly starving, they learned how to live on wild game [*thú rừng*]. In Nam Định, no one remembers this. Maybe it's in the family records somewhere? I don't know.

A major population center for Vietnamese Catholics, Nam Định, even in the ninteenth century, was a short trip from Hanoi but a much longer trip from Lào Cai. When people fled Nam Định in the 1880s, they sought refuge in the mountains to hide from the Black Flags. During the Sino-French War (1883–85), an event discussed extensively in chapter 4, the Black Flags fought for imperial Vietnam, which, together with the Qing Empire, resisted French control of northern and central Vietnam. In Nam Định, a city under French occupation, Black Flag soldiers, assuming the Vietnamese Catholic community to be secret allies of France, kidnapped and decapitated a young missionary, collecting a bounty of thirty silver bars from imperial officials.[13]

Yao, Tày, and Kinh stories form the larger story of imperial bandits and the culture of violence in the borderlands between China and Vietnam. This book tells that larger story, which begins in the mountains of southern China, continues in the uplands spaces of the borderlands and northern Vietnam, endures French colonial rule, and echoes in the oral traditions of borderlands communities. Along the way, the story of imperial bandits raises larger questions about the relationship between bandits and officials as agents of power, cultures of violence in borderlands spaces, and the role of oral traditions in historical research.

A rebellion and the deluge of armed groups that followed its collapse sent the first wave of imperial bandits into Vietnam from China during the 1860s. Tracing this flood of bandits to its source connects uplands rebellions, opium, mining, and overlapping Tai, Vietnamese, and Chinese cosmologies of power to the history of the borderlands. Two bandit groups, the Black Flag Army and the Yellow Flag Army, appear against the larger historical setting of the borderlands, their presence inciting official debates over statecraft in China and Vietnam and the violence of their actions lingering in the oral traditions of the mountains. While historical scholarship has tended to view the Black and

Yellow Flags in terms of the continuum between bandit and rebel, their shared history gives us space to reflect on the relationship of banditry to authority and on the ubiquity of violence as an element of power, both official and nonofficial, in the China-Vietnam borderlands.

The story of imperial bandits intersects with the beginnings of French colonial rule in northern Vietnam. Although later arranged into the French protectorates of Tonkin and Annam, northern and central Vietnam remained under Vietnamese imperial authority following the recognition of Cochinchina and other southern areas as zones of French control in the 1860s. While the arrival of a gun dealer named Jean Dupuis brings the Black and Yellow Flags into the backstory of French Indochina, we might also view the 1870s—the final decade of autonomous imperial Vietnam before the protectorates in Annam and Tonkin—from the perspective of imperial bandits and mountainous borderlands communities. Francis Garnier's invasion of the Red River Delta from Hanoi, which followed Dupuis' arrest, becomes not only an act of aggression against Nguyễn Vietnam, but also a threat to the Black Flags. Viewed from the periphery, the 1874 establishment of French consulates, which supported the gathering of information about conditions in the mountains and borderlands and played a pivotal role in shaping French understandings of uplands space, is more than a step toward French Indochina. The consulates, and the consular optic, appear as a source for the redemptive role of French rule in Vietnam, amplifying factions within the Vietnamese bureaucracy and tying colonial *mise en valeur* to the issue of imperial bandits.

Despite its name, the Sino-French War did not concern only the Qing Empire and the French Third Republic; it can also be seen as a borderlands conflict in which imperial bandits were transformed into colonial adversaries and allies. This view encompasses the large, conceptual stakes of the war, such as the end of the tributary system, as well as the range of experiences that the violence of war brings to the human condition. Rather than a radical break with the imperial past, the Sino-French War was an intensification of the personal networks, patterns of power and resistance, and debates over statecraft that all flow from the bandit flood of the mid-nineteenth century.

Just as the Sino-French War was not merely a break with the past, the establishment of French colonial rule does not represent a radical rupture in the history of the borderlands between China and Vietnam. The French colonial project largely continued to claim, or attempted to claim, a monopoly on violence through the modalities of power established during the final decades of autonomous imperial Vietnam. Imperial bandits played as much of an official role during French colonial rule as they did during imperial Vietnam, although the cast of characters is often reversed. In terms of cross-borderlands relations with China, elements of the French colonial project—whether the borderline, the telegraph, or the militia-based counterinsurgency—took on a twinned existence. They divided the officialdom in China and Vietnam into cooperative and hostile camps, usually characterized by attitudes toward French rule. However, these elements of colonial rule, particularly the borderline and the telegraph, also became tools in the service of the borderlands culture of violence. As the French colonial period began, imperial bandits transformed again, either into colonial officials or into anticolonial nationalists.

IMPERIAL BANDITS

> BANDE/BAND (of outlaws, rebels, or civil criminals). —This is the very example of an axiomatic language.
>
> —ROLAND BARTHES, *THE EIFFEL TOWER AND OTHER MYTHOLOGIES*

Bandits remind us that the terms of power are never completely settled. Particularly in borderlands spaces, bandits represent both the presence of formal authority and the trenchant anxieties of political projects. For communities in areas far from centers of political power, bandits (or, abstractly, *banditry*) signify naked force. Calling someone or some group a bandit lays bare a political language that otherwise dresses violence in the drag of civilization. Imperial bandits illustrate the role of force in formal political authority, even as the language of power, whether Vietnamese imperial, Chinese imperial, or French colonial, depends upon a claim to eradicate or curtail violence. They connect the exclusionary logic of imperial projects to cultures of violence. In the borderlands of China and Vietnam, *imperial* bandits played an essential role in political projects of empire. Bandits, in this sense, do not indicate a lack of *proper* authority; they help constitute proper authority itself.

Historians have connected banditry to weak states, postulating an inverse relationship between state authority and bandit power. Writing on the Mediterranean in the sixteenth century, Fernand Braudel remarked that the presence of bandits, who "lurked" in mountains and "frontier zones," meant a weakness of state authority.[14] Anton Blok echoed this theme in his study of the eighteenth-century "Dutch Frontier," claiming that banditry, "the easiest form of rebellion," flourished in "mountainous frontier zones where central authority is weak."[15] In the China-Vietnam borderlands during the nineteenth century, an understanding of bandits as an index of state weakness reflected the steady anxieties of imperial power, whether Vietnamese, Chinese, or French colonial.

However, the identification of bandits with imperial weakness sets, at best, a problematic tone for historical analysis, one that risks passive acceptance of official preoccupations. Other historians have connected bandits to dislocations wrought by social and economic change. Banditry becomes, for these historians, a very real, at times political, expression of frustration with the status quo. Perhaps the most well-known work of this sort comes from British historian Eric Hobsbawm, who connected the appearance of "social bandits" to agrarian economic change, arguing that certain bandits represented the interests of communities against predatory political states.[16] An early title for his iconic monograph on social bandits, *Primitive Rebels*, hinted at the evolutionary logic that supported his statements. For Hobsbawm, bandits existed as a discrete stage tethered to a particular set of socioeconomic relations. They were "primitive" rebels precisely because, from his Marxian perspective, bandits lacked the mature sensibilities of social revolutionaries, despite the resonance of romantic accounts (*Räuberromantik*) in oral traditions. Hobsbawm's work directly influenced the later writing of Jean Chesneaux, who attributed to the Black Flags a sense of "protonationalism."[17]

Still other historians view bandits not as administrative problems, infantile revolutionaries, or protonationalists, but as self-interested participants in political systems. For instance, in her study of the Ottoman Empire, Karen Barkey argued that the expansion of imperial authority depended on the transformation of bandits into bureaucrats.[18] Writing on Sicily, Anton Blok observed that administrative reforms designed to centralize or routinize state power often become a means for "local strongmen" to enhance their control over territory, people, and resources.[19] Whereas Barkey identified a transformation of bandits into bureaucrats, Blok found strongmen becoming powerbrokers, bridging and profiting from the distance between political authority and local community.

Specifically concerning China and Southeast Asia, historians have remarked on the close relationship between political power and bandits during the nineteenth century. Following the suppression of the Taiping Rebellion (1850–64), Qing imperial authorities often authorized surrendered rebels to take positions as militia leaders, rendering the distinction between outlaw and official a simple matter of sponsorship.[20] In another context, the Mataram Sultanate (1587–1755), in present day Java, bestowed the title of *petinggi* ("exalted person") on bandits too powerful to suppress. These royal employees found themselves "burdened with the duty to govern," a fact that nonetheless recognized their power and influence.[21] In this study of imperial bandits, we will see empires, whether Qing, Vietnamese, or French, attempt to buttress formal authority with powerful bandit allies.

However inclusive of bandits an imperial state might be, the claim to govern rests upon exclusion. Bandits are reminders of the terms of official power. They underscore the deep relationship between sovereign authority and exclusion. The word itself, as Giorgio Agamben has noted, tells us this. *Ban* is etymologically related to a Germanic term that meant "both exclusion from the community and the power of the sovereign," to "the fundamental structure of the law."[22]

Bandit does not represent the opposite of official, nor does it simply signify outlaw status. Bandits exist as fundamental aspects of imperial power. The appearance of bandits in the administrative paperwork of political states, or in the oral traditions of communities in the mountains, can be read as an index of the law itself, whether imperial, colonial, or, in the case of oral traditions, the everyday defense of community. However, as we will see in the case of the Black Flags, the very extension of imperial sovereignty depended not only on exclusion, but the often reluctant employment of the excluded in defense of empire.

As for the terminology of banditry, the various documentary sources and oral traditions that form the evidentiary basis of this book all deal with bandits in different ways. Bandit entered the English language from Italian sometime in the sixteenth century as a rendering of *bandito*, a word related to the verb *bandire*, meaning "to exile" or "to ban."[23] While French observers tended to use the terms *pirates, bandes* or, more infrequently, *brigands* for groups like the Black Flags (known in French as *Les Pavillons Noirs* or *Les Drapeaux Noirs*), terminology in other languages points to similar concerns about setting the line between the banishers and the banished.

Sources in classical Chinese—the common administrative language of China and Vietnam—as well as Tai, Yao, and Vietnamese oral traditions have very different vocabularies for talking about bandits. However, we can see a certain commensurability. For instance, reports filed by Qing and Vietnamese imperial officials describe bandits, as we might understand the term, as *fei* (V: *phỉ*). Historically, this character has meant many things.[24] However, only in administrative paperwork since the eighteenth century has it meant "bandit," a group or person acting beyond imperial law.

The precise meaning of *fei* is slippery and elusive. Other words are less ambiguous; *zei* (V: *giặc*) originally referred only to thieves, taking on the meaning of "bandit" in the *Rites of Zhou* (Zhouli).[25] While the classical Chinese term for "rebel" (C: *ni*; V: *nghịch*) is largely absent, mentions of *fei* or *phỉ* populate the official record: in the *Veritable Records* (C: Shilu; V: Thực Lục) or official histories compiled during both the Qing and Nguyễn eras as well as within the streams of paperwork that passed between officials and their respective courts, there are hundreds upon thousands of references to *fei* or *phỉ*, described as "local bandits" (C: *tufei*; V: *thổ phỉ*), "Miao bandits," "Yao bandits," and, in the case of imperial Vietnam, bandits from the Qing Empire.

Across multiple contexts, bandits reflect the traces of enforcement and contain the seeds of rebellion. As the line between bandit and official shifts, it reminds us that the formalities of power are constantly being rearranged, even long after the bandits in question have disappeared.

CULTURES OF VIOLENCE

In the nineteenth-century mountainous borderlands between China and Vietnam, power often meant violence. In the coming pages, we will see decapitation, dismemberment, displacement, murder, mutilation, rape, and resistance. Neither a transgression of the law nor an exceptional occurrence, violence connected sovereign power with imperial subjects. During raids, invasion, pillage, acts of murder, and a war with France, a culture of violence in the borderlands structured imperial authority, French colonialism, anticolonial revolt, and even early twentieth-century nationalism in China and Vietnam.

Rather than displacing violence, political power, bandit power, and communal resistance depended on violence. Holders of political power might explain their ends with the language of Confucian philosophy, administrative reform, or French civilization, but they shared a common reliance on brute force.

This study does not suppose that political formations, be they states, empires, or colonial protectorate regimes, eliminate violence. Historians have tended to view violence either as a problem to be solved or as an element of the human experience that endures regardless of social and institutional solutions.[26] Reducing violent phenomena, which are expressions or transgressions of power, to mere instruments fails to convey other dimensions of violence in historical contexts. In the early twentieth century, Walter Benjamin connected a sense of political order with a need to monopolize violence, stressing that uncontrolled violence threatens the law "not by the ends that it may pursue but by its mere existence outside the law."[27]

"Every state," said Leon Trotsky, "is founded on force."[28] If we may think of force as violence, then the claim to monopolize the legitimate use of violence, or the ability to sanction violence, becomes the defining characteristic of modern political projects. As Max Weber noted, the only legitimate use of force (violence) in the "modern state" receives either the explicit endorsement or the passive permission of formal authorities.[29] Beyond the state's control, beyond imperial control, violence threatens not just the political order, but order itself.[30]

Benjamin's "Critique of Violence" was aimed at the notion that societies solve the problem of violence. Weber's analysis investigated the presence of force (violence) in "modern states," elucidating the ways in which states control and deploy force or, at least, its legitimation. Both of these notions directly relate to the imperial bandits in this story—we will see the Black Flags and Yellow Flags thriving and enduring in the spaces between political power and community resistance, becoming sanctioned agents of imperial and colonial power, predatory entrepreneurs in violence, or aspirational figures of rebellion, often at the same time. However, the prevalence of this type of violence also suggests that the imperial regimes of China and Vietnam, during the nineteenth century, as well as French colonial regime, were modern political states.

VIOLENCE AND MODERN IMPERIA: CHINA, VIETNAM, FRANCE

Rather than a social aberration or a political problem, violence was a fundamental and ubiquitous feature of life in the China-Vietnam borderlands, one that set the modern terms of sovereign authority from the nineteenth and into the twentieth centuries. The Qing Empire (1644–1911), Nguyễn Vietnam (1802–1945), and the French Third Republic (1870–1940) each relied on violence to pursue imperial projects. Violence in the service of imperial power, sometimes mundane and other times grotesque, was nothing new; in East Asia, Southeast Asia, and elsewhere, empires since at least the third century BCE used war, conquest, mass killings, and disfigurement to establish, demonstrate, and protect sovereignty over subjects and land. By the nineteenth century, however, imperial violence increasingly became an element of rationalizing political projects.

In the Qing Empire and in Nguyễn Vietnam, separate yet related efforts to transform local rule by intensifying the reach of the imperial state took place in the eighteenth century (China) and the early ninteenth century (Vietnam). As James Scott has argued for twentieth-century political projects, both in Southeast Asia and elsewhere, beneath the dependable failure of ambitious attempts to alter the human condition, we find everyday forms of resistance, at times hidden from plain view.[31] For imperial China and Vietnam, below the surface of rhetoric, projects that reimagined the scope of political power depended on violence. Whether making subjects more legible to authority or simply securing the routine flow of tax revenues, the early modern political projects of empire in China and Vietnam both used violence as an instrument of imperial rule.

In China, the transformation of imperial power was nowhere more apparent than in the southwest. An official campaign known in Chinese as *gaitu guiliu*, a term variously translated as "bureaucratization" or "exchanging non-Chinese leaders for regular officials," began during the reign of the Yongzheng emperor (1722–35). In the southwestern borderlands, an area dominated by Tai-speaking elites and characterized by a diverse range of populations including Yao communities and others, this reform often replaced "native officials" or "indigenous leaders," deemed to have excessive power, with normally appointed imperial officials loyal to the Qing.[32] Some Tai leaders used the Qing reforms to their advantage, finding positions of influence within the new system.[33] However, these reforms were achieved through violence, much of it directed by a member of an elite Manchu clan, an imperial official named Ortai.

The ambitious project that Ortai executed in the southwest was the dismantling of a centuries-old system known in Chinese as the *tusi* (V: *thổ ty*). *Tusi* referred to appointments granted to individuals outside the normal bureaucracy, usually in areas where the presence of Chinese communities was historically insignificant.[34] During the second year of his reign (1723), the Yongzheng emperor decided to dismantle the *tusi* system, which he believed had for too long rewarded venal and oppressive local leaders, many of whom he deemed uncivilized, with positions of power and prestige.[35] His trusted official, Ortai, assured the emperor that ridding the southwest of *tusi* would render the Qing subjects of this remote region more receptive to the civilizing influence of imperial power, as the *tusi* themselves encouraged violent behavior among the common people.[36]

Ortai's appointment to a post in the southwestern province of Yunnan united the aspirations of the *gaitu guiliu* project with the system of imperial administration. Provinces, originally a military division during the Mongol Empire, had become a way to organize and govern territory during the Qing.[37] In 1725, Ortai served as the head official of the southwestern province of Yunnan with the additional position of governor-general, supervising governors for Yunnan and neighboring Guizhou.[38] Both these provinces became the setting for profoundly violent campaigns in the service of a routinized vision of imperial authority.

One of Ortai's early targets was the Miao. A term with rather derisive connotations, Miao (V: Miêu or Mèo) was a marker for groups living at high elevations, usually beyond the reach of imperial authority.[39] A label with a long history, Miao often referred to communities of Hmong speakers, a fact reflected in the persistence of the word as an ethnonym in contemporary China. For Ortai, the Miao, frequent rebels against imperial authority, could only be civilized through violence. "By killing one," he wrote, "you frighten a hundred, thus causing them not to repeat their rebellious behavior. Seen in this light, force really amounts to benevolence. Applying force and benevolence will yield rich results."[40]

Ortai ordered and led mass killings in Yunnan and Guizhou in an attempt to realize imperial reform, using violence in the service of a civilizing project in southern China. Toward the end of his time in Yunnan, Ortai, faced with Miao rebellions that would outlive his term as governor, began to reject the possibility that even violence would transform Miao into civilized subjects, referring to them as bestial, base, and cruel.[41]

While an important element in the Qing project to civilize the southwest, the *gaitu guiliu* campaign led by Ortai was not a unique example of imperial violence against uplands populations in Chinese history. In the 1520s, an official named Wang Yangming served the Ming Empire in areas far from the imperial center. Although best known as an innovator of Neo-Confucian philosophy, during his career Wang Yangming put his philosophical beliefs into political practice.[42] For Wang, the imperial political system could transform the innate moral goodness of all subjects, rendering groups previously described as uncivilized into civilized subjects.[43] Conventionally associated with Ming-era individualism, the philosophy of Wang Yangming also provided for a breakdown of the dualism of civilized and uncivilized as the dominant paradigm of Chinese/non-Chinese relations, as his understanding of civilizational transformation (C: *hua*; V: *hóa*) depended on the essential nondistinctness of Chinese and non-Chinese populations.[44]

However, Wang Yangming's philosophical outlook did not preclude the use of violent ends. His tenure in southern China included the suppression of rebellions led by non-Chinese groups, particularly the Yao and Miao. Wang's idea of "innate knowledge," which he claimed to have understood only "from a hundred deaths and a thousand sufferings," may seem at odds with his actions in the service of empire.[45] When he ordered, in 1528, the decapitation of three thousand "bandits," Wang celebrated the end of "a problem that has festered for some one hundred years."[46] That the bandits in question were Yao does not invalidate Wang Yangming's philosophical attitude about the transformative power of imperial rule, but rather reminds us that violence attends projects of empire, even when the agents of those projects explain their actions with the language of harmony and virtue.

In Vietnam, an explicit change in official attitudes toward uplands spaces, including the northern borderlands, connected the aspirations of imperial administration with the philosophical ideal of virtuous rule. The architects of Vietnamese imperial modernity, who sought to transform all subjects and areas of Vietnam into rationally governed, uniform administrative space, breathed new life into older Confucian intellectual traditions.

In the early nineteenth century, Vietnamese officials planned to intensify control over the expanse of their territory, from the Mekong Delta in the south to the borderlands with China in the north. Following the defeat of the Tây Sơn Rebellion in 1802, the Nguyễn lords established an independent dynasty. From the Nguyễn capital in Huế, in central Vietnam, the former Nguyễn lord Nguyễn Phúc Ánh proclaimed the beginning of the Gia Long reign (1802–19), the first imperial reign title of Nguyễn Vietnam. To govern the newly unified country the Gia Long emperor appointed powerful allies as heads of large military territories.[47] In 1820, when the Minh Mạng emperor succeeded his father, a new vision of imperial power took hold in Huế, one that demanded the dismantling of the military territories in favor of a novel feature of Vietnamese rule—the province.

Although the creation of the province as a unit of administration appears to be a case of Vietnamese leaders borrowing from China, the province, as a Vietnamese imperial institution, had a distinct role in the Nguyễn vision of empire. The transmutation of political institutions, in theory, went hand in hand with the transformation of imperial subjects. In 1820, a court official extolled the benefits of the province: "Those who rule will deal with misfortune by knowing how to swiftly increase virtuous governance, therefore reining in calamity and making all well."[48]

This observation, which referenced the *Spring and Autumn Annals* (Chunqiu), one of the core Confucian texts, laid the conceptual groundwork for the provincial system in imperial Vietnam. "Virtuous governance" (V: *đức chính*; C: *dezheng*) would flow through conventional political structures. In this sense, imperial Vietnamese officials connected the goals of reform in the early nineteenth century to a much older discourse of ethical statecraft, one that equated virtuous rule with the transformation of ordinary peoples' sensibilities.[49]

After the Minh Mạng reforms, which also brought change to central institutions such as the court in Huế, the idea of the province was violently translated into the structure of imperial power.[50] In southern Vietnam, a former beneficiary of the old military system, Lê Văn Khôi, launched a revolt against the imperial court upon the official dismantling of his power base in the 1830s.[51] After defeating this rebellion in the south, imperial authorities began enacting the court's mandate to transform all people living in Vietnam into loyal imperial subjects.[52] In northern Vietnam, a descendant of Nùng Trí Cao, a Tai-speaking rebel from the eleventh century, rebelled in similar circumstances. In 1834, Nùng Văn Vân revolted against Nguyễn authority in the mountainous borderlands of China and Vietnam.[53] Two years later, he died fleeing the imperial army, burned alive in the forest with his soldiers.[54]

Although much later in the nineteenth century, and with a different intellectual justification, French colonial authorities would also claim to act against violence, to bring civilization to the wider world while defending the sovereignty of France to do so.

While the idea of a civilizing mission (*la mission civilisatrice*), through the work of administrators and intellectuals, justified the global French imperial project, in the China-Vietnam borderlands French colonial rule did not substantially differ from the earlier Qing and Vietnamese empires. Despite the transformational rhetoric of colonial rule in Southeast Asia, the efforts of colonial administrators, especially in borderlands areas, connected the French imperial project to a long-standing culture of violence. In the story of the Black and Yellow Flags, French colonial institutions appear as elements in older forms of power and domination.

ORAL TRADITIONS

> I think that the current discussion can only conclude when we have collected materials among the people who live in areas that were once in the path of the Black Flags.
>
> —TÔ HOÀI (1962)

This book tells the story of bandits, their official allies, and the communities that endured the culture of violence in the China-Vietnam borderlands. In doing so, it takes into account stories about the past kept alive by communities in the borderlands and the Red River Delta. Oral traditions provide a means to understand the experience of communities, particularly at high elevations and in borderlands, communities that typically do not have a conventional archive at their disposal.

Eric Hobsbawm, whose seminal work on banditry informs our discussion of the Black Flags, also wrote dismissively about the stories the people tell. "Bandits," he tells us, "belong to remembered history, as distinct from the official history of books. They are part of the history which is not so much a record of events and those who shaped them, as of the symbols of the theoretically controllable but actually uncontrollable factors which determine the world of the poor; of just kings and men who bring justice to the world. That is why the bandit legend still has power to move us."[55] In the same work, Hobsbawm reminds readers that previous editions of his text perhaps relied too heavily on legends and stories, which transmit romanticized pictures of bandits and outlaws. The bandit tale, found in genres such as ballads and epics, he warns "is a very slippery source, and, like oral tradition, it is contaminated by the way in which it is passed through the generations."[56]

Although he does admit the limited usefulness of oral traditions, Hobsbawm denies them the status of historical evidence, a denial born of vigilance against myth making, against the promotion of legend as fact. However, oral traditions have a different sort of importance for this study of imperial bandits in the China-Vietnam borderlands. An examination of the stories that echo in the oral traditions of the mountain and valleys enables us to consider records of human experience at the core of history of the Black Flags. Where Hobsbawm sees "contamination," we might see an opportunity to tell a more inclusive, pluralistic, and enlivened story of life in the borderlands at the turn of the nineteenth and twentieth centuries.

Other historians brought oral traditions into the study of the past. For instance, Jan Vansina argues for a systematic qualitative framework for thinking about oral traditions, which he defines as distinct from oral *history*. However, he cautions that oral traditions represent a particular kind of source: "It follows that oral traditions are not just a source about the past, but a histology (one dare not say historiography!) of the past, an account of how people have interpreted it. As such oral tradition is not only a raw source. It is a hypothesis, similar to the historian's own interpretation of the past."[57]

Although oral traditions "have a part to play in the reconstruction of the past," they also create an analytical space for thinking about the historian's relationship to the past.[58] As "reported statements from the past beyond the present generation," oral traditions are a category of historical evidence that affords the opportunity for a more critical approach to historical research.[59] Although this kind of source has certain limitations—the lack of a comprehensive chronology and what Vansina calls the "interdependence of sources" being chief among them—historians using the "oral traditions hypothesis" can produce work that accounts for a broader range of voices from the past.

Historians of violence in imperial or colonial contexts have folded oral traditions into an evidentiary methodology. Writing about twentieth-century India, Shahid Amin has combined interviews of witnesses with documentary research in his study of the Chauri Chaura Incident, a violent attack by protesters on a colonial police station in the 1920s.[60] Amin laments that the "alternative accounts" generated from historical fieldwork would "soon be dead to the historian."[61] In Vietnam, Nguyễn Phan Quang has produced work that combines documentary research with oral traditions to study popular uprisings against the Minh Mạng reforms.[62] By examining oral sources about the 1830s, long past the time of living witnesses, Nguyễn Phan Quang has brought an inclusive sensibility to the study of the rebellions led by Nùng Văn Vân. Nguyễn Phan Quang puts a variety of sources into a conceptual framework, creating a lively balance among perspectives to produce a historical account that creates space for local actors, people often omitted from the grand narrative of nationalist historiography.

In China and Vietnam, oral traditions and the role of nondocumentary sources in historical research have been an explicit concern for those who have grappled with the history of the Black Flags. The work of Tô Hoài, Nguyễn Văn Bân, Trần Văn Giáp, Kiều Oánh Mậu in Vietnam and the historians affiliated with the Sino-French War Historical Research Group in the People's Republic of China collectively represent a range of perspectives on the role of oral traditions in historical research.

In Vietnam, the scholarly study of the Black Flags began during the French colonial period with historians making a vigorous case for oral traditions, particularly in the early twentieth century. Two classically trained scholars produced historical work that considered the stories people tell about the Black Flags and other imperial bandits. Kiều Oánh Mậu, a former imperial historian during the reign of Tự Đức (1848–83), published an account of Vietnamese victories against rebellion in 1901.[63] This study included oral evidence of atrocities committed by the Black and Yellow Flags, in particular a popular dirge in the area of Sơn Tây, outside Hanoi:

> Wu, Huang, Liu; Heaven help us! We still ask for assistance.
> They have stolen our property, burned our homes to cinders.
> They have taken our wives as concubines, our children as slaves.[64]

In the 1940s, decades after his death, more of Kiều Oánh Mậu's stories from the ground level appeared in the magazine *Tri Tân*, recording similar accounts of Black and Yellow Flag violence against ordinary people.[65] Everyday forms of violence emerge in these stories, stories that often challenge the preoccupations of official historiography.

As oral traditions recorded by Kiều Oánh Mậu began appearing in Hanoi journals, another Sơn Tây historian, Nguyễn Văn Bân, gathered more stories of the Black Flags. Although he was also classically trained, Nguyễn Văn Bân held an appointment in the French colonial administration in addition to an imperial examination degree.[66] In 1931 he published an anthology of Confucian philosophical texts translated into the romanized Vietnamese script (Quốc Ngữ).[67] He also collected stories, specifically about the Black Flags. After the French-sponsored Vietnamese journal *New Reports* (Báo-Mới) printed his initial essays, Nguyễn Văn Bân compiled several vignettes informed by oral traditions into a short book in 1941. Its title, *Black Flag Bandits* (Giặc Cờ Đen), left little doubt about Nguyễn Văn Bân's historical perspective. He considered the Black Flags a dangerous and terrorizing force that victimized ordinary people in Vietnam, rather than heroic champions of imperial sovereignty.[68]

In terms of methodological attitude, Nguyễn Văn Bân verged on an uncritical appreciation of oral tradition. The central problem in studying the Black Flags, he claimed, was that not everyone had heard the harrowing stories circulating in places like Sơn Tây. These were stories told by ordinary people, like Nga, a woman who survived abduction and rape to return to her family, and Cai Duy, a skilled military leader whose concern for the people of Sơn Tây led him to cooperate with the French army to fight the Black Flags in the 1880s. An old woman recalled the public decapitation of seventeen men by another bandit leader as he fled the Vietnamese imperial authorities in the late 1860s.[69] When Liu Yongfu, the Black Flags' leader, began working with the Vietnamese imperial authorities, a key event in our story of imperial bandits, local residents mocked the arrangement. "The Black Flags called themselves righteous but take whatever they see for themselves. Liu Yongfu cares about wealth and his underlings murder as they wish."[70] Although they would later be accused of denigrating the Black Flags to support their French colonial sponsors, Kiều Oánh Mậu and Nguyễn Văn Bân connected the study of the Black Flags and with the issue of oral traditions, a connection that echoes into the mid-twentieth century.

Despite oral traditions, Liu Yongfu, the Black Flag leader, has been celebrated as a symbol of Sino-Vietnamese cooperation. In 1958, for instance, Trần Văn Giáp, a former member of a French academic institute who lent his support to the Việt Minh in the 1940s, claimed that Liu Yongfu was a member of a heroic peasant uprising (*anh hùng khởi nghĩa nông dân*) who received the label "bandit" (*giặc*) from French colonial intellectuals and their feudal Vietnamese and Chinese lackeys.

In criticism of Kiều Oánh Mậu and Nguyễn Văn Bân, he wrote: "They have called him the 'Black Flag Bandit General' [*Tướng Giặc Cờ Đên*]. They say that Black Flag Bandits came to destroy Vietnam, to take women, kill children, raze houses, steal, and to throw people's rice and vegatables away to animals."[71] Stories about raids, for Trần Văn Giáp, were "ahistorical" (*phản lịch sử*), and "perversions of the truth" (*âm mưu xuyên tạc sự thực*).[72] Reflecting a materialist epistemological outlook that, as in Hobsbawm's work on banditry, forsakes reliance on oral traditions for the surety of documentary evidence, Trần Văn Giáp judged "oral sources" (*tài liệu truyền khẩu*) a poor basis for historical research.[73]

By the 1960s, a century after the Black Flags, historians in Vietnam began to ask new questions about oral traditions. Among many others, whose debates I discuss in the final chapter, Tô Hoài argued for the critical role that stories about the past should play in historical research. In a special issue of the journal *Historical Research* (Nghiên Cứu Lịch Sử) dedicated to the question of the Black Flags, Tô Hoài remarked that historians have a duty to understand the stories told by people in areas formerly raided by Liu Yongfu's army. Otherwise, he feared, no one would understand the experiences of ordinary people, believing instead the heroic image of the Black Flags offered by historians such as Trần Văn Giáp.[74] Tô Hoài reminded his readers that the dwindling population of people who had lived through raids in the nineteenth century, and the storytellers who lent their experiences new breath, were "the most precious archive."[75]

Oral traditions provide a conceptual space for the story of imperial bandits and the culture of violence in the China-Vietnam borderlands. The following chapters combine oral traditions with documentary sources to construct a history of these borderlands, taking into consideration relationships between different varieties of historical information, the methodological implications of oral traditions, and the location of the violent past in the everyday present.

The story of imperial bandits and the culture of violence in this region comes from the past, the nature of oral traditions notwithstanding, but the past is not a settled thing. Spaces existed between: territorial borderlands, flexible categories of official and bandit, and the shared terrain of oral tradition and documentary sources. This story illustrates the interplay between the past and the present, with stories told by the living complementing the words of the dead.

1

OPIUM AND REBELLION AT HIGH ALTITUDES

IN 1875, torrential rains devastated Tuyên Quang Province. Already poverty stricken, this region on the northern Vietnamese border faced the worst flooding in memory after dikes failed to contain the rain-swelled rivers. According to provincial official Vũ Trọng Bình, who witnessed the aftermath, "Everyone was poor, officials, ordinary people, even the bandits. Everyone was desperately poor."[1] Having watched the flood waters recede, Vũ Trọng Bình, a twenty-year veteran of the imperial bureaucracy, took a moment to record his thoughts. As he began to write, he found his hands covered in weeping sores, a physical manifestation of the related stress.[2]

Historically, flood control was a principal responsibility of imperial officials in Vietnam and China. In Nguyễn Vietnam, during the Tự Đức reign (1848–83), several officials in northern provinces proposed an aggressive expansion of dikeworks and irrigation canals as a way to prevent or ameliorate flooding.[3] Vũ Trọng Bình himself managed the strengthening of flood defenses in several provinces, including Tuyên Quang. However, another sort of flood also troubled him. "Our province," he lamented, "has been in dire straits for twenty years . . . all local officials agree that the bandits have the strength of an army."[4] A deluge of banditry overwhelmed the province as imperial officials anxiously looked on.

For Vũ Trọng Bình, banditry was a ubiquitous feature of the mountainous borderlands landscape. As unusually heavy rains threatened imperial dikeworks, so did uncontrolled bandit groups jeopardize imperial authority. Writing about the Mediterranean, historian Paul Saint Cassia has noted that banditry, as a label, evokes state power; "certain types of violent behavior" *become* banditry through an official, statist lens while this same behavior is "not necessarily seen in the same way at the grassroots."[5] In the borderlands, distinctions between *bandit* and *official* became subsumed by the culture of violence, the common currency of both imperial authority and the bandit power that flooded the borderlands. In northern Vietnam, where dikes channeled excess water, imperial authority faced a deluge of banditry.

Tracing the source of this flood takes us to the 1850s, when a series of uprisings erupted in the mountains. Groups carrying white flags led raids and attacks against imperial authority; these appeared in the official consciousness against the backdrop of the Yunnan opium trade, which intensified divisions between various communities in the borderlands. Following the outbreak of this rebellion, two groups of former rebels from southern China entered Vietnamese territory. One of these was the Yellow Flag Army, the subject of Vũ Trọng Bình's lamentations over Tuyên Quang. The other was the Black Flags, led by Liu Yongfu. The story of how these two groups came to dominate the borderlands is the subject of this chapter.

In the following pages, I discuss the common origins of the Black and Yellow Flags, their shared networks of mobility, their divergent paths to power, and their very different relationships to both imperial authorities and local communities in the uplands and valleys. The intertwined history of the Black and Yellow Flags illustrates the violence at the heart of imperial authority. One of the most significant events in this story, the Vietnamese authorities' employment of the Black Flags—an event that often inspires condemnation in oral traditions—represents neither a political abberation nor a fundamental weakness of the Vietnamese imperial system. Rather, the employment of the Black Flags, bandits working for the empire, was an imperial claim to monopolize violence. Especially in the uplands, we will see this claim challenged throughout the late nineteenth century, both by other bandits and by communities at the grassroots.

THE WHITE FLAG REBELLION

Although imperial bandits such as the Black Flags brought new violence to the mountains, it was a rebellion that began in the uplands that drew the Black Flags to Vietnam. As the trade in Yunnanese opium brought Chinese merchants into northern Vietnam, the White Flag Rebellion challenged Vietnamese imperial authority in areas where the empire had only a thin presence.

In the official record, the White Flag Rebellion first appeared in the mountains, in the borderlands between Nguyễn territory and the Qing Empire where Yao and Hmong speakers, identified as Man in Vietnam, maintained a loose historical relationship with communities at lower elevations.

The events known to Vietnamese administrators as the White Flag Rebellion present a special problem for historians. On the one hand, we can see violent, retributive acts by uplands populations against lowlands settlements occurring against the background of economic and demographic change, a culture of violence fed by dislocation. The Vietnamese Empire's encouragement of new settlements in the mountainous borderlands and the commercialization of Yunnanese opium provide the material context for these events. On the other hand, the term *rebellion* assumes a unity of action, a coherent organization, and a deeply held common purpose. In the administrative record, White Flag raids appear as an index of social dislocation and imperial anxiety in an environment of economic change.

Although I refer to the White Flags as a rebellion in the following pages, any ethnonationalist aims associated with the White Flags exclusively belong to the twentieth century. Anthropologists, ethnographers, and ethnohistorians in Vietnam folded the story of the White Flags into the historical background of Yao and Hmong communities in the northern uplands. Under the White Flag, these scholars claimed, Yao and Hmong speakers united against the oppressive feudal regime of precolonial Vietnam, laying the foundation for over a century of struggle.[6] During the nineteenth century, however, the White Flags emerged from the economic and demographic changes in the China-Vietnam borderlands.

OPIUM FROM YUNNAN

At the center of the White Flag Rebellion was opium. Although strongly associated with European imperialism, the cultivation and trade of opium, mostly for medicinal purposes, began in southern China perhaps as early as the eleventh century.[7] Opium from Yunnan became increasingly popular in the wake of the opium wars (mid-nineteenth century), a conflict that stemmed from the British trade in Indian opium to China.[8] Traditionally, users in China smoked sun-dried crude opium that produced a mild inebriation. The product from British India, sold under the brand name "Patna," had a higher potency and a higher cost.[9] By the mid-nineteenth century, domestically produced, more inexpensive opium from Yunnan began to push British Patna out of the consumer market.[10]

Even prior to the opium wars, the Qing Empire treated domestic and foreign opium very differently. In Yunnan, officials had to weigh the need to curtail opium consumption and its attendant problems against the livelihoods of local farmers.[11] A distinction between "foreign opium" (*yangyao*) and medicinal, "indigenous opium" (*tuyao*) reflected both agricultural and medicinal realities. The protection of a domestic good enabled Chinese farmers to compete against foreign opium from British India, which tended to have a higher price as well as a higher potency. During the eighteenth century, Ortai, the Manchu official who led a violent campaign to transform China's southwest, remarked on opium's reputed prophylactic qualities against disease, an endorsement that made opium an officially recognized regional necessity.[12] Opium enabled agents of the Qing imperial project to negotiate an otherwise hostile environment.

In Vietnam, however, opium drew condemnation from the imperial court. Since the 1820s, officials at Huế had taken a dim view of the product, deeming it a "poisonous substance." Although these criticisms applied to opium in general, the Minh Mạng emperor reserved particular ire for the trade in British Indian opium, noting that "foreign countries" supplied generous amounts of this "poison" to China.[13] For the Minh Mạng emperor, the defeat of China in the First Opium War (1839–42) manifested the deleterious effects of the British opium trade. China's defeat by Britain was also, he noted, a warning to other countries.[14]

Despite criticism from Huế, the Yunnanese opium trade was a powerful commercial force in the borderlands. By the 1850s, perhaps as early as the 1840s, opium flowed through a town called Lào Cai, in Thuỷ Vĩ County, Hưng Hóa Province, far from the court. Although Vietnamese officials referred to the town as Bảo Thắng, Lào Cai received its name from Chinese merchants; in Yunnanese (*guanhua*), Lào Cai means "old market" or "old road." In the mid-nineteenth century, Chinese merchants joined Tai-speaking populations in this borderlands town. Intercommunal tensions and a relatively thin administrative framework meant that imperial Vietnam could not depend on salaried officials in Lào Cai. Consequently, Tai powerbrokers and Chinese merchants dominated the area, with Vietnamese imperial authorities hiring official agents from the Tai elite.[15]

However, this improvised arrangement produced intercommunal tensions. It excluded populations indexed as Man who lived at altitudes above Tai elites and Chinese merchants.[16] The consequences of this exclusion became apparent in October 1860, when armed raiding parties struck Tai and Chinese settlements in the hills around Lào Cai. Although Tai miltia drove these raiding parties to the mountains in retreat, these eruptions of violence signaled a new disruption to Vietnamese imperial authority.[17] These raids in Hưng Hóa were a threat to trade and empire in a space where imperial authority relied on merchants and the Tai elite.

TENSIONS AT HIGH ALTITUDES

In the Vietnamese imperial imagination, the bustling river port of Lào Cai belonged to Hưng Hóa Province. During the nineteenth century, Hưng Hóa was one of the largest and most diversely populated provinces in Vietnam, containing all or part of the present day provinces of Điện Biên, Lai Châu, Lào Cai, Hà Giang, Yên Baí, and Sơn La.[18] When reforms in the 1830s called for the construction of a provincial system throughout Vietnam, an imperial territorial form—the province—became another layer in the complex political topography of the borderlands.

The official response to the White Flag Rebellion revealed the anxieties that informed Vietnamese imperial rule around Lào Cai. Tensions were often personal. In the winter of 1860, Nguyễn Kim Thọ, a Tai village leader near Lào Cai, reported a White Flag attack.[19] Frightened residents, he claimed, had fled in all directions. In several neighboring villages, the White Flags torched homes. Chased by local militias, the White Flags, two hundred strong and well armed, continued their raids elsewhere.[20]

In his report about the raids, Nguyễn Kim Thọ claimed that White Flag armies attacked from bases within southern China, coming across the borderlands to Vietnam. Such a claim would have invoked the official relationship between Nguyễn Vietnam and the Qing Empire, setting into motion a familiar, if not episodic, nineteenth-century pattern of cooperative counterinsurgency brokered by the court in Huế. Despite Nguyễn Kim Thọ's allegations, his superior, the provincial treasurer Nguyễn Huy Trạc, refused to press the imperial court to contact China about the raids. Nguyễn Huy Trạc confidently claimed that local militias and officials could handle this rebellion without the assistance or the interference of the Qing Empire. The prevention of further White Flag attacks and especially, as he emphasized, the protection of commerce, would be provided by soldiers and local militia already stationed in the mountains.[21]

In addition to asserting Vietnamese imperial sovereignty over Lào Cai, Nguyễn Huy Trạc's response to Nguyễn Kim Thọ betrayed an imperial prejudice against non-Vietnamese officials. He suggested that Nguyễn Kim Thọ failed to thoroughly investigate the extent of the White Flags' presence and offered a telling explanation as to why: "We know that the White Flags have entered into the village of Ngọ Phục in the county of Chiêu Tấn. They have gathered themselves in that area, yet there have been no reports from Nguyễn Kim Thọ about the difficulties related to these criminals. But on the other hand, [Nguyễn Kim Thọ] is Tai [thổ]. He does not know how to govern."[22] For his transgressions, Nguyễn Kim Thọ received forty lashes with a bamboo cane. Nguyễn Huy Trạc then designated a county-level, non-Tai official to complete the investigation of the White Flags.[23]

These criticisms of Nguyễn Kim Thọ illustrate the conflicts between Vietnamese and Tai officials, but they also show something else. In the paperwork generated by the investigation, Nguyễn Kim Thọ's official position is listed as a head of a village (V: *lý trưởng*). The description of a Tai leader with a term that explicitly referenced a Vietnamese administrative form highlights the layering of a rationalizing imperial vision over a Tai mode of power in the borderlands.

This Tai mode of power encompassed alternate terms for political authority. For instance, since at least the thirteenth century, *muäng* referred to the dominate political form in the expansive patchwork of Tai zones covering much of southern China and Southeast Asia. Until its replacement by *prathet* in 1941, *muäng* also formed part of a term for present-day Thailand (then Siam), *muäng* Thai or *muäng* Sayam.[24] Elsewhere in Vietnam, in the province of Hoa Bình, where Tai-speakers established communities or political collectivities, the Sino-Vietnamese reading of *muäng*, "mường," appeared as a highly localized term connecting uplands and lowlands, a term that endures in contemporary Vietnamese political geography.[25]

Scholars tend to emphasize the difficulty involved with translating this term into English. State, polity, kingdom, and principality all fail to capture the sense of flexible hierarchy and territorial ambiguity historically associated with *muäng*.[26] Moreover, *muäng* conveys three aspects of power in Tai contexts. Each *muäng* had one head (prince) or *chao*. Elders in the community appointed the *chao*, a leader that represented both the political power of the *muäng* and its cosmological justification. As a unit, the ordering *muäng* was decidedly hierarchical, although the terms of that hierarchy could often be quite flexible. It also reflected the importance of other political models in Tai zones, as the *muäng* leadership held power that derived, as a mandate, from heaven.[27]

In Vietnam, the official position of Nguyễn Kim Thọ as a *lý trưởng* was a claim to replace the traditional power of the *chao* with the modern imperial vision of a rationalized Vietnamese administration. However, the transformation of bureaucratic terminology, or the layering of the cosmology of imperial power, did little to change the perceived distance separating Vietnamese officials from their Tai colleagues.

Over the next eight years, the White Flag Rebellion spread from Hưng Hóa east to Tuyên Quang. As they created a fertile environment for other rebellions in northern Vietnam, the White Flags soon attracted the attention of the imperial court in Huế. In 1862, in the wake of raids in Hưng Hóa and Cao Bằng, the court appointed Nguyễn Bá Nghi to the post of military governor for Sơn-Hưng-Tuyên, giving him command of all military and militias in the provinces of Sơn Tây, Hưng Hóa, and Tuyên Quang. He was also given the additional position of military commander in charge of counterinsurgency."[28] His broad powers reflected the court's hope that Nguyễn Bá Nghi would defeat the White Flag Rebellion.

NGUYỄN BÁ NGHI

In selecting Nguyễn Bá Nghi, the court found a firm believer in the conventional extension of imperial authority. Born in Quang Ngãi Province in 1807, Nguyễn Bá Nghi received a *phó bảng* or "special appointment degree" in 1833.[29] After serving in various Mekong Delta provinces, he moved to Huế in 1859, spending time on the Privy Council and as head secretary of the Ministry of Revenue.[30] During the 1860s, he advocated negotiation rather than military resistance to French colonial ambitions in southern Vietnam.[31] After the recognition of Cochinchina and the subsequent suicide of Phan Thanh Giản, who had negotiated the disastrous Treaty of Saigon in 1862, the court entrusted Nguyễn Bá Nghi with the defense of the empire against the White Flags.[32] The loss of southern territory to France made the defeat of a rebellion in the northern uplands an even more urgent matter. Nguyễn Bá Nghi's background, his combination of central and provincial administrative experience, and his knowledge of international negotiations, qualified him, in the eyes of the court, to defend a diminished imperial Vietnam against internal rebellion.

However, his tenure soon became contentious. In 1865, Nguyễn Bá Nghi angrily intervened when Tuyên Quang provincial authorities captured the son of a suspected White Flag leader.[33] Ordering the suspect released, he complained to the court that provincial authorities too frequently harassed innocent people.[34] Nguyễn Bá Nghi then asked the court to relieve him of his post. His superiors in Huế refused, demoted him in rank, and sternly reminded him of his responsibilities. He now had a fixed term of three years in which to defeat the White Flags.[35]

Despite this reprimand, Nguyễn Bá Nghi still commanded a high degree of respect within the Vietnamese bureaucracy. In 1866, Phạm Phú Thứ, the head secretary of the Ministry of Revenue, solicited Nguyễn Bá Nghi's opinion about the possible establishment of semiautonomous areas, ruled by non-Vietnamese elites, in the northern uplands. Nguyễn Bá Nghi recommended posting more imperial armies to remote locations rather than arming local militias that, once empowered, might prove difficult to control.[36]

His skepticism extended to Chinese bandits. In 1866, the court dispatched Nguyễn Bá Nghi to Thái Nguyên Province to negotiate the surrender of a bandit leader from southern China.[37] Months later, when officials in another province demanded that this same bandit receive a position within the imperial government, Nguyễn Bá Nghi flatly rejected the idea. In an exchange forwarded to the Privy Council, another official complained that even as uplands bandits and White Flag sympathizers raided and burned military posts throughout the mountains, the provincial administration never received Nguyễn Bá Nghi's permission to hire this powerful, surrendered Chinese bandit who could have prevented such devastation.[38]

Nguyễn Bá Nghi, faithful to a more conventional projection of imperial power, refused to rely on bandits. Once hired, he warned, no one could effectively control them.[39] For the moment, his opposition held. For him, the fundamental issue was control; militias and surrendered bandits presented the same problem as the state could no more guarantee their loyalties than it could proscribe their actions.

Although the imperial court accepted his recommendation not to hire surrendered Chinese bandits, Nguyễn Bá Nghi's attempts to strengthen Vietnam through conventional means met serious resistance. In 1866, he requested permission from the court to open new training centers in borderlands provinces. Since the early nineteenth century, the imperial court had instituted training centers in non-Vietnamese populated areas to develop people of talent into civil and military officials.[40] Rather than enrolling cooperative powerbrokers as the situation demanded, Nguyễn Bá Nghi hoped to extend state power through traditional training institutions, identifying new talented candidates to staff the bureaucracy. This insistence on convention complemented his opposition to the employment of bandits as administrators. From his perspective, the path of education and instruction provided a means to suppress and prevent rebellions. However, the court refused his request, citing the abundance of such training centers and the limited funds for establishing more.[41] The employment of surrendered bandits as powerbrokers was a pragmatic option for a state that could not afford to strengthen traditional institutions.

MINES AND OPIUM

Although it emerged in the 1860s as a challenge to imperial rule around Lào Cai, the White Flag Rebellion also had a severe impact on commerce in the borderlands. While raids by White Flags disrupted the brisk trade in Yunnanese opium, their attacks on mines threatened a vital part of the imperial economy. For the Vietnamese authorities, the White Flag Rebellion portended a looming economic disaster.

As is the case with opium, historians tend to connect mining with European colonial rule in Southeast Asia. In Vietnam, the opening of mines was one of the principle economic motivations for French colonial rule, an element of the late nineteenth-century *mise en valeur*.[42] However, control over mineral resources has a much longer history in northern and central Vietnam.

Since at least the sixteenth century, mines played a significant role in imperial finance. The Trịnh lords (1539–1787), who administered northern Vietnam during the later Lê dynasty (1556–1778), relied heavily on mining revenues, establishing a relationship between political power and mineral extraction that continued through the Tây Sơn Rebellion at the end of the eighteenth century.[43] During the Trịnh period, Chinese miners, valued for technical expertise, received mining contracts and relocated to sites in the northern borderlands.[44] Assisting with mining and the collection of pit fees were Tai leaders, such as Nùng Văn Vân in Cao Bằng, whose rebellion partly stemmed from control of mines.[45]

By the Minh Mạng reign (1820–41), Vietnam actively taxed over one hundred mines in the north. Revenues appeared in imperial records, giving the outline of an imperial mine system tied to the provinces.

In the borderlands, protecting these mines meant cooperation with Chinese authorities. This was particularly true for the Tụ Long mine in Tuyên

TABLE 1.1. Northern Vietnam mines by mineral and province, circa 1830s

MINERAL	BẮC NINH	HẢI DƯƠNG	THÁI NGUYÊN	SƠN TÂY	HƯNG HÓA	TUYÊN QUANG	LẠNG SƠN	CAO BẰNG	TOTAL
Gold	1	0	6	0	4	10	9	5	35
Silver	0	0	10	0	2	1	0	0	13
Copper	0	0	0	0	5	2	0	0	7
Tin	0	0	1	0	0	0	0	0	1
Hematite	4	0	12	2	0	2	5	4	29
Zinc	0	1	9	0	0	1	0	0	11
Pig Iron	0	0	0	3	0	0	0	0	3
Salt	5	0	1	2	5	5	2	0	20
Sulfur	0	0	0	0	1	1	0	0	2
Cinnabar	0	0	0	0	0	1	0	0	1
Total	10	1	39	7	17	23	16	9	122

Source: Viện Sử Học, ed., *Khâm định Đại Nam hội điển*, 42:205–44.

Quang. During the 1840s, it generated copper for the minting of currency as well as eighty taels (V: *lặng*; C: *liang*) silver in annual pit fees.[46] In 1851, Tụ Long also became the site of a murder investigation involving both Vietnamese and Chinese authorities when thieves allegedly killed an official visiting from Yunnan.[47] This murder was not entirely unexpected, as armed groups frequently harassed miners and merchants, waiting in southern China to attack them as they crossed into Qing territory from Vietnam.[48]

Tụ Long also connected northern Vietnam to a major rebellion in southern China. During the 1850s, Du Wenxiu led a group of Chinese Muslims (C: Hui; V: Hồi) against the Qing Empire. Some followers of this rebellion (usually known in English scholarship as the Panthay Rebellion) fled to northern Vietnam.[49] In 1857, a scout from the provincial military informed Vietnamese officials in Tuyên Quang that Chinese Muslim rebels had occupied areas near the Tụ Long mines.[50]

Losing control of Tụ Long would have dealt a serious blow to the northern Vietnamese economy, which depended on copper currency for everyday transactions.[51] Reports surfaced from other Chinese merchants that mentioned ongoing efforts by Du Wenxiu's lieutenants to recruit followers among the miners in Tụ Long. A Chinese merchant, who was a registered resident of Hanoi, passed on news about Du Wenxiu's followers to imperial authorities in Nam Định, possibly while paying taxes there upon returning to Vietnam by boat from southern China.[52] Although Du Wenxiu's threat to imperial Vietnam subsided by 1860, the anxious response to Chinese Muslims from Yunnan revealed the importance of Tụ Long to the Vietnamese monetary system.[53]

Within three years, however, the White Flag Rebellion had made mining operations in Tụ Long impossible. In 1863, the Tụ Long copper mines, along with mines in other borderlands provinces, were abandoned. Violent White Flag attacks drove away what miners remained.[54] The following year, in Hưng Hóa Province, fees for gold mining at several sites went uncollected. Miners, just as in Tụ Long, fled the White Flags.[55] The White Flags further damaged the imperial tax base when their raids displaced farmers from their fields.[56] In 1864, the Ministry of Revenue in Huế, the body that handled taxation, granted tax amnesties to several counties and districts in Hưng Hóa, effectively declaring back revenue uncollectible.[57]

The White Flags then dealt a series of military defeats to a financially weakened Vietnam. In the summer of 1865, White Flags ambushed three hundred imperial soldiers in the mountains of Hưng Hóa. As soldiers lay dying, Vietnamese officials fled.[58] Months later, imperial soldiers only managed to capture a small group of twenty White Flags.[59] In 1866, the provincial authorities again requested a tax remittance from the Ministry of Revenue for four districts in Hưng Hóa.[60] The financial situation grew dim as Nguyễn Bá Nghi's use of conventional military forces failed to defeat the White Flags.

HE JUNCHANG

In the midst of rebellion, one merchant found a way to keep Yunnanese opium flowing and profitable. In 1860, a Chinese opium dealer named He Junchang devised a plan to protect the borderlands opium trade, recruiting soldiers from the Tai communities in the hills above Lào Cai.[61] Once he had insulated the opium trade from the White Flags, he began collecting a tax to fund his personal army. Some merchants even constructed a lavish temple in his honor, complete with expensive wood from southern China and large characters fashioned from gold, praising He Junchang's protection.[62] He Junchang effectively pushed the White Flags from Lào Cai, thereby guaranteeing the continued trade in Yunnanese opium through the borderlands.

He Junchang himself remains somewhat of a mythic figure. Documentary and textual evidence suggests that he acted to defend his economic stake in the opium trade during the White Flag raids. Some oral traditions claim that He Junchang was the founder of the White Flag Rebellion, almost certainly untrue. One story from Yunnan, collected by Chinese ethnographers in the early twentieth century, alleges that He Junchang actually worked as a French secret agent tasked with preparing the way for a French invasion of northern Vietnam and China.[63] While fascinating and dramatic, He's French connections are most certainly fictive.

Chased from Lào Cai by He Junchang, the White Flags continued raiding lowland settlements from bases in the uplands, expropriating money and supplies from villages.[64] Still using conventional tactics, Nguyễn Bá Nghi fought the White Flags by moving soldiers into rebel areas, pushing them into the hills. The White Flags, however, remained beyond his reach, hidden among the mountains. Frustrated, the court commented: "Being able to fight these uplanders is not difficult, but holding a newly won peace is quite hard."[65] While Nguyễn Bá Nghi chased raiding parties, the White Flags continued to raid the lowlands.

THE BLACK FLAG ARMY

For the imperial Vietnamese authorities, the solution to the White Flag Rebellion came in the form of the Black Flag Army. The elevation of the Black Flags to official status intensified an internal conflict over the shape of imperial authority, a conflict that would ultimately have consequences for the career of Nguyễn Bá Nghi. The arrival of the Black Flags also signaled the migration of their war with the Yellow Flags from China to Vietnam. Imperial sponsorship of the Black Flags and their protracted violent conflict against the Yellow Flags would shape the history of the borderlands, as well as northern mainland Southeast Asia, during the final decades of autonomous Nguyễn Vietnam, the period of French colonial rule, and into the twentieth century.

When Liu Yongfu organized the Black Flags in 1865, he broke away from a foundering armed movement tied to the Kingdom of Yanling, a short-lived rebellion that profited from the opium trade in southern China. In 1861, the Kingdom of Yanling existed in the remote orbit of the millenarian Taiping Heavenly Kingdom. Although lacking any religious agenda, Yanling provided Liu Yongfu with an organizational model that he brought to Vietnam along with the Black Flags.

Founded by Wu Lingyun, the son of a wealthy family, the Kingdom of Yanling expanded rapidly in southern Guangxi Province. Throughout the 1850s, Wu Lingyun led small, sporadic rebellions against the Qing, surviving and escaping custody with the help of a wide network of allies. A degree-holder who could not find official employment, Wu led these uprisings from a mountainous area called Dongmeng.[66] From his base in the hills, Wu Lingyun tied his rebellion to the domestic opium trade in Guangxi, collecting protection revenues as a form of taxation to fund his cause.[67]

Wu's organization grew through alliances, expanding beyond Dongmeng.[68] By 1853, Wu had several base areas and controlled some two hundred miles of Qing territory.[69] He also recruited new allies, including Xiao Zhangsan and Liu Yongfu. A bandit who raided lowlands settlements from the mountains in Tianbao, Xiao Zhangsan incorporated uplanders into his organization.[70] Liu Yongfu, the future founder of the Black Flags, was a former itinerant laborer with no formal education who came from a Hakka family with ancestral connections to Qinzhou in Guangdong Province.[71] As a member of the Long-Haired Army, which fought under the banner of "Oppose the Qing Restore the Han," Liu joined with Wu Lingyun in 1857.[72]

In 1861, Wu Lingyun proclaimed the Kingdom of Yanling, a challenge to Qing imperial rule in southern Guangxi in the shadow of the Taiping Rebellion.[73] Led by Wu and his sons, Wu Yazhong and Wu Zhuyuan, Yanling united smaller, scattered groups into a single organization.[74] Yanling stood in stark contrast to the Taiping—Wu Lingyun did not require his followers to adhere to a spiritual or ideological agenda, in contrast to the millenarian Christianity of the Taiping. Yanling was also limited; Wu Lingyun made no claim to wage war for all of China, only to supplant Qing authority in areas under his control.[75]

Although the contemporaneity of the Yanling and the Taiping would lead to the misidentification of the Black Flags as soldiers from the Taiping Heavenly Kingdom (particularly in French colonial sources), the two were fundamentally different movements.

Despite Wu's ambitions for a sustained rebellion, Yanling soon crumbled. In 1863, Wu Lingyun died in a battle with the Guangxi provincial army.[76] Leadership then passed to his son, Wu Yazhong, who ordered a massacre of Yanling followers accused of betraying his father.[77] Wu then led Yanling loyalists to Guishun in the far west of Guangxi.[78] There, they brutally occupied the town.[79] Guishun's wealthy residents and officials escaped to the surrounding mountains, while those who stayed behind aided Wu Yazhong in periodic raids of the wealthy refugees.[80] Those who had sought safety in the mountains became trapped. Hundreds if not thousands perished: according to one local story, five hundred people died of starvation while hiding from Wu, pinned in by constant attacks from the valleys below. Others committed suicide. The dead left behind bleached bones still visible in the early twentieth century.[81]

While the death of its founder pushed Yanling into crisis, Wu Yazhong continued to seek followers. To those who joined his rebellion, Wu proposed a balancing of accounts. "All those with more than the others, you are in my debt," he threatened. "All those in the middle, you can rest easy. As for those with less than the rest, follow me and next year you'll have your own oxen to plow your fields.[82] Wu wanted to secure a support base by appealing to the most impoverished segments of society. Promises of land and oxen specifically attracted those seeking a sedentary economic livelihood. As a self-conscious slogan, this pronouncement addressed potential members of Wu Yazhong's bandit organization as stakeholders in a more just economic order, albeit one that failed to speak to the interests of upland groups engaging in swidden or shifting cultivation. Wu offered a social bandit alternative for anyone willing to settle and till land.

This sloganeering did not persuade everyone. Liu Yongfu, who joined Yanling under the old leadership, soon broke away from Wu Yazhong. Outside Guishun, dwindling resources and strained alliances prompted Liu to form the Black Flag Army, gathering his followers in nearby Ande. Confronting Wu Yazhong, Liu insisted that his Black Flags could not survive under Wu's leadership.[83] Because of a lack of food, and possibly his unwillingness to forge marital ties with the Wu family, Liu Yongfu sent two of his lieutenants to scout the northern reaches of Vietnamese territory.[84] Liu Yongfu and the Black Flags soon left China for Vietnam.

While Liu Yongfu relied on personal contacts in the borderlands to move the Black Flags south, he took advantage of the White Flag Rebellion to gain a foothold in Vietnamese territory. Returning to Ande, a Black Flag scout provided Liu with a first-hand account of the White Flags: "These days in many places in Vietnam, White Miao and Yao bands act like bullies and demand exactions from the local population."[85] Armed with alliances and information about the White Flags, Liu led the Black Flags into Vietnam at a crossing bordering the province of Cao Bằng.[86]

While planning to confront the White Flags, Liu selectively forged bonds with other Chinese migrants in the Vietnamese uplands. He avoided joining forces with Liu Zhiping, for instance, who had struck a deal with the White Flags, essentially purchasing protection for all merchants in territory under his control.[87] Liu Yongfu sought an alliance with another Chinese bandit, Deng Wan. Also from southern China, Deng Wan had established himself in northern Thái Nguyên, south of Cao Bằng, prior to the Black Flags' arrival.[88] Finding a common enemy in the White Flags, Deng Wan and Liu Yongfu planned a united offensive.[89]

The Black Flags' defeat of the White Flags became an early example of the borderlands culture of violence that connected imperial bandits to uplands communities. Liu's pursuit of the White Flags led him and the Black Flags to Lục Yên, a river port in Tuyên Quang. Mountainous areas, rivulets, and small gorges dominated the landscape on either side of the river. Lục Yên sat in a lowland area west of the river and east of the mountains, its population mostly Tai and Chinese, with some uplanders from the hills.[90]

In February 1868, White Flag rebels expelled the last remaining Vietnamese officials from Lục Yên and proclaimed the area their own. Following this event, a clearer picture of the White Flags' leadership emerged. Bàn Văn Nhị, whose son had been briefly detained by Vietnamese authorities, and Lương Văn Lợi declared themselves the rulers of Lục Yên while another commander, Ngụy Thuận Chủ, defended the outskirts.[91] All were uplanders leading an expanding revolt against both Tai powerbrokers and Vietnam. After their seizure of Lục Yên, the leaders of the White Flags found themselves at the head of a rebellion that challenged Vietnamese imperial authority.

While the White Flags took control of Lục Yên, the Black Flags, newly arrived from China, were waiting. They developed a strategy to lay siege to the town, attacking White Flag camps on its outskirts. Other Chinese migrants joined the Black Flags, including Huang Shenglu, a rival of Liu Zhiping.[92] Vietnamese officials, also fighting the White Flags, briefly detained Liu Yongfu and Huang

Shenglu twice during their raids but released them on the understanding that they were merchants returning to Yunnan.[93] As he noticed several vacated villages in the outskirts of Lục Yên, Liu Yongfu believed that the residents "had been driven away" by the White Flags.[94] Decades later, Liu would describe his role in northern Vietnam in self-serving terms, as a defender of the Vietnamese and Chinese populations in a time of chaos and despair.

In March, less than one month after the White Flag victory, the Black Flags captured Lục Yên. According to Liu Yongfu's recollection, the Chinese merchants and Tai residents there welcomed the Black Flags, "Upon seeing me, they reacted as if a sweet and long-awaited rain had finally fallen."[95] Bàn Văn Nhị and Ngụy Thuận Chủ, White Flag leaders, both fled. To defeat a much larger White Flag force, Liu used entrapment tactics. A small group of cavalry rode out to catch the attention of the White Flag soldiers. As the cavalry returned, three lines of armed Black Flags fired, raining musket shot down on the White Flags. In the ensuing battle, between four and five thousand White Flag soldiers died.[96] The Black Flags then took one hundred captives, sliced off their fingers and scalps, and ordered them to walk into other White Flag camps as a visceral announcement of Liu Yongfu's victory.[97]

Maiming and public disfigurement announced the arrival of the Black Flags as a force in the borderlands. The decapitation of Bàn Văn Nhị, the White Flag leader who fled Lục Yên, brought Liu Yongfu to the attention of the imperial authorities. When Nong Xiuye, a Tai Black Flag lieutenant, captured a small group of White Flags in the outskirts of Lục Yên, one captive informed Nong that Bàn Văn Nhị had fled into the mountains east of the Red River.[98] In exchange for Nong sparing his life, the captive journeyed east and returned to Lục Yên with Bàn Văn Nhị's head. Liu Yongfu generously compensated the former White Flag in silver for the evidence.[99] Liu then alerted the Vietnamese authorities in Tuyên Quang that he had eliminated the White Flag leader, after which both he and the informant received regular positions within the bureaucracy.[100] In the mountains where the White Flags once dominated, Liu noted, people now cowered before the Black Flags.[101] As heads were exchanged for silver, violence created the conditions of submission.

However, Liu's official position also placed him under the suspicious eyes of Nguyễn Bá Nghi, the frustrated official tasked with defeating the White Flags.[102] In 1868, the court named Nguyễn Bá Nghi the official liaison for the Black Flags. He found himself forced to police a surrendered bandit who had succeeded where he could not. After receiving his new responsibilities, he promptly requested that the court permit him to resign from his post. Huế not only denied his request, it demoted him in rank and criticized his many failures and shortcomings over the past year.[103] To his great disappointment, the incorporation of cooperative bandits as pliant powerbrokers had replaced the provincial project in the borderlands. With the Black Flags, imperial bandits had become an element of Vietnamese rule.

THE YELLOW FLAG ARMY

Yet another group emerged from the ashes of the Kingdom of Yanling in southern China. This was the Yellow Flag Army, which crossed into Vietnamese territory on the heels of Wu Yazhong, the assumptive leader of Yanling who left Guishun in pursuit of Liu Yongfu. As China and Vietnam attempted to hunt down Wu Yazhong, the Yellow Flags, later led by Pan Lunsi, established a presence in uplands areas formerly held by the White Flags.

Wu Yazhong entered Vietnam at Cao Bằng after the Black Flags had defeated the White Flag Rebellion in 1868. Rather than pass through the province, however, Wu set up a base in its northern reaches near China.[104] His lieutenant from Guishun, Pan Lunsi, also known as Huang Chongying or Hoàng Sùng Anh, named the soldiers under his command the Yellow Flag Army and led them to the former White Flag stronghold of Hà Dương (present day Hà Giang), between Cao Bằng and Lào Cai.[105] The final remnants of Yanling, fleeing the Qing, had come to Vietnam.[106]

In contrast to Liu Yongfu, who targeted the White Flags, Wu Yazhong directly attacked the imperial Vietnamese authorities. In March 1868, Wu Yazhong and his followers, numbering perhaps in the thousands, robbed the grain warehouses in Cao Bằng.[107] He quickly overwhelmed the imperial army guarding the warehouse, which maintained a reserve supply of grain for times of famine, flood, or drought.[108] Wu then kidnapped the provincial treasurer, Nguyễn Văn Vỹ, holding him hostage to ensure the safety of his army.[109] Nguyễn Văn Vỹ himself had warned the Vietnamese court about Yanling bandits in southern China during the previous year. He now found himself captured by the same bandits who, as he had predicted, extended their networks from southern China across the borderlands into Vietnam.[110]

Meanwhile, Vietnamese authorities only slowly took notice of Pan Lunsi and the Yellow Flags. Since Wu Yazhong's attack in Cao Bằng had monopolized the attention of the provincial administration, Pan Lunsi was able to quietly establish himself in Hà Dương.[111] Unlike Liu Yongfu, Pan established friendly personal connections with uplanders formerly involved with the White Flags.[112] In October 1868, Pan Lunsi's army conducted raids throughout Tuyên Quang Province.[113] From their base at Hà Dương, the Yellow Flags reinvigorated the uplands revolt initially defeated by the Black Flags.

Monitoring the situation through reports in Huế, the Ministry of Military placed soldiers from various provinces under the command of Phạm Chi Hương to organize a campaign against Wu.[114] An experienced official, Phạm Chi Hương had previously succeeded in arresting members of a criminal gang in Bắc Ninh.[115] He was assisted in Cao Bằng by Ông Ích Khiêm, who, since 1867, was an acting High Commissioner for Pacification in recognition for his work fighting pirates on the northeast coast.[116] The court entrusted two experienced bandit hunters with the pursuit of Wu Yazhong and the recovery of the abducted imperial official.

As the court prepared an offensive, Wu Yazhong led raids beyond Cao Bằng. In neighboring Lạng Sơn, he ransacked villages near the provincial capital.[117] In May 1968, Wu left Nguyễn Văn Vỹ hostage in the mountains and traveled south. In Thái Nguyên Province, he recruited Chu Tường Lân, a bandit leader who had previously worked for Vietnamese authorities.[118] Phạm Chi Hương, who led the campaign to capture Wu Yazhong, had actually recommended Chu Tường Lân for an official position years earlier.[119] As Wu Yazhong began to forge his own network of alliances, his rebellion turned imperial allies into enemies.

Upon his return from Thái Nguyên, Wu soundly defeated Phạm Chi Hương and the imperial armies in Cao Bằng. Phạm Chi Hương's reports revealed a confused military effort. After fleeing the battle, he reported to Huế that Wu offered to surrender, provided that he could personally notify his followers in Thái Nguyên, after which he would return to submit to the Vietnamese authorities.[120] Predictably, when Wu Yazhong never returned, the Ministry of the Military ordered Phạm Chi Hương back to Lạng Sơn for a thorough investigation.[121] Because of his advanced age, Phạm Chi Hương received no punishment despite his neglect of duty. Two years later, he died while serving as an official in Thái Nguyên, his passing noted without mention of his failure to capture Wu Yazhong.[122]

FENG ZICAI, VŨ TRỌNG BÌNH, AND THE HUNT FOR WU YAZHONG

Although he was currently active in Vietnam, Wu Yazhong had come from China, a fact that did not escape Vietnamese authorities. They soon made Qing officials aware of Wu's activities beyond the borderlands. Initially, Su Fengwen, the Guangxi provincial governor, seemed satisfied that Vietnam could handle Wu Yazhong. However, the governor-general of Guangxi and Guangdong, a Manchu named Duanlin, warned that Wu planned to build a following in Vietnam in order to return to China.[123] If Wu treated the area as "one big bandit den," then Qing officials, according to Duanlin, should trap him inside.[124]

Meeting in Beijing, the Qing Grand Council sent Feng Zicai to Vietnam.[125] Feng's personal history with Wu Yazhong and his military experience made him an ideal choice. Hailing from a merchant family in Qinzhou, Feng had worked as a carpenter and cow-herder before joining a bandit army in the early 1850s.[126] Upon capture, Feng submitted to the Qing, choosing military service over imprisonment.[127] His official career eventually took him north in the late 1850s, where he fought against the Taiping Rebellion.[128] Four years later, he commanded Qing forces during the Fall of Nanjing, aiding the empire in vanquishing the Taiping and receiving an official post in Guangxi, where he helped suppress a Miao rebellion.[129] He also investigated another official, Xu Yanxu, who will reappear in this story in the 1880s, on charges of tax corruption.[130] Feng's military abilities had helped the Qing Empire recover from the Taiping Rebellion, while his lack of bureaucratic experience would ensure that personal loyalties would not interrupt official investigations.[131] The Grand Council ordered Feng to secure the protection of the southern borderlands as quickly as possible.[132] For the Qing Empire, bandit suppression in Vietnam, the goal of Feng Zicai's deployment, was an extended defense of the newly won post-Taiping peace.[133]

For the court in Huế, Feng Zicai's work in Vietnam had to take place in a manner that respected Vietnamese imperial sovereignty, which had been fractured in terms of its territorial reach. In 1862, while Feng Zicai put down rebellions in China, Nguyễn officials negotiated the Treaty of Saigon (1862) with France. Although this treaty brought an end to military hostilities between Vietnam and the Second Empire, which culminated in the French naval invasion of Đà Nẵng, it also ceded imperial territory in the Mekong Delta, including Saigon and the colony of Cochinchina, to France. Damaged by the Treaty of Saigon, the imperial authorities displayed an elevated sensitivity to sovereignty in northern Vietnam, evinced by the terms of Feng Zicai's employment.

The Vietnamese authorities needed a supervisor to monitor Feng Zicai and selected Vũ Trọng Bình as Feng's liaison. Originally from Quảng Bình, Vũ Trọng Bình had an early career in district and provincial-level administration, including a period as a supervisory censor.[134] His time as a censor earned him a reputation as a reliable ally of the court. In Nguyễn Vietnam, provincial-level censors advised Huế about domestic policy and the relative competency of its employees.[135] From censor, the court promoted Vũ Trọng Bình to borderlands patrol commissioner (V: *kinh lược sứ*).[136] In this capacity, he served as the link between the court and Feng Zicai, forwarding Feng's various requests to Huế while monitoring other officials who worked with Feng's lieutenants in Lạng Sơn.[137]

As he began his work in Vietnam in 1868, Feng's success against the Kingdom of Yanling, years earlier, began to yield positive results for the Qing. In Guangxi, thirty-three counties, all in former Yanling areas, had suspended tax collection in the 1850s and early 1860s, their tax burdens forgiven due to pillage and insurgency.[138] In 1868, the Grand Council mandated that all areas in Guangxi with forgiven tax burdens should now meet their full fiscal responsibility, ending the tax relief policy in the wake of Feng's successful efforts against Yanling.[139]

In Vietnam, however, Feng's arrival coincided with the further deterioration of the imperial state's ability to collect taxes. Despite the defeat of the White Flags, bandit raids, likely related to Wu Yazhong, caused four reliable tax posts to suffer heavy losses in Hưng Hóa Province.[140] Imperial finances dwindled further.[141] In August 1869, bandits ransacked two tax posts in Tuyên Quang.[142] One post had returned steady revenue since at least the 1820s only to be raided, its contents stolen.[143] As collected monies, mostly paid by merchants in the thinly populated borderlands, disappeared in the late 1860s, Huế had no alternative but to remit the stolen funds.[144] Wu Yazhong's raids eroded the fiscal health of imperial Vietnam at the precise moment that the costly relationship with Feng Zicai began.

Financial hardship continued. In March 1869, Vũ Trọng Bình, Feng's liaison, requested funds from the Ministry of Revenue on Feng's behalf.[145] The same month, Vũ Trọng Bình made another, more costly request, including ten pairs of ivory chopsticks, an elephant hair writing brush, and several varieties of incense.[146] Providing for Feng Zicai and the Qing army in northern Vietnam proved expensive. Less than a month after Vũ Trọng Bình forwarded Feng's requests, which the Ministry of Revenue satisfied, the governor of Hưng Hóa reported that bandits again attacked tax posts from the riverbanks, further depleting fiscal resources.[147]

Much of the money authorized for distribution to Feng Zicai funded local militia, a vital component to his successful approach—from the perspective of the Qing—to counterinsurgency. Feng first developed his militia strategy in Guangxi. Upon defeating bandit armies, Feng paid villagers to join sanctioned armed defense groups, which would alert the Qing military should bandits return.[148] Feng brought this approach to Vietnam. To villagers in areas raided by Wu Yazhong, he offered a choice: either enlist in a militia and receive a steady monthly salary, or return to the fields with a small, one-time copper payment.[149] Several divisions of Feng's army monitored the newly formed militia, organizations that gave ordinary people the opportunity to participate in the defense of their communities.[150] In June 1869, this combination of militias and soldiers chased Wu Yazhong from Cao Bằng and Lạng Sơn. Feng and his lieutenants, in cooperation with Vũ Trọng Bình, sealed off the northern borderlands with armed patrols.[151] As Duanlin had predicted, the "bandit den" of the China-Vietnam borderlands became a trap for Wu Yazhong.

However, backing Wu Yazhong into a corner had an unintended consequence. While Pan Lunsi and the Yellow Flags remained in control of Hà Dương, east of Lào Cai, several hundred Wu Yazhong loyalists allied themselves with Ngụy Thuận Chủ, one of the only surviving leaders of the White Flag Rebellion.[152] In the shadow of the hunt for Wu Yazhong, as the Yellow Flags remained unchallenged, the White Flag Rebellion slowly reemerged.

The defeat of Wu Yazhong was a tactical victory for Feng Zicai and Vũ Trọng Bình, and, for Vietnam, an opportunity to display the consequences of rebellion with a show of imperial violence. In late 1869, pinned into a small section of Bắc Ninh Province, Wu fled into western Thái Nguyên.[153] Gravely wounded, Wu Yazhong died hiding in Thái Nguyên.[154] In Bắc Ninh, Vietnamese and Qing soldiers beheaded almost two thousand of Wu's followers in a massive public display of force, an intimidating spectacle that spurred the surrender of other Wu allies.[155] They also discovered the body of a former Thái Nguyên military commander who, having failed to stop Wu, committed suicide at his post.[156]

Although it represented a defense of imperial power, the elimination of Wu also brought the final defeat of Nguyễn Bá Nghi, the official liaison for the Black Flags. His hopes for a conventional extension of imperial power in the far north effectively ended due to the success of Feng Zicai's hybrid approach to counterinsurgency. Although he worked with a division of Feng's soldiers to hunt down remnants of Wu's bandit network, Nguyễn Bá Nghi's role in policy decisions diminished steadily.[157] In 1870, after seeing Feng's liaison, Vũ Trọng Bình, elevated to higher rank, Nguyễn Bá Nghi died while serving as the treasurer of Sơn Tây.[158] With him perished the notion that routinized administration, rather than collaboration with surrendered bandits, should play the most significant role in the extension of Vietnamese political power in the mountainous borderlands. The passing of Nguyễn Bá Nghi was the rise of imperial bandits.

After the death of Wu Yazhong, small groups of his followers scattered across northern Vietnam. South of Thái Nguyên, Liang Tianxi fled to the uplands with over two thousand followers and tried to join forces with Pan Lunsi and the Yellow Flags in Hà Dương.[159] In Bắc Ninh, a Wu Yazhong loyalist calling himself Field Marshal Li continued the rebellion before his eventual capture.[160] To deal with the debris of Wu Yazhong, Vietnamese imperial rule increasingly became a hybrid of officials, militias, and, with the Black Flags, imperial bandits.

Vietnamese authorities next turned their attention supplying the Chinese soldiers aiding in the struggle against the Yellow Flags and their allies among White Flag loyalists.[161] To support Qing soldiers, Vietnamese officials developed a garrison arrangement. In Tuyên Quang, along the Lô River between Hà Dương and Yunnan, the Vietnamese official Đặng Xuân Bảng paid villagers (in silver) to cultivate crops specifically for the Chinese armies.[162] Meanwhile, elsewhere in Tuyên Quang, Ngụy Thuận Chủ and the White Flags led damaging attacks against lowland settlements.[163] Vũ Trọng Bình assured the court that Feng Zicai and Qing soldiers under his command would eliminate the last White Flag loyalist in Vietnam.[164]

Supplying militias and Chinese armies, however, created unexpected local opportunities. In Tuyên Quang, as Qing soldiers awaited the order to attack the Yellow Flags, militias from surrounding communities, some with questionable connections to the effort against the empire's enemies, began camping with armies from China and demanding rations. Đặng Xuân Bảng now had to supply rice and daily cash stipends for hundreds of newly arrived civilians who declared militia status.[165] For the court, providing for Chinese soldiers became a heavy burden.[166] For the militia, however, the Tuyên Quang government provided all provisions without the financial support of Huế.[167] Just as minor bandits tended to flock to stronger ones, the promise of a regular income and material comforts drove many borderlands residents to form or join militias.

In correspondence with the imperial court, Vũ Trọng Bình, in a year of floods, observed a dire situation in Tuyên Quang. In the years following Feng Zicai's campaign against Wu Yazhong, Vũ Trọng Bình mourned the enduring misery of Tuyên Quang and other areas that hosted Qing soldiers. In 1875, he watched as local officials struggled to control floods during the spring.

In addition to a tone of official woe, Vũ Trọng Bình's writings also express the limitations of the Vietnamese imperial project. During the floods of 1875, Vũ Trọng Bình writes that he and a delegation of officials planned to travel to Vĩnh Yên, in Tuyên Quang's southwest. As they charted their route, he writes, two obstacles stood in their way: floods and the Yellow Flag Army. On the road to Vĩnh Yên, Vũ Trọng Bình and his entourage found a small area under the control of uplanders.[168] As these "uncivilized" uplanders guided these vulnerable Vietnamese officials, the practice of imperial power relied on imperial subjects, a mode of mutuality that casts doubt on the totalizing fiction of empire.

POWER OVER RESOURCES: TAXING OPIUM

After the elimination of Wu Yazhong, the Black and Yellow Flags were all that remained of the Kingdom of Yanling. Each group sought a secure source of revenue and a base of operations in northern Vietnam. For the Black Flags, Yunnanese opium provided a lucrative, durable source of wealth. Their reliance on the opium trade established an enduring precedent for other groups in the China-Vietnam borderlands. Largely prevented by the Black Flags from profiting from opium, the Yellow Flags sought, and failed to find, a foothold in the mines. As these old rivals vied for a dependable economic base, they carried their struggle into a new setting.

Initially, each group sought a place in the imperial mining system. In 1868, Huế refused Liu Yongfu's request to open a mine in Lục Yên.[169] Although Tụ Long gradually returned to operation after the White Flag Rebellion's interference, other mining sites in Tuyên Quang and Hưng Hóa, which had dropped from five copper mines in the 1850s to one, lay dormant.[170] The court proved unwilling to entrust the Black Flags with mining, which had a central place in the imperial revenue stream. By requesting permission to mine, Liu Yongfu attempted to continue a well-established occupation for Chinese migrants in Vietnam. His rejection underscored a policy change in postprovincial Vietnam; mines would remain under direct imperial control. In 1868, when the Yellow Flag leader Pan Lunsi offered his surrender to the Vietnamese authorities in exchange for control of Tụ Long, Huế reiterated that only officials, not surrendered bandits, could control copper.[171]

The Black Flags and the Yellow Flags soon turned their collective attention to another source of revenue: opium. According to Liu Yongfu, his lieutenant Nong Xiuye once declined an official salary, choosing instead to collect protection fees on commerce, particularly Yunnanese opium.[172] Once scorned by the court, opium was traded widely throughout the country during the time of the Black Flags, creating a rich environment for improvised taxation and personal wealth.

Just prior to Liu Yongfu's arrival in Vietnam, the sale of opium became highly and openly profitable. In 1865, Huế repealed the ban on opium in Vietnam, a prohibition dating to the 1830s. Now legal, opium provided the empire with revenue, primarily through the sale of transport licenses.[173] Previously, illicit opium trafficking occurred in under-policed areas near the Red River. For instance, in the river port of Nam Định, southwest of Hanoi, merchants from China would stop briefly to unload their illegal cargo to avoid arrest in Hanoi, where Nguyễn government agents would more thoroughly inspect their ships.[174] A new license system was introduced along with the repeal of the opium ban, a system that directly benefited the Black Flags.

After the legalization of the opium trade, opium tax revenue largely reflected the empire's capacity to enforce the license system. Not surprisingly, the highest amount of revenue came from the well-patrolled town of Nam Định. The borderlands province of Lạng Sơn generated eight thousand *quan*, although nearby provinces failed to provide significant tax revenues. Returns in Hưng Hóa comprised less than 2 percent of the total for all Nguyễn Vietnam, despite the bustling trade in Yunnanese opium. In contrast, the court noted that French authorities in Cochinchina reported a total tax collection of 450,000 *quan* in the three former Vietnamese provinces of Gia Định, Định Tường, and Biên Hòa, over six times the amount generated by imperial Vietnam.[175]

TABLE 1.2. Opium tax revenues in northern Vietnam by province, 1865

PROVINCE	AMOUNT IN *QUAN*	PERCENTAGE OF TOTAL
Sơn Tây	4,800	7.04
Hà Nội	17,000	24.96
Hải Dương	10,600	15.56
Hưng Yên	1,300	1.90
Nam Định	24,000	35.24
Hưng Hóa	1,000	1.46
Lạng Sơn	8,000	11.74
Cao Bằng	600	0.88
Quảng Yên	800	1.17
Total	68,100	

Source: Dương, *Việt Nam: Những sự kiện lịch sử*, 47; Vũ, ed., *Lịch sử Việt Nam*, 253; original data culled from Viện Sử Học, ed., *Đại Nam thực lục*, 30:164.

While legalization did bring revenue, the decision to repeal the opium prohibition was not without controversy. The court solicited opinions from high-ranking officials, including Vũ Trọng Bình, whose concern for poverty informed his anxiety over legalized opium. He believed that any change in imperial policy should consider the possible effect of legalization on popular consumption. Taxes and transport fees, he recommended, should be prohibitively high, thereby discouraging widespread use while profiting from habitual users.[176] Although they initially concluded that the drug "poisons at home and abroad and should be prohibited," officials at court decided to repeal the opium ban, opting instead for severe taxation over moral suasion as a way to prevent mass addiction.[177]

To administer the high tax, the Vietnamese authorities issued imperial transport licenses, opium trading papers to be inspected at customs posts. By the end of the 1860s, Liu Yongfu and the Black Flags, on the basis of their official position in Vietnam, managed customs posts throughout Hưng Hóa Province. Liu also expanded his mandate for fee collection. As Yunnanese merchants moved oxcarts of salt through northern Vietnam, Black Flag soldiers charged them fees for passage, accepting payment in opium. For every two hundred pounds of salt, Liu charged a passage tax of two ounces of opium.[178] The product from Yunnan, now officially legal, provided the Black Flags with financial stability.

However, the Black Flags were not the only group tied to the borderlands opium trade. When Liu Yongfu occupied Lục Yên in March 1868, he began to hear stories about He Junchang, the Chinese merchant with a private army in Lào Cai.[179] Like the Black Flags, He Junchang controlled customs posts. On Liu's orders, two Black Flag lieutenants traveled from Lục Yên to Lào Cai to challenge He Junchang.[180] They established Black Flag posts south of Lào Cai, eventually forcing He's soldiers from a post at Long Lộ, on the outskirts of town.[181] At Long Lộ, the Black Flags seized ten large cannons, a few hundred muskets, gunpowder, musket balls, and a huge amount of food all left behind by He's fleeing army.[182] In late 1869, Liu Yongfu joined his lieutenants in Long Lộ and established two more Black Flag posts, each guarded by one hundred soldiers.[183] The Black Flags moved closer to Lào Cai and a confrontation with He Junchang, eyeing a more complete control of opium revenues.

COMMUNITIES IN THE CULTURE OF VIOLENCE: RAIDS AND RESISTANCE

Uplands communities found themselves positioned between the Black Flags and the Yellow Flags, and their competition for control of northern Vietnam's mines and opium trade. Many of these communities, including the Tai, Yao, and Hmong, suffered raids, kidnapping, assault, mass killings, and displacement. Acts of resistance in the mountains, transmitted in the oral traditions of the borderlands, occurred beneath the surface of the war between the Black and Yellow Flags.

Like the White Flags before them, and, in the case of Liu Yongfu, following the example of other groups in southern China, these armed migrants carried out raids against communities. Unlike the White Flags, however, Black and Yellow Flags raids, at least initially, focused on the uplands.

Raids brought food and conscripts. At the entrance to a settlement, a raiding party would announce their presence with a loud explosion, either a gunshot or the detonation of loose gunpowder. Alarmed residents hid while the pillagers took rice, grain, chickens, and pigs.[184] Then the raiding party demanded all able-bodied men and young boys emerge from their dwellings, after which they pressed many into forced labor, taking them as they retreated.[185] Community leaders often feared that failing to appease the bandits would result in the massacre of the entire village.[186]

Supplementing opium revenue and, in the case of the Black Flags, government salaries, these powerbrokers also appropriated grain and rice from Tai communities in between the Red and Clear rivers. Subject to imperial monopoly, salt could only be traded by authorized merchants. Targeting Tai populations for land would have likely yielded foodstuffs, access to irrigated fields, as well as potential base areas below the higher elevations.

Raiding parties also targeted young women from mountain villages, forcing them into marriage or raping them.[187] According to one story, uplands (Yao) women in Bảo Thắng, south of Lào Cai, developed a technique for resisting abduction. Noticing that bandits kidnapped villagers on their way to the market, a group of women began selecting young men from the village to pose as husbands. If stopped, a woman could claim marriage to her male companion, reducing the risk of abduction.[188] In other instances, women in Bảo Thắng and Văn Bàn, southwest of Lào Cai, avoided capture by hiding in the woods, in ponds, or in temples.[189] As villagers became more familiar with the raids and with the desires of the pillagers, women began to develop new tactics for resistance.

According to other oral traditions, women in the uplands began altering their physical appearance to avoid abduction. Following the rape and murder of a young woman in Bảo Thắng, women in one settlement took steps to disguise themselves.[190] Rather than using a neighbor as a stand-in husband, they smeared their faces and hair with dirt and manure. When a raiding party arrived, they ventured outside and behaved in an erratic manner, feigning insanity, and thus discouraged their would-be kidnappers.[191]

Raids also threatened children in uplands communities. As a means to exact payment from families without daughters, bandits would take small children to a cooking fire. After tying them at the ankles and wrists, the bandits would lay each child on a roasting spit over the flames. Children often burned to death and those who survived bore permanent and painful scars. This form of torture also sent a warning to nearby communities, as the valleys filled with the noxious scent of singed hair and the desperate screams of young victims.[192]

During the 1860s and 1870s, the Black and Yellow Flags spread into the hills of northern Vietnam, carrying with them familiar tactics of pillage and abduction. As uplands communities resisted raids, the Black and Yellow Flags continued to assert their authority. The Black Flags, under imperial sanction, established a parallel state, controlling taxation, the use of force, and even the lives of human beings with an intimacy that dwarfed the aspirations of the imperial court. In the 1880s, these same tactics were visited upon lowland populations as the Black Flags become involved in the Vietnamese military struggle against France.

Although Liu Yongfu's army competed with the Yellow Flags for resources and the control of populations, he identified He Junchang in Lào Cai as his principal rival for control of opium taxation. As Liu led the Black Flags to Lào Cai, He Junchang forged a defensive alliance with the Yellow Flags.[193] In April 1869, Pan Lunsi ordered his army from Hà Dương to join He, uniting with the weakened forces of the Chinese merchant. As Vietnamese officials quietly tracked the Yellow Flags' migration to Lào Cai, the opium-trading hub became the stage for a bloody confrontation between these three well-armed groups.[194]

An uneasy and brief détente between the Black Flags and the Yellow Flags soon followed. Relaying a message through a Black Flag lieutenant, Pan Lunsi offered Liu Yongfu a stake in Lào Cai, a gesture that seemed deeply suspicious to the Black Flag leader.[195] According to Pan Lunsi's proposal, Lào Cai would become four territories, with the Yellow Flags and He Junchang occupying three and the Black Flags one.[196] This arrangement quickly fell apart, as Yellow Flag soldiers began demanding protection payments from the Black Flags.[197] Yellow Flag soldiers then injured Nong Xiuye, the Tai Black Flag lieutenant, during an attack at the Long Lộ customs post. Furious, Liu Yongfu planned a counterattack.[198] Open war between the two groups, years in the making, finally erupted in Lào Cai.[199]

The battle was brief and intense. Pan Lunsi, claiming to seek peace, lured Liu Yongfu to a neutral location. Scouting the rendezvous site, Black Flag soldiers saw several well-armed Yellow Flags hidden within shooting distance of the meeting place. In response, Liu ordered Black Flag riflemen into concealed sniping positions. When Liu and Pan met, over a thousand Yellow Flags, armed and carrying pouches of gunpowder around their waists, confronted Liu's army. The Black Flag riflemen fired, igniting the pouches.[200] After a thunderous explosion, one that ripped apart many of Pan Lunsi's soldiers, the Black Flags wandered the bloodied field, driving away or executing the wounded.[201] Although Pan Lunsi himself escaped to the east, the Black Flags had driven the Yellow Flag Army from Lào Cai.[202]

In the immediate aftermath of victory, Liu Yongfu, as he had done years earlier in Ande, claimed to witness a celestial event. As three thunderclaps resonated from the heavens, echoing across the battlefield like cannon shot, the mountains, streams, and forests came alive with lively sounds. Above the trees, two bright stars battled in the sky. One fell to earth, and three more thunderclaps boomed. Heaven itself, in Liu's retelling, acknowledged the power of the Black Flags.

After their victory in Lào Cai, the Black Flags became doubly sanctioned imperial bandits, recognized by both China and Vietnam. Despite the fact that Liu once sought to overthrow the Qing, officers from Feng Zicai's army, still in Vietnam after the hunt for Wu Yazhong, offered the Black Flag leader official recognition from China in exchange for his assistance with the Yellow Flags.[203] A cooperative offensive then drove Pan Lunsi's remaining followers deeper into the mountains.[204] In March 1870, the founder of the Black Flags received a hereditary title from the Tự Đức emperor, and Liu found himself enjoying the recognition and flattery of both the Qing and Vietnamese empires.[205]

Regardless of their official status, however, the ways in which the Black Flags exercised their dominance often interfered with local authorities. In Lào Cai, for example, the battle over the opium trade made routine tax collection impossible, causing the Ministry of Revenue to order tax offices moved far from the city.[206] As Nguyễn Bá Nghi had warned, sponsorship of powerbrokers like Liu Yongfu did not guarantee control. In November 1869, one of Liu's raids against the Yellow Flags spilled over into Tuyên Quang. In response, a provincial official attempted to convince the court that all "Qing bandits," with no distinction between the Black and Yellow Flags, should be driven out at any cost.[207] In rejecting this proposal, the court replied flatly: "That is not how the situation is being managed."[208] The defense of Nguyễn rule now rested with pliant bandits and former rebels, over the loud objections of officials suspicious of the status quo.

OPIUM, VIOLENCE, AND IMPERIAL RULE

In the 1860s, when White Flag raids struck communities in Cao Bằng and Hưng Hóa, the high-altitude tensions of the Vietnamese Empire collided with the borderlands trade in Yunnanese opium. In Lào Cai, as Chinese merchants feared a loss of livelihood, He Junchang organized a personal militia to combat the White Flags. The opium trade, however, brought a more powerful, and more violent, group of migrants across the borderlands. Combining intimidating raids against uplands populations with displays of gruesome force against the White Flags, the Black Flag Army ended the 1860s as imperially sanctioned powerbrokers in the borderlands. Their leader, Liu Yongfu, effectively became the head of an organization that not only profited from the opium trade, but also ensured its short-term survival in the form of territorial control.

As the 1870s began, the Black Flags continued their war against the Yellow Flags for domination of the opium trade and control of the mountainous borderlands. Now an official of the Vietnamese Empire, Liu Yongfu would become intimately involved with the coming struggle against French imperialism. For the Yellow Flags, however, survival came in the form of a relationship with

France; first in the form of an arms dealer and, later, as soldiers under French command during the 1880s.

The networks connecting French agents of empire with the Black and Yellow Flags, the twinned vestiges of a Chinese rebellion vying for power in Vietnam, are the subjects of the following chapter.

2

COMMERCE, REBELLION, AND CONSULAR OPTICS

On the morning of November 20, 1873, Nguyễn Chăm, an interpreter for the French colonial administration in Saigon, found himself translating something quite out of the ordinary while on temporary assignment in Hanoi. A French naval officer by the name of Francis Garnier, addressing himself as the "Great Official Garnier," had unexpectedly announced the end of Vietnamese imperial authority in the city and throughout the Red River Delta.

Within an hour, the French tricolor flew over the northern, southern, and western gates of Hanoi. Garnier declared the Red River, from Nam Định in the south all the way to Lào Cai in the borderlands, open to foreign commerce.[1] Tariffs and taxation, he promised, would be standardized and transparent. Under his authority, foreign residents and merchants could now purchase property throughout northern Vietnam, which Garnier referred to as Tonkin.[2]

In his pronouncement, Garnier reassured the traditional elite: "We have no wish to seize Tonkin for ourselves and expel all officials. We wish merely to find men from this country to place in authority over the people."[3] A potential changing of the guard resonated with those few members of the elite still loyal to the Lê dynasty, which had passed from power with the end of the eighteenth century.[4]

In the nineteenth century, Lê restorationists remained a consistent if easily resolved threat to Nguyễn rule. In 1854, Cao Bá Quát and Lê Duy Cự rebelled against the Nguyễn in the name of the Lê in the Red River Delta, a challenge the imperial authorities swiftly defeated.[5] Twelve years later, as White Flag raids dotted the north, Tạ Văn Phụng, a Vietnamese soldier in a French military division, left southern Vietnam for the Red River Delta. Proclaiming himself the Emperor Lê Duy Minh, Tạ Văn Phụng led a rebellion from a base in Bắc Ninh before being captured and executed.[6] Although largely defeated decades before

FIG. 2.1. La Rue Jean Dupuis in Hanoi (1875). From Franchini and Ghesquière, eds., *Des photographes en Indochine.*

his proclamation, some two thousand Lê loyalists joined Garnier in 1873 in a failed attempt to restore the fallen dynasty.

Appeals to Lê loyalists aside, Francis Garnier's 1873 declaration spoke most directly to the culture of violence in the borderlands between China and Vietnam. His reason for traveling to Hanoi, his dictation of a grand pronouncement to Nguyễn Chăm, and his death the following December all connected him to the networks of imperial bandits and officials that emerged during the 1860s.[7]

CONTESTED HILLS

A few years before Garnier's 1873 announcement in Hanoi, the Yellow Flags had regrouped in the mountains. Although the Black Flags had driven them from Lào Cai, Pan Lunsi and his army were preparing to challenge Black Flag control of the opium trade. As the Yellow Flags struggled against the Black Flags and their Vietnamese imperial allies, and as ordinary people coped with raids from both the Black and Yellow Flags, the Qing Empire entered into a war between imperial bandits.

In 1870, Pan Lunsi seized control of his former base at Hà Dương in Tuyên Quang. From the surrounding hills, the Yellow Flags launched attacks on Vietnamese soldiers.[8] One Vietnamese official, wounded by a Yellow Flag attack, fled from Tuyên Quang north into China, which caused the imperial court in Huế to order his arrest and return on charges of abandoning his post.[9] With the provincial government defeated, the Yellow Flags effectively controlled Tuyên Quang, posing a threat to the Black Flags from east of Lào Cai.

The Yellow Flag victory stimulated debate in Huế. In January 1871, the grand secretariat issued a damning report to the six ministries and the court. Its central theme was the ineptitude of officials in northern Vietnam. Directly criticizing Nguyễn Huy Kỷ, the governor of Hưng Hóa, the report noted that Pan Lunsi, along with Liu Yongfu, continued to evade capture. "If current officials cannot shoulder their responsibilities more effectively, there are many others who can replace them."[10] This report, which grouped the Black Flags and Yellow Flags together into a single administrative problem, demonstrated the lingering discord about the employment of the Black Flags. In response, the court confirmed the official status of Liu Yongfu, who would soon become indispensable to the fight against the Yellow Flags.[11]

Premature reports of the Yellow Flags' demise began to circulate as Pan Lunsi aggressively challenged Liu Yongfu. Soon after he was criticized at court, Hưng Hóa governor Nguyễn Huy Kỷ informed Huế that Liu had killed Pan Lunsi in Lào Cai. Reports from Tuyên Quang later contradicted news of Pan's death, confirming that he remained alive in Hà Dương, having only sustained a gunshot wound.[12] Pan then led groups of Yellow Flags into positions near all major Black Flag camps.

Concerned, Liu Yongfu left Lào Cai in the hands of lieutenants and took one hundred followers and their families to Muăng Ba, a Tai area west of the Red River.[13] Liu's forays into Tai territory would result in the extension of his personal network beyond Vietnam into other areas of Southeast Asia, linking the Black Flags to powerbrokers in the *muăng* or Tai polities of the Black River Basin.

As the war between the Black and Yellow Flags intensified, Vietnamese officials took note of further damage to imperial finances. In the winter of 1871, "bandits" robbed the tax collection post in Bảo Thắng, in the hills south of Lào Cai.[14] Later that year, Trần Đình Túc, the newly appointed Hưng Hóa governor, alerted the Ministry of Revenue in Huế about an impending population crisis. In three counties where village authorities had reported bandit raids, tax funds had been stolen and fields deserted. As crops went untended, land fell fallow, reversing the gains of Ngụy Khắc Tuấn's efforts to encourage cultivation in the 1850s.[15]

Pan Lunsi combined overtures of surrender with attacks on villages, creating a refugee crisis in the northern uplands. On two occasions, in 1871 and again in 1872, Pan Lunsi offered his submission to officials in Tuyên Quang and Hưng Hóa. Both times, the Ministry of Military and the court in Huế rejected him.[16] In March 1871, between surrenders, the Yellow Flags attacked communities in Tuyên Quang. As had happened in Hưng Hoá, people abandoned their homes. To support the displaced people, the Tuyên Quang government purchased emergency rice with funds from the provincial treasury.[17] The Yellow Flag offensive continued for three months. Moving south, they occupied several Nguyễn military encampments near Sơn Tây, outside Hanoi. Militias and provincial armies from Sơn Tây and Hưng Hóa pushed the Yellow Flags back into Tuyên Quang.[18] Afterward, the Yellow Flags again raided Tuyên Quang, swelling the ranks of fleeing refugees.[19]

In a symbolic and a geographic sense, the Yellow Flags took the place of the White Flag Rebellion. As raids raged into the summer of 1871, Hoàng Kế Viêm, the Black Flags' supervisor, notified Huế that Pan Lunsi held bases throughout former White Flag strongholds in Tuyên Quang. According to Hoàng Kế Viêm, Pan Lunsi planned to expand his territory through the mountains west into Hưng Hóa, where people had once joined the White Flags.[20]

Communities, the imperial Vietnamese authorities, and other armed migrants responded to the growing strength of the Yellow Flags.[21] In July 1871, two hundred and fifty villagers in the mostly evacuated Hưng Hóa counties of Thủy Vĩ and Văn Bàn formed militias to defend their communities from further pillage.[22] Soldiers from other provinces moved to Hưng Hóa to attack the Yellow Flags.[23] Pan Lunsi's resurgence also created an opportunity for other bandit leaders. Liu Zhiping, one of Liu Yongfu's early contacts in northern Vietnam, began to reassert his own power in Thái Nguyên in the wake of Yellow Flag attacks.[24]

In 1872, as the military effort against him intensified, Pan Lunsi again offered his submission to Nguyễn authority. In exchange for his loyalty, Pan demanded food and weapons.[25] The court's response, relayed through Hoàng Kế Viêm, revealed no interest in negotiations with Pan or the Yellow Flags.[26]

Although Pan Lunsi had brought the Yellow Flags back into a position of power in the borderlands, the destruction and dislocation that accompanied his war with the Black Flags galvanized opposition to the Yellow Flags at all levels, from community militias to the court. In need of an ally, Pan Lunsi received an unexpected visit from a French gun dealer in 1872. The events leading to Francis Garnier's attempted overthrow of imperial Vietnam began to unfold when Pan Lunsi met Jean Dupuis.

THE ARMS DEALER: JEAN DUPUIS AND THE BORDERLANDS

Ten years before he met Pan Lunsi, Jean Dupuis was in Egypt. In 1859, he left the family textile business in France to seek work on the Suez Canal. Eager to travel, he befriended an elderly naval veteran named Leroux who, with financial backing from France, supplied Dupuis with a cargo of wines, liqueurs, and preserved fruits to resell in Hong Kong.[27] With a ship and 50,000 *francs* salary, Dupuis left Egypt on his first commercial expedition.[28]

After delivering his cargo in Hong Kong, Dupuis attached himself to the expeditionary forces of General Cousin de Montauban in inland southern China.[29] Along with many of Montauban's followers, Dupuis settled in Shanghai in 1860, joining a growing European expatriate community that included his future colleague Ernest Millot. In 1861, Dupuis moved west to the river city of Hankou and built a business through his merchant contacts.[30] In Hankou, Dupuis decided to supplement his inventory with decommissioned European and American field rifles that he hoped to sell to China.[31] He developed a reputation as a reliable arms dealer, selling weapons to the Qing Empire at a time when it struggled against internal rebellions such as the Taiping Heavenly Kingdom, the Du Wenxiu or Panthay Rebellion, and the fledgling Kingdom of Yanling.[32]

To fulfill contracts for weapons, Dupuis began scouting river routes through the China-Vietnam borderlands. When Ma Rulong, Yunnan's provincial military commander in Kunming, offered Dupuis payment for a shipment of rifles and ammunition, Dupuis decided to deliver the weapons by leading ships from Hong Kong to the Vietnamese port of Haiphong, returning to Kunming via the Red River.[33] Although this was a way to avoid overland travel, the route would bring Dupuis and his shipment into contact with the Black Flags.

In May 1871, from southern Yunnan, Jean Dupuis scouted the area around Lào Cai and proclaimed the navigability of the upper Red River for small merchant craft.[34] To share this news with his French contacts in Shanghai, Dupuis paid a Black Flag soldier to deliver a letter to Macao.[35] His willingness to rely on Black Flag assistance would soon yield to a deep distrust of Liu Yongfu and his Vietnamese imperial allies. To Dupuis, his experiences over the next two years would demonstrate the inherent hostility of imperial officials to open commercial activity.

Although he held a contract with the Qing administration in Yunnan, Dupuis never attempted to reach an understanding with the Vietnamese authorities about his activities. According to Dupuis, the legitimacy of his business in the Red River area derived from the vassalage status of Vietnam vis-à-vis the Qing Empire, a claim that testifies to his utilitarian and highly selective understanding of Vietnam's relationship to China during the nineteenth century.[36] Nonetheless, he did receive support from French officials. The following spring, Admiral Dupré, the governor-general of Cochinchina, assured Dupuis that Commandant André Senez, captain of the *Bourayne*, would meet the gun dealer at Haiphong and facilitate introductions with Vietnamese officials.[37]

Dupuis was confident in the face of risk. When he scouted Lào Cai, he noticed that the Black Flags defended the city with sixteen double-barreled hunting rifles and various other flintlock guns. They presented, he assured Dupré, no significant challenge to a well-armed commercial vessel.[38] Assured of the feasibility of the venture, Dupré recommended Dupuis' plan to Admiral Pothuau, the head of the Ministry of the Navy (Ministère de la Marine) in Paris.[39] Enthusiastic, Pothuau wrote in support of Dupuis' further exploration of a commercial route connecting Yunnan to Haiphong and, potentially, Saigon. However, he stressed Dupuis would receive no official sponsorship from France. If he or his men died en route, Pothuau "could not intervene to avenge" them.[40]

This qualified support for Dupuis' proposal reflected the fragility of the colonial idea in French politics during the early 1870s. The Ministry of the Navy had long maintained an interest in the advancement of French commercial interests abroad. In the late 1850s, when Napoleon III considered a military withdrawal from Cochinchina in the wake of French defeat in Mexico, officials from the ministry, along with influential clergymen and shipping magnates, dissuaded the emperor from abandoning an overseas presence in Southeast Asia.[41] In the 1870s, Pothuau's refusal to officially support Dupuis' expedition evinced a disinterest in the colonial enterprise that was typical during the early Third Republic. In the wake of the disastrous Franco-Prussian War and the recent suppression of the Paris Commune, there remained very little political will in France for an aggressive policy abroad. Some politicians, such as Eugène Étienne, did favor "prudently and practically conducted" colonial enterprises for the enrichment of France, although not the political incorporation of colonies themselves.[42] In this domestic political environment, officials and politicians could only furtively pursue a colonialist agenda while observing Dupuis' efforts in Vietnam.

With the support of Dupré in Cochinchina, and the recognition of the Ministry of the Navy, Dupuis acquired ships for his Red River arms shipment. In Hong Kong, he purchased two British gunboats (appropriately named the *Hong-Kiang* or "Red River" and the *Lao-Kai*, an alternate spelling for Lào Cai), one steam ship (the *Son-Tay*), and an unnamed *jonque* for transporting weapons to Kunming. The order included six to seven thousand rifles ("chassepots et remington"), thirty pieces of field artillery, and over twelve tons of ammuni-

FIG. 2.2. Haiphong (Cửa Cấm; 1875). From Franchini and Ghesquière, eds., *Des photographes en Indochine.*

tion.[43] Dupuis assembled a crew of 130, including people from China, France, Britain, and the Philippines. Ernest Millot from the Millot Trading House in Shanghai joined, having previously helped Dupuis recruit an expeditionary team for the trip from Yunnan southward into the Red River Delta.[44] A former mercenary named Georgios Vlavianos, a British subject of Greek origin, served as the captain of the *Hong-Kiang*.[45] The ships prepared to leave Hong Kong in October 1872.

In November 1872, an impatient Dupuis arrived at Haiphong, a place known in Nguyễn paperwork as Cửa Cấm.[46] In Haiphong, scheduled to rendezvous with Commandant Senez and the *Bourayne*, per Dupré's instructions, Dupuis received word that Senez had sailed south to Hanoi. Impatient, Dupuis decided to proceed unescorted. He spent a week trying to navigate the various streams around Haiphong, ultimately failing to find a path to the Red River. Dupuis moored his ships at Đồ Sơn, a cape between Haiphong and Cát Bà Island. There, a Christian convert from the Dominican mission at Hải Dương delivered a letter stating that Senez would meet Dupuis in Haiphong upon his return from Hanoi.[47] Disregarding this news, Dupuis refused to return, choosing instead to await Senez at Đồ Sơn.

Unknown to Dupuis, the twinned provinces of Hải Dương and Quảng Yên (Hải-An) had a recent history of unrest. The governor of Quảng Yên, Hồ Trọng Đĩnh, had recently pacified the coast after several attacks by pirates prior to Dupuis' arrival.[48] In the summer of 1871, a group of Hải-An officials led by Tôn Thất Thuyết, who reappears later in this story, and Lê Tuấn captured and summarily executed a band of thieves without first consulting the imperial court, an action that cost them each a demotion in rank.[49] By September, piracy became such a significant problem on the coast that the Vietnamese court allowed Senez and the *Bourayne* to attack ships under the guidance of Hải-An officials.[50] Senez, like the Black Flags in the uplands, was incorporated into the projection of imperial authority. His participation in coastal counterinsurgency quickly expanded; when Dupuis arrived in November, Senez had responsibility for patrols along the coast of Quảng Yên and seaports between Haiphong and Huế.[51]

Unlike Senez, however, neither the provincial bureaucracy nor the Huế court knew Jean Dupuis. A meeting between Dupuis and the Hải-An authorities did little to allay suspicions. On November 18, Lê Tuấn, now the Hải-An borderlands patrol commissioner, received a letter from Senez about Dupuis. Lê Tuấn sailed down from Quảng Yên to Haiphong, approximately fifteen kilometers to the southwest, to inspect the gun dealer's ships and verify his credentials.[52] According to Jean Dupuis, Lê Tuấn doubted the navigability of the Red River into Yunnan, warning Dupuis that, even if he succeeded in reaching Yunnan, the rebels and bandits in the far north would surely kill him.[53] Dupuis responded by attesting to his direct experience with the area. According to Dupuis, Lê Tuấn's order for him to wait in Haiphong while Huế verified his Chinese paperwork was merely a thinly veiled attempt to stall his travel.[54] After a tense meeting with Lê Tuấn, Senez departed Haiphong, leaving Dupuis to await official permission, forwarded through Lê Tuấn, to proceed.[55]

In his first reports to Huế about Dupuis, Lê Tuấn emphasized certain irregularities. For instance, Senez had claimed that Dupuis wanted to use the Red River as a commercial waterway, but Lê Tuấn discovered during his inspection that Dupuis' ships carried guns and ammunition. Although Lê Hữu Thường, the Hải-An governor-general, informed Lê Tuấn that Dupuis presented a contract with China for the weapons, no one in the Hải-An administration had prior knowledge of this contract or his cargo.[56] Despite the presence of the French colony of Cochinchina in the south, the imperial court still ruled northern and central Vietnam. The presence of a French gun dealer contracted by provincial officials in the Qing Empire to deliver weapons via the Red River necessitated the submission of paperwork to the Ministry of Rites in Huế and from there to the local government in Hải-An. Lack of information and Dupuis' seeming ignorance of protocol triggered deep suspicion.[57]

The fifteen-day wait proved too brief for a complete investigation into the French trader's credentials. According to Jean Dupuis, Lê Tuấn sent a messenger to inform him that since the verification of his paperwork would take longer than expected, Dupuis might enjoy spending time in Saigon or Hong Kong, but not in an uncomfortable place like Haiphong. Angered, Dupuis piloted his ship to Quảng Yên to meet Lê Tuấn face to face.[58] Dupuis insisted that he would not wait and, if bandits and rebels impeded the court's approval of his travels, then he would contact Feng Zicai, the Chinese official stationed in Vietnam to fight the Yellow Flags, and propose to work with him to bring peace to the area. According to Dupuis, Lê Tuấn ignored his suggestion and continued to delay him.[59]

Frustrated, Dupuis decided to search for an entrance to the Red River on his own. With a small crew, he piloted the *Son-Tay* from Haiphong along the Thái Bình River, arriving the next day at the office of Lê Hữu Thường, the Hải-An governor-general and Lê Tuấn's superior. When Dupuis, who carried a small arsenal with him, demanded provisions for his crew who remained moored in Haiphong, Lê Hữu Thường offered him large portions of rice and several pigs, chickens, and ducks. In return, Dupuis gave the governor-general a 12mm Lefaucheux carbine rifle, one hundred cartridges of ammunition, and a pair of binoculars.[60] After Lê Hữu Thường inspected his ship, Dupuis returned to Haiphong.

On the morning of December 4, 1872, Dupuis and his entourage began a meandering journey along the networks of Red River tributaries, which took them through several provincial jurisdictions en route to Hanoi. At Hải Dương on December 15, after failing to find a way to the Red River from the Thái Bình River, Dupuis ignored the exhortations of provincial officials that he stop for inspection. Three days later, the Dupuis party finally reached the Red River, an event celebrated with cannon shot. Shortly thereafter, officials in Hưng Yên, alarmed by the sounds of cannons, ordered the military into defensive positions as Dupuis approached.[61] Dupuis recalled that although he did not personally meet the governor in Hưng Yên, he nonetheless received rice, pigs, chickens, and ducks upon his arrival. In exchange, as in Hải Dương, Dupuis offered a Lefaucheux. On December 22, 1872, continuing along the Red River, the Dupuis party arrived in Hanoi, again ordering cannons shot to announce his presence.[62] Bùi Thức Kiên, the governor-general of Hà-Ninh (Hanoi-Ninh Bình), notified Huế that he could not stop this well-armed gun dealer.[63] Jean Dupuis' travel from Haiphong to Hanoi was filled with cannon-shot and gifts from local governments. He had in effect pillaged these communities, unwittingly emulating raids led by the White Flag rebels and imperial bandits, raids announced by gunshots at the village gate.

According to Dupuis, he received a mixed welcome when he finally arrived in Hanoi. Sensing hostility from Vietnamese officials, Dupuis recalled that the Chinese merchant community seemed enthusiastic about him, perhaps due to their own tensions with the imperial authorities.[64] Shortly after his arrival, Dupuis claimed to receive a response to his antibandit proposal, which came from Feng Zicai. Feng, according to Dupuis' secretary, was not interested in the possibility of collaboration.[65] Upon learning of his arrival, Lê Tuấn insisted that the French gun merchant await the imperial court's confirmation of his credentials before leaving Hanoi again. In his memoirs, Jean Dupuis described the myriad delays he suffered in Hanoi as dogged efforts by Lê Tuấn to impede his progress.[66] Dupuis cast Vietnamese officials like Lê Tuấn as the chief enemies of commerce, progress, and prosperity. In the 1880s, a commercially minded argument for French colonial intervention in northern Vietnam would echo Dupuis' interpretation, ascribing malice to the routine rhythms of imperial bureaucracy.

As in Haiphong, the local context in Hanoi influenced official anxieties about the French arms dealer. When Bùi Thức Kiên, the provincial governor of Hanoi, failed to detain Dupuis, he also failed to police an area that was, from the court's perspective, verging on chaos.[67] In the months prior to Dupuis' arrival, bandits from southern China attacked the area north of Hanoi, taking the lives of forty-four Vietnamese soldiers.[68] Farther north in Thái Nguyên, Hoàng Kế Viêm and Feng Zicai maintained an uneasy collaboration against Pan Lunsi and the Yellow Flags.[69] Jean Dupuis, well armed and ambitious, had sailed into a situation where imperial authority seemed, to those wielding it, precarious and under pressure.

Again ignoring official orders to wait, Dupuis left Hanoi. The Vietnamese authorities responded by tracking his ships. Lê Tuấn ordered a military patrol to scout north into Hưng Hóa, where the Black Flag lieutenant Nong Xiuye served as an imperial military commander.[70] As officials followed Dupuis, Hoàng Kế Viêm, liaison for the Black Flags, ordered Hưng Hóa officials to detain the arms dealer and, if possible, force his return to Hanoi.[71]

While the court and provincial authorities collected reports about his credentials and his movements, Dupuis' voyage continued, bringing him into contact with the Black and Yellow Flags. On January 25, when Dupuis reached the provincial capital of Hưng Hóa, Nong Xiuye and one hundred Black Flag soldiers inspected his ships, performing an action typically reserved for imperial authorities.[72] A few days later, Dupuis reached a government outpost on the north bank of the Red River controlled by Ông Ích Khiêm, the recently retired Vietnamese military official who once assisted in the campaign against Wu Yazhong.[73] Dupuis offered Ông Ích Khiêm a revolver and a Lefaucheux in exchange for his assistance in procuring the aid of a Black Flag officer, stationed across the river, who then supplied the gun merchant's ships with provisions.[74] As Dupuis navigated personal networks, he found imperial officials as necessary as imperial bandits.

However, his encounter with a group hostile to imperial authority would have long-lasting consequences. In February 1873, as he proceeded north along the Red River, Jean Dupuis developed an especially close relationship with Pan Lunsi's Yellow Flag Army. On February 9, he arrived at a Yellow Flag post.[75] For a week, Dupuis enjoyed the hospitality of Pan Lunsi's lieutenants. They informed him of their hope to safely return to southern China, fleeing the Black Flags and the Vietnamese authorities. When Pan Lunsi arrived to meet with Dupuis, they discussed the ongoing war between the Black and Yellow Flags as well as Pan's desire for absolution for his earlier rebellion in China.[76] For Pan Lunsi, meeting Jean Dupuis was an opportunity to broadcast his intentions to the Qing Empire. As someone with official connections to the Chinese bureaucracy, Dupuis might relay a message of atonement on Pan's behalf. For Jean Dupuis, the Yellow Flags provided crucial intelligence and assistance as he moved arms across the Red River. For imperial Vietnam and the Black Flags, however, this relationship meant that the Yellow Flags had the potential to forge contacts with French merchants who, in the case of Dupuis, acted outside the control of the imperial authorities.

Concerned about Dupuis, imperial officials requested information from Jean Gauthier, a French Catholic priest in Huế. In early February, Gauthier provided the Privy Council a letter detailing Dupuis' activities.[77] After meeting with Gauthier, Phan Đinh Bình, secretary at the Ministry of Rites, recalled the priest evading questions and stressing the complexity of his knowledge about Dupuis.[78] Still uncertain about Dupuis' true intentions, court officials anxiously awaited further reports from the north.[79]

Continuing his journey north, Dupuis arrived in Lào Cai on February 20. He noted the utter desolation of the once vibrant trading port. Local merchants, he claimed, confided in him that they desperately longed for an end to Black Flag rule.[80] He coupled his friendship with Pan Lunsi and the Yellow Flags with a condemnation of Liu Yongfu, who, in Dupuis' narrative of events, was an enemy of free trade and progress.

After three months on the Red River, Dupuis delivered his cargo to the Chinese authorities in Yunnan and prepared to descend again for Hanoi. Hoping to forestall his delays with the Vietnamese authorities, who still tracked his ships, Dupuis met with Qing officials in Yunnan to assure the validity of his travel documents and the delivery of paperwork to Huế. He also offered to mediate the surrender of Pan Lunsi, preparing a letter that formally requested the help of the Yellow Flags in the exploration of mining sites in northern Vietnam.[81] He hoped that he could provide a means to clemency for Pan Lunsi in exchange for intelligence about mineral resources in the mountains.

Unknown to Jean Dupuis, as he traveled to Yunnan, Huế received reports of his time with the Yellow Flags. "The upland areas of Hưng Hóa," declared the Privy Council in an edict dated March 19, "are rife with bandits."[82] The Privy Council ordered a detailed account of Dupuis' travels, noting that fresh reports of Yellow Flag raids seemed to follow Dupuis' arrival in China.[83] A French merchant, it seemed, was actively arming enemies of Vietnam.[84]

When he returned to Hanoi in May, after procuring salt and rice from a local merchant and hiring a guide, Dupuis informed the authorities that he intended to journey again "through upland areas" to Yunnan.[85] As Dupuis left, local reports from the mountains of Hưng Hóa claimed that he had sold weapons to Pan Lunsi.[86] Once made aware of the allegations, Dupuis' secretary sent a report to Huế denying any assistance to the Yellow Flags. However, the evidence against Dupuis, in the eyes of the Court, was damning.[87]

Dupuis' actions during his second visit to Hanoi only made matters worse. As they approached Hanoi, at a place called Kim Liên, his entourage fired on two Vietnamese officials, wounding one and killing another. When he moored his ships in Hanoi, the warm reception from the Chinese merchant community did nothing to allay imperial fears of an insurgent conspiracy.[88] Assured of his bad intentions, the court ordered Dupuis arrested, dispatching Nguyễn Tri Phương, a senior military officer and borderlands patrol commissioner, to detain him.[89] Held in the Hanoi citadel, Jean Dupuis awaited assistance from the French colonial authorities in Saigon. Francis Garnier, *le grand mandarin*, soon came to his defense.

FRANCIS GARNIER, A FAILED INVASION, AND FRENCH COLONIALISM

Long before his arrival in Hanoi, Francis Garnier had expressed his belief that France should expand its presence in the world. "France," he wrote to his parents while still in his teens, "is the arbiter of Europe, only using its influence to spread happiness and improve people's morality."[90] For Garnier, the very future of French civilization depended on empire. "Nations without colonies," he warned, "are dead."[91]

Convinced of the necessity of colonies, Garnier began his overseas career in Cochinchina. A French colony since 1858, Cochinchina became a rich source of empirical evidence for the young naval officer. When he arrived in 1862, Garnier decried the neglect of Cochinchina's natural resources at the hands of Vietnamese officials. French rule, he argued, would bring the benefits of Cochinchina's riches to all.[92] Garnier depicted the imperial bureaucracy as venal and contemptible, an enemy of development, and an impediment to commerce. Jean Dupuis, as of yet unknown to Garnier, would share this interpretation.

In 1866, Garnier put his colonialist sensibilities into practice as a member of the Doudart-Lagrée expedition. This expedition sought a viable commercial path to China from Cochinchina, a path that would open southern China to the very same forces of development and commerce that Garnier claimed to defend in Cochinchina.[93] When the expedition stopped short in southern Yunnan, Garnier remarked that the Red River, which Jean Dupuis would chart some four years later, could serve as a connective pathway from Saigon to China.[94] Although the search for the source of the Mekong failed, the expedition provided Garnier with an opportunity to appreciate a potential commercial link between French Cochinchina and Yunnan.

That link, Garnier thought, would lead to wealth. The "Yunnan myth," a popular assumption that the southern Chinese province of Yunnan contained vast riches, motivated his participation in the expedition, which aimed to "penetrate and exploit" Yunnan's immense copper and tin reserves.[95] For Garnier, the Red River was a path to mineral wealth and, consequently, national prestige for France.

The Red River also inspired religious leaders, who saw a pathway for missionary work. In 1869, Paul Puginier, the apostolic vicar of Western Tonkin, proposed charting the river in a letter to the Société des Missions Étrangeres. Missionaries, he speculated, could easily travel the river from Hanoi to Yunnan.[96] Where Puginier saw a route for the church, Garnier saw an artery for empire.

In 1870, following the end of the Doudart-Lagrée expedition, Francis Garnier briefly returned to France. He witnessed the national humiliation of the Franco-Prussian War, which only intensified his desire for empire.[97] Garnier's vision of empire as national rejuvenator anticipated the later work of Anatole Leroy-Beaulieu, author of *De la colonisation chez les peuples modernes* (1874).[98] Leroy-Beaulieu would argue that France should acquire colonies for commercial and national benefit, thus inducing the evolution of "inferior peoples toward civilization."[99] These ideas, before they were articulated on the page, became the inspiration for Garnier's aggression in the Red River Delta.

Following a stay in France, Francis Garnier returned to Cochinchina as Jean Dupuis was arrested in Hanoi. In Saigon, Admiral Dupré, head of the Cochinchinese administration, assigned Garnier the task of negotiating the gun dealer's release. According to a letter sent to his brother, Garnier boasted that Dupré gave him carte blanche in the pursuit of justice for Dupuis, as well as unofficial orders to secure the commercial opening of the Red River for the benefit of France.[100] In a letter sent to Dupuis in October 1873, written at the Dominican mission at Đồ Sơn en route to Hanoi, Francis Garnier promised not to abandon the cause of opening the Red River.[101] Upon his arrival in Hanoi, together with two hundred French marines, Garnier claimed that Dupuis' predicament reflected the imperiled condition of the court's authority in northern Vietnam, a region dominated by the Black Flags.[102] Presenting a list of demands to the imperial authorities, Garnier awaited a response at the side of Jean Dupuis and his entourage.

In Huế, the court had formed a disquieting picture of Francis Garnier, one that paralleled their understanding of Dupuis. Trần Tiễn Thành, a veteran of the bandit wars of the 1860s, expressed his suspicions about Garnier's true intentions. At the same time, Đặng Xuân Bảng, the governor-general of Hải-An who fought against Wu Yazhong, reported the appearance of five other French ships at the Cape of Đồ Sơn.[103] From the perspective of the court, hostile forces were gathering in the north.

After receiving no response to his demands, Garnier dictated his statement declaring the end of Nguyễn authority over the Red River to Dupuis' interpreter, Nguyễn Chăm, and ordered the attack on Vietnamese positions in Hanoi. His invasion surprised many, including Paul Puginier.[104] Initially, Puginier discouraged Garnier from military action, fearing reprisals against Catholic communities in the wake of an uprising.[105] Once Garnier seized Hanoi, however, Puginier dispatched Père Six, a convert and priest from Phát Diệm, to establish relations between the newly proclaimed administration and Catholic communities.[106] Puginer's sense of caution gave way to a guarded optimism about a potential new order in northern Vietnam.

Garnier's aggression brought about the death of Jean Dupuis' arresting officer, the Vietnamese military official Nguyễn Tri Phương. As Giorgios Vlavianos, who was detained as a member of Dupuis' crew, commanded an assault on the eastern gate of the city, Garnier led a strike at the southern gate.[107] During the siege of the southern gate, Garnier's division injured Nguyễn Tri Phương and killed his son, Nguyễn Lâm.[108] Gravely wounded and mourning his son's death, Nguyễn Tri Phương refused food and water after being taken prisoner by Garnier. He died the following month.[109]

In response to the attack on Hanoi, imperial opinion was divided between the court and regional military officials. In Huế, Nguyễn Văn Tường implored the French representative Paul Philastre to have Garnier remove his forces from Hanoi and the surrounding area, under Vietnamese military escort if necessary.[110] Meanwhile, in northern Vietnam, Hoàng Kế Viêm guided Liu Yongfu and several hundred Black Flag soldiers to positions west of Hanoi.[111] As the court pursued negotiation, provincial military and imperial bandits prepared an offensive.

Garnier soon expanded his presence. From Hanoi, he dispatched French marine units to other provinces along the Red River.[112] However, enforcing his claim to open the river to free commerce required a show of force that left his small army strained. Returning to Hanoi in December, Garnier received word from Paul Puginier that the Black Flags and Hoàng Kế Viêm waited to attack from west of the city.[113] To preempt the offensive, Garnier led a charge from the western gate with a few dozen well-armed allies.

What happened next immeasurably enhanced the reputation of the Black Flags. According to Liu Yongfu, as Garnier's small party advanced, a Black Flag platoon, led by Wu Fengdian, opened fire from a concealed position, killing and wounding several of the French soldiers. Wu Fengdian then ordered the decapitation of five bodies, including those of Francis Garnier and the officer Adrien Balny d'Avricourt.[114] Wu and Liu Yongfu, following the precedent set with their victory over the White Flags, received a large silver payment for delivering heads of fallen enemy soldiers.[115] As soon as news of Garnier's death reached Huế, court officials ordered Hoàng Kế Viêm and Tôn Thất Thuyết to move Liu Yongfu and his followers back to Hưng Hóa to prevent any further escalation of hostilities.[116]

When Wu Fengdian and Liu Yongfu exchanged the severed heads of French military officers for silver, their actions continued an imperially sponsored culture of violence. Once turned over to imperial authorities, heads were displayed as a visceral statement of a rebel's defeat. In this case, the rebels were French. The defeat of Garnier's invasion and failed coup were an act of sanctioned violence in defense of imperial authority.

In the aftermath of Garnier's death, Jean Dupuis recalled an encounter with a Black Flag lieutenant in Hanoi. According to Dupuis, Lin-Tchi, a monstrous figure with an abnormally large head and neck, arrived to assure peaceful relations between France and the Black Flags. For Dupuis, Lin-Tchi represented the Black Flags' unjust oppression of the Yellow Flags and their upland allies. Dupuis also claimed that imperial officials discovered huge caches of opium and weapons with Lin-Tchi's entourage. He prepared, Dupuis speculated, to take revenge on those Lê restorationists and Catholics who sided with Garnier against the Black Flags.[117]

The defeat of Garnier brought Huế and Paris into formal negotiations. After the failed coup, Dupré lost his position in Saigon as governor of Cochinchina and the ministry in Paris ordered the immediate evacuation of the French military from northern Vietnam to facilitate the negotiation of a treaty.[118] The Red River remained under the control of imperial Vietnam and the borderlands remained the domain of the Black Flags. Francis Garnier's effort to launch an uprising had seemingly come to nothing.

DISMEMBERED BODIES

At 7:00 a.m. on November 3, 1875, according to paperwork sent to the French colonial government in Cochinchina, five bodies were exhumed from the Red River Delta. Along with the corpse of Francis Garnier, the headless bodies of Adrien Balny d'Havricourt, a *sergent de la flotte* named Dagorne, a *breveté* named Sorre, and a sailor named Bonifay were found in the moist earth. All five had perished during the failed insurrection two years earlier.[119]

Unlike Garnier and his colleagues, Jean Dupuis did not die in 1873. Following the order to evacuate, Dupuis went first to France and then to Hankou, the town in China where his career began. Until the end of the 1870s, he sent letters to France asking for restitution of expenses incurred on the Red River. Citing correspondence between himself and French officials at the legation in Beijing, Francis Garnier, and the French consulates in Hanoi and Haiphong, Dupuis argued that he had performed an essential service to France. In 1879, following a lengthy investigation, the Chambre des Députés in Paris refused to acknowledge Dupuis' contribution, denying him official recognition, and thus restitution, for his actions in the 1870s.[120]

In 1874, despite orders for French citizens to evacuate the city, several people formerly attached to Dupuis' expedition chose to remain in Hanoi. These included Antoine Ernest Constantine from France, John Brown from Britain, and "Madame Ghislain-Beljonne," who later opened a small cabaret in Hanoi.[121] Giorgios Vlavianos, the captain of the *Hong Kiang*, reappeared in the written record as head of security for the French consulates that were established in 1874. Later in the decade, Vlavianos's career in Vietnam would bring him face to face with both the Yellow Flag Army and the Qing military official Feng Zicai. Ernest Millot, another member of Dupuis' expedition, returned to Shanghai after the evacuation order. In the 1880s, Millot would return to work on the Tonkin-China telegraph network, an element of French infrastructure that, in the early twentieth century, would provide a platform for imperial bandits as well as colonial officials.

As for Jean Dupuis, he eventually returned to Europe. In Paris, he cultivated a reputation as a savant of all things Tonkin. A celebrity in France, he made connections with leaders in the emerging field of geography, which connected the study of unfamiliar places with commercial exploitation. In 1875, as French officials discovered the remains of Francis Garnier in the Red River Delta, Dupuis became a member of the Société de Géographie Commerciale (SGC) in Paris, an organization founded by an aristocrat named Brau du Saint-Pol Lias.[122] Like Francis Garnier, Brau viewed the acquisition of colonial territories as a vehicle for the renewal of France, particularly after the Franco-Prussian War. "Colonization," he wrote "is the most effective spring from which the powers of a people can be refreshed."[123] For Brau, "colons-explorateurs" such as Dupuis provided valuable opportunities for connecting the French nation with the rejuvenating spring of colonialism.[124] During this period, Dupuis focused on publicizing his personal involvement with Garnier as well as the vast commercial potential of northern Vietnam.

On November 28, 1912, Jean Dupuis died in Monaco at the age of eighty-three. A British academic journal eulogized him as the one individual most responsible for the sequence of events that enabled France to establish colonial rule over Tonkin and Annam, and, consequently, all of Indochina.[125] The obituary noted that he helped navigate the Red River into Yunnan, overcoming "difficulties with the Annamite authorities."[126] A large figure in nineteenth-century geography, Jean Dupuis passed away in the early twentieth century, largely ignored by the very country that inherited the consequences of his actions.[127]

FRENCH CONSULATES AND *MISE EN VALEUR* IN LATE IMPERIAL VIETNAM

In 1874, imperial authorities brokered a treaty with France. This agreement, the Philastre Treaty, or Giáp Tuất Treaty in Vietnamese historiography, introduced some fundamental changes to the French presence in imperial Vietnam, including the establishment of two official consulates in Hanoi and Haiphong. These two offices provided the wider network of French observers, including colonial authorities in Saigon and representatives in Huế and Beijing, with information about northern Vietnam and the China-Vietnam borderlands. However, this information, taken from reports produced by consular authorities, was raw data for the development of a *mise en valeur*, a view of the untapped potential of natural resources in imperial Vietnam.

Paul Philastre, a French representative in Huế, signed the treaty together with two Vietnamese officials: Lê Tuấn, who had helped track Jean Dupuis, and Nguyễn Văn Tường, a member of the imperial court who would later be implicated in an insurrection against French colonial authority. On the surface, the Philastre Treaty benefited both sides.[128]

According to the treaty, France promised material goods and respect for imperial rule in exchange for an endorsement of a change in the official relationship between the Huế court and the French Third Republic.[129] Paris provided Vietnam with five steam ships, one hundred cannons, and various small arms. These arms included about one thousand *tabatière* rifles with ammunition.[130] According to the Philastre Treaty, the rifles Vietnam received were at least a decade behind the weapons Jean Dupuis traded. In the 1880s, during an attack on central Vietnam, these rifles would prove ineffective against French ships.

As a sign of the new relationship, imperial Vietnam granted France the right to establish consulates. Consulates in Hanoi and Haiphong could sponsor commercial expeditions by French citizens in Tonkin.[131] These expeditions, although not outlined by the treaty, would provide information about domestic political events in northern Vietnam.

Le Comte de Kergaradec, the first head of the Hanoi consulate, used commercial expeditions to generate an account of the untapped natural resources of northern Vietnam. A *lieutenant de vaisseau*, de Kergaradec had a career in the French navy prior to working in Hanoi.[132] Upon his appointment, he requested reports from merchants and visited with Paul Puginier, still the vicar apostolic of Western Tonkin.[133] On October 10, 1875, de Kergaradec reported to the colonial authorities in Cochinchina about the precarious condition of French interests in northern Vietnam. There were, in his estimation, two principal barriers to commerce and trade in the north: imperial Vietnamese officials and the Black Flags.[134]

De Kergaradec decided to travel through the Red River Delta in order to supplement his initial picture of northern Vietnam. In January 1876 he visited Sơn Tây, a major market and political center on the Red River outside Hanoi. There he met briefly with Vũ Trọng Bình, who once fought floods and bandits in Tuyên Quang. He was, to de Kergaradec, a powerful senior official with a reputation for honesty and fairness.[135] Despite his praise of Vũ Trọng Bình, de Kergaradec lamented the general state of affairs in the north. He reserved particular scorn for the role of Liu Yongfu and the Black Flags, who, he complained, had a stranglehold on commerce in Lào Cai.[136]

Motivated, as was Garnier, by the putative riches of Yunnan, de Kergaradec saw wealth in the borderlands. Unlike Garnier, however, de Kergaradec primarily sought to profit from preexisting patterns of trade, hoping to acquire Lào Cai and its opium revenues for France. To this end, and without the knowledge of the Vietnamese authorities, de Kergaradec initiated direct negotiations with the Black Flags. On March 22, 1876, in response to a request he made through an intermediary, three people claiming to represent Liu Yongfu paid a visit to de Kergaradec in Hanoi.[137] No one from the Black Flags sought official permission to enter discussions with the consulate, and no French official contacted imperial authorities in Huế or Hanoi. The delegation itself consisted of a lieutenant identified as Hoàng Nhị, one relative of Liu Yongfu, and one secretary.[138]

According to de Kergaradec, the Black Flag delegation posed three questions: (1) Does France seek revenge for the death of Francis Garnier? (2) Does France intend to take Lào Cai by force? (3) Will France entertain an offer to purchase Lào Cai from the Black Flags? The envoys presented financial compensation as the only way for the Black Flags to leave Lào Cai, an outcome that would remove what de Kergaradec viewed as a significant barrier to commerce along the Red River.[139]

During his meeting with Black Flag representatives, de Kergaradec attempted to placate their concerns. No one, de Kergaradec assured them, would seek revenge for the death of Garnier. Nor would anyone, acting on behalf of France, try to take Lào Cai from the Black Flags by force. However, de Kergaradec requested a guarantee that French ships and merchants could pass through the area in peace.[140] In response, the Black Flag representatives advised him that any official journeys up the Red River into Black Flag–dominated territory must include a small security force provided by the consulate.[141]

De Kergaradec made such a journey almost two years after his clandestine meeting with the Black Flags. In November 1876, he assembled a group of twenty, including a photographer named Émile Gsell, which traveled from Hanoi to Sơn Tây and met an official escort for the journey to Lào Cai.[142] Although ostensibly surveying the commercial potential of the area, this expedition kept detailed records of the system of customs fees along the Red River from Sơn Tây to Hưng Hóa town (near present-day Việt Trì). Salt, for instance, a government monopoly good, attracted a 3 to 10 percent duty from Nguyễn authorities in Hưng Hóa. One hundred piculs of salt, valued at 320 *quan*, brought in thirty-two *quan* in fees for the local government, fees that contributed to the costs, broadly understood, of transporting the salt to markets.[143] De Kergaradec also observed that annual fees paid by customs posts to the provincial government placed an additional burden on the salt trade.[144]

Additionally, the expedition recorded that customs posts in Black Flag territory farther to the north demanded a much higher duty. In Bảo Hà, a market center along the Red River, de Kergaradec learned that posts charged a 60 percent duty on salt, payable either in silver, opium, tea, or tin. The post in Bảo Hà assessed additional fees of seemingly arbitrary category, including transport fees, inspection fees, and vendor fees.[145] Although he only briefly visited Lào

Cai, de Kergaradec valued customs duties collected there at over 90,000 *francs* a year for the Black Flags.[146]

Through this consular expedition, de Kergaradec developed an understanding of the political situation in northern Vietnam that cast uplands populations as potential allies to French interests. This theme, also present in French colonial correspondence about the uplands of central Vietnam, became a key justification for the expansion of French colonial rule later in the nineteenth century.[147] When Vietnamese officials in Lào Cai relayed a message from the leader of the Black Flags outlining the proper conduct for foreign visitors, de Kergaradec saw imperial weakness.[148] With local officialdom working as couriers for the Black Flags, de Kergaradec commented that their powerful leader, Liu Yongfu, was "an ignorant, unyielding, and mistrustful bandit who has lived by raping the mountains for these past twenty years."[149] He cast the Black Flags as the enemy of uplands populations.[150] He also hoped to use his personal connection with the Black Flags, from their secret meeting in Hanoi, to create a fatal schism in Liu's organization.[151] For de Kergaradec, weakening the Black Flags would not only remove a barrier to the commercial development of northern Vietnam, it would also ensure a positive role for France as defenders of the mountains.

As de Kergaradec held meetings and visited Lào Cai, the Black Flags continued their struggle against the Yellow Flags with imperial support. Still the Black Flag leader, Liu Yongfu received a promotion to vice military commander in the Vietnamese imperial bureaucracy. An order from the court granted all Black Flags who played a part in Garnier's defeat a significant monetary reward.[152] Black Flag soldiers now existed in a parallel relationship to officials with imperial titles, even as their roles as imperial bandits at times conflicted with the Vietnamese administration.

Liu Yongfu's promotion and the rewards granted to his soldiers preceded the transfers of two high-ranking Black Flag allies to positions of considerable power. In 1874, Hoàng Kế Viêm served as governor-general of Sơn-Hưng-Tuyên and Tôn Thất Thuyết as the governor of Sơn Tây and counselor for military affairs.[153] These two officials helped to escalate the campaign against the Yellow Flags, aiding Liu Yongfu's war with Pan Lunsi. In early 1874, they sent armies to chase the Yellow Flags from Tuyên Quang. In recognition of this accomplishment, the Privy Council in Huế emphasized the need to either gain the awed submission of the Yellow Flags or carry out their swift and thorough elimination.[154] The Black Flags, as imperial bandits, strengthened their alliance with the Vietnamese Empire.

For the imperial court, especially after the new treaty, the defeat of the Yellow Flags remained a priority. To subdue Pan Lunsi, the Privy Council briefly considered sending requests both to China and, strangely, even the French military stationed in Hanoi.[155] While authorities in Huế deliberated, attacks by the Yellow Flags triggered a minor rebellion in Cao Bằng, as members of uplands populations blocked salt and rice shipments in borderlands areas close to Guangxi.[156] In response, the Cao Bằng administration requested permission from Huế to have cannons transferred to Cao Bằng from Guangxi, an action that would have involved the cooperation of the Qing Empire and the provincial Guangxi officials. However, the grand secretariat and Ministry of Military denied their request, signaling a desire to defeat the Yellow Flags without the assistance of China.[157]

For months, the struggle against Pan Lunsi continued. In August, imperial soldiers, who came from as far away as the central Vietnamese coast, dealt a blow to the Yellow Flags outside Sơn Tây.[158] The Yellow Flags went north into the Black Flag stronghold of Hưng Hóa.[159] In September, Pan Lunsi offered his surrender in a letter to Hoàng Kế Viêm.[160] The court, unimpressed, ordered Hưng Hóa governor Nguyễn Huy Kỳ to demand Liu Yongfu capture Pan Lunsi as quickly as possible.[161]

Huế continued to rely on the alliance between the Black Flags and the imperial armies until evidence of new financial devastation emerged. According to reports, tax funds in the beleaguered province of Tuyên Quang had dwindled in the wake of Yellow Flag raids.[162] In the wake of this news, the court approved a radical overhaul of the provincial system to defeat Pan Lunsi. Four "routes" (V: *đạo*) would be led by four military commanders. This change put Liu Yongfu in charge of the route of Hưng Hóa (coterminous with Hưng Hóa Province) and three other officials in charge of similarly delimited areas.[163]

While this change expanded the official power of the Black Flags, it also consolidated military authority through northern Vietnam. The imperial reaction was to endorse a form of military rule that recalled the commandery system of the early nineteenth century, a system officially dismantled with the introduction of the province during the Minh Mạng reign. The provincial project, designed in the 1830s to routinize imperial power, was now in full reverse.

As it authorized radical changes in northern Vietnam, the Privy Council also tried to control the actions of Liu Yongfu, its most high-profile imperial bandit. In January 1875, it observed that Liu's new official position came with responsibilities. The Black Flag leader had to follow the mandates of the court as well as his immediate superiors. Despite orders to defend Tuyên Quang and all of Hưng Hóa Province against the Yellow Flags, the Privy Council complained that Liu's primary concern was the Black Flags' presence along the upper Red River. Concerned about French-sponsored merchants encountering the Black Flags, the council ordered Liu Yongfu to concentrate on the extermination of Pan Lunsi, an assignment that would take him far from the trading port of Lào Cai.[164]

In Beijing, the Qing Grand Council, which followed reports from Guangxi, soon became involved in the hunt for Pan Lunsi.[165] Within months, the Grand Council identified the Yellow Flags as a threat to the security of China, citing Pan Lunsi's contact with the French and his looming threat to the security of the borderlands.[166] In March, after the Yellow Flags humiliated the provincial administrations of Bắc Ninh and Thái Nguyên, the Vietnamese Imperial Court accepted Chinese assistance, assigning Tôn Thất Thuyết to work with the Qing military against Pan Lunsi.[167] At this point, assistance from China, while not wholly welcomed, was unavoidable.

The defeat of Pan Lunsi was a coordinated effort. Qing armies, led by Li Yangcai and Liu Yucheng, flushed most of the Yellow Flags from Thái Nguyên as the Black Flags and Nguyễn soldiers awaited them at Pan's old base area in Hà Dương.[168] When the Yellow Flags sought refuge there, they were ambushed. The war with Pan Lunsi ended with the Yellow Flag leader drawn and quartered in the fields around his former stronghold.[169] Mutilated and dismembered, the body of the Yellow Flag leader signaled the end of an uncooperative imperial bandit, a victory born from the bond between the Black Flags, Vietnam, and, most recently, the Qing Empire.

However, victory over the Yellow Flags exacted some severe costs. After Pan Lunsi's execution, Tôn Thất Thuyết reported that residents displaced by Chinese military operations refused to return to their villages.[170] The aftermath of counterinsurgency meant lasting dislocation for communities caught between the Yellow Flags and their enemies. According to oral traditions in the area west of Hanoi, residents openly taunted the leader of the Black Flags, whom they believed complicit in displacing villagers: "The Black Flags called themselves righteous yet take whatever they see for themselves; Liu Yongfu cares about wealth and his underlings murder as they wish."[171]

For Liu Yongfu, victory over the Yellow Flags was lucrative. In February 1878, he began receiving a monthly salary and supplies directly from Huế. The Ministry of Revenue also granted Liu a monthly allowance in copper, rice, and salt for the more than 1,400 registered members of his personal militia.[172] Later that year, the grand secretariat authorized the award of a special dispensation for Liu Yongfu on the occasion of the fiftieth year of Nguyễn Hồng Nhậm, the Tự Đức emperor. He received a *Phi Long* (Flying Dragon) payment of 30 *quan* gold, recommended by Bùi Văn Dị and authorized by the emperor.[173] The court issued *Phi Long* dispensations to mark special events and recognize meritorious service to the empire.[174] Although the court now embraced Liu Yongfu, not all members of the imperial bureaucracy accepted the Black Flags, an issue that would characterize domestic politics in imperial Vietnam for much of the next decade.[175]

As the Black Flag's liaison to the court, Hoàng Kế Viêm tried to mollify their critics. He encouraged Liu and his lieutenants to lead their followers in land cultivation around Lào Cai, binding them to one location. However, this plan failed. Accustomed to living on customs duties and raids, most Black Flags lacked basic agricultural skills or, at least, the will to acquire them. The local population, as one of Hoàng Kế Viêm's assistants learned, offered no help—no one, he reported, actually believed the Black Flags intended to settle anywhere.[176] Similar to Ngụy Khắc Tuấn decades earlier, Hoàng Kế Viêm hoped to bring sparsely populated regions under sedentary cultivation, ensuring a reliable tax base while controlling powerful imperial bandits in the process.[177] However, Liu Yongfu had no interest in either agriculture or leaving Lào Cai.

With its conventional armies depleted after the war against the Yellow Flags, the Vietnamese court received reports of militias fending off bandit raids on their own. East of Lào Cai in Cao Bằng, a bandit leader named Ông Thất pretended to surrender to the imperial authorities in 1877.[178] However, after offering his submission, he raided villages in search of food.[179] According to Nguyễn Đình Nhuận, the Cao Bằng governor, an uplands militia drove Ông Thất away, chasing him into hiding and defending communities from pillage.[180] In October, Ông Thất fled south to Thái Nguyên.[181] Although they briefly cornered him there with three hundred followers, Vietnamese officials lost track of Ông Thất for the next two years.[182] He reemerged in January 1880 when, together with the Black Flag rival Liu Zhiping, he led a series of raids in Guangxi, allegedly targeting Catholic converts in southern China.[183]

Already resistant to agriculture and politically controversial, the Black Flags further disrupted life in the borderlands. Liu's soldiers refused to pay imperial rates for copper and lead, an action that put them at odds with provincial and court authorities.[184] In March 1878, long after the defeat of the Yellow Flags, Black Flags raided settlements in Hưng Hóa Province, prompting a weak assurance from the provincial authorities, directed at the court, that Liu Yongfu's army could be controlled.[185] Meanwhile, officials in Hanoi demanded, through the court in Huế, a full report of Liu's activities, citing heightened tensions between the Black Flags and de Kergaradec.[186] Hoàng Kế Viêm assured the court that he would complete a full investigation into Liu Yongfu, providing an account of his alleged crimes against imperial authority.[187]

As the division separating pro–Black Flag officials and opponents of Liu Yongfu began to deepen, evidence emerged that demonstrated the true strength of these imperial bandits. As late as 1881, imperial officials in Hưng Hóa had to remind merchants and porters carrying goods to market that they must present their paperwork first to the Vietnamese authorities, even if they delivered to the Black Flags.[188] In areas under Liu Yongfu's control, imperial Vietnamese authority began to seem almost secondary, an afterthought to the power of imperial bandits.

THE LI YANGCAI REBELLION: VIOLENCE THROUGH CONSULAR OPTICS

For de Kergaradec, who gathered information from his post at the Hanoi consulate, the employment of imperial bandits and the borderlands culture of violence became a study in chaos, inefficiency, and disorder. In 1878, only four years after the establishment of the consulate, a rebellion led by a Qing officer named Li Yangcai provided de Kergaradec the opportunity to see, and produce an understanding of, cooperative counterinsurgency involving China and Vietnam. As with his investigation of customs posts, de Kergaradec's reports on Li Yangcai emphasized the endemic chaos, thick banditry, and the threat to French interests in the borderlands.

Before he rebelled, Li Yangcai commanded Qing armies against the Yellow Flags, an experience that left him with a detailed knowledge of the borderlands.[189] After Pan Lunsi's defeat, Li recruited a few thousand followers from Qinzhou and announced his intention to overthrow the Nguyễn dynasty. In its place, he planned to reestablish the Lý dynasty, which had vanished from political power six centuries earlier.[190] From China, Li crossed into Vietnam at Lạng Sơn, seizing market centers as a base of operations.[191]

Provincial authorities in Vietnam and China coordinated their response to Li Yangcai's insurgency. Within days of Li attacking Lạng Sơn, Yang Zhongya, the governor of Guangxi, provided the governor of Lạng Sơn and Cao Bằng, Nguyễn Đình Nhuận, with information about the size of Li's personal army and his last known whereabouts.[192] Nguyễn Đình Nhuận then led imperial armies in pushing the Lý pretender deep into the mountains of southern Lạng Sơn.[193] To assist in the hunt for Li Yangcai, the Guangxi governor recommended that Feng Zicai, who had recent experience hunting bandits in Vietnam, assist the Vietnamese military.[194] Over the next two months, Feng and several thousand soldiers from Guangxi helped drive Li Yangcai and his followers even further south into Bắc Ninh and Thái Nguyên.[195] As he fled, Li commanded his followers to loot market towns, stealing resources as they moved south.[196]

Some of Li's victims began reporting his activities to the Vietnamese authorities. Among these was Xie Pangping, a member of a Chinese merchant association in Bắc Ninh. On December 16, 1878, the court in Huế received a communication from Xie Pangping, who identified himself as an *An Nam Đông Kinh Thượng Khách* and an *An Nam Bắc Ninh Thượng Khách*, both of which indicate that Xie was a Qing subject legally residing in Vietnam. In his report, Xie claimed that Li Yangcai's band had dwindled to half its original size due to defeat, starvation, and illness.[197]

As the authorities in Nguyễn Vietnam coordinated with Qing officials and relied on intelligence reports from Chinese merchants, the campaign against Li Yangcai attracted the attention of French representatives in Beijing. On November 7, 1878, an official at the French legation, Gabriel Devéria, supplied Louis Lafont, the governor of Cochinchina, with the transcript of a conversation between Devéria and a member of the Qing Grand Council.[198] In the transcript, Devéria initially asked about a "Guangxi insurrection," to which the Qing official replied that he knew nothing about a rebellion in Guangxi Province. Once Devéria mentioned Li Yangcai, the Qing official outlined the cooperative effort involving the Nguyễn government, even citing the anti–Wu Yazhong campaign ten years earlier as a precedent.[199] Later that month, when another French legation official contacted a Qing official in Guangxi about the possibility of French assistance, the Qing official replied that any such proposals to send foreign soldiers to Vietnam must pass through the Huế court.[200] In Beijing, French representatives attempted to intervene in a case of cooperative counterinsurgency, and much like Dupuis years earlier, officials expressed disinterest, keeping France at arm's length.

French officials in Saigon, in contrast to Devéria in Beijing, had another source for information about Li Yangcai: the Hanoi consulate. In December, a military officer attached to the consulate filed an account of Li Yangcai's raids in Bắc Ninh and Thái Nguyên. This report detailed Li's claim to overthrow the Nguyễn and reestablish the Lý, providing a far more complete picture of the rebellion than did reports from the French legation.[201]

Into 1879, Li Yangcai and the campaign against him created a fertile atmosphere for the revival of long-dormant rebellions. In the wake of Li's uprising, a Yellow Flag lieutenant, Gao Shi'er, who fled in the wake of Pan Lunsi's execution, occupied villages in Hưng Hóa.[202] In Tuyên Quang, uplanders formerly tied to the White Flag Rebellion of the 1860s renewed raids of lowland villages.[203] In Thái Nguyên, Liu Zhiping, the rival of Liu Yongfu who had recently submitted to Nguyễn authority, renounced his loyalty to Vietnam and attached himself to Li.[204] Also in Thái Nguyên, two unknown thieves identified as Lý Lục and Lý Thất ransacked lowland villages throughout the summer of 1879. When Nông

Đức Đàng, a militia leader who had tracked the two Lýs into the mountains, reported their arrest to the provincial authorities, he noted that they declared their loyalty to the rebel Lý dynasty of Li Yangcai.[205]

As reports from the Qing and Nguyễn bureaucracies generated conflicting evidence about the strength and popularity of Li's rebellion, the French consulate in Hanoi gathered intelligence through investigation. In April 1879, de Kergaradec dispatched Giorgios Vlavianos, Jean Dupuis' former colleague who had stayed in Vietnam and worked for the consulate, to Thái Nguyên. Once there, Vlavianos claimed that he was graciously offered a meeting with Feng Zicai, the Qing official leading an army against Li Yangcai. In his report of this meeting, Vlavianos described the rifles used by the Qing and Nguyễn as outdated and poorly maintained.[206] According to Vlavianos, Feng's plan to defeat Li by trapping him in the mountains was proving difficult. Military rice convoys, which transported food to Feng's soldiers, became targets for those uplanders who were, like the Lý brothers in Thái Nguyên, sympathetic to the rebellion. Li Yangcai, despite Feng's best efforts, maintained a steady supply of food by robbing or diverting convoys bound for Feng's soldiers.[207]

Upon his return to Hanoi, Vlavianos supplied the consulate with a letter from Feng Zicai warning against future voyages north. In the letter, Feng cautioned the Hanoi consulate that Liu Yongfu and the Black Flags, despite their cooperation with the Nguyễn and Qing governments, would kill anyone they did not recognize.[208] Heeding this warning, de Kergaradec commissioned no further expeditions, although he continued to update the governor of Cochinchina with news of Li's rebellion.[209]

In his correspondence with Lafont, de Kergaradec developed a depiction of the campaign against Li Yangcai that emphasized the long-term threat posed by China and the Black Flags to French interests.[210] He claimed to have secured the assistance of Feng Zicai with the gradual exit of the Black Flags from areas near the Red River, thus removing a barrier to French control of trade in northern Vietnam.[211] The Black Flags, once the object of diplomatic overtures, became a lethal threat to French interests. De Kergaradec noted that, with the assistance of sympathetic Vietnamese officials such as Hoàng Kế Viêm, the Black Flags were training civilian militia in Sơn Tây, just west of Hanoi. Besides the obvious military dangers they presented, de Kergaradec argued that the Black Flags also interfered with the establishment of a borderlands customs service, a key provision of the 1874 treaty and a personal priority of de Kergaradec.[212]

Advocates of French interests operated outside the consulate as well. Although de Kergaradec envisioned an alliance between France and uplanders, an early ally of the consulate emerged from within the Vietnamese imperial bureaucracy. Nguyễn Hữu Độ, the governor of Hanoi Province, suggested that all Chinese soldiers return north as soon as possible. Li's rebellion, he argued, did not pose a significant threat to Vietnam. Moreover, a long-term Chinese military presence would irrevocably harm the population.[213] Although the court rejected Nguyễn Hữu Độ's proposal, his position placed him at odds with Nguyễn officials and the Black Flags, as well as evincing a sympathy for the interests of de Kergaradec.[214] In fact, Nguyễn Hữu Độ, who would become a powerful official under the French protectorate after 1883, also claimed to have defeated similar bandits without Chinese assistance.[215] The symmetry between the agenda of this rather controversial official, described by Đặng Phong as an "enthusiastic servant" of French interests in Vietnam, and that of the Hanoi consulate had a basis in their shared hostility toward both Chinese military assistance and the Black Flags.[216]

After leading a thirteen-month rebellion in northern Vietnam, Li Yangcai was finally captured in late October 1879. According to Feng Zicai, a militia in Thái Nguyên assisted his soldiers to fight Li and his followers. After taking Li alive, Feng reported that most of Li's followers either starved in the mountains or drowned in the surrounding lake as they fled.[217] De Kergaradec excitedly relayed news of Li's capture to Lafont in Saigon, speculating the eminent return of all Qing soldiers to China.[218] After his return to Guangxi as a prisoner of China, Li Yangcai was decapitated. To prevent the continuance or reappearance of his rebellion, the Qing Grand Council, on the advice of authorities in Guangxi, allowed Vietnamese officials in Thái Nguyên and Lạng Sơn to display Li's disembodied head as a graphic warning.[219] Just as the head of Garnier signaled the defeat of his invasion in 1873, Li Yangcai's head became a visceral reminder of imperial Vietnamese sovereignty.

For de Kergaradec, the execution of Li Yangcai did little to resolve the obstacles to French interests that he saw throughout northern Vietnam. Smaller Chinese bandits that had forged connections with Li during his brief uprising remained hidden in the mountains of Thái Nguyên and Tuyên Quang.[220] Viewed through the consular optic, these small bands, as well as uplands militias, were substantial threats. Not only did small groups of bandits threaten the safety of expeditions, de Kergaradec also believed that the Vietnamese state would take the existence of these bands as a pretext for blocking the commercial development of northern Vietnam.[221] Furthermore, there was still the issue of the Black Flags. When the bulk of Liu Yongfu's army returned to Lào Cai in January 1880, de Kergaradec reiterated his worries about their disruptive effects on commerce.[222] The following summer, when a French merchant ship encountered problems during a voyage from Hanoi to Lào Cai, de Kergaradec blamed the Black Flags.[223] The consulate's increased level of observation, in effect, provided de Kergaradec with numerous opportunities to discover the enduring threats to French interests in northern Vietnam.

MINES AND MAPS: CHARTING THE BLACK FLAGS AND THE *MISE EN VALEUR*

De Kergaradec, through his role at the Hanoi consulate, also developed an interest in the mineral resources of northern Vietnam. As discussed in chapter 1, mines long played a major part in the imperial economy and monetary system. However, as with Lào Cai and the opium trade, de Kergaradec struggled to compile useful information about mines. Mineral expeditions—gathering intelligence about a vital part of the imperial revenue system under the guise of charting natural resources—became a priority for consular officials. The consular optic, which shaped French official perceptions of the borderlands culture of violence during Li Yangcai's rebellion, also informed the *mise en valeur* that characterized French interests in northern Vietnam. In the 1880s, consular interest in mines took the tangible form of maps, cartographic representations of mineral space.

These maps were plans for the future of French Tonkin. In the case of Jean Dupuis, geography as a form of knowledge was grounded in the French colonial project. Although he lacked Francis Garnier's faith in the restorative properties of overseas colonies for France, Dupuis remained connected to the imperial ideal through his work with the Société de Géographie Commerciale in Paris. In his writing and his map of the Red River, Dupuis presented an estimation of commercial possibilities, forging a link between knoweldge of terrain and the ability to profit from human exchange. In the 1880s, mineral maps were no less an expression of imperial ambition.[224] They represented a more detailed contribution to the emerging picture of northern Vietnam, a picture drawn from the data provided by the consulate offices.

In 1875, de Kergaradec, on the basis of his personal travels and meetings with officials, published an itemized estimation of mining in northern Vietnam.

This rather thin data, de Kergaradec hoped, would be improved with the cooperation of the imperial authorities. As early as spring 1876, the court granted the Haiphong consulate permission to send surveyors into the mountains to search for mining sites.[225] In the 1880s, with the Yellow Flags and Li Yangcai defeated, de Kergaradec hoped that empirical evidence could supplement his initial estimates.

However, compared with information from older sources, unavailable to de Kergaradec, the 1875 figures suggest a drastic reduction in imperial mining.

The contradiction between these tables shows two things. First, de Kergaradec's information was likely wrong. Even considering the deleterious effects of rebellion and banditry on mines, which were frequently abandoned, the consular figures are dwarfed by the decades-old imperial data. Second, and

TABLE 2.1. Mines by mineral and province according to de Kergaradec, 1875

MINERAL	TUYÊN QUANG	HƯNG HÓA	THÁI NGUYÊN	LẠNG SƠN	TOTAL
Copper	1	1	0	1	3
Silver	0	0	5	0	5
Gold	0	0	2	0	2
Total	1	1	7	1	10

Source: CAOM. AGC12986: "Rapports du Consul de France à Hanoi a.s. de l'ouverture du haut du Fleuve Rouge, renseignements sur les ressources minières au Tonkin." De Kergaradec to Duperré, Oct. 10, 1875.

TABLE 2.2. Northern Vietnam mines by mineral and province, ca. 1830s

MINERAL	BẮC NINH	HẢI DƯƠNG	THÁI NGUYÊN	SƠN TÂY	HƯNG HÓA	TUYÊN QUANG	LẠNG SƠN	CAO BẰNG	TOTAL
Gold	1	0	6	0	4	10	9	5	35
Silver	0	0	10	0	2	1	0	0	13
Copper	0	0	0	0	5	2	0	0	7
Tin	0	0	1	0	0	0	0	0	1
Hematite	4	0	12	2	0	2	5	4	29
Zinc	0	1	9	0	0	1	0	0	11
Pig Iron	0	0	0	3	0	0	0	0	3
Salt	5	0	1	2	5	5	2	0	20
Sulfur	0	0	0	0	1	1	0	0	2
Cinnabar	0	0	0	0	0	1	0	0	1
Total	10	1	39	7	17	23	16	9	122

Source: Viện Sử Học, ed., *Khâm định Đại Nam hội điển*, 42:205–44.

perhaps most crucially, de Kergaradec's data demonstrated the weakness of the consulates' ability to gather information.

To address this shortcoming, de Kergaradec and the head of the Haiphong consulate, de Champeaux, organized a mineral expedition in 1881. They selected two men with military and engineering training: Julien Courtin and Horace Villeroi. Previously attached to the Haiphong consulate, Courtin and Villeroi had no serious experience with mineral science or mining, but both young men, born in 1855, proved more than willing to join an expedition.[226] On September 6, de Kergaradec received authorization from imperial officials in Tuyên Quang and Hải Dương, securing the agreement of the Vietnamese authorities for a survey of mineral deposits.[227] A week later, Courtin and Villeroi arrived in Hưng Hóa town, at the confluence of the Red and Black Rivers. From there, a Vietnamese guide accompanied them north.[228] For the entire month of September, Courtin and Villeroi ascended the Red River without incident.

On October 7, however, the expedition ran into trouble. As Courtin and Villeroi approached a Black Flag customs post, their ship was fired upon, fatally wounding one of their porters.[229] After the pair surrendered, a Black Flag soldier inspected their papers and informed them that he could not allow them to pass. Consequently, Courtin and Villeroi returned downriver to Hưng Hóa, where they found a large group of Black Flags visiting the offices of the provincial governor. The pair contacted de Kergaradec for assistance, after which a Vietnamese official in Hanoi assured the consulate that the entire incident stemmed from a simple misunderstanding.[230]

In the days after the alleged incidents in Hưng Hóa, a cook identified only as "Loc" visited the Hanoi consulate. On October 13, Loc learned that a large delegation of Black Flags, including their leader Liu Yongfu, were planning a lengthy stay in Hưng Hóa. When he arrived at Hưng Hóa, Loc saw over two hundred Black Flag soldiers, armed with swords, rifles, and pistols. They stayed as guests among Hưng Hóa's residents, Loc claimed, and dined with local officials while making ritual offerings to several temples.[231]

Loc's information helped explain the problems faced by Courtin and Villeroi, but also provided, for de Kergaradec, further proof of the barriers the Black Flags posed. Loc claimed that Liu Yongfu ordered an attack on the two Frenchmen in Hưng Hóa. The provincial governor then intervened, according to Loc, mollifying Liu and protecting the French engineers. The next day, Liu and the bulk of his entourage departed.[232] To de Kergaradec, the Black Flags had actively interfered with the mineral expedition, blocking the tide of progress in northern Vietnam.

After the incident in Hưng Hoá, Courtin and Villeroi turned their attention to the Black River, which flowed into Vietnam's northwest. By November 25,

1881, they had produced an annotated map that detailed both the limitations of their expedition and the extent of Black Flag control along the waterways of northern Vietnam.[233]

As a document, it charts the failure of their plans. Although Lào Cai ("Lao Kay") sits at the top of the Red River, neither Courtin nor Villeroi reached the Black Flag river port. "Long Lỗ," a Black Flag customs post south of Bảo Hà, appears as a location of interest, along with Hưng Hoá, the site of their encounter with Liu Yongfu's army. Although they intended to map rivers, and despite the usefulness of this map for later expeditions, Courtin and Villeroi's cartography says even more about the complex patchwork of imperial bandits and Vietnamese officials in the mountains and borderlands. Courtin and Villeroi, who both died on the banks of the Black River on January 1, 1882, were followed by two vastly more experienced engineers.[234]

In late 1881, just prior to the deaths of Courtin and Villeroi, Edouard Saladin and Edmond Fuchs arrived in Huế.[235] They met with Henri Rheinart, the chargé d'affaires for France, and with Vietnamese officials at court, securing imperial permission for a study of mines. Their initial report emphasized Vietnam's historical reliance on Chinese labor for mining and commented on the general anemia of mineral exploitation.[236]

In Huế, Fuchs and Saladin gained only a limited picture of the mineral resources of northern Vietnam, a fact largely due to their restricted access to data. In December 1881, with the support of the imperial authorities, they visited zinc mines in central Vietnam.[237] After traveling north to survey mineral deposits in Quảng Yên, near Haiphong, Fuchs and Saladin were prevented by the court from further expeditions. Much to the displeasure of de Kergaradec, the mountainous regions of Thái Nguyên, Tuyên Quang, and Hưng Hóa provinces remained, for French engineers, undocumented.[238] Frustrated, Fuchs and Saladin returned to Haiphong.[239] Once there, ignoring their lack of official permission, they surveyed mineral deposits in the surrounding area. Their efforts brought them into contact with a group of Black Flags, who detained the engineers, to the anger of de Kergaradec, before ordering them away.[240] They soon left for Saigon, subsequently conducting surveys of mineral deposits in Cambodia before returning to France in March.[241]

Following their return from Vietnam, Saladin and Fuchs published articles in the *Annales des Mines*, pieces that interwove empirical data with colonial ideology. Trained as mineral engineers, with experience in France as well as work in Vietnam, Fuchs and Saladin viewed their work as part of the larger project to spread free trade and civilization. Mineral surveys would "open the Red River to the free travel of civilized people."[242] These articles appeared as a commercial-colonial agenda developed in Paris. Politicians such as Eugène

Etiénne, an associate of Léon Gambetta and Jules Ferry in the Third Republic, argued that colonial expansion should involve a series of businesses "prudently and practically conducted" to "strengthen, extend, and enrich France."[243] As with the Red River or the Mekong in the eyes of Francis Garnier, mines cut a path to national prestige through empire.

Like Garnier and Dupuis, Fuchs and Saladin seemed to anticipate the later theoretical work of Leroy-Beaulieu. Their call to open the Red River as a commercial artery for "civilized people" appeared in print two decades prior to Anatole Leroy-Beaulieu's *La renovation de l'Asie* (1901), which developed the theme of renewal through colonial rule.[244]

Their publications also included maps of significantly more detail than those of Courtin and Villeroi. Compiled from their own research as well as earlier maps by Jules Harmand and others, the 1882 mineral map captures Fuchs and Saladin's view of the developmental potential of Vietnam while tracing the fault lines of imperial bandit domains. As the words "Royaume d'Annam" fall over the Black River in the northwest and along the Central Highlands, "Pavillons Noirs" (Black Flags) marks the domain of Liu Yongfu (fig. 2.4).

Whereas Jean Dupuis explained his experiences in the language of the geographical movement, Saladin and Fuchs emerged as engineers of empire.[245] Concerned less with the Yunnan myth and more with a full account of mineral resources, Fuchs and Saladin set out to document the potential for trade and development in northern Vietnam. As an element of the consular optic, their work produced knowledge about minerals that was laced with condemnations of the Vietnamese Empire, thus creating a redemptive role for France in Vietnam.

FRANCE AND IMPERIAL VIETNAM

The identification and defense of French interests, the surveillance of Vietnamese counterinsurgency, and the cartographic representation of northern Vietnam's mineral resources all flowed from the establishment of consular offices. Consular optics, the particular way of seeing sponsored by de Kergaradec in Hanoi, resulted in a picture of disorder, a refracted vision of Nguyễn Vietnam composed to complement the interests of those advocating colonial rule. To paraphrase Henri Bergson, de Kergaradec's charge of disorder cloaked what he was really thinking of—namely, the introduction of an ordering, commercially attuned, and development-inducing French colonial authority.

As de Kergaradec made the case for French interests, complained about Chinese interference during the Li Yangcai rebellion, and commissioned expeditions for mines and maps, his concerns complemented those of Nguyễn Hữu Độ.

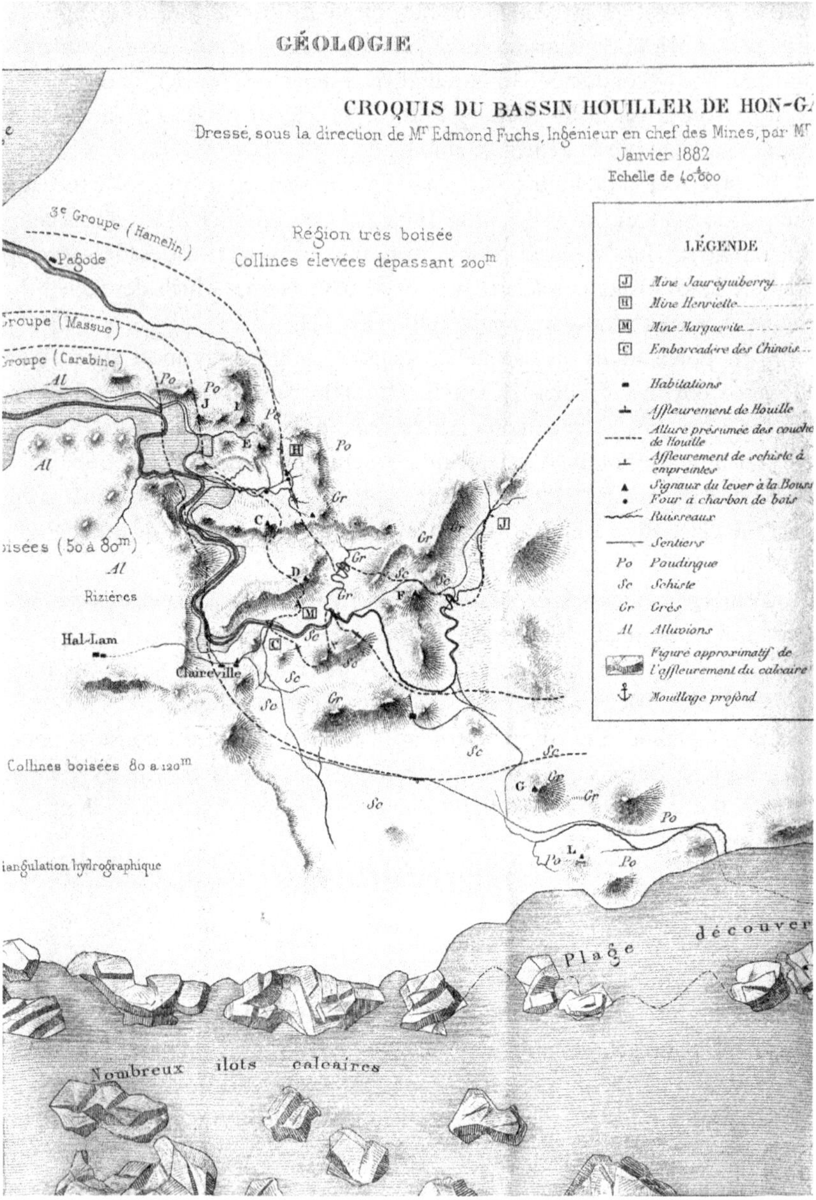

FIG. 2.3. Fuchs and Saladin's "Hon-Gac" map. From Fuchs and Saladin, "Mémoire sur l'exploration des gites de combustibles et quelques-uns des métallifères de l'Indo-Chine," *Annales des Mines* 2, no. 5 (1882).

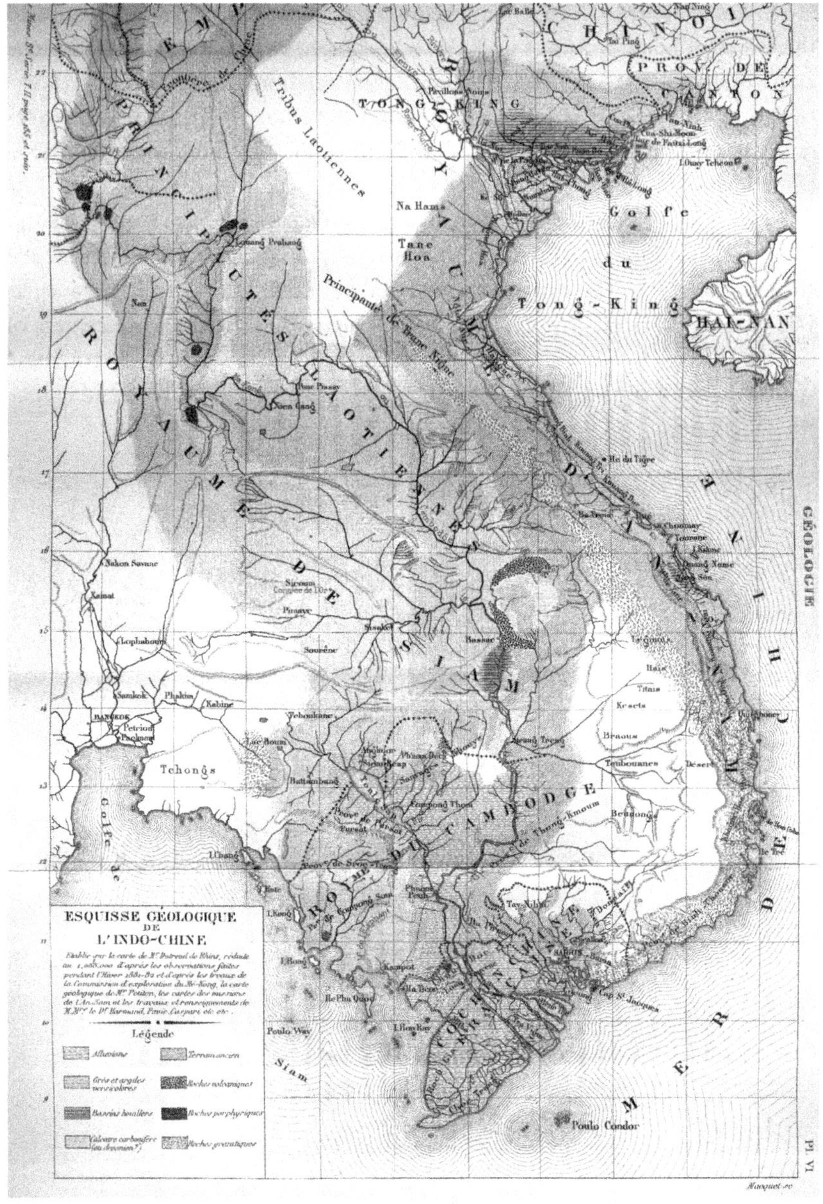

FIG. 2.4. Fuchs and Saladin's mineral map of Vietnam. From Fuchs and Saladin, "Mémoire sur l'exploration."

On October 19, 1880, Nguyễn Hữu Độ sent a report to the Privy Council and the Office of Foreign Affairs in Huế. He identified two chief problems that the court had to resolve in order to secure good relations with France. First, the court had to break the Black Flags' monopoly over commerce in Lào Cai. Second, tax administration, especially in the China-Vietnam borderlands, suffered from an endemic corruption that had to be eliminated.[246]

The congruence between the claims in Nguyễn Hữu Độ's 1880 report and the agenda promoted by de Kergaradec seems, at first glance, solid evidence of cooperation. However, this consistency tells us something else. The consular way of seeing in northern Vietnam was a refractive lens for the advancement of not only French interests, but also for factional concerns within the Vietnamese state. Much the same can be said for the coming war between China and France over Vietnam.

3

IMPERIAL BANDITS AND THE SINO-FRENCH WAR

DEEP in the night of March 26, 1883, a declaration appeared on the wall of the Hanoi Citadel. According to Commandant Berthe de Villers, the French officer who found it, the note came from Liu Yongfu, the leader of the Black Flags.

The mighty warrior [*le guerrier robuste*] Liu makes the following declaration to the French:

> You are nothing more than bandits before the law; other nations could not be lesser than you. Wherever you go, you say that you come to teach the one true religion. This is only a cover for your attacking good people; you lie yet again when you pretend to come for trade, you come to rape the land and nothing else.
>
> You have the heart of a vile animal and your behavior is that of wild beasts.
>
> Since your arrival in Vietnam [*le royaume d'Annam*], you have done nothing but take over citadels and murder imperial officials.
>
> Your crimes are as numerous as the hairs on your head.
>
> You impair trade and industry [*des douanes et faites*], the base of economic production, a crime that merits death.
>
> You are the cause of the people's misery and the country lies on the verge of ruin.
>
> All the people are irritated and heaven [*ciel*] cries for vengeance.

The note concludes with a violent ultimatum to all French military in Vietnam: Cut off the heads of the Consul [de Kergaradec], the Commandant en Chef [Henri Rivière], and the Chef de Bataillon [Berthe de Villers] and bring them to me at my camp; only then will I show mercy by not hunting you down and killing you.[1]

In all likelihood, this declaration is misattributed to Liu Yongfu or, at the very least, its French translation reflects some broad interpretive license. For instance, the historian Etienne Võ Đức Hạnh claims that Liu Yongfu used colloquial Vietnamese terms to refer to himself and the French.[2] The note also may have been written by a French military officer with assistance from a Vietnamese imperial official—a telling detail from Liu's supposed description of the might of his armies seems to reference the Battle of Thermopylae. In the note, Liu claims: "I have led my soldiers to Phu Hoai Duc [outside Hanoi]; my battle flags and my spears block out the sun, my rifles and my swords are as numerous as the trees of a forest."[3] This sentence conjures up a picture of an embattled French military in the Red River Delta, hiding in the Hanoi Citadel, waiting to wage war against an enemy that threatens not only France, but civilization itself.

That war came soon. When the note appeared in Hanoi, Commandant de Villers stood guard over the citadel while his superior, Commandant Henri Rivière, led a small force of soldiers to Nam Định, southeast from Hanoi along the Red River. Rivière's actions over the next few months would set the course for a violent conflict involving France, the Qing Empire, Vietnam, and, most significantly, imperial bandits in the mountains.

In contrast to Francis Garnier, whose ill-fated séjour in Hanoi transpired a decade earlier, Henri Rivière lacked any intellectual interest in colonialism.[4] However, he did have practical experience in colonial situations; while serving in the French navy in New Caledonia in 1878, Rivière led a group of European settlers in defense of their property during a violent anticolonial revolt.[5] Unlike Garnier, however, Rivière never mentioned the need to redeem the world through French civilization. His time in Vietnam, during his mid-fifties, should have preceded a position in Paris en route to a quiet retirement.

After becoming commandant de la division in Cochinchina in 1881, Rivière soon found himself leading the French forces in northern Vietnam, arriving in Hanoi from Saigon on April 10, 1882.[6] Appraising the situation in the north, Cochinchina governor Le Myre de Vilers argued that a French military presence could defend the gains of the 1874 treaty against the Black Flags. In a letter to Rivière, de Vilers described Liu's army as "pirates" who threatened lawful commercial activity.[7] In another letter, he cited the case of Saladin and Fuchs, the mining engineers Liu Yongfu detained, as evidence of the vast threat the Black Flags posed to French interests.[8] If Vietnamese imperial officials could not help resolve the apparent contradiction between the provisions of the 1874 treaty and the frustrations of French-sponsored expeditions, then de Vilers would send French forces north. Believing the imperial court and the provincial administration either unable or unwilling to enforce the treaty, de Vilers dispatched Rivière to confront the enemies of progress in the Red River Delta.

In the declaration posted on the Hanoi Citadel wall, Liu Yongfu set a deadline for the French to turn over their leaders to the Black Flags: May 10, 1883. By May 19, Henri Rivière would be dead. His death would provide the spark for war in Vietnam, a war over Nguyễn sovereignty and the Black Flags, the issue of free trade in the borderlands, and the relationship between Vietnam and the Qing Empire. The events of this conflict, their relationship to the Black Flags and the Qing-Nguyễn relationship at the end of the nineteenth century, and the endurance of the borderlands culture of violence during the war between France, China, and Vietnam are the subject of this chapter.

This war, conventionally referred to as the Sino-French War, brought together a series of interconnected and complex personal networks. More than just a military conflict between China and France over the issue of French interests in Vietnam, the Sino-French War occurred at intersections of mobility and violence. Although seen, in tactical terms, as a battleground for a land war, the borderlands between China and Vietnam played a central role in this conflict, which was less a clash of universalist worldviews and more a violent contest between modalities of power, notions of development, and fragile arrangements of imperial sovereignty.

THE SINO-FRENCH WAR (1883–1885): TERMS OF CONFLICT

As a label, the Sino-French War presents a problem. While it captures the sentiments of the nineteenth-century diplomats and officials of the French Third Republic and the Qing Empire, who tended to view the conflict in terms of China and France, it obscures not only the Vietnamese imperial authorities, but also networks of borderlands mobility. A historical explanation of this conflict should not rely too heavily on diplomatic definitions. Underneath the conventional analysis of the Sino-French War, webs of conflict and collusion resist reduction to official discourse and elite epistemologies.

Historians, echoing official concerns from the late nineteenth century, have established a narrative of the Sino-French War that emphasizes the radical rupture caused by French colonial rule. According to Lloyd Eastman, the war resulted from the shock of a new mode of international power: the post-

Westphalian *staatensystem*. In his view, a novel form of sovereignty disrupted centuries of precedent and introduced a fatal contradiction: "the essential incompatibility between their (Chinese) traditional view of interstate relations, in which China was a universal empire rightfully superior to other states, and the Western concept of a *staatensystem*, in which all sovereign states are legally equal."[9] Eastman also attributed the conflict to the pervasive disharmony between regional (provinces, districts) and central (Grand Council) authorities in the Qing Empire, making the war essentially an outgrowth of China's domestic predicament in the decades after the opium wars (1839–1842, 1856–1860) and the Treaty of Nanjing (1842).

Eastman's excellent grasp of elite concerns in late nineteenth-century China notwithstanding, framing the Sino-French War in *weltanshauung* terms creates two analytical blind spots. First, official decisions become occasions for tracking the disintegration of a tutelary "traditional view of interstate relations," an emphasis that ignores alternate modes of official and everyday interaction in the borderlands. Although significant, diplomatic language does not constitute the entirety of historical context. Second, framing the conflict in binary terms, as China versus France, overlooks the borderlands that were at the very center of the conflict.

Eastman's "traditional view of interstate relations" refers to the tribute system, the formal recognition of Chinese regional authority by smaller states, kingdoms, and empires and "a substitute for more forceful domination."[10] The failure of overt domination brought the tribute system into existence, Eastman argues, and marked the limits of unmediated Chinese political control. Although the nineteenth century posed certain challenges to this traditional worldview, Eastman reminds us that the official response was to see tributary states "as buffers against the encroachment of the Europeans."[11]

However, official Chinese attitudes about tributary states should not inure us to the ontological concreteness of Chinese superiority. Any discussion of the formal relationship between China and a tributary state should take into account the perspective of the tributary state itself and should not presume the uncontested nature of the claim to Chinese civilizational centrality that accompanied acceptance of tributary status. As a functional concept, "the 'tribute system' is a Western invention for descriptive purposes."[12] Particularly for the nineteenth century, a more nuanced assortment of official contacts, economic relationships, and intellectual exchange should replace the more generalized concept of "tribute" in the historical imagination. In examining events at a time when other countries built empires that effectively displaced the traditional interstate relations system of tribute, a critical and contextual appreciation of the formal relationship between China and tributary states can help us understand the diverse factors that bound the Qing Empire to countries beyond its direct administrative control.

Although a rites-based arrangement connected the Qing Empire to Nguyễn Vietnam, adopting this "model of engagement" as the basis for a historical Sino-Vietnamese relationship obscures the importance of domestic Vietnamese politics and personal networks, particularly for the borderlands.[13] When considering relations between these imperial states, we should pay attention to not only the "context of diplomatic ritual," but also to borderlands networks of mobility and violence.[14]

THE FALL OF HANOI AND THE DEATH OF HOÀNG DIỆU

In March 1883, the borderlands, in the form of Liu Yongfu's alleged warning to the French military, went south. During the final months of Henri Rivière's life, the Black Flags spread to the Red River Delta. For the second time in a decade, Liu Yongfu stood poised to defend the authority of imperial Vietnam against France. Before another confrontation between France and the Black Flags, the French occupied Hanoi, an action that sparked a range of responses.

In Huế, internal discourse over statecraft revealed doubts about the reliability of the Black Flags. Concerned about a possible armed conflict after Rivière's deployment to Hanoi, the imperial court ordered Hoàng Kế Viêm and Nguyễn Hữu Độ to conduct a thorough investigation of Liu Yongfu and his lieutenants.[15] There could not have been two officials more mutually opposed; during the 1870s, Nguyễn Hữu Độ openly advocated for a peace settlement with France and loudly distrusted the Black Flags while Hoàng Kế Viêm became the chief ally of Liu Yongfu in the imperial bureaucracy. To deprive Rivière of a pretext for hostilities, the court also commanded Hoàng Kế Viêm to move the Black Flags far from Hanoi, where Nguyễn Hữu Độ served as provincial governor.[16] A renewed French military presence in Hanoi intensified official divisions over the Black Flags.

Despite the intentions of Huế, efforts to forestall conflict quickly fell apart. After less than ten days in Hanoi, Henri Rivière sent a threatening letter to the provincial military commander, Hoàng Diệu.[17] The letter, which staff at the French consulate in Hanoi translated from French into classical Chinese, spelled out specific French grievances against imperial Vietnam. According to Rivière, no one from the provincial bureaucracy had assured him that they could control the Black Flags, the largest barrier to free commerce on the Red River and in the borderlands. He pressed Hoàng Diệu to guarantee either the submission or the eradication of Liu's army.[18] If Hoàng Diệu failed, Rivière would seize Hanoi.[19] Hoàng Diệu received this ultimatum as the court awaited its commissioned report on the Black Flags. With no allowance for the cumbersome rhythms of the Vietnamese bureaucracy, Rivière orchestrated a scenario for military action by making one provincial official impossibly accountable for the entire imperial administration.

Consistent with his threat, but to the great shock of Hoàng Diệu, Rivière occupied Hanoi on April 26. The entire attack lasted less than an hour, and ended with only four French soldiers wounded.[20] Hoàng Diệu, defeated and ashamed, sat down to compose a short statement before taking his life.[21] His final piece of prose, entitled "Defeat" (Di biểu), expressed Hoàng Diệu's profound regret over, to his mind, *his* loss of Hanoi. Calling it the most important administrative center in northern Vietnam, he encouraged imperial officials to follow the example of the late Nguyễn Tri Phương, who attempted to defend Hanoi against Garnier in 1873.[22] Hoàng Diệu lamented the turmoil of the country: "The French armies came to ground from their ships and terrified the people."[23] The violence brought by Rivière set loose "streams of blood that flow as far as the distance to the heavenly gates."[24] Amid Hoàng Diệu's poetic cries and unheeded pleas, Hanoi fell to France.[25]

The loss of Hanoi exacerbated the imperial schism between those seeking negotiation and those wanting revenge. The court placed Nguyễn Hữu Độ in charge of direct negotiations with France. At the same time, Hoàng Kế Viêm, the liaison for the Black Flags, prepared for war in the northern provinces.[26] Their hostility quickly became personal. Weeks after Rivière's attack, Hoàng Kế Viêm issued a damning report about Nguyễn Hữu Độ's alleged failure to render promised funds to Liu Yongfu, funds supposedly intended to assist the Black Flags in their return to Lào Cai.[27] In response, the court reminded the two officials of their shared responsibility to investigate Liu Yongfu's army, an investigation that would founder as the rift between them deepened.[28]

Their twinned, contradictory roles, Nguyễn Hữu Độ as a contact for French representatives and Hoàng Kế Viêm as an advocate for armed resistance, would survive the coming conflict with France.

HENRI RIVIÈRE IN HANOI

Like Francis Garnier ten years earlier, Henri Rivière issued a proclamation to the people of Hanoi. Asserting his reluctance to resort to violence, Rivière explained that the unabated insolence of the Black Flags compelled him to act. In the name of commerce, the military under his command would chase down all bandits, especially Liu Yongfu, whom he claimed blocked trade and travel along the Red River. For Rivière, French soldiers came to "protect our nationals and crush the insolent Black Flags," but not, as he addressed the sympathetic elite, "to imperil your country."[29] Henri Rivière blamed the late Hoàng Diệu for any peril that Tonkin might face. "The reprehensible conduct of Hoàng Diệu" he wrote, "forced us to attack the Hanoi Citadel."[30] To the residents of Hanoi and Tonkin, Rivière promised "peace, except for *pirates* and brigands who we will treat with the utmost harshness."[31] He positioned himself as a defender of the population and a protector of commerce, a combination of Dupuis and Garnier.

Using the Red River as a pathway, Rivière quickly expanded the French military presence in northern Vietnam. With a force of four armed ships, four hundred and fifty infantry marines, and a small band of non-French support laborers he occupied administrative and military centers.[32] In Hanoi and elsewhere, he also damaged the ability of both the Black Flags and the imperial Vietnamese authorities to collect taxes; marines who stormed the Hanoi Citadel and other military centers seized the imperial tax coffers guarded therein.[33] To strangle the revenue stream of the Black Flags, who relied on customs posts, Rivière pressed the imperial court, through de Kergaradec and the Hanoi consulate, for a French military outpost in Sơn Tây. A river port west of Hanoi along the Red River, Sơn Tây was a Black Flag stronghold and, at least since the late 1870s, a lucrative hub for custom posts. In Huế, where Henri Rheinart negotiated with imperial officials, the court refused to grant authorization for a French outpost in Sơn Tây, in effect defending the interests of the Black Flags against Rivière.[34]

For Henri Rivière, the reticence of the court signaled hostility. He identified Hoàng Kế Viêm as a particularly corrosive influence, an official whose relationship with Liu Yongfu had doubtlessly, to Rivière's mind, influenced other provincial authorities to ignore French demands.[35] To resolve this, Rivière asked Rheinart to broker direct negotiations between him and court officials.[36] Rheinart, who possessed an excellent grasp of court politics, agreed with Rivière and the Hanoi consulate that the Black Flags posed a barrier to commerce and development in Tonkin.[37] In Nguyễn Hữu Độ and a court official named Trần Đình Túc, he found two high-ranking officials with incidental sympathies. Their common opposition to the Black Flags and Hoàng Kế Viêm, although for dissimilar reasons, provided the basis for a pragmatic alliance.

The bond of this alliance, the Black Flags, quickly became a serious threat to Rivière's occupation of the north. By August 1882, the French authorities in Cochinchina had limited Rivière to a defensive role.[38] This decision contradicted advice from other French military officers, including Commandant Beaumont in Saigon, who believed that any diplomatic solution between the French authorities and the imperial court would collapse under the weight of mutual mistrust. War with the Black Flags, Beaumont pressed, was certain.[39]

Ignoring this advice, Rivière's superiors elected to scale back his ambitions in the Red River Delta. They could not, however, scale back his anxiety over the Black Flags and a potential Chinese intervention against France.

FEARS OF CHINESE INTERVENTION

Seven days passed between the decision to limit Rivière's operations and his receipt of these new orders. By the time he received the new directive, Rivière had already commanded his troops to detain all Chinese soldiers discovered in French-controlled Vietnamese territory.[40] Although he immediately rescinded this order, Rivière's paranoia about a Chinese intervention inspired an appeal for assistance to Admiral Jauréguiberry in Paris.[41] For the commander of French military in northern Vietnam, control over the delta meant forestalling the potential military threat from the Qing Empire.

From the Hanoi consulate, de Kergaradec began gathering new reports about Chinese soldiers in Vietnam, reports that fueled Rivière's fears. During the summer of 1881, A. Aumoitte, the *chancelier du consulat* (consular secretary) in Hanoi, traveled north to Bắc Ninh and Lạng Sơn to gather information for a map of the China-Vietnam borderlands. Aumoitte returned to Hanoi with detailed notes about the number, weaponry, and health of Chinese soldiers who remained in Vietnam after the campaign against Li Yangcai.[42] As de Kergaradec did in the late 1870s, Aumoitte depicted imperial authority in the borderlands as skeletal and tenuous, thereby inviting French military intervention.

Some voices within imperial Vietnam called for the easing of French anxieties. Bùi Văn Dị proposed that Hoàng Kế Viêm compose a letter explaining the official role of the Black Flags to the French consulate in Hanoi. Bùi Văn Dị hoped this gesture would demonstrate that Vietnam harbored no grievances against France and might provide an opening for negotiating the return of Hanoi.[43] Despite this plea for negotiation, Hoàng Kế Viêm and the Black Flags continued to prepare for war.

In China, Qing officials followed the situation in Hanoi. Believing that the French military only provided security for consular staff and protection for merchants, the Grand Council in Beijing initially maintained a policy of friendly diplomatic engagement with France.[44] The strategic concerns of powerful Chinese officials such as Li Hongzhang, who emphasized the threat of Japanese invasion in Korea, did not prioritize the defense of Vietnam.[45] However, this began to change in the early 1880s. The Grand Council, based on reports from Yunnan and Guangxi, now believed that the invasion of Hanoi and the Red River Delta was only the beginning of a French plan to use northern Vietnam as a path to invade southern China.[46]

As the mutual suspicion between French and Chinese authorities intensified, the Grand Council in Beijing believed it had uncovered a French agent in southern China. In 1881, prior to Rivière's occupation of Hanoi, Qing authorities in the borderlands province of Guangxi detained and questioned an individual named Li Yuchi. A former low-ranking official in Hubei Province, Li Yuchi had worked as a private secretary for Jean Dupuis, the French gun dealer whose arrest sparked the Garnier affair in 1873.[47] Zhang Shusheng, the governor of Guangxi, informed the Grand Council that Li Yuchi nurtured a furtive relationship with France.[48] Knowledge of this potential agent of France, who served within the Qing bureaucracy, pushed members of the Grand Council to advocate, in opposition to Li Hongzhang, for an alliance with the Black Flags in defense of the southern Chinese borderlands.[49]

In April 1882, the Qing Empire prepared to defend itself and Vietnam against imminent aggression. To finance domestic defense, the Grand Council diverted funds from Sichuan, north of Yunnan, to Guangxi and Yunnan.[50] Following Rivière's occupation of Hanoi, provincial military from Yunnan and Guangxi were sent to northern Vietnam.[51] The same borderlands that hosted fleeing Black and Yellow Flags twenty years earlier now became a staging area for the struggle against French imperialism. Almost certainly without realizing it, the Grand Council was fulfilling Rivière's fears of Chinese intervention.

Chinese armies, despite the relationship between China and Vietnam, also worried imperial Vietnamese officials. When three Yunnanese military divisions approached a borderlands post in Hưng Hóa, the provincial governor, Nguyễn Quang Bích, sent a skeptical report to the imperial court. The Qing armies, he warned, might stay in Vietnam if allowed to help against the French.[52] Anxious about a possible erosion of Vietnamese sovereignty, Nguyễn Quang Bích saw his country trapped between an extensive Chinese military presence in the north and an aggressive French colonial administration in the south.

Rather than asking China for assistance, officials at the imperial court in Huế addressed Rivière's invasion through the framework of the 1874 treaty.[53] In contrast to Garnier's invasion of 1873, Rivière's occupation of Hanoi could be resolved through negotiations because the French commandant acted on behalf of a country officially represented in Vietnam through its consulates in Hanoi and Haiphong and with Rheinart at Huế. The court expected a diplomatic resolution.

French representatives, fearing war, tried to directly contact provincial Chinese officials. In September 1882, Henri Rheinart learned of direct correspondence between the court in Huế and the Yunnan government, correspondence that did not, as was the convention for paperwork from China sent to Vietnam, pass through the Ministry of Rites. Rheinart then wrote directly to Cen Yuying, the Yunnan-Guizhou governor-general, in an unsuccessful request for information about Chinese military positions.[54] The Qing Empire, it became clear, was preparing for war.

THE INTERRUPTION OF FRENCH INTERESTS

While concerned about a Chinese intervention, Henri Rivière also consistently argued that a more insidious menace threatened the safety of his soldiers and the long-term interests of France in Tonkin. This menace was the incompetence, according to Rivière, of imperial officials. During the Sino-French War, claims of Vietnamese official ineptitude accompanied both arguments for defending French interests and imperial proposals for Chinese intervention. However, allegations of incompetence and venality obscured the more complex reality of the intersections between imperial authority and the culture of violence.

For Rivière, a putative lack of official control over the upper reaches of the Red River threatened French commercial interests protected by the 1874 treaty. Merchant vessels could not safely move goods, discouraging international investment.[55] In August 1882, a French investor living in Japan contacted French officials in Beijing to arrange, through the Hanoi consulate, a passport for travel to Vietnam. Although he could not secure financial backing for his expedition, which would have involved the shipment of manufactured products from Hanoi to Yunnan, the French national did receive the support of de Kergaradec, who wrote Beijing on his behalf.[56] A route forged through impatience and transgression by Jean Dupuis in 1873 now attracted interest from the international French business community, although investors were reluctant to finance ventures into such an uncertain area.

In Vietnam, the impending confrontation between France and China pushed an elderly official into action. Vũ Trọng Bình, the former liaison for Feng Zicai who anxiously reported floods and raids in the 1870s, had been the governor-general of Nam Định-Hưng Yên since 1881. At the age of sixty-nine, Vũ Trọng Bình took an active role in accommodating Qing soldiers, whose presence was now a reality, by reappropriating provincial tax funds to garrison Chinese troops in Nam Định.[57] When one of Rivière's ships scouted Nam Định, Vũ Trọng Bình requested four to five hundred soldiers from Hanoi to assist the Chinese armies against a possible French attack.[58] The imperial court agreed but stressed that these preparations should remain confidential. Vũ Trọng Bình, who had prior experience with the Qing military, gathered forces for a defense of Nam Định, determined to resist further French encroachment.

From Rivière's perspective, the defense of Nam Định was quite different. Rather than a protective measure, the French commandant viewed the gathering of Chinese and Vietnamese soldiers around the southern Red River port as a plan for ambush. Prior to his journey to Nam Định, Paul Puginier, who had earlier advised Garnier, informed Rivière of a secret plan to launch a war against France, likely exaggerating the confidential defensive preparations managed by Vũ Trọng Bình.[59] When Rivière's ship approached Nam Định, no official imperial representative emerged to greet it. Instead, the Vietnamese soldiers trained their cannons on the ship. Having narrowly avoided a violent confrontation, Rivière received an official apology from the imperial court.[60]

With conflict imminent, the court suspended two infrastructure projects outlined by the 1874 treaty. To the bewilderment of Rheinart, who communicated his shock to Rivière, the court refused French engineers permission to survey for railroads and telegraph lines.[61] In Rheinart's view, these projects would serve the communication and transportation needs of the French consulates, international and domestic merchants, and the military. After their suspension, Rheinart hoped that the death of the reigning Tự Đức emperor would cause a factional realignment at court. Under a new emperor, he might have an opportunity to instill enthusiasm for railroads and telegraphs in the Vietnamese sovereign.[62] For the moment, however, these projects, and Rheinart's vision, remained at a standstill.

CHINESE NARRATIVES OF NGUYỄN INCOMPETENCE

In January 1883, as tensions deepened around Nam Định, a Qing official with no prior experience in Vietnam made a sudden and unexpected appearance at the imperial court in Huế. This official, Tang Jingsong, wanted to personally contact Liu Yongfu to enlist the Black Flags in the coming war with France. Much like Jean Dupuis in the 1870s, Tang Jingsong developed an opportunistic understanding of Vietnamese political economy to serve an agenda focused elsewhere.

Tang Jingsong's travel to Vietnam followed negotiations in the Chinese city of Tianjin that established a working agreement between China and France. In November 1882, the Li-Bournée Convention, signed by Frédéric Albert Bournée and Li Hongzhang, temporarily diffused tensions over Vietnam.[63] Although not a treaty, the convention stipulated three things. First, all Chinese military would withdraw from Vietnam, in return for which France would assure the Qing Empire that it did not intend to invade sovereign Vietnamese territory. Second, Lào Cai, the base of Black Flag power in the borderlands, would become a free-trade zone policed by the French military but open to all merchants. Third, a neutral area would be established within the China-Vietnam borderlands, with patrolling duties divided by a French "protectorate administration" and the Qing Empire.[64]

The second and third provisions clearly targeted the Black Flags. Jean Dupuis, Francis Garnier, de Kergaradec, and now Henri Rivière had all painted Liu Yongfu as the chief enemy of progress and development, abetted by corrupt Vietnamese officials. At the level of elite diplomacy, French negotiators seemed to agree. However, conventions signed in Tianjin did not necessarily echo in the provinces of the Qing Empire or imperial Vietnam. The Black Flags remained in control of borderlands commerce and would soon join the war against France in defense of territory and revenue.

Before the war, however, the Black Flags were visited by Tang Jingsong, who had traveled from Beijing to Vietnam. Tang's interest in Liu Yongfu carried him across his home province of Guangxi into northern Vietnam. In preparation for his trip, he used his official position in the Ministry of Personnel in Beijing to consult with Yunnan provincial authorities about the Black Flags.[65] Tang's journey to Vietnam would, he argued, enable him to give a report about the Black Flags upon his return. In the years before the telegraph supported the rapid spread of information across the borderlands, Tang's firsthand investigation could have been crucial.[66]

Despite his suspicion of France, Tang Jingsong shared the opinions of several French officials concerning the imperial Vietnamese administration. According to Tang, Vietnam was at the mercy of a venal, incompetent government. "They have generals and they have armies, but they have no idea what to do with them," he remarked.[67] Tang's notion of Nguyễn incompetence stemmed from a lack of familiarity. Not only was he unfamiliar with borderlands arrangements of power and the role of the Black Flags, he had no knowledge of factions within the imperial officialdom.[68]

Moved by this limited understanding, Tang resolved to assist Vietnam for historical and political reasons. China and Vietnam shared more than a history, they also shared borderlands. In Tang's estimation, the threat posed by bandits more than justified Chinese assistance.[69] Moreover, he believed that a French invasion of Yunnan would shortly follow the fall of northern Vietnam, as merchants and military flowed north along the Red River.[70] From Tang's perspective, help for a tributary state meant the prevention of a European invasion of the Qing Empire. Saving Vietnam was saving China.

For Tang Jingsong, Liu Yongfu was a glimmer of hope. Impressed by the Black Flag leader's perseverance and his victories over the Yellow Flags, Tang felt Liu's ability to sustain his followers through taxing commerce opened a possible future role for his soldiers in the borderlands.[71] Once in Vietnam, Tang planned to go to Lào Cai, examine the situation, and meet face to face with the formidable leader of the Black Flags.

Regardless of his intentions, Tang's sudden appearance in Huế alarmed the

Vietnamese authorities. In January 1883, on a ship from Shanghai, Tang arrived at court. Following protocol, he displayed a letter issued by the Qing Grand Council that explained his rank and position to the Vietnamese Ministry of Rites. The ministry secretary, Nguyễn Văn Tường, incredulously asked what business brought an official from Beijing to Huế.[72]

Through correspondence in classical Chinese, Tang asked Vietnamese officials about the state of the country. He learned of the precarious condition of the China-Vietnam borderlands. In the northwest, as Nguyễn Văn Tường told him, bandits vied for control over the gold mines in the hills of Sip Chao (V: Thập Châu), a Tai area contested by the Black Flags and Yellow Flags. In central Vietnam, the French demanded the right to mine for coal.[73] To Tang Jingsong, Vietnam seemed surrounded by enemies and disorder.

Spurious allegations of Nguyễn corruption bolstered Tang's claim that the Black Flags could help China rescue Vietnam from French aggression. In his memoir, Tang would accuse Nguyễn Văn Tường of profiting from the taxation of Qing subjects living in Vietnam. According to Tang, corrupt officials such as this dominated the court.[74] He inveighed against Nguyễn incompetence, even criticizing the hiring of Chinese mercenaries to fight for Vietnam.[75] Tang singled out Hoàng Kế Viêm, the official liaison for the Black Flags, as an exception to the general venality of Vietnamese officialdom. As a consistent advocate for Liu Yongfu, Hoàng Kế Viêm was, in Tang's opinion, the one Nguyễn official who could help halt the erosion of sovereignty in Vietnam.[76]

Tang Jingsong clearly had great adulation for Liu Yongfu, whom he finally met the following March. The Black Flags' defeat of Francis Garnier in 1873, for Tang, had proven the strength of Liu's army and its value for the coming war with France.[77] Tang hailed Liu as an exceptional individual, someone who had overcome childhood poverty and a lack of education to wield enormous power. Tang hoped that Liu would use this power to benefit the Qing Empire, proposing that the Black Flags might protect exploited Chinese merchants, train Vietnamese soldiers, and share revenue with southern Chinese provinces from borderlands commerce.[78] However, Tang's ambitious praise neglected borderlands realities. Perhaps due to a lack of information, he mentioned nothing about Lào Cai except that, as he was told in Huế, it returned only meager tax revenue.[79] Tang's motivations, his concern for the defense of China, also blinded him to the violent practices of the Black Flags, which he would soon witness firsthand.

Over the objection of Nguyễn Văn Tường, the court granted Tang Jingsong permission to travel in Vietnam. Nguyễn Thuật, an imperial tutor and secretary in the Ministry of Personnel, served as Tang's guide on a carefully regulated tour that began in the province of Hà Tĩnh and continued north to Bắc Ninh and Hải Dương.[80] Alarmed about bandits along the Red River, Nguyễn Thuật would later recall that he continually worried about his guest's safety.[81] During the trip, Tang saw his guide's anxiety as evidence of the need for Chinese intervention. As he would later write, he believed that France, through ties with uplands communities, threatened to take over northern Vietnam as Nguyễn officials "abandoned themselves to inaction."[82] Tang's guided tour provided him with empirical justification for his imperial paternalism. In his eyes, Vietnam needed a Chinese intervention to survive.

Soon after becoming Tang Jingsong's official guide, Nguyễn Thuật took up a position that brought him into close contact with the borderlands culture of violence. During the negotiations between French and Chinese representatives in Tianjin, Li Hongzhang insisted that a Vietnamese representative attend the talks, thereby stalling the negotiations.[83] Following the orders of the Huế court, Nguyễn Thuật left Tang Jingsong in Haiphong and traveled north to Tianjin.[84] Along with Phạm Thận Duật, formerly governor of the borderlands province of Hưng Hóa, Nguyễn Thuật spent eight months in China as a member of the Vietnamese delegation.[85]

In February 1883, as he passed through Lạng Sơn on his way to Beijing, Nguyễn Thuật sent some disturbing reports to Huế. Villagers living in the borderlands, he claimed, had been abducted from their homes and then sold in southern Guangxi as slaves. The perpetrators were the very Chinese soldiers that assisted Vietnam with the capture of borderlands bandits, namely those under the command of Feng Zicai.[86] The court responded that an investigation would commence at once.[87] However, the Sino-French War halted any inquiry into the alleged human trafficking across the borderlands.

As his former guide traveled north, Tang Jingsong met with Vietnamese and French authorities in Haiphong. In February 1883, he met with the French consulate. According to Tang, Giorgios Vlavianos, the Greek-born British subject who had worked for de Kergaradec in Hanoi, led one hundred or so surrendered Yellow Flags who served as the consular defense force.[88] While the Black Flags continued to serve as Vietnamese officials, enjoying imperial protection for their activities, the former followers of Pan Lunsi found employment with the French consular authorities. The association of the Yellow Flags with France would endure the coming war and last well into the twentieth century.

BORDERLANDS VIOLENCE IN THE DELTA: NAM ĐỊNH, 1883

In March 1883, as he continued his quest to meet Liu Yongfu, Tang was enjoying a dinner with Vietnamese officials in Bắc Ninh when he learned that Henri Rivière's army had attacked the southern Red River Delta city of Nam Định.[89]

He would remain in Vietnam as the war between China and France drew the Black Flags into another confrontation outside Hanoi.

Although the situation in Nam Định had been tense for weeks, Rivière's attack was carefully planned. From Saigon, Governor Charles Thomson placed an additional 125 marine infantry under Rivière's command in January 1883, giving him the means to widen the war.[90] Rheinart, the French representative in Huế, reported directly to Rivière about the visit of Tang Jingsong and its potentially devastating consequences for French interests. Chinese subjects, he warned, might gain the exclusive right to mine in northern Vietnam. According to Rheinart, when Tang Jingsong arrived in Huế, he consulted with the Ministry of Revenue, which oversaw mines.[91] In February, during Tang's stay in Haiphong, Rheinart notified Rivière that a Chinese emissary had formally requested the right to open a mine in nearby Quảng Yên Province.[92] Officially, Governor Thomson ordered that Rivière avoid all conflict with Qing armies.[93] However, perceived threats to French interests, fueled by Rheinart's reports, soon motivated a unilateral, aggressive action.

Events in France further alarmed French representatives in China and Vietnam. When Jules Ferry's government came to power in March, the Li-Bournée convention died. A radical anticlericist who envisioned colonial territories as a means to enrich France, Jules Ferry advocated military intervention, not negotiation, in Vietnam.[94] Direct, preemptive action became politically possible with the formation of Ferry's government.

When Paris cancelled his diplomatic assignment, Bournée imparted a surprising, perhaps incendiary piece of information to his counterpart, Li Hongzhang. French mining interests, he told Li, would use the Ferry government to press for the removal of the Black Flags, effectively opening up Vietnam to mineral exploration.[95] After watching the collapse of negotiations, and duly warned about French intentions, the Chinese leadership prepared for war in Vietnam.[96] As during the rebellions of the previous decades, the control of mineral resources was at stake.

Mineral resources also clearly motivated French military operations. On March 14, 1883, acting on Rivière's orders, Chef de Bataillon Berthe de Villers conducted reconnaissance in Quảng Yên. He hoped to establish a "petit Gibraltar en miniature" to check the expansion of British commercial influence and challenge the power of the Black Flags.[97] De Villers' fears were largely based on reports, again from Rheinart in Huế, that Chinese miners had sold rights in Quảng Yên to a British company.[98] For Rivière and de Villers, French control of Quảng Yên would enable the completion of mineral surveys begun by Saladin and Fuchs, the engineers whom the Black Flags detained some years earlier.[99] De Villers announced that the site designated for the British mining concern was now under his control. Upon learning of de Villers' announcement, the Vietnamese court protested directly to the French consulate in Haiphong but received no response.[100]

On March 19, just weeks after the formation of the Ferry government in Paris and days since de Villers' occupation of Quảng Yên, Henri Rivière commanded two armed river craft in an invasion of Nam Định.[101] Imperial Vietnam lost control of a major population center in the southern Red River Delta as a spirited defense of the city, prepared by Vũ Trọng Bình and aided by soldiers from Hanoi, faltered.[102] Unknown to Rivière, the Nam Định administration had reduced the number of men guarding the river port just prior to the attack in an effort to disentangle military affairs from tax collection, gravely weakening its defenses. In the aftermath of the defeat, Vũ Trọng Bình was criticized and demoted for exceeding the court's limitations on salary provisions for Chinese soldiers as he tried to enhance the city's defenses.[103]

After receiving news of the invasion of Nam Định, Tang Jingsong traveled to Sơn Tây, west of Hanoi, where he made contact with Hoàng Kế Viêm and met with several Black Flag lieutenants.[104] His conversations with them confirmed his confidence in their ability to help Vietnam and defend China, a matter made more urgent by the fall of Nam Định to Rivière. The recent exploits of Huang Shouzhong, a Black Flag lieutenant who had just returned from the northwest, particularly impressed Tang. In Huế, Tang learned from Nguyễn Van Tường that the Tai-dominated areas of the mineral-rich northwest were rife with disorder. Huang Shouzhong's success there meant, to Tang, that the Black Flags could bring order to turbulent areas through both conquest and alliances with Tai elites.[105]

When Tang Jingsong finally met Liu Yongfu in Sơn Tây, the Qing official overheard an ambitious plot to strike at the heart of the French empire in Cochinchina. According to Tang, Hoàng Kế Viêm initiated a conversation with Liu about an offensive against Saigon in response to Rivière's aggression in Nam Định.[106] Hoàng Kế Viêm proposed that Huang Shouzhong and a select group of Black Flags invade Saigon, disrupting communications between Saigon and Paris and imperiling French supply lines.[107] Although rejected by Liu, Tang Jingsong would later pose this plan to other Chinese officials as a way to prevent northern Vietnam from coming under French control.[108] The Black Flag invasion of Saigon, which remained purely hypothetical, demonstrated the hope that Liu Yongfu's army inspired in Vietnamese and Chinese officials during the war. Once the enemies of the Qing, the Black Flags now represented a new, anticolonial version of the China-Vietnam relationship in official consciousness.

Although the details remain difficult to corroborate, some discussion of Liu Yongfu's relationship with the Qing Empire also transpired in Sơn Tây. According-ing to Liu Yongfu, Tang Jingsong offered him food, weapons, and official titles for the Black Flags in exchange for their loyalty to China.[109] In Lào Cai and the Tai areas of the northwest, Tang promised that the Qing Empire would recognize an independent state ruled by the Black Flags. In exchange, Liu Yongfu would defend China against France.[110] According to Tang, however, Liu Yongfu himself requested Chinese endorsement and Tang only expressed cautious optimism.[111] Tang also claimed that some Black Flag lieutenants asked to return to China, citing low salaries and an irregular food supply in Vietnam.[112]

As Tang met the Black Flags in Sơn Tây, personnel changes and factional shifts in Huế created momentum for an imperial reaction to Rivière's aggression. In April 1883, Rheinart left his post and returned to France, depriving Rivière of a reliable source of information about court politics.[113] At the same time, local resistance to Rivière's army slowly grew under the leadership of Phan Đình Bình, a former secretary in the Ministry of Military, who personally led militias and provincial soldiers against the French occupation in Nam Định.[114] Deeming a recapture of Nam Định impossible, Hoàng Kế Viêm and Liu Yongfu left Tang Jingsong in Sơn Tây and moved their soldiers, numbering perhaps as many as thirty thousand, to the villages west of Hanoi, near the site of Garnier's death in 1873.[115] When Rivière returned to Hanoi in April, he had already been warned about the Black Flags through a letter from de Villers.[116] The Black Flags, as they did ten years earlier, waited in the outskirts of Hanoi.[117]

BLACK FLAGS, THE CULTURE OF VIOLENCE, AND THE DEATH OF HENRI RIVIÈRE

When he left Hanoi to face the Black Flags on May 19, 1883, Henri Rivière knew the great risk he was taking. Having recently persuaded the French authorities in Saigon to send him more soldiers, he felt prepared for a violent confrontation.[118] For Catholic communities and the Vietnamese imperial authorities, however, the looming showdown between Rivière and the Black Flags brought a terrifying anxiety.

Paul Puginier, who saw the Red River as a pathway for mission work, claimed that the Black Flags posed a grave challenge to the work of the church. During the intensification of hostilities in 1883, he received distressing reports from missionaries in Hanoi about the Black Flag harassment of Vietnamese Catholics and priests.[119] In the late evening and early morning of May 15 and 16, several hundred Black Flags occupied a Catholic community in a village outside Hanoi, stabbing a Vietnamese priest before retreating.[120] The attack, a warning to all missionaries, was an effect of the growing hostility between Rivière and the Black Flags.

Officials at the imperial court also took a dim view of the tensions in the Red River Delta. On May 18, Trần Đình Túc, who helped negotiate the 1874 treaty, sent a letter to de Kergaradec at the Hanoi consulate. As the secretary of the Office for Foreign Affairs, which handled relations between France and Vietnam during this period, Trần Đình Túc reminded de Kergaradec that the treaty guaranteed peace and promised respect for imperial sovereignty, guarantees betrayed by the French military presence and, most importantly, the theft of tax funds by soldiers under Rivière's command.[121] Trần Đình Túc's appeal to the treaty failed to move de Kergaradec or any other representative of France in Vietnam.

By May 1883, the French military command fully anticipated war with China. From on board his ship off the northeast Vietnamese coast, Commandant Meyer, head of the French navy for China and Japan, warned Governor Thomson, in Saigon, that China had dispatched a force of ten thousand soldiers from Yunnan to northern Vietnam.[122]

On the afternoon of May 19, with war looming on land and at sea, Henri Rivière, Berthe de Villers, and an expeditionary force of one hundred French soldiers departed Hanoi to search for Black Flag camps.[123] Black Flag scouts quietly tracked them. As the small French force moved, the scouts motioned other Black Flags and Vietnamese soldiers into position, surrounding Rivière's party on three sides. Once the French soldiers moved within rifle range, the Black Flags closed ranks, releasing a heavy volley of musket fire and bullets.[124] Fatally wounded during the attack, Rivière lay dying while an injured Berthe de Villers led the French forces in a quick retreat.

The next morning, the Black Flags displayed the heads of twenty vanquished French soldiers, including Rivière, outside the western gates of Hanoi.[125] Decapitation served a familiar purpose. An act of performative violence, it produced a spectacle for witnesses, a demonstration of the power of the Black Flags. Display of the heads was proof of victory. As with Garnier a decade earlier, any lingering loyalty to France in the Red River Delta would have to account for the confirmed elimination of an armed force. A disembodied head was a reminder as much as an announcement.

Writing about the death of Henri Rivière, Bùi Văn Dị, who earlier hoped to mollify French fears, described the event with a combination of solemn acknowledgment and learned allusion. In his poem, "Upon Hearing News of a Great and Welcome Victory at Cầu Giấy," he celebrated the fact that "the prosperity of Thăng Long [Hanoi] has not yet been exhausted."[126] He praised the victorious armies, saying that they recalled the bravery of great field marshals of the Han dynasty. However, his verse also betrayed an uncertainty about the future of Vietnam. He described the unnamed prevailing forces, the Black Flags and Hoàng Kế Viêm, as "unlike Tang Weibo."[127] A military commander during the ninth century, Tang Weibo's death inspired his loyal soldiers to commemorate him as a wise leader.[128] Although he acknowledged the defeat of enemy armies outside Hanoi, Bùi Văn Dị's omission of the Black Flags and his loaded reference to a celebrated Chinese martyr revealed his own unease as his country was defended by unreliable heroes.

According to oral traditions from Sơn Tây, the popular reaction to Rivière's defeat was no less ambiguous. As the Black Flags worked closely with Vietnamese soldiers, they brought the borderlands culture of violence down to the valleys around the lower Red River. Into the twentieth century, people recalled lamentations. "Wu, Huang, Liu; Heaven help us! We still ask for assistance."[129] "They have stolen our property, burned our homes to cinders. They have taken our wives as concubines, our children as slaves."[130] They "looted our wealth and torched our homes, raped our wives and left our children to starve."[131] These dirges enshrine loss at the hands of the Black Flags, the damage to lineage, property, and livelihood that they brought to lowland villages.

Despite the Black Flags' violent occupation of the delta, Tang Jingsong, who still waited in Sơn Tây, saw their victory over Rivière as an expected success. He noted that the Black Flags returned from the battle with an image of French soldiers as dehumanized adversaries.[132] Regardless of this victory for Vietnam and, in Tang's mind, for China, distrust sprouted between Tang Jingsong and Hoàng Kế Viêm. When Hoàng Kế Viêm handed Tang an order to return to Beijing, Tang refused to comply, claiming the paperwork forged.[133] Tang, perhaps increasingly unwelcomed, remained with the Black Flags in Vietnam.

For Catholic communities in northern Vietnam, Rivière's defeat put them in even greater jeopardy. Puginier warned against violent reprisals against Catholic villages, priests, and individuals who would now be seen as Rivière's failed collaborators. In response to Puginier's concerns, the French military provided defense for Catholic communities throughout the Red River Delta, including Nam Định.[134] During the summer of 1883, as Puginier prepared mass, a group of Black Flags torched his cathedral in Hanoi, after which Puginier called on the French army for assistance.[135] In Nam Định, one day after Rivière's defeat, a young missionary named Béchet attempted to hide from the anti-French resistance, the leaders of which suspected his complicity in the occupation. Upon finding Béchet, Vietnamese soldiers bound and decapitated him, collecting a bounty in silver from Nam Định officials.[136] Those hostile to the French presence in northern Vietnam viewed Catholic communities as agents of collusion between Catholics and the French military, and many Catholics found themselves caught between two hostile armed forces.

THE YELLOW FLAGS AND FRANCE

For another group, the Yellow Flags, the death of Rivière meant a new opportunity. Two hundred Yellow Flag soldiers previously stationed at the Haiphong consulate joined the French military effort in Hanoi.[137] According to Émile Duboc, a *lieutenant de vaisseau*, the help of Liu Yongfu's old rivals improved the chances of a French victory over the Black Flags.[138] During the summer of 1883, 450 Yellow Flags patrolled the northern and western sections of Hanoi under the command of Giorgios Vlavianos.[139] On July 30, French colonial officials met in Haiphong to confirm their commitment to the eradication of the Black Flags, a goal they hoped to achieve with the assistance of the Yellow Flags.[140] In August, when the French military retaliated against the Black Flags and their allies outside Hanoi, the Yellow Flags joined them.[141] A relationship that began with contacts between Pan Lunsi and Jean Dupuis in 1872 continued as the Yellow Flags became allies to the French colonial occupation of northern Vietnam.

However, like the Black Flags under Vietnamese sponsorship, the Yellow Flags resisted strict discipline, often pursuing power on their own terms. In September 1883, following the campaign outside Hanoi, a French officer discovered that Yellow Flag soldiers, in defiance of his orders, had looted several villages. Furious, the French officer captured and beheaded the leaders of the raids before their fellow soldiers. He then seized the weapons of the remaining Yellow Flags and expelled them from the camp.[142] French sponsorship, as Émile Duboc noticed, could not reform these otherwise "loyal and brave allies."[143] The reliance of French authority on ostentatious violence and unpredictable allies would continue long after the end of the Sino-French War.

INTERNATIONAL MEDIA

Beyond Vietnam, the defeat of Henri Rivière sparked international interest in the Black Flags. In May 1883, a background piece on Liu Yongfu introduced him to the readership of *Shenbao*, a Chinese-language newspaper. Although the article detailed Liu's victories, it also mentioned the deleterious effects of the war between the Black and Yellow Flags for people in the borderlands.[144] The following June, as the Black Flags harassed Catholic communities in the wake of Rivière's defeat, another article clarified the terms under which the Black Flags aided Vietnam. Although China previously governed territory the Nguyễn now ruled, the article contended, Vietnam became an independent country almost a millennium ago. Therefore, Liu Yongfu acted at Vietnam's request, taking no orders from China.[145] Chinese media coverage described the Black Flags' employment by Vietnam without the language of condemnation used by Tang

Jingsong. The assertion of an independent Vietnam on the pages of the *Shenbao* presented events without recourse to simplified notions of tribute, offering an interpretation of the Black Flags as an anticolonial volunteer army.

More implausible mythologies about the Black Flags appeared in English-language media. In the United States, the *New York Times* carried news of their victory over Rivière, including some specious information about Liu Yongfu's followers, the "Kroumirs and Zulus of Tonquin." According to a July 1 article, "They are pirates of every nationality on the globe; they existed in 1863, and since then their ranks have been recruited by swarms of adventurers from all parts of Europe, Asia, and Africa, and especially from France."[146]

This *räuberromantik* interpretation of the Black Flags as an international mercenary army, while baseless, contrasts with another image of Liu Yongfu.[147] On the evening of December 22, 1883, six months after the death of Rivière, G. Champagne's *Les Pavillons Noirs ou la Guerre du Ton-kin* opened in Paris at the Théâtre des Batignolles. In the play, a young French army officer rescues his kidnapped lover from a wicked bandit army, the Black Flags, monstrous villains at once comical and menacing.[148]

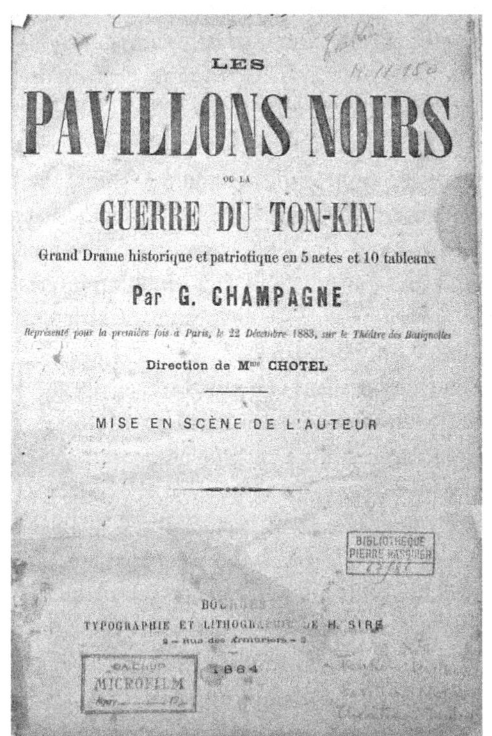
LES

PAVILLONS NOIRS

OU LA

GUERRE DU TON-KIN

Grand Drame historique et patriotique en 5 actes et 10 tableaux

Par G. CHAMPAGNE

Représenté pour la première fois à Paris, le 22 Décembre 1883, sur le Théâtre des Batignolles

Direction de Mme CHOTEL

MISE EN SCÈNE DE L'AUTEUR

TYPOGRAPHIE ET LITHOG[illegible] DE H. SIRE

1884

FIG. 3.1. *Les Pavillons Noirs* playbill. Champagne, *Les Pavillons Noirs ou la Guerre du Ton-Kin.* 1883.

THE HARMAND CONVENTION: COURT FACTIONALISM, THE BLACK FLAGS, AND A NEW ORDER

In the aftermath of the Black Flag victory, an event in Huế altered the political landscape in Vietnam. Two months after Rivière's defeat, Nguyễn Hồng Nhậm, reigning emperor of the Tự Đức reign, died.[149] The violent succession struggle that Rheinart had predicted, but could not witness, began. As the struggle developed, a new French representative, Jules Harmand, pressed for a diplomatic settlement to the hostilities in northern Vietnam. That settlement, the Harmand Convention, outlined the basic structure of the French colonial protectorate in Tonkin. It also paid particular attention to the Black Flags.

While regional differences certainly influenced the factionalism at court following the death of the Tự Đức emperor, the issue of the Black Flags provided a definitive wedge between officials calling for peace and those advocating armed resistance to French expansion.[150] The situation in the provinces and the borderlands influenced the officials selecting the next Nguyễn emperor.

When the Tự Đức emperor fell gravely ill in July 1883, he had no biological sons. Among his three adopted sons, all nephews, he selected Nguyễn Ưng Chân to follow him as the emperor of the Dục Đức reign. After the Tự Đức emperor's death on July 17, a row erupted at court among the three regents nominated to guide the young monarch. One regent, Trần Tiễn Thành, claimed that the other two—Nguyễn Văn Tường, who had reluctantly arranged Tang Jingsong's travel, and Tôn Thất Thuyết, a former official in Quảng Yên—directed a grievous personal insult at him during the enthroning ceremony.[151] Citing their dissatisfaction with the selection of Nguyễn Ưng Chân as emperor, and perhaps personally offended, Nguyễn Văn Tường and Tôn Thất Thuyết moved to marginalize their coregent. They arrested the would-be Dục Đức emperor, imprisoning him at his former study hall where he died of starvation weeks later.[152] Consequently, the Dục Đức reign lasted only three days.

The next imperial reign lasted four months and contained some contradictory decisions by the throne regarding negotiations with France. With the support of the regents who had conspired against the Dục Đức emperor, Nguyễn Hồng Dật became the Hiệp Hòa emperor. During his short reign, the court promoted Liu Yongfu to a position of even greater authority and granted Hoàng Kế Viêm broad powers in northern Vietnam.[153] However, the Hiệp Hòa emperor also ordered the court to enter into talks with Jules Harmand, a decision that galvanized Nguyễn officials into two definitive camps: those concessionary to the French presence and those who viewed armed struggle as the only means to defend the withering autonomy of the Vietnamese empire.[154]

Jules Harmand capitalized on instability and factionalism to convene a new relationship between Vietnam and France. A physician who participated in the Garnier delegation to Hanoi in 1873, Harmand had previously served as the French representative to the Siam court in Bangkok, and made several trips to Cambodia.[155] Like Jean Dupuis, Harmand also published academic work, including a defense of French colonial rule and its redemptive power for Asia and the world.[156] From his position in Huế, Harmand turned the divided court to his advantage, using differences among officials to further the development of a new, more lucrative French role in northern Vietnam.

Other events benefited Harmand's efforts to forge a new agreement. On August 21, 1883, under the command of Admiral Courbet, the French military laid siege to Huế and the port of Thuận An, between the ocean and the Hương River in central Vietnam.[157] The imperial army attempted to defend Huế but abandoned their positions after their cannon and rifle volleys, fired from outdated weapons received from France as a provision of the 1874 treaty, failed to damage the French ships.[158] The war with France now extended to the seat of imperial power.

Following Courbet's attack, the emperor and officials at court began to press for negotiations with Harmand. The condition of the Vietnamese military, from the perspective of Trần Đình Túc and Nguyễn Trọng Hiệp, two officials who sought negotiations, did not justify an aggressive stance.[159] In northern Vietnam, the French military established encampments to enforce the gains made by the late Henri Rivière.[160] With Huế under attack and the court divided, the Hiệp Hòa emperor authorized direct talks with Jules Harmand and Palasne de Champeaux, the former head of the Haiphong consulate.[161]

The result was the Harmand Convention of 1883.[162] Signed by Harmand, de Champeaux, Trần Đình Túc, and Nguyễn Trọng Hiệp on August 25, this document, containing twenty-seven articles, granted France protectorate status over the remaining territories of imperial Vietnam.[163] In exchange for French "protection," the Vietnamese court recalled to Huế all officials hostile to France. Also, the signatories promised to enforce the general opening of Vietnam to European commerce.[164] The convention revived plans for a Saigon-Hanoi telegraph network, which would connect French Cochinchina directly with the rest of Vietnam and, eventually to China. It also established the framework of the résidence system in northern (Tonkin) and central (Annam) Vietnam, whereby French officials would oversee Vietnamese imperial officials governing at the lower levels, and authorized the occupation of mountain passes above Huế by the French military.

The Harmand Convention also formalized the alliance between France and those Vietnamese officials who opposed the Black Flags. According to Article 23: "Henceforth, France will guarantee the integrity of the lands governed by the Annam king, defend the sovereign against all outside aggression and internal rebellion, and pursue just claims against foreign governments. *France and France alone is charged with chasing from Tonkin the bands known as "Black Flags" and the assurance of secure and free commerce for the Red River.*"[165]

Article 23 gave France the sole power to contend with Liu Yongfu and the Black Flags. Like the convention itself, it represented less an initial stage in the French conquest of northern Vietnam than it did a victory for the anti–Black Flag faction within the court, which now possessed a signed document that detailed their alliance with France. If the convention of 1883 reflected the colonialist ambitions of Jules Harmand, to an even greater degree it fulfilled the political aspirations of Trần Đình Túc and Nguyễn Trọng Hiệp, two court officials fully opposed to the administrative employment of Liu Yongfu and the Black Flags.

The Harmand Convention, while not ratified by the Third Republic and therefore not legally binding in France, had immediate consequences for the Hiệp Hòa emperor and his allies at court. Opposed to the convention, two officials, Nguyễn Văn Tường and Tôn Thất Thuyết, orchestrated a violent coup. Claiming that he had consorted with the enemy and sold the country to France, they brought the Hiệp Hòa emperor before the court, declared him unfit to rule, and placed him under guarded arrest in his royal residence.[166] With the emperor detained, the two coconspirators worked with Ông Ích Khiêm, the aging bandit hunter then living in Huế, to murder Trần Tiễn Thành and other Hiệp Hòa sympathizers.[167] Although intended as a document to bind Vietnam into a protectorate system, the Harmand Convention also enabled rival factions to identify and attack one another in Huế as Rivière's army occupied the north.

QING VIETNAM STUDIES AND THE SINO-FRENCH WAR

Far from the violent events in Huế, the war between China and France in the borderlands soon drew Qing Vietnam experts into the conflict. These officials held administrative positions in southern Chinese provinces, positions that afforded them opportunities to become familiar with the networks that coursed through the borderlands during the nineteenth century. The Qing Empire intentionally deployed borderlands experts in the war with France, a form of late Qing area studies that demonstrated the harmony of intellectual knowledge with military mission.

The first expert sent to Vietnam was Cen Yuying. A member of a Tai-speaking community in Guangxi, Cen combined knowledge of terrain with extensive experience in counterinsurgency.[168] In the 1870s, from various positions in the Yunnan and Guizhou, he oversaw the defeat of an uplands rebellion, termed the "Miao Rebellion" by Qing officials, as well as the suppression of the Panthay Rebellion led by Du Wenxiu.[169]

Cen Yuying's experiences in Yunnan informed his suspicions of France. After Garnier's invasion in 1873, Cen claimed that the Yellow Flags were coordinating with the French military to overthrow Vietnamese authority in the Red River Delta, citing Pan Lunsi's meeting with Jean Dupuis as evidence.[170] In the 1880s, Cen accused French merchants and military officers of taking "trade and commerce as a mere pretext to get to Yunnan."[171] Despite Jean Dupuis' previous role as a supplier of arms for China, Cen suspected Dupuis of scheming to arm Yunnan's Muslim population and reincite the former followers of Du Wenxiu.[172] When Cen led the Yunnan provincial army into Vietnam on May 15, 1883, he brought with him a distrust of France forged during a decade of counterinsurgency work in southern China.

Cen was accompanied by other officials with similar counterinsurgency experience and borderlands knowledge. These included Tang Jiong, who already had a long career in provincial administration when he arrived in Vietnam. His family, originally from Jiangxi, joined the civil bureaucracy during the Ming dynasty. After his father died fighting the Taiping Rebellion, Tang Jiong began his own career in the late 1860s, advocating the use of surrendered bandits to suppress rebellions in the uplands. In the 1870s, he reformed salt taxation in Sichuan, establishing a system by which the provincial government directly controlled the salt trade rather than selling licenses to private merchants.[173]

The most scholarly of these borderlands specialists, however, was Xu Yanxu. Although he came from Shandong Province in northeastern China, Xu developed a deep concern for Vietnam during the 1860s and 1870s, when he held a supervisory position monitoring the borderlands.[174] In 1867, the fight against Wu Yazhong, who raided the Cao Bằng granary and kidnapped Vietnamese officials, brought Xu into Vietnamese territory.[175] A decade later, he published a historical study of the country, a volume that narrated the various dynastic powers that controlled Vietnam since the tenth century. He framed his study, which included a map of lands governed by the Nguyễn, in terms of contemporary issues. According to Xu, a consistent stewardship of the borderlands concerned all Chinese dynasties since the Qin (255–209 BCE).[176]

Xu Yanxu commented that disorder and unrest in the borderlands consistently threatened the long-standing relationship between China and Vietnam. In the 1860s, he witnessed Wu Yazhong's followers destroying the Zhennan Gate, an embodiment, for Xu, of Vietnam's tributary status.[177]

Xu's version of the China-Vietnam relationship, as well as his conception of the borderlands as the setting for the defense of that relationship, granted a paternalistic role to China, albeit without the judgmental commentary of

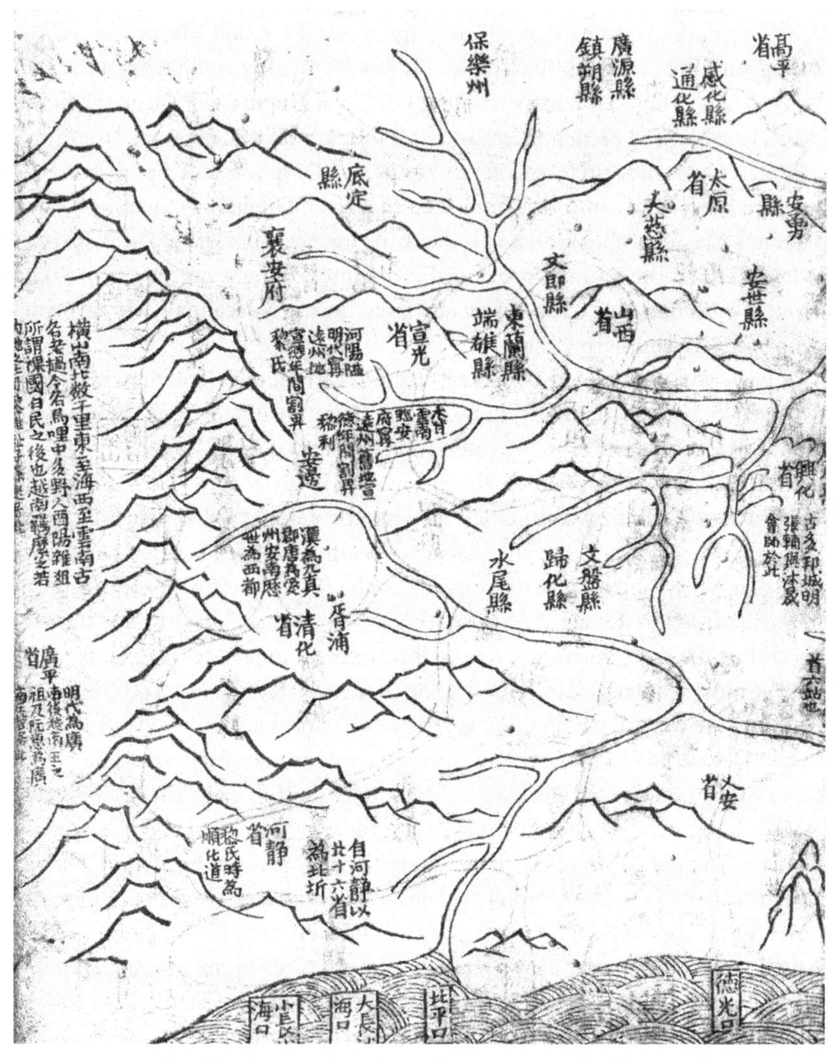

FIG. 3.2. Xu Yanxu's map of northern Vietnam. From Xu, *Yuenan Jiluo*.

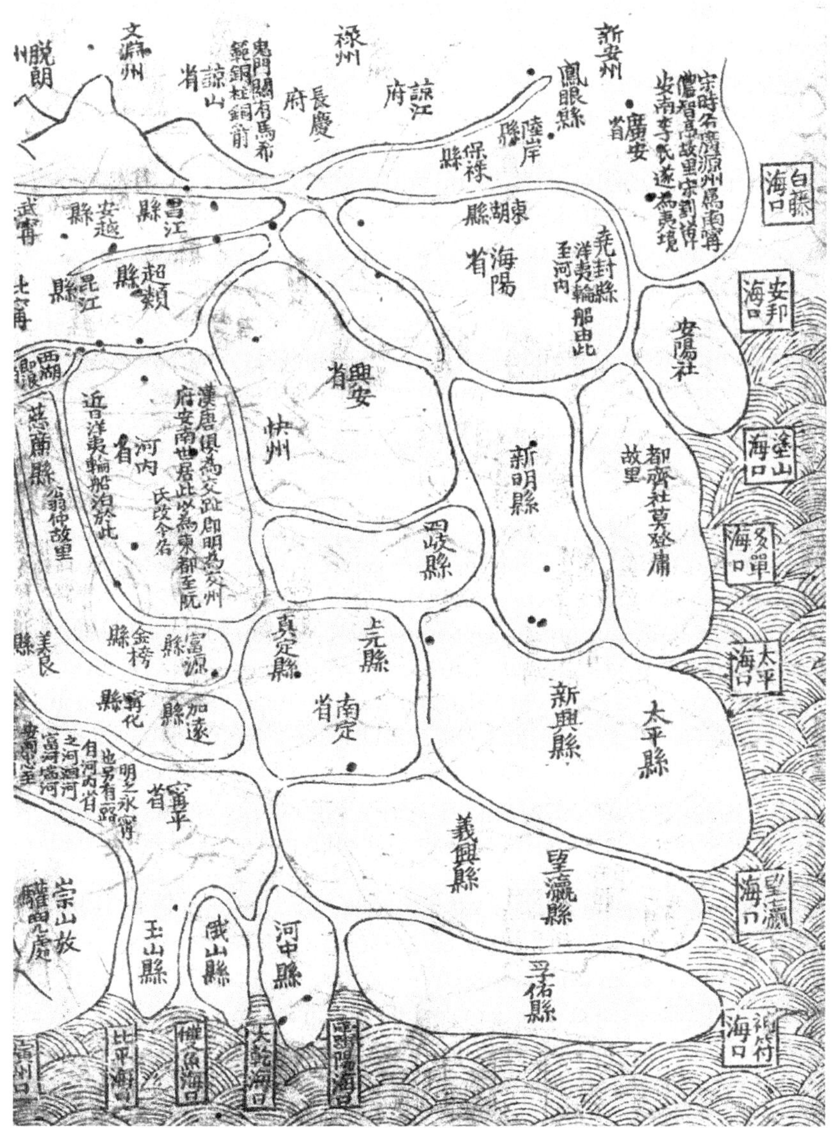

FIG. 3.3. Xu Yanxu's map of northern Vietnam, including Lào Cai. From Xu, *Yuenan Jiluo*.

Tang Jingsong. The ideological and political context of Xu's experience in Vietnam shaped his characterization of the China-Vietnam relationship as an eternal historical category.

In April 1883, as Xu Yanxu, Tang Jiong, and Cen Yuying crossed into Vietnam, their defense of Vietnamese sovereignty was a way to protect both China and its traditional relationship with Vietnam.[178] The Vietnamese official Bùi Văn Dị, who bore poetic witness to Rivière's coup, echoed this sentiment when he claimed that Chinese assistance would enable Vietnam to preserve its traditional relationship with its northern neighbor.[179] By the end of the war, these borderlands specialists met differing fates: two would be imprisoned in China for insubordination, while one, Cen Yuying, would try to render Chinese sponsorship of the Black Flags into an enduring pathway for anticolonial resistance.

BLACK FLAGS AT WAR

From September 1883 to February 1885, the Black Flags fought on behalf of Vietnam and China, extending the war against France that had begun with their ambush of Henri Rivière outside Hanoi.

Victories came quickly. In September 1883, the Black Flags defeated the French army west of Hanoi at Đan Phượng.[180] Since the death of Rivière in May, Liu Yongfu and Hoàng Kế Viêm had been awaiting a French counterattack when ships carrying French and Yellow Flag soldiers confronted them at Đan Phượng.[181] The new arrivals found themselves significantly outnumbered by the Black Flags in heavily flooded terrain.[182] After three days of intense fighting, the French and Yellow Flags retreated with four ships and three hundred soldiers lost.[183] Despite the Black Flag victory, Huang Shouzhong, a trusted lieutenant of Liu Yongfu, suspiciously fled, raising doubts about his loyalty.[184] The Black Flags had stopped the French army, but Huế ordered them to retreat, ostensibly to prevent another French offensive.[185]

Two different perspectives of the events in Đan Phượng emerged. From his camp in Bắc Ninh, the Chinese official Xu Yanxu heard that a Black Flag lieutenant, likely Huang Shouzhong, had fled and interpreted this to mean defeat for Liu Yongfu. His report was forwarded to the Qing Grand Council in Beijing in late September.[186] From Huế, Jules Harmand reacted to the news differently. In October, he assured the French military that only they could defeat Liu Yongfu and pacify northern Vietnam, as evinced by this apparent French victory.[187]

However, the immediate objective of the French expedition to Đan Phượng in September 1883 was not a military one; they had gone in search of Henri Rivière's remains. On the basis of information provided by the Catholic leader

Puginier, the French military found Rivière's head along a road near the village of Phù Diễn.[188] A witness recorded the gruesome discovery: "The eyes were gone, the sockets filled with limestone and dirt."[189] Villagers also led the French military to another location, where they found thirty more heads in various states of decomposition. No corpses remained. The Black Flags, they claimed, had tossed the lifeless bodies into the river.[190] With the assistance from a local Catholic community, the French and Yellow Flags were able to locate what little remained of Rivière's corpse.[191]

The French authorities in northern Vietnam established commemorations of Henri Rivière and Francis Garnier at Cầu Giấy, their common site of death west of Hanoi. People would now gather to celebrate the sacrifice of two French citizens whose passing "decided the acquisition of our *belle colonie*."[192] At the same time, the French government in Cochinchina formally inducted Francis Garnier into a colonialist pantheon, commissioning a statue of his likeness and transporting it to Saigon.[193] These two military casualties became colonial martyrs, unliving witnesses whose dissembled bodies, once signs of their violent death, occasioned reverence and remembrance.

As Rivière and Garnier were formally celebrated, war continued. In December 1883, a second French offensive targeted Sơn Tây, west of Hanoi where Tang Jingsong had met Liu Yongfu. Five battalions of Chinese soldiers had joined the Black Flags.[194] The Grand Council in Beijing had abandoned its earlier plans to launch a direct strike against French-occupied Hanoi, choosing instead to gather forces in Sơn Tây.[195] Admiral Courbet, who led the French offensive, believed that as many as 25,000 Chinese soldiers awaited him.[196]

Courbet's attack on Sơn Tây pushed the Black Flags back into the borderlands. In reality, only a few thousand Chinese soldiers supported the Black Flags in Sơn Tây.[197] An Algerian regiment easily chased the Black Flags and their allies north along the Red River to Hưng Hóa.[198] Tang Jingsong, who hid from the French attack inside the Sơn Tây Citadel, escaped with the help of Vietnamese officials.[199] Sơn Tây fell to France.

Courbet's victory at Sơn Tây had an immediate impact on China's war preparations. Fournier, the French negotiator in Tianjin, speculated that Li Hongzhang's opinion of the Black Flags as useful proxies for the indecisive Grand Council began to waver after Sơn Tây.[200] He was correct. Within weeks following the occupation of the Sơn Tây Citadel, Zhang Shusheng, a Qing Black Flag supporter, received orders to travel to Hubei Province.[201] This temporary assignment took him far from the field of action in the borderlands.[202] In Beijing, enthusiasm for an aggressive posture toward France began to wane.

During the Sino-French War, divisions within the Qing Empire fell into two main factions: officials such as Li Hongzhang who decided to negotiate with France, and officials who consistently endorsed armed resistance. Advocates of war identified themselves with an older Chinese intellectual tradition referred to as Qing Yi. Qing Yi, which had roots in the Han dynasty as a process of determining moral fitness through mutual critique, became, by the Ming dynasty, an instrument of the "self-appointed guardians of Confucian values."[203] In the nineteenth century, adherents of this attitude advocated force in response to foreign aggression.[204] In terms of Vietnam policy, Qing Yi officials, such as Zhang Shusheng, evinced a "penchant for war" and opposed negotiation with France.[205] The defeat of the Black Flags at Sơn Tây weakened the Qing Yi position on Vietnam.

BẮC NINH

After the fall of Sơn Tây, the Black Flags went north of Hanoi. In March 1884, they met Xu Yanxu, the scholarly Qing Vietnam expert who commanded soldiers from Guangxi Province in Bắc Ninh. The Vietnamese officials gathered with him included Nguyễn Quang Bích, who had revised his earlier reservations about Chinese assistance, and Hoàng Tướng Hiệp, the governor of Tuyên Quang.[206]

France soon attacked. The French general Théodore Millot, a veteran of the Franco-Prussian War, joined generals François de Négrier and Brière de l'Isle in an attack on Bắc Ninh on March 12.[207] After the first day of battle, the Black Flags and their allies withdrew to Hưng Hóa.[208] The French tricolor now flew over citadels in Hanoi, Sơn Tây, and Bắc Ninh.[209]

Logistical problems plagued the defense of Bắc Ninh from the outset. Although Li Hongzhang, while still negotiating, sent a warning via telegraph to the Grand Council before the French attack, the information could not be relayed to Xu Yanxu in a timely manner.[210] Cen Yuying confirmed his receipt of Li Hongzhang's advice in the same report to the Grand Council in which he announced the loss of Bắc Ninh to the French, news that the council had already received via telegraph from Tianjin.[211] Tang Jingsong, the official who had promised yet failed to provide more current information to Beijing about developments on the ground in Vietnam, fled with the Black Flags to Hưng Hóa.[212]

The French occupation of Bắc Ninh also had consequences for Tang Jiong and Xu Yanxu. Later that month, Beijing ordered them taken into custody upon their return to China.[213] The Ministry of Punishments in Beijing declared them both culpable for the defeat and called them both to the capital for a full investigation. Xu Yanxu died in custody that April. Tang Jiong, after learning in January 1885 of the reduction of his punishment to life imprisonment, passed away while under arrest in Beijing.[214]

Thrice defeated, the Black Flags began what would be their final attempt to defend base areas in the borderlands. However, their actions turned allies into adversaries. The Black Flag lieutenant Huang Shouzhong, who had fled from the French army in Sơn Tây, detained Hoàng Tương Hiệp, the Vietnamese official who aided the Black Flags in Bắc Ninh, on suspicion of collusion with France.[215] According to Huang Shouzhong, Hoàng Tương Hiệp bore responsibility for the Black Flags' defeat.[216] After he seized the contents of the provincial treasury in Tuyên Quang for the Black Flags, Huang marched Hoàng Tương Hiệp into China and arranged for his indefinite detention in Longzhou, where the former Tuyên Quang governor died the following year.[217] As Huang Shouzhong demonstrated, the Black Flags not only acted independently of Vietnamese authority, they also had the power to dispense with imperial officials at will.

THE BLACK FLAG DEFENSE OF LÀO CAI

As the French army occupied their bases and customs posts, the Black Flags retreated to the borderlands. Vietnamese officials who remained in Tuyên Quang fled to Hanoi, and the French army pushed the Black Flags all the way to Lào Cai.[218] In May 1884, General Millot announced a French victory in Tuyên Quang. Forced out, Black Flag lieutenant Wu Fengdian, who led the attacks on Garnier and Rivière, prepared a final offensive to defend Lào Cai and Black Flag control of the opium trade.[219]

French representatives in China quickly used these military victories to establish a new governing convention. In Tianjin, Ernest Fournier, a veteran of campaigns in Cochinchina and the Franco-Prussian War, signed the Li-Fournier Convention with Li Hongzhang on May 11, 1883.[220] According to this convention, France guaranteed naval protection for the coastal waters of southern China and northern Vietnam. In exchange, Li Hongzhang confirmed that the Qing Empire would remove its military from Vietnam, assure the safety of the borderlands, and agree to negotiate new commercial treaties with France.[221] Six days after this agreement, Fournier sent a telegram to General Millot. By June, according to his estimation, the French military could occupy the entire borderlands, including Lào Cai.[222]

THE PATENÔTRE TREATY AND THE OUTLINES OF THE PROTECTORATE

A new treaty in Huế soon followed the initial agreement between officials in Tianjin. With the French military outside Huế after Courbet's invasion of Thuận An, the Nguyễn emperor ordered officials to negotiate a treaty with Jules

Patenôtre, Harmand's replacement in Huế. According to the Patenôtre Treaty, an official representative of the Third Republic would now interact directly with the Vietnamese court.[223] The provincial bureaucracy would continue to function under the authority and supervision of a French protectorate administration. A series of *résidents* would represent French authority in Vietnam. The new government, the treaty noted, would defend both commerce and Catholic communities, two things threatened by the existence of the Black Flags.[224]

The Patenôtre Treaty also contained provisions for tax reform and population surveillance, which, in turn, threatened the Black Flags. Customs, transportation fees, and taxes for goods such as opium became the sole domain of the protectorate administration.[225] This new legal reality placed the protectorate in direct competition with the Black Flags, who had enjoyed a steady source of revenue through customs posts since the 1860s. To control the movement of people to and from northern Vietnam, the treaty also called for a system of passports and registration.[226] The French protectorates of Annam and Tonkin now supplanted the authority of the court, the provinces, and the most powerful imperial bandits in the borderlands.

During treaty negotiations, the imperial court, seeking peace, issued a general recall of officials. This exposed some surprising divisions. Nguyễn Quang Bích, along with most of the officials serving with the Black Flags, refused to comply, thereby maintaining command of the provincial military and militias. However, Hoàng Kế Viêm, the Black Flag liaison, returned as ordered to Huế in the spring of 1884.[227] Promptly demoted, the formerly powerful official now served as the supervisor of the Ministry of Public Works under supervision of the French protectorate.[228] Hoàng Kế Viêm's trust in imperial institutions led to his punishment by the colonial regime. The following year, as discussed in the next chapter, these divisions would fuel an elite-led movement to restore Vietnamese imperial authority, known as the Cần Vương.

THE TELEGRAPH

In addition to mandating a recall of officials and a new administrative order, the Patenôtre Treaty, like the Harmand Convention which it replaced, also revived the construction of a telegraph network connecting Saigon to Hanoi, which the court had suspended earlier that decade. The telegraph network would now have relay stations built on land granted to the protectorate by Huế.[229]

With the establishment of this system, the protectorate matched the technological capacities of Vietnam with those of China. A Danish-based corporation, the Great Northern Telegraph Company, began constructing a telegraph network from Shanghai in the 1870s. By the 1880s, they had set up service between

Beijing and Tianjin, the site of the French concession.[230] Li Hongzhang, who negotiated the Tianjin Treaty, advocated the telegraph as a technological advancement in the service of "self-strengthening," or enabling China to resist foreign aggression through domestic reforms.[231] Li Hongzhang's enthusiasm for the device, as his failure to communicate with Cen Yuying about Bắc Ninh made clear, often outpaced the physical infrastructure needed to support it. As he would later celebrate, the Patenôtre Treaty formalized the protectorate's commitment to the construction of telegraph lines throughout northern Vietnam, connecting the French administration with China and the larger region, asserting, through telecommunication technology, the Qing Empire's place in the imperialist world.

Despite the diplomatic-level talks at Tianjin and the Patenôtre Treaty, the Sino-French War reemerged in June 1884. Following a general armistice, French forces were patrolling the area between Bắc Ninh and Lạng Sơn when they found themselves surrounded and outnumbered by several thousand Chinese soldiers who had yet to receive word of the armistice.[232] The ensuing event, described by one French author as the "ambush" at Bắc Lê,[233] resulted in the deaths of twenty-seven French soldiers and—interpreted as a violation of the ceasefire—became a justification for the French army's full occupation of northern Vietnam.[234]

France also expanded its war with China to the sea when Admiral Courbet blockaded the island-province of Taiwan.[235] After destroying most of the Chinese navy in Fuzhou, he ordered the occupation of the eastern province of Fujian.[236] As Li Hongzhang attempted to maintain the dialogue with Fournier in Tianjin, the second phase of the Sino-French War saw China increasingly imperiled. Assistance to Vietnam, in terms of official policy, became secondary to the preservation of China.

Early in 1885, war threatened to come over the borderlands. The Qing Grand Council learned, via a telegram from Guangxi, that the French army planned to attack the border pass at Lạng Sơn.[237] By February 13, two French divisions had captured Lạng Sơn and nearby market centers, encroaching on an area used by China to supply its armies in Vietnam.[238] To isolate Chinese soldiers, General de Négrier ordered laborers attached to his brigade to set fire to the surrounding hills.[239] The uplands and all those within them became active targets of military violence.

Under de Négrier's command, the French army in Lạng Sơn began physically transforming the landscape in other ways. They built the initial infrastructure for telegraph relay stations in Lạng Sơn, feeding lines that would eventually connect with stations in southern China.[240] From poles anchored into the earth, these lines in the air towered over the rubble of a stone gate, a former boundary marker that de Négrier ordered detonated.[241] He felt the destruction of the gate was an adequate riposte for the "ambush" at Bắc Lê. De Négrier then placed placards amongst the rubble below the telegraph poles, which read: "The respect of treaties surely protects a country from its ports to its borders."[242] In place of boundary markers, telegraph poles suspended wires above the debris of the old order.

With de Négrier in Lạng Sơn, the Black Flags reoccupied Tuyên Quang. Liu Yongfu, along with Black Flag lieutenants Wu Fengdian and Huang Shouzhong, was joined by Cen Yuying, the Qing official who was fast becoming a dependable ally of the Black Flags.[243] In communication with the Grand Council, Cen requested a significant increase to the salaries of Liu Yongfu and the three thousand Black Flags under his leadership.[244] However, de Négrier's blockade of Chinese supply lines prevented these funds and any provisions from reaching them.[245] When aid from China never arrived, Liu Yongfu received assistance from Nùng Hồng Nghĩa, a Tai ally in nearby Cao Bằng.[246] Personal networks sustained the Black Flags, even during their official employment by China as soldiers in the war with France.

As the Black Flags waited, another old ally of Vietnam reappeared to fight the French at Lạng Sơn. Feng Zicai, who had led the struggle against Wu Yazhong in the late 1860s, was recalled from retirement to field an army.[247] When Lạng Sơn fell, he gathered a largely voluntary force from Guangxi Province.[248] On March 21, Feng Zicai led an attack on French positions.[249] Within a week, the French army, thinned by patrols and preparing a siege of Tuyên Quang, suffered heavy losses and retreated.[250]

At camps in the hills above Lạng Sơn, an optimistic Brière consoled his soldiers. "Men of the second brigade, remember well that since the world began, no Chinese army has ever forced European soldiers into a defensive position."[251] For Brière, the war over Vietnam had become a war over civilization, a conflict of racialist dimensions between China and Europe.[252]

Feng's victory at Lạng Sơn had instantaneous effects in both France and China. When the news reached Paris, the government of Jules Ferry, who had loudly advocated for French military intervention in Vietnam, collapsed. Alexandre Ribot and Georges Clemenceau seized upon the defeat in Lạng Sơn to criticize Ferry's imperialist policies, citing them as the reason for the economic depression in northern France.[253] In Beijing, advocates for war failed to capitalize on the victory. Citing the need to defeat rebellions in southern China, the Grand Council ordered Feng back to Qing territory when it received word of the attack on Lạng Sơn.[254] Li Hongzhang, resolved to prevent any loss of territory, convinced Fournier that China had no intention of tolerating any violation of the Tianjin Treaty.[255] Feng Zicai had won a victory, but one ultimately defeated by diplomacy.

On April 6, 1885, the Sino-French War in the borderlands ended as Chinese armies and the Black Flags returned north.[256] Two Chinese officials offered different perspectives on this defeat. Su Yuanchun, from Guangxi, stated that French armies had overwhelmed the Black Flags.[257] However, Cen Yuying, the longtime Black Flag ally from Yunnan, claimed that Liu Yongfu's army lost because the Black Flag lieutenant Huang Shouzhong had deserted his post in Tuyên Quang.[258] Defeated, Cen Yuying himself escorted Liu Yongfu back to China.[259] Huang Shouzhong, whom Cen blamed, traveled to Yunnan where he served in a Longzhou militia.[260] After some difficulty finding a place to settle, Liu Yongfu moved back to Qinzhou at the invitation of Feng Zicai.[261] His official salary suspended, Liu temporarily retired to a less eventful existence.[262]

After the end of the Sino-French War, Cen Yuying attempted to lay the groundwork for a Chinese-supported resistance in Vietnam. In May 1885, Cen sent an official telegram to the Grand Council in Beijing. He claimed that Nguyễn Quang Bích, who had fought with Cen and the Black Flags in Tuyên Quang, wished China to officially recognize a former Black Flag ally in the borderlands, the Tai leader Đèo Văn Trì. According to Cen, Nguyễn Quang Bích wanted Đèo Văn Trì recognized as the *tusi* of an area along the Black River in Vietnam's northwest, recalling a system largely dismantled during the eighteenth century in China.[263] Although the Grand Council never acted, Cen's proposal, which brought a largely defunct imperial institution into an anticolonial context, showed that Black Flag allies in the borderlands retained a compelling amount of power. As we will see, Cen Yuying's personal esteem for the Black Flags continued well after Chinese recognition of French colonial rule.

IMPERIAL BANDITS AND THE WAR OVER IMPERIAL VIETNAM

In 1883, as a military conflict between France and the Qing Empire escalated in northern Vietnam, the Black Flags moved from the borderlands into the Red River Delta. They also moved from the administrative outskirts of the Vietnamese Empire into the center of imperial politics as the issue of their presence animated divisions in Huế and the colonial ambitions of French officials.

Despite the diplomatic (and historiographical) labelling of this conflict as the Sino-French War, and its supposedly essential role in the expansion of the post-Westphalian *staatensystem* in nineteenth-century Asia, the violence of the 1880s was a continuation of the violence of the 1860s. The Black and Yellow Flags, mobile networks that tied a failed Chinese rebellion to the respective projections of Vietnamese and French imperial power, nourished their own dominance of communities in the uplands and lowlands throughout the conflict.

Factional divisions typified official discourse in both Vietnam and the Qing Empire. An emerging anti–Black Flag sentiment among Vietnamese officials found a new ally in the French military. Qing officials, including some experts on the borderlands, weighed a defense of China against an assertion of China's place in the imperialist nineteenth century.

Although the end of the Sino-French War brought the end of the Black Flags in Vietnam, the borderlands networks that sustained Liu Yongfu's army provided a compelling foundation for Vietnamese anticolonialism. The civilizing institution of French political order, the central conceit of arguments for French intervention, also continued the culture of violence of the previous decades. As we will see in the next chapter, not only did French authorities fail to completely control the borderlands, their claim to establish colonial rule depended on harnessing the very violence, and *pirates*, that they claimed to displace.

4

BORDERLINE, RESISTANCE, AND TECHNOLOGY

In 1891, Vietnamese members of the Garde Civile Indigène at the French military outpost of Động Mới filed the following report to the French *vice-résident* stationed at Bảy Sậy. "During the night, either on the first or the second of March, a strong band [*une forte bande pirates*] attacked the post from three sides with only a fraction of their strength. They entered the village of Nghĩa Lộ and took six buffalos, two cows, and a horse. They also left with eighty piastres. The band had secured all of the roads leading up to the military post prior to the attack, catching us all by surprise. They numbered two hundred-fifty or three hundred, with sixty or seventy rifles."[1] Both in tactics and in estimated size, the nameless band in this report resembled the Black Flags and Yellow Flags of decades earlier. Although they targeted French military outposts rather than Vietnamese soldiers, bandits continued to take resources from local populations, raiding villages in displays of power that supplied them with food, opium, and human beings. They also, as before French colonial rule, were intimately connected to the projection of imperial power.

The *vice-résident* of Tuyên Quang referenced the recent events in Bảy Sậy in his report on "*colonnes de police*." He criticized the French colonial government. Raids conducted by imperial bandits nominally under protectorate control reminded him of the earlier history of Tuyên Quang, the situation lamented by Vũ Trọng Bình decades earlier. "The main leaders of Chinese bandit gangs," he wrote, "have given us their submission, for which we give them weapons to destroy other rebels. But," he mused, ". . . to be blunt, this system is no different than the court in Huế employing Liu Yongfu against the other Taipings."

This expression of colonial anxiety contains a telling factual error, namely, the myth that the bandits that flooded northern Vietnam in the 1860s had been directly connected to the Taiping Heavenly Kingdom. A millenarian movement founded by a charismatic civil exam candidate who claimed to be the younger brother of Jesus Christ, the Taiping became a major threat to the Qing Empire during the mid-nineteenth century. Although their rebellion, as well as the imperial reaction to it, changed the social, political, and economic landscapes of southern China, the Taiping never reached the China-Vietnam borderlands, unlike the Panthay Rebellion of Du Wenxiu.

Although no connection existed between the Taiping Heavenly Kingdom and the Kingdom of Yanling—it was the collapse of the latter that sent the Black and Yellow Flags to Vietnamese territory through the borderlands—and despite the fact that the Black Flag founder, Liu Yongfu, never fought "other Taipings" in Vietnam or elsewhere, the myth of Taiping connections endured. It reduced the complex array of networks, personal connections, and armed groups at play in the middle and late nineteenth century to a concise accusation of Taiping contagion, indirectly blaming the Chinese imperial authorities for the *pirates* disrupting French colonial rule. For enemies of French colonialism, conflating post-Yanling bands with the Taiping connected, in a positive sense, the actions of Liu Yongfu and other imperial bandits to what Jean Chesneaux once called a "proto-nationalist" consciousness, one exemplified, according to certain interpretations, by the Taiping.

Historical inaccuracies notwithstanding, the *vice-résident*'s statement underscores the links between colonial rule and imperial bandits. As French officials claimed to control Tonkin, fulfilling the earlier aspirations of Dupuis, Garnier, and de Kergaradec, the structure of the protectorate reflected the ambitions and uncertainties of French colonial rule, a claim to sovereignty interwoven with the enduring culture of violence in the borderlands.

This chapter addresses how the culture of violence in the borderlands shaped both French colonial institutions and anticolonial responses in northern Vietnam. Raids, imperial bandits, communal resistance, and performative violence not only endured the beginning of protectorate rule, they each played a fundamental role in the projection of French imperial authority. As the *vice-résident* of Tuyên Quang suspected in 1891, French Tonkin had a great deal in common, historically and politically, with the imperial Vietnam it supposedly vanquished.

French colonial institutions, according to colonialist rhetoric, attempted to rationalize power, introducing an element of civilization through the control of force and the elimination of wanton violence. As de Kergaradec's pointed observations made clear in the 1870s, the Black Flags were the chief authors of devastation and misery, one of the targets of French civilization. As colonial rule, particularly in the China-Vietnam borderlands, responded to the existence and potential renewal (and contagion) of bandit violence, its institutions can be read as an index of colonial anxiety.

Anticolonialism, as a term for the range of violent responses to colonial rule in Vietnam, appeared both outside and inside the folds of French administration. An early rebellion led by Vietnamese officials tried to forge a connection between the goal of a restored Nguyễn government and the power of the Black Flags. Two central technologies of French colonial rule—the international telegraph and the borderline between Tonkin and the Qing Empire—became pathways for continuing the borderlands culture of violence, much to the surprise of the architects of the French empire in Southeast Asia.

ANTICOLONIAL VIOLENCE AND ITS BLACK FLAG CONNECTIONS: THE CẦN VƯƠNG

In Vietnam, rebellion against French rule predated the establishment of colonial institutions.[2] As part of a *maquis* (resistance movement) in the hills above Huế, an official composed an argument for rebellion in the political language of imperial Vietnam. The leader of this rebellion, using a stolen imperial stamp to authenticate orders to other officials, issued an edict of loyalty, a line from which provided the movement with a name: Cần Vương ("save the sovereign" or "save the king"). A rallying cry for traditional elites, the Cần Vương also had direct connections to the imperial bandit networks of the mid-nineteenth century, particularly the Black Flags.

The Cần Vương connected Vietnamese scholar-officials who rejected the French protectorate with the culture of violence in the borderlands that sustained imperial bandits. During the course of the rebellion, the defense of the Vietnamese imperial sovereign became imbricated with the Black Flags, so much so that some individuals had a kind of twinned existence, both as Cần Vương partisans and imperial bandits.

The rebellion began after the death of the Hiệp Hòa emperor. In July 1885 two officials worked to place Nguyễn Ưng Lịch on the throne as the Hàm Nghi emperor. These officials, Nguyễn Văn Tường and Tôn Thất Thuyết, each opposed the French protectorate. An imperial regent, Nguyễn Văn Tường had negotiated the Patenôtre Treaty but now began developing plans for an opposition to French rule led by the newly appointed emperor.[3] While Nguyễn Văn Tường had experience with the imperial court in Huế, his colleague, Tôn Thất Thuyết, had a long alliance with the Black Flags, as well as a penchant for violent actions in defense of imperial sovereignty.

After the enthronement of the Hàm Nghi emperor, Tôn Thất Thuyết planned an attack on the French military to incite an uprising. Scouting French soldiers in Mang Cá, an area outside Huế, he watched as they wearily returned to their encampment. In preparation for an ambush, he ordered several divisions of Vietnamese imperial soldiers to surround the camp. However, the attack backfired. Panicked, Vietnamese soldiers set the area around the camp ablaze. The French army responded by quickly defeating the forces under Tôn Thất Thuyết's command, driving the would-be commander of the armed resistance back to Huế in retreat.[4]

The next morning, what would become the Cần Vương Rebellion moved into the hills above Huế. Together with the Hàm Nghi emperor, Tôn Thất Thuyết fled to an uplands base area called Tân Sở ("New Base"), from where he issued the edict that gave the rebellion its name.

However, not all elites participated. Despite his role in selecting the Hàm Nghi emperor, Nguyễn Văn Tường refused to answer the call to revolt, opting to stay behind in Huế. When General de Courcy, head of the French forces in Huế, demanded that the reluctant official capture Tôn Thất Thuyết, Nguyễn Văn Tường found himself hunting his former ally. Upon failing to capture Tôn Thất Thuyết, Nguyễn Văn Tường was deported to the island prison at Poulo Condore en route to Tahiti.[5] Imprisoned, he tried unsuccessfully to communicate with Tôn Thất Thuyết and the *maquis*.[6] In February 1886, Nguyễn Văn Tường arrived in Tahiti, only to die five months later.[7]

Another official who resisted the call to rebel was Hoàng Kế Viêm, the former Black Flag liaison. Following the launch of the rebellion, Hoàng Kế Viêm, demoted when he returned to Huế during the Patenôtre recall in 1884, retired to his home village in Quảng Bình, where he dedicated himself to teaching at the local school. However, oral traditions in Quảng Bình question the sincerity of Hoàng Kế Viêm's disinterest in the Cần Vương. At least two stories claim he maintained covert connections with the *maquis*, smuggling arms to Tôn Thất Thuyết and planning the eventual overthrow of the protectorate. Another story commemorates an encounter one villager had with Hoàng, during which the retired official offered some thoughts on Vietnam's future as they drank cups of rice-alcohol. "Local officials must protect our children," he said. "They must guard our fields and crops. Whenever that happens, the people will honor and be grateful to them. For now, bottoms up." According to the story, Hoàng Kế Viêm, dispirited, quaffed his drink and wandered home.[8]

Hoàng Kế Viêm's obsolescence compared favorably with the fate of others who refused to join the rebellion. As bases of resistance, areas controlled by the Cần Vương recognized neither the Huế court, which existed under French control, nor the French protectorate. All officials linked with the French-sponsored imperial court were active enemies of the rebellion. In the case of Đặng Huy Xán, a recent exam graduate, this categorical distinction had fatal consequences. In the fall of 1885, the French-sponsored Huế court sent him to Bình

Định Province to assume administrative duties. However, before reaching his post, he was killed by a Cần Vương–led ambush.[9]

More than simply a violent response to French colonial rule, the Cần Vương also drew out the long-term factionalism within the imperial Vietnamese bureaucracy and court, a fact the French Catholic leader Paul Puginier noted. In June 1885, prior to the launching of the Cần Vương, Puginier passed along court documents, received from Catholic priests in Huế, to the Office of the Gouverneur in Saigon, the French authority in Cochinchina. These documents included correspondence between the Privy Council and the Foreign Affairs Office that proved Tôn Thất Thuyết's involvement in the obstruction of French interests prior to the Cần Vương. From his position in the Ministry of Military, the future *maquis* leader conspired against the Patenôtre Treaty, which established the protectorate system in Vietnam.[10] Tôn Thất Thuyết, who, like Hoàng Kế Viêm, once allied himself with the Black Flags, never attempted to conceal his disdain for French rule. With the Cần Vương Rebellion, he transformed that disdain into insurrection.

With the beginning of the elite rebellion against France, imperial Vietnam had two courts. From the mountain base of Tân Sở, the Hàm Nghi emperor and Tôn Thất Thuyết claimed authority over the empire and orchestrated a call to resist foreign occupation. At the same time, the Đồng Khánh emperor, the candidate chosen to replace the absconded Hàm Nghi emperor, ruled from Huế, where the other Vietnamese court existed under French control.

The two courts competed for personnel and allies. While the Huế court continued to manage the imperial bureaucracy, the Tân Sở court recruited officials through a series of edicts. Authored by Tôn Thất Thuyết, although attributed, through the imperial seal, to the Hàm Nghi emperor, these edicts outlined a radical restructuring of Vietnamese imperial authority, a change that interwove the *maquis*' claim of imperial sovereignty against French rule with the culture of violence that sustained imperial bandits.

These titles and positions combined old and new. Hoàng Đình Kinh's Bắc Ninh judgeship (Án Sát), the governor appointment of Nguyễn Văn Giáp, the treasurer appointments of Nguyễn Cao and Nguyễn Thiện, and the governor-general appointments of Lã Xuân Uy and Nguyễn Đình Nhuận all adhered to the imperial standards established during the 1830s. An unconventional post was granted to Nguyễn Quang Bích: Broad Supervisor of the Realm (Hồng Lô Tự Khanh). As an official title, this appointment recalled military positions from as far back as the third-century Han dynasty in China, representing the hope that an official with military experience could marshal a general resistance to France within Vietnam.[11]

The Cần Vương Rebellion also embraced Liu Yongfu, the former leader of

TABLE 4.1. Tân Sở court appointments for northern Vietnam, July 1885

OFFICIAL	POSITION	AREA
Hoàng Kế Viêm	Military Affairs Chief	Vietnam
Lã Xuân Uy	Governor-General	Lạng-Bằng
Nguyễn Đình Nhuận	Governor-General	Sơn-Hưng-Tuyên
Tạ Hiện	Military Governor	Thái Nguyên
Nguyễn Văn Như	Military Commander	Thái Nguyên
Nguyễn Văn Giáp	Governor	Sơn Tây
Nguyễn Cao	Treasurer	Sơn Tây
Nguyễn Thiện (Thuật)	Treasurer	Hưng Yên
Nguyễn Quang Bích*	Supervisor of the Realm	Vietnam
Hoàng Đình Kinh	Provincial Judge	Bắc Ninh

Source: Zhong Fa zhanzheng shi yanjiu hui, ed., *Zhong Fa zhanzheng*, 7:473. 越南咸宜元年諭告, Việt Nam Hàm Nghi Nguyên Niên Dụ Cáo.
* Nguyễn Quang Bích is identified as Ngô Quang Bích.

the Black Flags. Although he had fled north to China by the end of the Sino-French War, Liu Yongfu continued to command the attention of the Vietnamese court. Two weeks before the rebellion, when the Hàm Nghi emperor still ruled from Huế, the court rescinded all official titles from Liu Yongfu as a criticism in absentia.[12] After launching the rebellion, the newly announced Tân Sở court reversed this decision, announcing that it reserved an unspecified amount of silver to encourage the Black Flags to return to Vietnam and fight the French.[13]

The rebellion called on other imperial bandits. Nguyễn Quang Bích recruited a lieutenant, Đốc Ngữ, to expand the *maquis* in the northwest, bringing in Tai and uplands populations of the Black River Basin.[14] In the Tai area of Sip Chao, a former battleground for the Black and Yellow Flags, Nguyễn Quang Bích nourished an alliance among imperial officials and Tai powerbrokers, including Nguyễn Văn Quang; Sa Văn Nọi, a Tai leader in Mộc Châu; Cầm Bun Hoan

TABLE 4.2. Cần Vương base areas led by people with ties to the Black Flags

BASE AREA	LOCATION	LEADER(S)	YEARS ACTIVE
Tuyên Hóa	Quảng Bình, Hà Tĩnh	Hàm Nghi emperor and Tôn Thất Thuyết	1885–1888
Kiến Xương	Đông Triều,Quảng Yên, Bãi Sậy, Phả Lại	Tạ Hiện	1885–1887
Hữu Lũng	Bắc Sơn, Lạng Sơn, Phủ Lạng Thương	Hoàng Đình Kinh (Cai Kinh)	1885–1887
Cẩm Khê, Việt Trì	Hưng Hóa, Sơn Tây, Hoà Bình, Thanh Hóa	Nguyễn Quang Bích, Nguyễn Văn Giáp, Đốc Ngữ, Đề Kiều	1885–1892
Bãi Sậy	Hưng Yên, Hải Dương, Hà Đông, Bắc Ninh	Đinh Gia Quế, Nguyễn Thiện Thuật, Nguyễn Thiện Kế	1885–1892
Hùng Lĩnh	Thanh Hóa	Tống Duy Tân, Cao Bá Điển, Nguyễn Sự Chí	1885–1892

Source: Dương, *Căn Cứ Địa trong Phong Trào Cần Vương Chống Pháp*, 229–32.

in Muäng La (Sơn La); and Đèo Văn Trì, who would later work for the French, in Muäng Lai (Lai Châu).[15]

In the borderlands, the Cần Vương also relied on opium.[16] The trade in Yunnanese opium had previously sustained the Black Flags and had, for a brief while, generated additional revenue for imperial Vietnam. Overlap—in terms of territory, people, and sources of revenue—between Cần Vương loyalists and the Black Flags challenged the French military effort to pacify Vietnam.[17] Imperial bandits and borderlands commerce provided the Cần Vương with a convenient network for armed insurrection.[18]

In some cases, connections between the Black Flags and the Cần Vương were personal. In the 1870s, Tạ Hiện, named as the Thái Nguyễn military governor by the Tân Sở court, helped defeat remnants of Pan Lunsi's Yellow Flags.[19] In 1883, he led four thousand Vietnamese soldiers against Henri Rivière in Nam Định.[20] After the 1885 edict, Tạ Hiện commanded Cần Vương rebels in northeastern Vietnam, although he was captured in the early 1890s.[21] Another rebel with personal ties to the Black Flags was Nguyễn Văn Giáp.[22] An official in Sơn Tây during Rivière's siege in 1883, he refused to acknowledge the authority of the French protectorate, hiding in Sơn Tây.[23] Once word of the Cần Vương reached him, he promptly joined the revolt, adopting the nom de guerre Bố Giáp.[24]

In response to the Cần Vương, the leaders of the French protectorate presented their own alternate ordering of administrative space, one that linked imperial officials loyal to the Huế court to the projection of French colonial power throughout Vietnam. The Office of Borderlands Patrol Commissioner (Kinh Lược Sứ) connected the French administration to the Nguyễn bureaucracy. Prior to the protectorate, borderlands patrol commissioners held power over military affairs related to areas bordering the Qing Empire. Under French rule, however, the office became one of the most powerful positions in Vietnam, arbitrating all court decisions.[25] One of the first French colonial borderlands patrol commissioners, Nguyễn Hữu Độ, combined a career of endorsing French rule with a personal enmity for the Black Flags and their allies, making him an ideal choice for defending the protectorate through counterinsurgency.

Administrative changes also came to the local level. In each province, still nominally governed by the Vietnamese imperial bureaucracy, a *résident* oversaw the Vietnamese civil and military administrations.[26] Beginning in 1886, the *résident supérieur*, based in Hanoi, coordinated decisions and issued mandates to provincial *résidents*.[27] The same year, Paul Bert, the first *résident supérieur*, formalized the use of *chasseurs annamites*. Initially recruited in Huế to hunt down Cần Vương partisans, *chasseurs annamites* came from the royal army and local militia. Modeled on the *tirailleurs tonkinois* who fought for France during the Sino-French War, the *chasseurs annamites* were the basis for the formation of the Garde Indigène, a project led by Paul Bert.[28]

Territorial arrangements also changed. In northern Vietnam, the protectorate redrew boundaries in the most extensive overhaul of the local political economy since the provincial reforms of the 1830s. For instance, the province of Hưng Hóa, previously a vast and diverse territory, was divided into several pieces. Lào Cai, now under French control, became a province. Another part of Hưng Hóa, along with a section of Tuyên Quang, became Yên Bái. The protectorate separated the Tai-dominated areas of Sơn La and Lai Châu, with the latter a territoire militaire and later placed under the control of the Đèo clan, a decision that accommodated older Tai modalities of power such as the Muäng and Chao. Hà Giang, the former Yellow Flag stronghold, also became a territoire militaire, a decision that took land from Hưng Hóa and Tuyên Quang.

TABLE 4.3. Northern borderlands provinces and *territoires militaires*

NGUYỄN VIETNAM (1830–1885)	PROTECTORATE TONKIN (1885–1945)
Hưng Hóa	Lào Cai, Yên Bái (partial), Sơn La, Hà Giang (Territoire Militaire III, partial), Lai Châu (Territoire Militaire IV)
Lạng Sơn	Lạng Sơn, Bắc Giang (partial)
Cao Bằng	Territoire Militaire II
Tuyên Quang	Tuyên Quang, Yên Bái (partial), Hà Giang (Territoire Militaire III, partial)
Thái Nguyên	Bắc Cạn, Thái Nguyên, Bắc Giang (partial)
Quảng Yên	Quảng Yên, Hải Ninh (Territoire Militaire I)

Source: Dương, *Căn Cứ Địa trong Phong Trào Cần Vương Chống Pháp*, 104–6, map inset 216–17.

Amid this reordering of official space, Paul Puginier, who remained in Vietnam during the protectorate, reminded the French authorities of their special responsibility to Catholic communities. In his estimation, the survival of these communities, as well as the mission of the church, depended on the protectorate.[29] A viable Catholic presence in Vietnam would enable the church to avoid a repeat of its experiences in Laos, where missionary efforts failed, he believed, largely due to the lack of security for priests and parishioners.[30] In August 1886, Puginier sent a lengthy report to the *résident supérieur* in Hanoi. He claimed that Cần Vương partisans conducted violent reprisals against priests and Vietnamese Catholics, echoing the earlier abuses by the Black Flags. In his estimation, armed resistance to French rule was a toxic threat to the church.[31]

NGUYỄN HỮU ĐỘ HUNTS THE CẦN VƯƠNG

Nguyễn Hữu Độ, the borderlands patrol commissioner who had opposed the Black Flags during the 1880s, coordinated the capture of Cần Vương partisans. In September 1888, he reported the arrest of Lê Đàm, a son of Tôn Thất Thuyết. Two provincial officials captured Lê Đàm in the hills above Huế and secured his pledge of loyalty to the protectorate.[32] Based on his continued success, Nguyễn Hữu Độ became the borderlands patrol commissioner for life in 1889.[33]

From atop the imperial bureaucracy, Nguyễn Hữu Độ managed a project that made visible the enemies of the French protectorate. From May to July 1891, provincial governments and the military and civil authorities of the French protectorate submitted intelligence reports about *pirates*.[34] These reports constituted a catalogue of bandit and rebel groups, mapping such groups to locations in northern Vietnam. While intended as an act of analysis, these surveys also record the limits of pacification.[35] As an attempt to make banditry legible, the 1891 surveys signaled both the ambitions and frustrations of French rule in northern Vietnam.

The contents of this catalogue are a blend of Cần Vương rebels and other groups, a blending that closes the gap between banditry and political rebellion in the optics of the French colonial state. However, the lingering connections between the Cần Vương and the Black Flags, as seen in borderlands networks, underscore the importance of Nguyễn Hữu Độ's role and the basic harmony between the prerogatives of the borderlands patrol commissioner and the French colonial state, a harmony that goes beyond collaboration. We find French rule as an element in an ongoing domestic struggle.

In the northwestern province of Hưng Hoá, the epicenter of the Black Flags and, later, Nguyễn Quang Bích's Thập Châu army, the bandit survey claimed that six hundred fifty Cần Vương loyalists fought France under the command of Hoàng Văn Thụy, who also took the name Đề Kiều. Nguyễn Quang Bích's lieutenant, Đề Ngữ, and a Cần Vương rebel named Đốc Đại led another well-armed militia that extended its reach from Hưng Hóa east to Sơn Tây, within a day's journey of Hanoi.[36]

These surveys recorded the fragility of alliances forged by the protectorate with surrendered bandits, a fragility that seemingly confirmed the doubts recorded by the *vice-résident* of Tuyên Quang in 1891. This fragility also threatened to create the conditions for a return of the Black Flags. In Lào Cai, Hoàng Thắng Lợi, a low-ranking commander in Liu Yongfu's army during the 1870s, recruited another band led by Nguyễn Triệu Trung in a campaign to recapture former Black Flag base areas throughout the borderlands.[37] To the east, in Tuyên Quang, Nguyễn Triệu Trung bestowed official appointments on anyone who agreed to work with him, borrowing the language of the Vietnamese imperial bureaucracy to create a miniature *maquis*.[38] Based on reports from military patrols, French officials soon learned that this band was an extensive network, armed with Winchesters and reaching into the mountainous northwest. A lieutenant within Hoàng Thắng Lợi's band, "Bang Sang," originally came from the Tai-dominated area of Sơn La to Lào Cai area as a soldier with the *tirailleurs tonkinois*, who fought under French command. His defection to a group seeking to revive the Black Flags stoked colonial anxieties.[39] Further reports

TABLE 4.4. Quantitative data for rebellious groups in Tonkin, 1890–1891

PROVINCE	NUMBER	REMARKS
Bắc Ninh	41	
Cao Bằng	12	
Hà Nam	10	
Hà Nội	20	
Hòa Bình	3	
Hải Ninh	13	
Hải Dương	132	
Hưng Yên	24	
Hưng Hóa	21	
Hải Phòng	6	
Lạng Sơn	3	all "Cai Kinh"
Lục Nam	8	
Thái Nguyên	2	Ba Kỳ & Tạ Văn Diệu
Nam Định	1	
Sơn Tây	80	
Thái Bình	10	
Quảng Yên	20	
Tuyên Quang	31	

Source: NAVN. RST, 76319. Summary report, May 1, 1891.

revealed that Nguyễn Triệu Trung also came from Sơn La, indicating that the renewal of the Black Flags meant cooperation between enemies of French rule from Tuyên Quang to the northwest.[40]

On December 27, 1891, two Vietnamese officials in Tuyên Quang sent a panicked report to Nguyễn Hữu Độ. The report claimed that bandits from China, moving across the borderline, had joined forces with Nguyễn Triệu Trung and remnants of the Black Flags. After occupying a series of lowland villages, they abducted eight men, fourteen women, and several small children. Retreating to the hills, they stole livestock and set fire to the communal hall.[41] Despite the return of Liu Yongfu to China, and in defiance of the border and French attempts to control movement across it, former imperial bandits openly challenged colonial rule, joining forces with rebellious officials who refused French authority.

French colonial rule, with surveys and cooperative imperial officials, did not eradicate *pirates*. Imperial bandits merely changed form, adapting to a new set of negotiable barriers and categories. Even the institutions of colonial rule, such as the borderline and the telegraph, became elements in the borderlands culture of violence.

A LINE IN THE EARTH: A BORDER AND ITS LIMITS

. . . and now a line ran through the woods, although you could not see it.

—WILLIAM FAULKNER, 1948

After the end of the Sino-French War, French colonial representatives and Chinese officials set a borderline.[42] Although this line was only the latest effort to distinguish sovereignties in the borderlands, the French colonial borderline represented fixity and security to the official imagination. The barrier between China and Vietnam became another element of the borderlands, which continued as a mode of power and human interaction even after the borderline was drawn. An attempt to control space and movement, this line created a new context for old activities at the hard edges of empire.

Vietnamese states, particularly following periods of direct Chinese rule, often concerned themselves with concrete symbols of sovereignty over borderlands territory.[43] Prior to the French protectorate, the Nguyễn imperial authorities, at court and in the provinces, exhibited a studied sensitivity over Vietnamese sovereignty.[44] In both Vietnam and the Qing Empire, officials used empirical surveys of lands and populations to determine the extent of imperial power in liminal areas.[45]

While the French protectorate continued the practice of making territory more visible to state authority, concern for control of the borderlands motivated the drawing of a firm division between French Tonkin and the Qing Empire. A Boundary Commission determined the mutual extents of Chinese and French territorial control. Less than twenty years after the Bayonne Commission formalized the Pyrenean border between Spain and France, cartographers, *géographes*, and colonial officials met with their counterparts from China to draw a line in the earth.[46]

Advocates for empire accorded a central role to the borderline. In March 1884, before the end of the Sino-French War, James Duncan Campbell, an employee of the Chinese Maritime Customs Service, informed French prime minister Jules Ferry that the fixing of a boundary between China and Tonkin, to the obvious advantage of France, could only take place in peacetime. It also, Campbell advised, would require the formation of a special commission.[47] Following the war, settling the border became a priority, something essential to the territorial integrity of French Tonkin.

On April 9, 1885, Charles de Freycinet, the French minister of foreign affairs, received word from French representatives in Huế that the Qing Grand Council had accepted the Paris Convention, which ended the Sino-French War and put the Tianjin Treaty into effect as a legal document.[48] However, communication problems hampered the immediate withdrawal of Chinese soldiers. In an exchange with French representatives, Li Hongzhang cautioned that the war in Vietnam had damaged the newly constructed telegraph network that linked the southern Chinese provinces to Beijing.[49] As before the telegraph, memorials and edicts between Beijing and the provinces now traveled on horseback through relay stations. News that, with the advent of the telegraph, once arrived quickly now took weeks to reach its destination.

Communication problems notwithstanding, French officials authorized a Boundary Commission the following August, months after the war. It had five delegates, including Paul Neïss, a naval doctor who became the unofficial chronicler of the commission.[50] In November 1885, after several delays, the Boundary Commission arrived in Hanoi to begin consultations with their Qing counterparts.

From Beijing, the Grand Council sent two officials with no experience in borderlands administration to meet the commission. Both Zhou Derun, a native of northern Guangxi, and Deng Chengxiu, from inland Guangdong, belonged to an informal group within the Qing officialdom known as the Southern Faction. Deng and Zhou warned of "territorial dismemberment" and opposed commercial treaties that favored foreign countries.[51] During the Sino-French War, Deng Chengxiu proposed a broad, consensus-based decision-making process for the development of political policy, in line with the Qing Yi approach that typified those supporting war with France. Deng's vision of Qing rule incorporated the perspectives of even the lowest-ranking local official into the formation of Grand Council decisions.[52] A wide consideration of elite opinion, while the philosophical apex of Qing Yi, was anathema to Li Hongzhang, who opened negotiations with France. Li Hongzhang and the Grand Council selected two officials from a faction that had fallen out of favor to settle the borderline with France.

Both Zhou Derun and Deng Chengxiu openly criticized the decision to sign a treaty with France in 1885. To Deng, the defeat of China and Vietnam in the Sino-French War made little sense. "If their generals had saved themselves and backed down, that would have been the best policy. If the enemy attacked and then fled without pursuit, then our commanders would be left with rotten provisions . . . but to refuse to declare war and then, having gone to fight anyway, refuse again to call a victory a victory—that is no policy at all!"[53] A vocal opponent of peace with France and a member of a faction out of favor with the Grand Council leadership found themselves traveling south to Vietnam. Indebted to Li Hongzhang for their continued professional relevance, they now had orders to enforce a decision in which neither believed.

Unsurprisingly, some initial discord between the two sides ensued. De Freycinet requested that the meeting of the French commission and the Qing delegation take place on the southeastern Chinese coast.[54] Zhou and Deng protested that, since they would travel by land through Yunnan and Guangxi, they would be too far from the coast to change course.[55] Infuriated, de Freycinet accused China of attempting to sabotage the Boundary Commission.[56] Eventually, they accepted a proposal to meet in the borderlands, with Zhou in Lào Cai and with Deng in Lạng Sơn.[57]

Although not the head of the Boundary Commission, the group's doctor, Paul Neïss, kept a detailed travelogue. Selected for his experience in Cochinchina, Neïss had himself led an earlier expedition in 1880 to contact the Baria, a powerful uplands group in central Vietnam. Neïss's 1880 expedition, and his subsequent reports, helped contribute to a French "ethnographic model" for surveys of unfamiliar areas, one that relied on the military as a protective force.[58] He brought this ethnographic model to his work in the borderlands.

Beginning in 1885, Neïss wrote ethnographic essays based on his experiences with the Boundary Commission. Published as serials in *Le tour du monde*, his writings commented on the surrounding countryside. The very landscape itself, he noted, characterized by calcareous rock formations, caves, and occasionally impassable rapids, seemed designed to shelter bandits.[59] Neïss voiced a particular concern for Tai communities in the borderlands, who had "been incessantly exposed, for long years, to the continuous invasions of *pirates*."[60] Neïss's concern for the Tai was matched in intensity by his contempt for other populations. When his dog failed to return to camp one evening, the doctor angrily attributed its disappearance to the culinary predilections of non-Tai villages or Chinese merchants.[61]

In these articles on the borderlands, Neïss paid special attention to commercial goods. Using distilling devices Neïss characterized as "very simple but effective," Qing subjects—Chinese residents of the borderlands that lived in Vietnamese territory—processed anise, cultivated and supplied by Tai villages, into an oil that they sold to traveling customers.[62] Citing botany research by Benjamin Balansa, Neïss predicted that French rule in Tonkin would gradually bring the benefits of a more scientific and more "rational" method of processing anise to Tai cultivars, obviating the need for Chinese technicians in the process.[63] French rule meant sovereignty over subjects and territory, but also over products, effectively removing Chinese contributions to the borderlands economy.

Writing for a French audience, Neïss also explained the commercial possibilities of Yunnanese opium. In his view, Chinese involvement in the production and distribution of opium hampered the development of a profitable colonial enterprise. He noted that in Lạng Sơn, where the Boundary Commission met Deng Chengxiu, the trade in Yunnanese opium depended upon silver as a means of exchange. Control of the opium trade, even for the inferior Yunnanese product, meant control of a considerable portion of the silver flow in the borderlands. As with anise, Neïss saw the potential for a higher quality, more profitable product with Yunnanese opium. These improvements, he believed, could only come from French involvement in opium production.[64] For Neïss, the removal of the Black Flags from the borderlands opium trade, as with the removal of Chinese involvement from anise oil production, would create a space for French colonial rule to render a local product into colonial profits.

After gathering information about borderlands commerce, Neïss traveled from Lạng Sơn to Lào Cai, where he heard stories of Liu Yongfu and the Black Flags. These stories haunted his account. On June 22, the commission held a debriefing with Colonel de Maussion, who had occupied Lào Cai since March.[65] According to de Maussion, resurgent Black Flag loyalists, likely those later identified as Hoàng Thắng Lợi's band, had been disrupting survey work. When de Maussion dispatched civil engineers to the outskirts of Lào Cai, a group of Black Flag loyalists fired on them from across the Red River.[66] Although Liu Yongfu had left for southern China following the end of the Sino-French War, the Black Flags continued to violently challenge the establishment of French colonial rule in Vietnam.

According to Neïss, Lào Cai, which once bustled with Chinese and Tai merchants moving opium from the uplands and across the borderlands, bore the scars of the Black Flags. Describing it as a "skeleton of a city," he related a story that someone told him about life under Black Flag rule.[67] The former head of the Black Flags had filled ponds with the headless bodies of his disposed enemies.[68]

Other stories claimed that, upon Liu Yongfu's retreat to China, the remaining Black Flags set the entire town ablaze, sparing only a large temple on the west bank of the Red River.[69] In the villages above Lào Cai, Neïss saw entire villages filled with only women and children, the men conscripted to fight in the ranks of the Black Flags.[70] To Neïss, Liu Yongfu's domination and destruction of Lào Cai seemed at once impressive and terrifying.

Eventually, the Boundary Commission itself came under attack in Lào Cai. On August 19, as its ships coursed down the Red River toward Bảo Hà, a former Black Flag customs post, the commission came under fire. Upon hearing the shots, the commission's military escort, some thirty members of the *tirailleurs tonkinois*, jumped into the river and swam to shore. Although unguarded, Neïss and the rest of the commission managed to escape unscathed.[71] Nonetheless, in a very real sense, Black Flag loyalists threatened the work of etching the borderline into borderlands.

Over the next two years, the Boundary Commission and their Chinese counterparts managed to establish a borderline separating the French protectorate of Tonkin from the Qing Empire. Between Longzhou and Guangxi, the commission identified three roads, long used for envoys and tribute missions, as reference points for determining the new boundary. However, the roads, which ran from Longzhou to Đồng Đăng and then diverged along various paths, proved a cumbersome model.[72] In May 1886, to resolve this difficulty, the Boundary Commission began authorizing the transfer of entire villages previously under Vietnamese jurisdiction to China.[73] The initial proposed borderline was also moved north four kilometers to accommodate the Cao Bằng district of Bảo Lạc, a Tai area that had previously been the domain of Nùng Văn Vân in the 1830s.[74]

In addition to roads, the Boundary Commission also sought to control movement. After settling the border, French authorities restricted Chinese merchants and laborers to three sites for registered entry: Lạng Sơn, Thất Khê, and Lào Cai.[75] For centuries, Lạng Sơn had served as an official gateway between China and Vietnam. Although its arched gate, which separated Lạng Sơn from Pingxiang, was demolished by de Négrier during the Sino-French War, Lạng Sơn remained an easily defended area along established trade routes.

Unlike Lạng Sơn, Thất Khê and Lào Cai owed their existence largely to borderlands commerce. In Thất Khê, Tai communities lived in the hills while Minh Hương, people with ties to the former Ming dynasty who settled in Vietnam, lived in the lowland areas.[76] Despite its river connections to Longzhou, Thất Khê had no appreciable Kinh or lowland Vietnamese population.[77] Lào Cai, due to its centrality to borderlands commerce and its proximity to China, was a natural choice for a crossing point. By integrating Lào Cai into the borderline, the protectorate claimed control over a former Black Flag base area, a strategic position within sight of China, and a lucrative node of the Yunnanese opium trade.

In his writing, Neïss envisioned the borderline as a response to the sufferings of Tai communities in the borderlands. As with so many efforts to control, pacify, and develop the borderlands, the borderline brought surprising consequences. As the Boundary Commission continued its work, people fleeing the French military entered southern China. After the borderline, new groups with ties to old imperial bandits used displaced populations to claim territory. The borderlands, and its culture of violence, endured the line in the earth.

ADMINISTRATIVE REFUGEES: TAI POWERBROKERS AND BLACK FLAG PRETENDERS

Officials created the border and the border created refugees. Following the settling of a terrestrial line between the Tonkin protectorate and the Qing Empire, many residents of borderlands communities moved into Chinese territory. For the Yunnan provincial government, the appearance of these "refugees" (C: *nanmin*) required a response that combined relief with eventual return. As temporary settlements became available, administrative refugees from northern Vietnam posed new challenges to Yunnan's administrators.[78] When the issue of refugee return transformed into a problem of refugee rebellion, Ngụy Danh Cao, a Tai leader who claimed a close relationship with the Black Flag Army, proved the plasticity of the supposedly permanent borderline.

In contrast to an imagined era of peace and discipline, the settlement of the borderline brought significant demographic dislocation. Refugees from the protectorate administration poured into the southern Chinese provinces of Guangxi and Yunnan. In Guangxi, the provincial government began redrawing political geography to accommodate these new arrivals.[79] To the west in Yunnan, China offered migrants land and emergency aid.[80] Rather than halting population flows, the attempt to demarcate sovereignty with lines in the earth effectively pushed people into southern China.

The borderlands refugee crisis reached its apogee in the summer of 1889. According to the Yunnan government, people fleeing French Tonkin appeared in two waves. The first, numbering between twenty to thirty thousand people, followed the Tai powerbroker Đèo Văn Trì out of northwest Vietnam to Mengzi, in the southern reaches of Yunnan.[81] The second wave of several thousand, guided into Yunnan by a relatively unknown figure named Ngụy Danh Cao, arrived in Kaihua District, east of the Red River.[82] The first wave would eventually, and peacefully, return to Tonkin. However, the lingering presence of Ngụy Danh Cao's group caused a minor crisis in the Tai area of Muăng La (C: Mengla).

Located in the southwestern part of Yunnan Province, Muăng La had been under the rule of a single Tai clan since the mid-seventeenth century. The multiple names for this hierarchical Tai group attest to the complicated political and social networks at work in the borderlands. Although contemporary Chinese (PRC) sources refer to this family as Dao, Qing imperial paperwork from the period identifies the family in Muăng La as Diao, which, in Sino-Vietnamese, is Đèo. In imperial Chinese documents, *diao*, which carries a derogatory meaning, approximated a Tai term for "hill." In 1658, in the first decades of the Qing Empire, the Diao first came to power in Muăng La.[83] Either through selection or inheritance, a member of this family kept control of Muăng La until 1932, their position dismantled by the changes of the twentieth century.[84]

In 1890, as refugees poured into Mengzi and Kaihua, Yunnan's provincial administration provided emergency aid while preparing for the refugees' eventual return to Vietnam. Tan Qunpei, the provincial governor, monitored the situation. In January 1890, he reported that, while Đèo Văn Trì and his followers had returned as expected, the refugees led by Ngụy Danh Cao had not. Moreover, the latter had begun harassing villages and officials in the area around Hekou, the river-port bordering Lào Cai.[85] What had begun as a provincial administrator's attempt to assist a band of people in need quickly transformed into a counterinsurgency operation. The refugees became rebels against China under the leadership of Ngụy Danh Cao. This rebellion provided an early test of the borderline policed by China and France.

Ngụy Danh Cao's transformation from a shepherd of refugees to a bellicose rebel occurred against the background of postborderline demographic dislocations, but it also coincided with the death of an important Black Flag ally within the Qing bureaucracy. Seven months separated the arrival of several thousand people in Yunnan under Ngụy Danh Cao's command and reports from Governor Tan Qunpei of the Tai powerbroker's apparent malevolence. During this time, the Qing government had developed a profile of Ngụy Danh Cao, largely through an investigation by Cen Yuying, a veteran of war with France who knew Liu Yongfu. In a report to the Grand Council in Beijing, Cen Yuying portrayed Ngụy Danh Cao as a trustworthy ally to China. This depiction reflected Cen's own personal experiences during the Sino-French War as well as his perspective on the current state of affairs in French-governed Vietnam. In 1889, and near the end of his life, Cen Yuying interviewed this displaced powerbroker-turned-rebel who sought refuge from the very French authority against which Cen Yuying had fought.

Following the first reports of refugees from Tonkin, Cen Yuying traveled to Hekou, across the Red River from Lào Cai, to meet Ngụy Danh Cao.[86] According to Cen Yuying, Ngụy Danh Cao had initially crossed into China from Lai Châu, the *territoire militaire* controlled by Đèo Văn Trì. Cen recommended that Ngụy Danh Cao and his followers be permitted to break ground in uncultivated lands, with the understanding that some might remain as settlers.[87] As it had done since the refugee crisis began, China permitted migrants to cultivate new lands in Yunnan, thereby absorbing people fleeing northern Vietnam.

According to Cen Yuying's report, Ngụy Danh Cao testified to his connections with the Black Flag Army. For Cen, this evoked his own personal relationship with Liu Yongfu, the former Black Flag Army leader.[88] By referencing a personal connection with the Black Flags, Ngụy Danh Cao convinced a powerful Qing official of his own importance. He persuaded an agent of formal state authority of a direct connection between him and the Black Flags in an attempt to make himself invaluable.

Despite his success with Cen Yuying, a series of events quickly led to the unraveling of Ngụy Danh Cao's reputation. In June, shortly after authoring his laudatory report on Ngụy Danh Cao, Cen Yuying died.[89] His replacement as governor-general, Wang Wenzhao, had no personal ties to the Black Flags or Liu Yongfu. Without a sympathetic ally in the Qing government, and after remaining in southern Yunnan throughout the summer and fall, Ngụy Danh Cao announced his intention to wage a protracted struggle against the Diao for control of Muäng La with his personal army in January 1890.[90] Just as Liu Yongfu once had Lào Cai, Ngụy Danh Cao now sought his own base area. Ngụy Danh Cao's failure, as explained later, demonstrated both the changes and consistencies in the postborderline region.

Both the Yunnan government and the Grand Council in Beijing roundly condemned Ngụy Danh Cao despite his connections to the Black Flags. A subsequent investigation alleged that, far from being a leader of refugees, Ngụy Danh Cao had crossed into China as a transporter of people taken and held against their will. After defeating his attempt to take over Muäng La, the Qing authorities began exercising their newly established formal relationship with the French Tonkin protectorate to hunt down Ngụy Danh Cao.

Signaling a break with the late Cen Yuying, Wang Wenzhao called Ngụy Danh Cao the "Vietnamese Black Flag leader."[91] For Wang, a relationship with Liu Yongfu and the Black Flags was not a cause for concern. Moreover, Wang's identification of Ngụy Danh Cao as "Vietnamese" referred to territory only nominally governed by Vietnam yet actually controlled by the French protectorate of Tonkin. Wang Wenzhao's pairing of the words "Vietnamese" and "Black Flag leader" identified Ngụy Danh Cao with this place and, by extension, to a new system of territorialized rule. In the context of the recently fixed borderline, "Vietnam" signified a territorialization of responsibility. Wang Wenzhao's relative disdain for Ngụy Danh Cao marked a generational difference in attitudes about both the Black Flags and the issue of territorial responsibility. Rather than a vestigial trace of the Sino-French War, Liu Yongfu's former army became a matter of administrative concern for French Tonkin.

To eliminate the threat Ngụy Danh Cao posed to the established order in Yunnan, China relied on another Tai powerbroker. Ngụy Danh Cao's uprising in Muäng La had challenged the authority of Diao Zhangyu. A member of the powerful Diao clan, Diao Zhangyu assisted the provincial army in a siege against Ngụy Danh Cao. After four days, Ngụy Danh Cao and his personal army were defeated. As his followers were captured and many publicly decapitated, he fled back into Vietnam.[92] The Yunnan government defended one Tai powerbroker against an interloper, sending the "Vietnamese Black Flag" back into French territory.

After the victory in Muäng La, Wang Wenzhao reported the results of his investigation. In full contradiction of the late Cen Yuying's original claims, Wang Wenzhao contended that Ngụy Danh Cao had entered Yunnan not as a benevolent shepherd of refugees, but with a formidable personal army leading a large group of captives. His claims of Black Flag connections notwithstanding, Ngụy Danh Cao's only and original intention was to establish a base in Muäng La.[93] On the basis of Wang Wenzhao's report, the Yunnan government now officially recognized Ngụy Danh Cao as a criminal and a possible smuggler of human beings. It also recognized him as the responsibility of the French protectorate.[94]

Following his defeat in Muäng La, French authorities pursued Ngụy Danh Cao in Tonkin. He and his surviving followers, once in custody, negotiated a position within the Tonkin protectorate. Rather than dissipate the borderlands networks flowing from the Black Flags, the importance of which, for China, had effectively died with Cen Yuying in 1889, the French administration bricked them into the state apparatus. The personal power of Ngụy Danh Cao, as with that of other figures, was folded into the fabric of colonial rule.

On July 31, 1890, the Zongli Yamen, the bureaucratic organ responsible for relations between China and other nontributary states, received a report from Vietnam concerning the fugitive Black Flag. The French authorities agreed with and substantiated Wang Wenzhao's allegations, claiming that Ngụy Danh Cao was a destitute troublemaker with a history of banditry and theft.[95] His failed uprising and subsequent flight made the common objective of France and China quite clear. Tonkin and Yunnan not only shared a border, their administrations also resolved to mollify disruptive powerbrokers whose transgressions, against each state and its respective territorial limits, threatened to undo a fragile, albeit forced, tranquility.

The military administration of Sơn La, on the border with Lai Châu in Vietnam's northwest, had no problem capturing Ngụy Danh Cao. By mid-August, he had formally surrendered to the French military. In exchange for his life, Ngụy Danh Cao agreed to four conditions: (1) to relinquish his weapons, (2) to receive a modest stipend for his followers, (3) to submit to French authority and assist with operations to establish and ensure security, and (4) to cease all hostilities against China.[96] The reporting French military officer further proposed that Ngụy Danh Cao's followers could find work with the French military. Ngụy Danh Cao himself, along with his family and personal entourage, remained in Lai Châu under the double supervision of the French military and the Tai powerbroker Đèo Văn Trì.[97]

The conditions that followed Ngụy Danh Cao's surrender represented part of a broader effort by the protectorate to fold borderlands powerbrokers into the colonial state. The surrender of powerbrokers such as Ngụy Danh Cao established a model for agreements between the protectorate and imperial bandits.[98] Within two weeks of Ngụy Danh Cao's submission, a band of 184 *pirates* surrendered and offered to serve as auxiliary forces for the French military.[99] Several other powerbrokers, many with bases in the borderlands, also volunteered, accepting status as *soumissionaires*, or "surrendered rebels."

Ngụy Danh Cao's transformation under French rule was part of larger pattern. Over the next four years, other power figures, most notably Ba Kỳ in Thái Nguyên and Hoàng Hoa Thám in Yên Thế, offered their submission.[100] While *soumissionaire* status did not guarantee loyalty to the protectorate, the policy of incorporating former *pirates* into French authority effectively brought personal networks into the French claim of authority in Vietnam. From the perspective of Wang Wenzhao in Yunnan, the policy of hiring former *pirates* into the protectorate was a reassurance that their' subjects would not harass China's southern provinces.[101] The Tonkin administration cast some *pirates* as *soumissionaires*, providing a political distinction between cooperative powerbrokers and those who remained enemies of the state.[102]

Ngụy Danh Cao's arrest and return to Tonkin brought more than his brief rebellion to a close. It also ended the ability of other potential borderlands powerbrokers to forge relationships with China on the basis of Black Flag connections. Although the Black Flags and Liu Yongfu would later become valuable allies to anticolonial activists in the early twentieth century, any positive currency that association with the Black Flags carried, from the perspective of the Qing Empire and the French authorities, was exhausted by Ngụy Danh Cao's rebellion.[103]

Despite his rebellion's failure, Ngụy Danh Cao proved that the new borderline was a porous division between Tonkin and southern China. In the post-borderline period, the establishment of French colonial rule relied to a great extent on the coerced cooperation of borderlands powerbrokers, continuing the practice of incorporating imperial bandits into state authority begun by the Nguyễn decades earlier.

THE CAI KINH: A FRENCH PROSE OF COUNTERINSURGENCY

> We know very well that the regular Chinese troops will evacuate the city without any difficulty, but we do not know whether some of Cai-Kinh's gangs might not try to resist.
>
> —PAUL NEÏSS, 1885

As the newly drawn borderline created a new context for imperial bandits, the struggle to impose colonial rule in the borderlands generated a French "prose of counterinsurgency," a novel rhetoric of political order that resonates with precolonial practice.[104] As Ranajit Guha reminds us in the case of British India, colonial officials tend to develop and deploy a particular idiom when discussing rebellion.[105] Describing a rebellious act as *banditry* or rebels as *pirates* hid the political significance of the act, buttressing the notion that the only politics are colonial politics. For colonial officials, rebellion was criminal, "a matter of administrative concern" never to be regarded as the political challenge it often represented.

However, the French prose of counterinsurgency also tells us something else. A more long-term connection between banditry and governance typified life in the borderlands, a place suited to the disruption of staid categories. The power to ban creates both the banished (bandit) and the banishers (official) as the wielders of political authority rely on a practice of exclusion. Rebellion becomes the ultimate criminal act, a violation not only of the law, but, to the mind of the law-giver, the very conditions of legality.

During the period of French colonial rule in Vietnam, rebels and bandits blended within official rhetoric, in the "grammar," recalling Barthes, of European empire in Southeast Asia. The blending of outlaws and partisans was not only a feature of the French prose of counterinsurgency, it also reflected a deeper relationship between outlaw and law-giver, between bandit and official, between the Black Flags, in this instance, and the rebels of the Cần Vương.

The case of Hoàng Đình Kinh exemplifies this interweaving. Known in French sources as Cai Kinh, Hoàng Đình Kinh fulfills a colonial narrative role as a foil to French military efforts to pacify Tonkin. He has a mirrored existence in Vietnamese history as a member of the Cần Vương who waged a protracted struggle against foreign domination. These different lives of Cai Kinh share a common point of origin in the 1890s.

Until his death in 1890, Hoàng Đình Kinh held power over much of Lạng Sơn, Cao Bằng, and the northern part of Bắc Ninh. His organization, which connected the borderlands culture of violence to the aims of the Cần Vương, survived him. Much of the mythology surrounding the Cai Kinh stems from encounters with the French military after the death of its eponymous founder.

According to French colonial historian Paul Munier, Hoàng Đình Kinh was the scion of an influential family near present-day Bắc Giang.[106] In the mountains of Hữu Lũng, Hoàng Đình Kinh served as a low-level administrator during Li Yangcai's rebellion, cooperating with the Chinese commander Feng Zicai.[107]

Hoàng Đình Kinh existed in a borderlands space marked by ethnic diversity and demographic scarcity. Into the 1890s, the area around Hữu Lũng had a very small Vietnamese population, who relied on uplanders for medicine and food.[108] The historical patterns of upland-lowland relations in Hữu Lũng never became a serious subject for the architects of the French protectorate. According to one geographical source, the area had "not yet been settled."[109]

The Cai Kinh first became known to French officials when it blocked the work of the Boundary Commission following the Sino-French War. Upon reaching Lạng Sơn in 1885, Paul Neïss remarked that Cai Kinh controlled territory through alliances with other groups, making themselves "masters of the country."[110] In May 1886, the Boundary Commission declared that the Cai Kinh virtually governed Thất Khê, one of the official border crossings for Chinese merchants and laborers traveling to Vietnam.[111] The Cai Kinh directly challenged the power of the French protectorate to police its borders.

It also threatened to become the most powerful branch of the Cần Vương, one that relied heavily on borderlands networks that the border could not contain. Another bandleader from southern China, Liu Qi had come to Vietnam sometime before the Sino-French War. According to French reports, he engaged in opium trafficking and the theft and sale of women and children while leading guerrilla strikes against the French army.[112] In 1884, Liu Qi and his followers opened fire on a French river patrol, killing thirty-three French marines.[113] During the Battle of Lạng Sơn, Liu Qi disrupted French supply lines throughout the area of Chợ Chu.[114] Liu Qi continued to harass the French military as an ally to the Cai Kinh and, by extension, the Cần Vương Rebellion.

Sometime in 1888, Hoàng Đình Kinh, having survived an assassination attempt by his brother-in-law, was captured by a Vietnamese militia and turned over to the imperial authorities.[115] To prevent his escape, the Vietnamese governor of Lạng Sơn, loyal to the Huế court, incapacitated Hoàng Đình Kinh with chloroform. The following morning, the leader of the Cai Kinh was decapitated, his head displayed in public as a warning to current and future followers.[116]

After the death of Hoàng Đình Kinh, leadership passed to the Chinese bandit Liu Qi. As Cai Kinh leader, Liu Qi ordered the kidnapping of two children of a French official as his family traveled near Hữu Lũng.[117] At the time of the kidnapping, Liu Qi led the Cai Kinh across several provinces and maintained his own personal army of four hundred followers. He robbed French supply convoys and sporadically raided communities in the hills and valleys.[118] Following the kidnapping, the French army drove Liu Qi from Hữu Long. Liu fled deep into the mountains.[119] In February 1892, Liu Qi, the feared leader of the Cai Kinh, was shot by a French soldier who caught Liu butchering an officer's horse.[120] Hoàng Thái Nhân, Liu's widow, led the Cai Kinh until its gradual demise in 1894.[121]

During Hoàng Thái Nhân's brief tenure as head of the Cai Kinh, the band once associated with the Cần Vương partisan Hoàng Đình Kinh became the target of a concerted French campaign of counterinsurgency. As acts of violence against local communities and the French military intensified, a French officer in Cao Bằng, the second *territoire militaire*, began to develop an alternative method. An application of counterinsurgency techniques honed in Africa, this approach, "La Méthode Galliéni," resonated with earlier antirebellion efforts. Combined with a policy of recruiting surrendered bandits as *soumissionaires*, Galliéni's method provided a sense of temporary stability. It also afforded borderlands powerbrokers the means to ensure their own authority.

A veteran of the Battle of Bazeilles during the Franco-Prussian War, Joseph-Simon Galliéni arrived in Tonkin in 1892. Previously, he had served in Réunion and then in Senegal, where he incorporated local militia into efforts to establish and defend French colonial rule.[122] Galliéni viewed the French army in Tonkin as the defender of economic development and social stability, a role that included protection of the railroads and local markets as well as the involvement of the army in road construction.[123] During his own appointment in Lạng Sơn, Galliéni employed a tactic he referred to as "a drop of oil" (*une tâche d'huile*) to secure the cooperation of the local population with the French military. Galliéni's personal account and subsequent retellings of the Galliéni method claimed that this novel, pragmatic approach involved only a slight use of force, thereby reducing causalities.

In 1893, Galliéni took up his post in Cao Bằng. In this borderlands territory, he had two basic duties: to protect the railroads and to secure the border with China. In his estimation, the borderlands between China and Vietnam housed violent bands that engaged in kidnapping, the sale of women and children, and the opium trade. Echoing Paul Neïss, Galliéni identified the Cai Kinh as the most powerful of these groups and the most significant threat to French rule in the mountainous northeast.[124]

Initially, he established a counternetwork of small militias to compete with the Cai Kinh for popular support.[125] Within the first months of his tenure, however, the Cai Kinh abducted three French soldiers, taking them back to their stronghold in the mountains. Galliéni then ordered an offensive against the Cai Kinh. When he arrived at the bandit compound, he claimed to have found the captured soldiers, still alive, along with dozens of abducted women from southern Lạng Sơn whom he promptly ordered released.[126]

The victory over the Cai Kinh provided Galliéni with instant recognition. Three other leaders swiftly offered their submission: Hoàng Hoa Thám in Yên Thế, Liang Sanqi in Chợ Chu, and Ba Kỳ in Chợ Mới.[127] Two of these submissions would not last a year, but for the moment Galliéni had won the loyalty of major figures in the borderlands.

Galliéni developed a militia and community defense strategy that bore a consistent yet unacknowledged similarity with Feng Zicai's efforts in the 1860s and 1870s. In both cases, the localization of military authority folded communities into the structure of state rule. For instance, Galliéni promoted the recruitment of Tai community leaders in Cao Bằng, especially those opposed to the historically dominant Nùng clan.[128] As he toured Cao Bằng and Lạng Sơn in March 1894, Galliéni noted that all mountainous settlements, whether Tai, Yao, or Hmong, had fortifications against attack from outside.[129] The French military presence notwithstanding, he assumed that the structures guarded the communities from attacks by "*pirates chinois*."[130] In describing the situation this way, Galliéni joined a long chorus of administrative and communal voices that identified violent borderlands powerbrokers as "Chinese bandits." The French prose of counterinsurgency shared a template with similar projects that associated borderlands bandits with groups from the Qing Empire. The Taiping contagion of the 1880s became the *pirates chinois* of the 1890s.

Galliéni coordinated his program to suppress banditry, thereby confirming the authority of the protectorate in the borderlands, with the Chinese government in Guangxi. He sought out the assistance and endorsement of the governor of Guangxi, paying him two personal visits in 1894 and 1895. In the 1860s and 1870s, China fought Pan Lunsi and Li Yangcai in Vietnam. Now, in the 1890s, Galliéni hoped to secure assistance from China in defense of French rule.[131] On March 10, 1894, he traveled to Longzhou, crossing the border at Lạng Sơn and Pingxiang, the long-standing point of passage for tribute envoys from Vietnam to China.[132] In Longzhou, he consulted with Su Yuanchun, the

Guangxi military commander and a veteran of the Sino-French War.

Although less than ten years had passed since he commanded divisions against the French army, Su Yuanchun confirmed his commitment to cooperation in securing the border. He supervised patrols to prevent bandits or anticolonialist activity from entering the Tonkin protectorate.[133] By 1894, the prevention of borderlands banditry in southern Guangxi and Yunnan became a priority for China. Contrary to accommodation, as in the case of Ngụy Danh Cao in Yunnan, waves of armed bands fleeing Vietnam were met with the full force of the Guangxi army as smaller divisions and militias patrolled the borderline.[134] The securitization of the border became a shared concern.

Even as Galliéni collected *soumissionaires* and worked with China, the infrastructure of the protectorate came under attack.[135] In 1895, Ba Kỳ, the *soumissionaire* based in Chợ Mới, rebelled and ordered his followers to attack a French telegraph relay station. They captured one engineer and killed another as they damaged a vital telecommunications link.[136] On April 11, Galliéni received orders to capture Ba Kỳ and broker no negotiations.[137] According to Galliéni, Ba Kỳ possessed an almost occult power over the inhabitants of areas under his control. This charisma, combined with a reliance on the opium trade and firearms smuggled from southern China, made Ba Kỳ too dangerous for conventional warfare.

To defeat Ba Kỳ, Galliéni employed "the drop of oil," an incremental increase of French allies and infrastructure around the enemy to spare the local population.[138] He drained the water, to appropriate a phrase from the Chinese official Zeng Guofan, around Ba Kỳ with such completeness that Ba Kỳ offered his submission and directed his followers to work under Galliéni's command, constructing railroads and roadways in Lạng Sơn.[139]

The combination of the *soumissionaire* policy and Galliéni's "drop of oil" method dispersed and rerouted imperial bandit networks in northern Vietnam. In the language of the protectorate, this was pacification. For people such as Ba Kỳ, pacification provided avenues to maintain a semblance of authority as the formal modalities of power shifted. The French prose of counterinsurgency turned rebels into allies, but, on its underside, its allies still held the means to pursue insurgent ends.

Galliéni's tactics in the mountainous northeast had a ripple effect to the west in the former Black Flag stronghold of Lào Cai. From 1890, when the French administration monetized the total amount of trade that passed through Lào Cai, the sum value of commerce conducted through Lào Cai reached just over five million *francs*.[140] By 1892, after the establishment of the Cercle de Lao Kay as an administrative unit, that figure rose to over ten million.[141] In 1895, after two years of Galliéni's method, over thirteen million francs worth of trade passed through Lào Cai.[142] The overland route from Lào Cai to Yunnan also saw heavier commercial traffic under the military protection of Galliéni.[143]

Defeat or incorporation of imperial bandits engaged in borderlands commerce drove down the cost of shipping goods through Lào Cai. In 1892, the price of moving products along the Red River through Lào Cai began to fall, a development that reflected a perceived increase in security. From a high earlier that year of 40 percent relative to the value of the goods shipped, transportation fees fell close to those assessed in Haiphong, largely due to the decrease in the likelihood of robbery.[144] According to Eugène Franquet, the protectorate had a special responsibility in Lào Cai, namely the rejuvenation of an area ravaged by the Black Flags. Lào Cai had only 40,000 inhabitants, a low figure attributed by Franquet to the bandit groups and wars of the nineteenth century. He envisioned the role of French colonial rule as restorative, returning Lào Cai to its former splendor and providing renovation and repopulation. The stimulation of commerce, he claimed, was the first step toward the rebirth of Lào Cai.[145]

In 1898, after Galliéni's success in Tonkin and the stabilization of trade in Lào Cai, Lieutenant Courjon, a French military officer at the former Black Flag base area of Bảo Hà, made a passing remark about civil and military officials. Between the uplands area of Bảo Hà and Phó Lũ, the protectorate employed "*chinois*." All of these *chinois*, Courjon noted, "were once pirates."[146] Attesting to the axiomatic quality of terms like *pirate* or *bandit*, Courjon's comments demonstrated the power of exclusion wielded by the French protectorate; the inclusion of formerly banished groups into French administration was the recasting of imperial bandits in different roles. The power to "ban," to rule, was the power to include erstwhile "bandits" within the projection of colonial authority.

The axiomatic quality of *bandit* was often cofigured with stories of heroic resistance. For instance, in the twentieth century, the Cai Kinh, Galliéni's first great adversary in Tonkin, were folded into the narrative of "resistance to foreign aggression," a key trope of Vietnamese revolutionary historiography.[147] In 1986, the Hà Bắc Provincial History Council published a history of the former Cai Kinh base areas in Hữu Lũng, casting Hoàng Đình Kinh as a participant in the "righteous uprising against the French colonial invasion."[148] This history, however, excluded the Chinese bandit Liu Qi. In 2002, Hoàng Đình Kinh again entered popular commemoration when the Peoples Committee of Lạng Sơn Province, to which the Hữu Lũng area now belongs, officially designated the site of his uprising as a historical landmark.[149] A former Cần Vương partisan and adversary of French colonialism became a local expression of a national Vietnamese historical narrative.

In the 1890s, through the recruitment of surrendered bandits, building infrastructure, and the protection of commerce, Galliéni had turned imperial bandits into allies of the protectorate project. However, the employment of *soumissionaires*, as administrators in Thái Nguyên would soon realize, carried certain unforeseen risks.

LINES IN THE AIR: BORDERLANDS NETWORKS, VIOLENCE, AND THE TELEGRAPH

> We could link up with the French telegraph station just outside of Zhennan Gate, then to Tonkin and even on to Saigon, where we would be connected via British telegraph networks to Burma and other colonies.
>
> —LI HONGZHANG, 1888

After the war, telegraph lines crossed the borderlands.[150] In 1885, a relay station in Qinzhou connected southern China with Tonkin.[151] Twice delayed, the completion of this network captured the imagination of Li Hongzhang, the Qing official who negotiated the end of the war with France. Over the lines built in cooperation with France, Li hoped China would communicate with the world, projecting its influence and presence on a scale befitting its rightful status as a major power. In 1888, Li happily reported to Beijing about the union of lines. "Northern Vietnam," he noted "will be connected with the preexisting telegraphs lines in China."[152] The Qing Empire would then have the ability to communicate with the wider wired world.

As with the Boundary Commission, China and France collaborated over the telegraph. In Vietnam, stations in Mong Cai, Đông Đang, and the former Black Flag base of Bảo Thắng, in the hills above Lào Cai, handled Chinese telegraphic traffic to all points within Indo-China and beyond.[153] From the northeast corner of Vietnam westward, lines in Mong Cai connected to a Chinese station in Dongxing, Đông Đăng with Zhennan Gate, and Lào Cai with the Mengzi/Manhao line.[154] China was now wired into a transregional communications network.

The construction of this network also brought about the death of a French citizen with long ties to Vietnam. Ernest Millot, a supporter of the Dupuis mission in the 1870s, had returned to Hanoi in 1889. Together with Jean Dupuis, Millot had an audience with the Đồng Khánh emperor in Huế.[155] Dupuis, in frail health, then returned to Europe, but Millot stayed, starting a business importing *cyclopousses* from Japan before gaining a contract with the Compagnie des Postes et Télégraphes.[156] Millot hoped to investigate the Black River area while supervising the installation of telegraph stations and lines in the northwest. His own curiosity intersected with the protectorate's need to extend

FIG. 4.1. French telegraph station, Lào Cai Provincial Museum (author's photo).

its communication lines. In May 1891, his plans were cut short. While traveling in northern Vietnam, Ernest Millot died of fever. His family in France received the news within a week, via telegram.[157]

The telegraph also provided a new pathway for former imperial bandits, even for those seemingly embedded in the protectorate project. One such person was the *soumissionaire* Liang Sanqi. In the late 1860s, as a member of Pan Lunsi's Yellow Flags, Liang occupied Thái Nguyên. Together with his family and a collection of followers, he settled in the market town of Chợ Chu, near the boundary of the Thái Nguyên and Tuyên Quang provincial border.[158] Over the next two decades, Liang survived raids by rival groups as well as counterinsurgency campaigns while entrenched in Chợ Chu, which he ruled as an autonomous area during the Sino-French War.[159] His power remained unchallenged until March 1890, when he formally requested to surrender to the French military.[160]

The decision to accept Liang's surrender caused strong debate within the protectorate. Reports from Vietnamese officials alleged that Liang's personal army routinely conducted raids against uplands communities and extorted protection fees from merchants.[161] When a special commission convened during the summer of 1890 to consider his offer, the Huế court representative demanded that Liang Sanqi be integrated into the Nguyễn bureaucracy as an assistant military commander (*phó lãnh binh*).[162] Such a measure would have enabled the Nguyễn bureaucracy to police Liang's actions and report any transgressions by the *soumissionaire* directly to the protectorate. Stern opposition to Liang's employment came from Commandant Boylié, a veteran of the Sino-French War and the French military liaison to the commission. Boylié stated his trenchant mistrust for Liang, suggesting that if this troublemaker received the sanction of the protectorate, then the French military must encircle Chợ Chu with soldiers standing ready to eliminate him should he violate his agreement.

Despite these reservations, the commission issued official conditions of surrender for Liang Sanqi on August 15, 1890. In exchange for official recognition, tax exemption for villages under his direct control, and a salary for his personal army, the commission demanded the following:

- Help secure and pacify northern Thái Nguyên.
- Protect local villages from raids by bandit gangs.
- Stop the transportation of women and children in areas under his control.
- Prevent the passage of weapons bound for insurgent groups.
- Keep in regular and frequent contact with the *résident* in Thái Nguyên.[163]

With this agreement, Liang Sanqi became an official ally of the French protectorate. Although the Tonkin authorities hoped to use powerbrokers such as Liang to secure control of the borderlands, Liang's own agenda consistently interfered with the establishment of routine colonial authority.

Liang Sanqi maintained an active and hidden interest in furthering his own power at the expense of the protectorate. Liang's abiding self-interest can best be found in two instances: his apparent support for the kidnapping and smuggling of human beings and his attempt to foment rebellion against China via secret telegrams.

Allegations that Liang's army participated in the kidnapping and selling of human beings became known to the Thái Nguyên *résident* soon after the *soumissionaire*'s surrender. In February 1891, bandits raided a village in northern Thái Nguyên near Chợ Chu. They stole three buffalo and abducted two young women. According to the protectorate's investigation, the women claimed that Liang Sanqi's army had cooperated with the bandits.[164] In the wake of these events, another protectorate official in Tonkin warned that surrendered bandits hired by the state would erode legitimacy and bring about a systemic weakness of the rule of law, just as they did for the Nguyễn, he claimed, during the 1860s.[165]

These cautionary comparisons of French Tonkin with Nguyễn Vietnam failed to persuade the protectorate leadership that Liang Sanqi posed any sort of uncontrollable threat. However, the evidence continued to mount. French officials around the mountainous region of Tam Đảo accused Liang of running secret opium farms and selling his product throughout the surrounding valleys, outside the control of the protectorate's opium monopoly.[166] Throughout the 1890s, in the vicinity of Liang's base, merchants and even tax clerks reported that armed groups of bandits robbed them of their goods and currency.[167] French authorities pledged that they would warn Liang about his activities but emphasized that the usefulness of this *soumissionaire* outweighed the potential risks Liang posed for the protectorate.[168] Despite Liang's value, an event happened that both substantiated the anxieties of the Thái Nguyên government and demonstrated the durability of Liang's own personal power.

In 1907, Liang Sanqi attempted to incite rebellion through the joined telegraph lines connecting China and French Tonkin. In August, a French civil servant named Émile Courandy received several strange telegrams at his post in Thái Nguyên. They were encrypted, but undecipherable with the standard encryption key.[169] The mysterious telegrams sparked an investigation that led the protectorate authorities to a small house in Hanoi, the home of a Chinese tailor named A Pik. After some forceful persuasion, A Pik divulged that he had in his possession a key for decrypting the messages.[170] Their contents alarmed the French authorities.

The telegrams transmitted a manifesto for revolt against the Qing Empire. "Europeans," Liang's first transmission began, "are causing great misery for everyone."[171] He assured the people of Vietnam that forces dedicated to the overthrow of the Qing, which had allowed southern China to be carved up by European concessions, were waiting for an opportune moment to bring the venal empire to its knees.[172] But the people of Vietnam, Liang promised, need not fear this uprising. They could "continue living their lives and practicing their trades."[173] No one would need to fear abduction or conscription by these waiting rebels, who would gather their forces with a threat, enforced by Liang, of "immediate decapitation" should harm come to any innocent person in Vietnam.[174]

As was the case with the previous allegations against him, Liang's plot to overthrow the Qing Empire from within Vietnam did not bring the revocation of his *soumissionaire* status. The investigation into the seditious telegrams collapsed under the weight of Liang's alliance with the protectorate authorities. Shortly after the events of 1907, Liang offered a new demonstration of his worth when he provided the protectorate and French military with information about the whereabouts of Hoàng Hoa Thám, a former *soumissionaire* linked to a growing anticolonial movement.[175] However, in Thái Nguyên, the provincial authorities remained suspicious. When Liang Sanqi passed away on November

7, 1924, the French military and Thái Nguyên government seized his personal property and scattered his followers by ordering them to take up posts far from their former base area.[176] Liang's power did not outlive him. The effort to establish durable protectorate rule in Tonkin had lost an unpredictable, perhaps dangerous ally.

Despite the novelty of the medium, Liang's rebellious message was nothing new. When Wu Yazhong promised new lands and bountiful crops to the farmers of southern China in the 1860s, his aims were identical to those of Liang Sanqi some forty years later. Only communication technology distinguished Wu's broadcast from Liang's. Had the protectorate not intercepted Liang Sanqi's message, the long dormant rebellious agenda of the Kingdom of Yanling would have coursed through the telegraph lines connecting Tonkin and southern China. Li Hongzhang's vision of a strengthened, "modernized" Qing Empire would have been undone by one of the very technological improvements that made it attainable.

LIU YONGFU AND THE TELEGRAPH

In China, the lines of the telegraph network also carried more than just administrative instructions. They also offered a means for Liu Yongfu, the former leader of the Black Flags, to exercise his personal power.

When the San Na Rebellion, a tax revolt against the Qing authorities, erupted in Guangdong Province, the leader of the rebellion, Liu Siyu, sought refuge in Liu Yongfu's Qinzhou home.[177] As government soldiers tried to enter Liu's residence to apprehend them, the former Black Flag threatened them with armed resistance, eventually negotiating for the safe return of the San Na rebels to their home villages.[178] After the San Na leaders were arrested, Liu Yongfu ordered his secretary to send a telegram urging mercy for Liu Siyu. The former Black Flag leader played a role in the pardoning of the San Na rebels, with whom he found common cause.[179]

Celebrated by the Chinese nationalist Sun Yatsen, the San Na Rebellion brought a new generation of borderlands powerbrokers into the Chinese political revolution.[180] Huang Mingtang, a grain clerk in Guangdong Province, openly sympathized with the rebels and called for an end to the heavy tax burden that inspired them.[181] In 1907, Huang Mingtang joined Sun Yatsen's Revolutionary League, connecting the generation of Liu Yongfu to a new generation of revolutionary nationalists in China.[182]

Liu Yongfu's successful defense of the San Na rebels followed a period of employment in the Qing Empire after his return from Vietnam. During the Sino-Japanese War (1894–95), Liu was deployed to Taiwan. After the Japanese navy attacked the island, Tang Jingsong, Liu's old admirer from his time in Vietnam, and Liu Yongfu prepared to defend Taiwan. When Li Hongzhang signed the Treaty of Shimonoseki, ceding the island to Japan, Tang declared the Republic of Taiwan, with Liu Yongfu as vice president.[183] However, faced with the Japanese military, neither stayed long in Taiwan. Liu Yongfu reportedly fled Taiwan dressed as a woman to avoid detection by the Japanese military.[184]

LIU YONGFU IN QINZHOU

After leaving Taiwan, the former Black Flag became a focal point for Vietnamese anticolonialism. For one activist, Liu Yongfu represented the promise of victory against French colonial rule. Phan Bội Châu, the classically trained scholar and educator who founded the Restoration Society in 1900, tried to gather an anticolonial resistance among Vietnamese intellectuals with the assistance of Liu Yongfu.

Phan Bội Châu initially expressed his anticolonialism in terms of the shared literary traditions of China and Vietnam, eventually expanding the scope of his activism to Japan. Born too early to join the Cần Vương *maquis*, Phan Bội Châu criticized the protectorate, and French colonial rule in general, for its abject hypocrisy. He condemned colonialism with citations from such diverse intellectuals as Mencius, Rousseau, and the Italian nationalist Mazzini.[185] He also actively recruited imperial bandits to his cause.

One of the first imperial bandits Phan Bội Châu sought was Hoàng Hoa Thám. An adversary of Liang Sanqi in Thái Nguyên and a former lieutenant in the Cai Kinh, Hoàng Hoa Thám came from a humble background in Hưng Yên to lead his own army in Yên Thế, which bordered the former Cai Kinh base area in Hữu Lũng. Phan Bội Châu celebrated Hoàng Hoa Thám as the "George Washington of Vietnam," a reference to the Yên Thế leader's guerrilla warfare expertise.[186] He briefly met Hoàng Hoa Thám in 1902 to evaluate the remnants of the failed Cần Vương, before turning his attention to Liu Yongfu.[187]

In 1905, Phan Bội Châu journeyed to meet Liu Yongfu, whom he hailed as a defender of Vietnam despite the tragic outcome of the Sino-French War.[188] He argued that without Liu, "our people would not have had a single drop of blood left to wash the enemy's neck."[189] Liu's house served as a meeting place for Vietnamese anticolonial activists, hosting not only Phan Bội Châu but also Phan Châu Trinh and Nguyễn Thuật, the Cần Vương veteran and former guide for Tang Jingsong.[190] In January 1907, Phan Bội Châu stayed with Liu after returning from Japan, where he had arranged scholarships for Vietnamese students participating in the Đông Du ("Go East") Movement.[191] Although Phan Bội Châu's plans to form an anticolonial army failed, his attempt to transform the former Black Flag leader and his allies into agents of political revolution illustrated the endurance of borderlands powerbrokers in the Vietnamese anticolonial consciousness. "Liu was now an old man, but as we talked over the old days in northern Vietnam, from time to time he pounded the table and let forth a great roar, reminding me of the power he used to display when he fought the French at Cầu Giấy near Hanoi."[192]

In 1911, Liu Yongfu gained an official position in Sun Yatsen's newly established Republic of China. The former head of the Black Flags became the militia commander for Guangdong Province.[193] However, his power seemed chiefly cosmetic. His final communication with the Republican government, a telegram protesting concessions to Japan made in 1915, received no reply.[194] Liu Yongfu died on December 16 the following year, at his compound in Qinzhou, on the gates of which he inscribed his last official Vietnamese title, "Military Commander of Tam Tuyên."[195]

IMPERIAL BANDITS AND FRENCH COLONIAL RULE

With the deaths of Liu Yongfu and Liang Sanqi, the generation of imperial bandits that began with the Kingdom of Yanling in southern China came to an end. From the failed rebellion in Guishun, the Black and Yellow Flags crossed into Vietnamese territory, competing for resources, land, and state recognition. As the Tonkin protectorate in northern Vietnam took shape following the Sino-French War, the technology of French colonial rule often became an element of revolt or, at the very least, a new pathway for imperial bandits to pursue their own ambitions.

The elements of the technology of French colonial rule, intended to transform northern Vietnam into a vibrant, civilized, and commercially profitable outpost, proved difficult to control. The borderline dividing China from Tonkin contributed to a refugee crisis. Powerbrokers with ties to the Black Flags participated in a *maquis* with the support of a rogue emperor and his regents. Counterinsurgency and quantitative data about bandits only made enemies of the protectorate more visible, not necessarily more obedient. Even the telegraph network, which China saw as a harbinger of respectability as well as a means of efficient communication, became a conduit for sedition in Vietnam, and, for Liu Yongfu, a means to lobby for the next generation of rebels in China.

In his book *Chasseur de Pirates!* (1928), Albert de Pouvourville, who also published under the name Matgioi, described the drug-induced hallucinations of an anonymous French *commandant* stationed to the former Black Flag stronghold of Bảo Hà. Given to smoking up to seventy-five pipes of opium a day, this unnamed, dispirited officer became convinced that the tall, slender figures that surrounded his post were not trees in a "virginal forest," but high-ranking French generals. Deeply inebriated, he would salute the trees, believing, through his narcotic haze, that not doing so would be a breach of military conduct.[196]

Through this fictive *commandant*, who calls into question the fitness of the French military against the confusion of conquest, Pouvourville criticized colonial authority in Tonkin. The station at Bảo Hà, where the addict officer served, lay at one end of a system of customs posts established by the protectorate with the help of the French military. At the other end was Lào Cai.[197] Below the surface of Pouvourville's critique, an older order endured in the borderlands.

As the *vice-résident* in Tuyên Quang observed, the French protectorate's arrangement of allies bore a strong resemblance to the earlier policies of imperial Vietnam. The Black and Yellow Flags, imperial bandits who traced their origins to the Kingdom of Yanling, linked the establishment of colonial rule to the imperial project of Nguyễn Vietnam. Between both, the borderlands culture of violence set the terms of political authority and resistance, becoming, by the end of the nineteenth century, a mode of power also shared by the anticolonial Cần Vương Rebellion.

Attempts to control the borderlands during the French protectorate featured new techniques—a charted borderline and a telegraphic network—but largely continued, even in their failures, the imperial projects begun by Nguyễn Vietnam and the Qing Empire. In the place of the Black Flags, the French alliance with the Yellow Flags, which had its origins with Jean Dupuis in the 1870s, tethered the projection of French authority to the borderlands culture of violence. Whether as security personnel under the command of Vlavianos or as sanctioned powerbrokers in Thái Nguyên, the Yellow Flags thrived under French rule.

However, as with the employment of the Black Flags by the Nguyễn and, later, the Qing, sanction did not ensure loyalty. Nor did it restrain the activities of imperial bandits. As the case of Liang Sanqi demonstrates, *soumissionaire* status never guaranteed the surrender of rebellious aspirations. Folding pliant bandits into colonial rule availed them of the technologies of empire.

Even the borderline itself, which Neïss believed would end the suffering of uplands communities who endured the rule of the Black Flags, was repurposed. Although a collaboration between Qing and French representatives, the borderline never completely embodied a strict delineation of territorial sovereignty. The useful vagaries of the borderlands, changes in the control of commerce, the shifting loyalities of imperial bandits, and movements of populations across altitudes, never took on the predictable consistency promised by the borderline. As the case of Ngụy Danh Cao makes clear, a line in the earth allowed imperial bandits to seek new bases of operation across the borderlands in southern China.

In addition to the similarities between French and Vietnamese imperial projects, and the persistence of borderlands modalities of power underneath both, technological changes intended to streamline communication were put to alternate uses. While Li Hongzhang's ambition for a Qing Empire assured of its place in the region through the telegraph fueled his demand for the Indochina-China telecommunications network, the "lightning wires" carried missives regardless of their author, be they official reports, calls for revolt, or, in the case of Liu Yongfu in Qinzhou, pleas of clemency for impoverished rebels. In the early twentieth century, at the twilight of imperial bandits and the dawn of revolutionary nationalism in China and Vietnam, the former leader of the Black Flags dictated telegrams in defense of the younger generation, forging a connection between the bandits that inundated the borderlands and the activists that would begin the intertwined struggles for postimperial China and postcolonial Vietnam.

CONCLUSION

Flags in the Dust

> In Latin, *terminus* means "limit, border." It was originally the name of a divinity who was still represented in the classical age as an anthropomorphous figure whose body gradually faded away into a dot firmly planted on the ground.
>
> —GIORGIO AGAMBEN, *POTENTIALITIES*

> Because they're locals.
>
> —BORDER GUARD, PINGXIANG/LẠNG SƠN, 2004

ON September 26, 2004, I was waiting at the border of the People's Republic of China and the Socialist Republic of Vietnam. A slender pole, which a young soldier raised and lowered with a rope, was all that separated the two countries. From Pingxiang, a Chinese border town and commercial hub, I had traveled to Friendship Pass, a structure marking the end of one national sovereignty and the beginning of another. Behind the stone gate, I approached the borderline across which was the Vietnamese province of Lạng Sơn.

This line between China and Vietnam cuts through the region where imperial bandits waged war during the nineteenth and early twentieth centuries. As the Black and Yellow Flags struggled over opium and territory, they generated a culture of violence intimately connected to both imperial power and popular resistance. Vietnamese and Chinese imperial rule—and even the establishment of French colonial rule—would have been impossible without imperial bandits. In the borderlands, stories of this culture of violence resonate in the oral traditions of Yao, Tai, and Vietnamese communities.

FIG. 5.1. Friendship Pass (author's photo).

Stories of the Black and Yellow Flags also resonate in the historical research produced in China and Vietnam during the twentieth century. Scholarly remarks on Liu Yongfu, Pan Lunsi, Wu Yazhong, and others are an index of historical judgment, not dissimilar to the role of banditry as an index of law.

BLACK FLAGS AND REVOLUTIONARY MARXIST-LENINISM

In the 1950s, historical scholarship on the Black Flags tended to emphasize their role in the struggle against France. During a time when the People's Republic of China (PRC) worked with the Democratic Republic of Vietnam (DRV) and the People's Army of Vietnam to forge a revolutionary relationship, Liu Yongfu became a symbol of friendship and solidarity. Before the 1960s, historical studies produced in the PRC and the DRV downplayed or dismissed stories of raids, rape, and human trafficking.

The first Vietnamese historian to publish an academic study of the Black Flags was Trần Văn Gíap. Although other writers briefly profiled Liu Yongfu and his army, including Trần Văn Giàu, head of the Việt Minh in southern Vietnam, and Nguyễn Khắc Viện, a French-trained physician and activist for independence, Trần Văn Giáp was the first to author a book solely dedicated to the Black Flags.[1] A former member of the École française d'Extrême-Orient whose loyalty to national independence led him to leave the French organization after World War II, Trần Văn Giáp produced a detailed monograph on the Black Flags that reflected his intellectual role in the DRV.

Trần Văn Giáp's book, *Liu Yongfu: Black Flag General (A Soldier from the Taiping Heavenly Kingdom Fighting France in Vietnam*, trafficked in the notion that Liu Yongfu had a direct relationship to the Taiping Rebellion, a myth that often served the interests of French colonial authorities in Vietnam. This myth has endured in the official historiography. Although other studies in Vietnam have challenged the notion that Liu Yongfu had a connection to the Taiping, including a rumored 1937 pamphlet by the pseudononymous Ché Thuyết, *The Schemes of Liu Yongfu*, and an unpublished manuscript from the 1960s, the myth of the Black Flags' Taiping link persists.[2]

In his version of the Black Flag story, published in 1958, Trần Văn Giáp defended the reputation of Liu Yongfu against charges of "banditry" (V: *giặc*). For Trần Văn Giáp, this condemnation of the Black Flags and their leader were "perversions of the truth" (*âm mưu xuyên tạ sự thực*). He reminded his readers that the name of a street in Hanoi from the French colonial period, La Rue des Pavillons Noirs, today's Mã Mây Street, was an attempt by French engineers to "engrave this ugly picture of Liu onto the mind of the people."[3] For Trần Văn Giáp, oral traditions that substantiated accusations of Black Flag violence, which formed the core of Nguyễn Văn Bân's earlier work on the subject, did not stand up to scrutiny.[4] Liu Yongfu's banditry was a creation of the French colonial authorities and, in the case of Nguyễn Văn Bân, their Vietnamese lackeys.

When Trần Văn Giáp claims that French officials carved negative images about Liu Yongfu into the urban landscape of Hanoi, he appeals to the role of Vietnamese speakers as leaders of revolutionary Vietnam. Vietnamese, in its romanized form (Quốc Ngữ), was the language of political power. "The mind of the people" signifies the Vietnamese people in a socialist revolutionary sense. The "people" in this connection may be a general political term, but we might note that Trần Văn Giáp, elsewhere in his book, repeatedly references "the Vietnamese people" (*nhân dân Việt Nam*), yet expresses no concern for the "minds" of other communities, such as the Tày, Nùng, Yao, or Hmong. This framing of the story of the Black Flags reinforces the ethnopolitical supremacy of Vietnamese speakers as arbiters of historical truth.

BLACK FLAGS AND ORAL TRADITIONS

In Vietnam, the authoritativeness of Trần Văn Giáp's Black Flag monograph did not last long. Both in the DRV and in the Republic of Vietnam (1955–75), historians asked fundamental questions about Liu Yongfu. Revisionist work on the Black Flags, particularly in Hanoi, sparked a trenchant debate about the China-Vietnam relationship, rumors of violent behavior in the borderlands, and the nature of historical research itself.

The Black Flags were a topic of debate for historians in the DRV.[5] In the pages of the journal *Historical Research* (Nghiên Cứu Lịch Sử), a spirited discussion took place in the early 1960s. Through these debates, we see the methodological and thematic fault lines that divided scholars in the DRV, who did not form, with respect to the Black Flags, a united front.

Contradicting Trần Văn Giáp's earlier exclusion of oral evidence, articles in *Historical Research* challenged the idea that the stories of ordinary people have no place in the study of the past. Trần Đức Sắc, who published under the name Văn Tân, defended oral traditions, citing Kiều Oánh Mậu, who published popular dirges about the Black Flags in the early twentieth century.[6] A native of Hoài Đức, the district outside Hanoi where both Garnier and Rivière died in the ninteenth century, Trần Đức Sắc investigated oral traditions himself, visiting village elders and recording the stories that people told about life under the Black Flags. In one village, people recalled that when the Black Flags set up camp in the 1880s, residents heard the sound of pigs being slaughtered in the distance. Only later did they realize that these sounds actually were the panicked screams of people in neighboring villages.[7]

However, not all oral traditions were equal. With the assistance of the Culture Office (Ty Văn Hoá) in Thanh Hoá Province, Trần Đức Sắc transcribed a song from a Mường community that lamented their hardship under the Black Flags. As an ethnonym, *mường* comes from French colonial efforts to classify speakers of a Mon-Khmer language closely related to Vietnamese. It also refers to Tai political cosmology, *mường* being the Vietnamese pronunciation of *muăng*. During the nineteenth century, the imperial political project attempted to displace Tai modalities of power with the province. In the 1960s, Trần Đức Sắc dismissed the Mường song from Thanh Hoá as unreliable for the purposes of judging (*đánh giá*) the Black Flags.[8] This disregard was a marginalization of other, non-Vietnamese historical perspectives, buttressing ethnopolitical supremacy through claims of evidentiary worth.

Trần Đức Sắc cited the work of other researchers who shared his concern for Vietnamese oral tradition. In Thái Nguyên Province, which included Chợ Chu, previously ruled by the French-sponsored imperial bandit Liang Sanqi, a local historian who wrote under the name Thế Văn gathered stories about the Black Flags for Trần Đức Sắc's research. A professor at Thái Nguyên Normal University, Thế Văn investigated stories from the village of Võ Nhai about a band of Black Flags that terrorized the local population in the late 1860s. One villager, in his eighties, recalled that the Black Flags conscripted seven hundred men for their army and raided food and opium before leaving. Thế Văn learned that one area in Võ Nhai, Hang Thẳm, was rumored to be the place where the Black Flags massacred those villagers who resisted them. A century later, the people of Võ Nhai still avoided traveling through Hang Thẳm.[9]

Trần Đức Sắc also connected the Black Flags to the Yellow Flags. In the example of Liang Sanqi, he characterizes the distinction between Yellow and Black Flags as flexible. According to Trần Đức Sắc's research, Liang Sanqi began as a low-level officer in the Black Flags, claiming to be a Yellow Flag only after Liu Yongfu returned to China in 1885. Although difficult to corroborate, this detail evinces the lingering hostility to Liang Sanqi in Thái Nguyên. Even into the early twenty-first century, local cultural authorities describe the former Yellow Flag and *soumissionaire* as deeply opportunitistic, a bandit that wanted to make himself "into a king" (*làm vua*) at the expense of the local population.[10]

Despite these stories of violence and duplicity, Trần Đức Sắc resisted denigrating the heroic reputation of the Black Flags. Referencing Trần Văn Giáp, he stressed that the objective material conditions of the late nineteeth century, the period of feudalism (*thời phong kiến*) according to the Marxist narrative of Vietnamese history, necessitated such depraved actions by the Black Flags. Acts of violence, pillage in particular, were superstructural manifestations of material conditions.[11] Echoing Trần Văn Giáp, Trần Đức Sác concluded by characterizing the Black Flags as rebels against imperialism, albeit rebels forced into predatory banditry by the iron law of history.

Regardless of his appeal to historical materialism, Trần Đức Sắc's essay on the Black Flags incited a firestorm of debate in the pages of *Historical Research*. Chương Thâu, formerly a Chinese translator, assailed the notion that Liu Yongfu could have responsibility for abductions, rapes, and mass killings. In defense of the Black Flags' historical reputation, Chương Thâu claimed that Liu Yongfu had actually saved the people of Vietnam from harm at the hands of Chinese officials, citing somewhat specious evidence that the leader of the Black Flags had prevented the Qing official Cen Yuying from kidnapping women from Vietnamese villages and selling them into sexual slavery in China.[12]

Ultimately, the *Historical Research* debate over the Black Flags produced no clear consensus. The last words went to the historians Đặng Huy Vận and Dinh Xuân Lâm, who reminded readers that more remained to be done.[13] Tô Hoài, a journalist and travel writer based in Hanoi, offered some poetic concluding thoughts, encouraging historians to engage the oral traditions of communities formerly under the Black Flags. Village elders, he believed, were "a precious archive," one that disappeared with each passing life.[14]

In the Republic of Vietnam, based in Saigon, Trương-Bá-Phát published the lone scholarly article on the Black Flags in the journal *Sử Địa*. "Black Flag Thugs Assasinated Francis Garnier" (Bọn Cờ Đen Hạ Sát Francis Garnier) appeared in 1973, during the final years of the republic.[15] Focusing almost exclusively on the death of Garnier a century earlier, Trương-Bá-Phát claimed that eyewitness accounts provided terrific details about the Black Flags in the Red River Delta. This view of oral traditions, as supplementary material in the service of a perfected empiricism, stands in contrast to earlier work in the DRV. However, Trương-Bá-Phát's emphasis on the "assasination" of Garnier occludes a more complex hisorical grounding of the Black Flags as well as the brazen illegality of the French officer's actions.

In the People's Republic of China, the Black Flags provided an enduring metaphor for the relationship between China and Vietnam, a relationship that has never been a uniform set of interactions.[16] Claims to a Sino-Vietnamese relationship, whether born of amiability or animus, serve particular political, cultural, ideological, or ideological interests. During the 1960s, the Black Flags embodied the socialist revolutionary relationship that connected the DRV with the PRC.

Scholarship on the Black Flags in the PRC also elucidated the image, cultivated during Liu Yongfu's lifetime, of the Black Flags as allies in the global struggle against imperialism. The image of Liu Yongfu as a bridge between China and Vietnam appeared with Li Jian'er's *Biography of Liu Yongfu* (1957), a book republished in Taiwan (Republic of China; ROC). Liu Yongfu's army connected the era of the opium wars and the Taiping Rebellion, times of severe political and economic dislocation, with the burgeoning spirit of agrarian revolt against European imperialism.[17] Li Jian'er's inclusion in a volume published in Guangxi by the Qinzhou Municipal Historical Research Group (2003) demonstrated the usefulness of Liu Yongfu as a linkage between the otherwise disparate historiographical traditions of the PRC and ROC.[18]

In China, a significant shift in the historical narrative around the Black Flags ocurred in the late 1970s. There were two reasons for this. First, the war between the PRC and the Socialist Republic of Vietnam (SRV; 1976–present) inspired vitriolic political writings that used the story of the Black Flags to comment on twentieth-century events. Second, the climate of cultural and intellectual openness that attended domestic reform in China after 1978 encouraged a renewed emphasis on local history. The image of Liu Yongfu as an ally of Vietnam became a counterpoint to the allegations of Vietnamese betrayal that fueled the Sino-Vietnamese War in 1979. After the end of the Great Proletarian Cultural Revolution (1966–76), openness about local history in China created an atmosphere wherein historians could investigate the role of the borderlands in the story of the Black Flags.

In China, a defector from New Zealand crafted the emblematic statement about Liu Yongfu during the postreform period. A long time resident of the PRC, Rewi Alley had traveled to China before the founding of the People's Republic and joined the Chinese Communist Party in Shanghai.[19] In his book *Refugees from Viet Nam in China* (1980), Alley laid the blame for the Sino-Vietnamese War of the previous year—during which the People's Liberation Army (PLA) of the PRC invaded and then withdrew from several border towns in Vietnam—squarely on the Vietnamese leadership. In Alley's estimation, they had "forgotten the tough fight put up by the Black Flags in defense of Vietnam."[20] The army of Liu Yongfu, he wrote, were "Chinese volunteers waving black flags [who] helped the Vietnamese in defense of their country . . . under the command of General Liu Yongfu."[21]

The context of Alley's comment was a conflict that brought defeat to the PLA and devastation to borderlands communities. Deng Xiaoping, China's reformist leader, once characterized the Sino-Vietnamese War as a "preemptive counterattack" against Vietnam.[22] Launched against the regional background of the Hoa refugee crisis and the Vietnamese invasion of Cambodia, which toppled the Khmer Rouge–led Democratic Kampuchea in 1978, the Chinese invasion of Vietnam only lasted a matter of weeks. Despite the deployment of the national military to Cambodia, Vietnamese militias pushed back the human-wave tactics of the PLA. As they retreated to China, after occupying the cities of Lạng Sơn, Lai Châu, Hà Giang, Cao Bằng, and Lào Cai, the PLA followed orders to use all munitions brought with them. As a result, these cities faced remarkable destruction. In terms of the human toll, over 50,000 Vietnamese citizens, mostly militia and civilians, died, twice the number of PLA casualties.[23]

In addition to Rewi Alley's postwar hagiography, the 1980s marked a period of renewed local historical interest in the Black Flags. While much of the work produced after the Sino-Vietnamese War was fatuous—such as a 1981 survey of Sino-Vietnamese relations that claimed Liu Yongfu brought land reform to the hills around Lào Cai—a general reassessment of the Black Flags had begun.[24] Ma Honglin, in an essay from 1986, argued that Liu Yongfu promoted the cultivation of the land by securing populations under his control, a perspective that entirely evades rumors of violence.[25] For Guo Weiyong, writing in the same period as Ma, the Black Flags conveyed the spirit of Chinese peasant rebellion to the people of Vietnam, an interpretation that neglects the established and rich tradition of "uprisings" that animates both Chinese and Vietnamese historiography.[26]

However, the shadow of the Sino-Vietnamese War continued to loom large. Some historians in the PRC, including Yuan Shiqi and Zhang Maolin, took

FIG. 5.2. Lào Cai after the Sino-Vietnamese War, Lào Cai Provincial Museum (author's photo).

the story of the Black Flags as an opportunity to excoriate the Vietnamese imperial state. Although some Nguyên officials, such as Hoàng Kế Viêm and Nguyễn Quang Bích, trusted Liu Yongfu, the imperial authorities squandered their chance to prevent the loss of their country to France. French colonial rule, according to Zhang Maolin, could have been prevented had the Vietnamese court decisively supported the Black Flags.[27] This perspective seems to unconsciously echo the aborted plan, discussed by Tang Jingsong in Bắc Ninh in the 1880s, to push the Black Flags to invade Saigon. In both cases, the failure to make use of Liu Yongfu becomes an accusation against the leadership of Nguyễn Vietnam.

In China and Vietnam, historians produced competing images of the Black Flags. In Hanoi, the Black Flags occasioned a spirited debate over the nature of evidence in an age of dialectical materialism. In China, historians combined fantastical claims of land reform with more sophisticated criticisms of Nguyễn Vietnam. Despite the lively contentiousness of historical research, the story of the Black Flags is the story of the borderlands and, most importantly, of the resonance of oral traditions on the ground.

IMPERIAL BANDITS AND BORDERLANDS HISTORIES OF THE PRESENT

In Qinzhou, where Liu Yongfu retired, the former home of the Black Flag leader is now a museum. Visitors pass a large stone tablet as they enter the compound. The tablet bears two inscriptions, one in Chinese and another in Manchu, both attributed to the Guangxu emperor (1875–1907), that celebrate Liu Yongfu's role in the war against France and his later participation in the failed resistance to Japan in Taiwan. At the back of the main house, a statue of Liu Yongfu, with the title "National Hero Liu Yongfu," stares at the front panel separating two open doorways. Side rooms contain porcelain bowls, furniture, weapons, and cartoon-like illustrations of other Black Flags.

Particularly since the end of the Cultural Revolution, museums in the PRC have played an essential role in the stewardship of public memory.[28] At the Liu Yongfu Museum in Qinzhou, many of the walls feature portraits of the Black Flag leader in meetings. One painting has Liu dictating remarks to a secretary; another shows a candlelit meeting between Liu Yongfu, Phan Bội Châu, and Nguyễn Thuật. Yet another portrait depicts Liu Yongfu in a doorway grasping his sword, in front of the nervous visage of a blond-haired captive doffing his hat. In each of these images, Liu Yongfu conveys power and authority. The leader of the Black Flags connects the anticolonial movements of the nineteenth century to the budding nationalism of the early twentieth century.

Although he retired to his ancestral home of Qinzhou, Liu Yongfu founded the Black Flag Army in Ande. From Qinzhou, reaching the town of Ande means crossing most of Guangxi Province. Near the border with Yunnan, Ande sits among modestly sized hills, a short drive from Jingxi, where the Việt Minh trained soldiers during the war with France. In the 1860s, when Liu Yongfu founded the Black Flags and broke away from Wu Yazhong, Liu gathered a few hundred followers in a cave-like temple carved into on a small hill, waiting out a thunderstorm.

According to stories people tell in Ande, the temple outside town is the same one that hosted the Black Flags in the nineteenth century. Inside, visitors find two sets of paintings on the stone walls. One depicts the kings of hell, a common theme in the Daoist iconography of the underworld. The other, in text painted in blood red, tells the story of the Black Flags.

The area around Ande is connected to more than just the story of the Black Flags. Identified by arches above the main road as the "uprising site" (*qiyi di*) of Wu Sangui, who led a revolt in the eighteenth century, Ande has been at the center of several rebellions against imperial authority. It also has connections

FIG. 5.3. Liu and two Vietnamese revolutionaries, Liu Yongfu Museum (author's photo).

FIG. 5.4. Statue of Liu Yongfu, Liu Yongfu Museum (author's photo).

FIG. 5.5. Liu Yongfu dictating a memo, Liu Yongfu Museum (author's photo).

FIG. 5.6. Portrait of Liu Yongfu, Liu Yongfu Museum (author's photo).

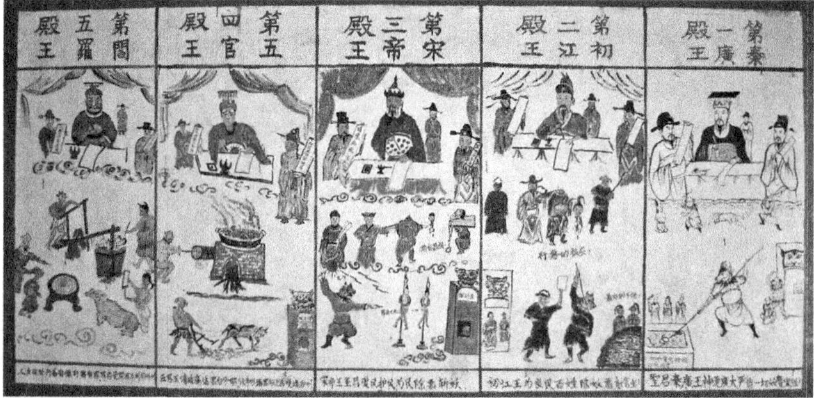

FIG. 5.7. Ande mural, Ande, Guangxi (author's photo).

to powerful Tai lineages, such as the Cen family, and to grandly mythologized *tusi* who traced their lineages to events around Ande.[29]

The painted text on the temple wall binds the Black Flags to this tradition. Likely painted after the end of the Cultural Revolution, it places Liu Yongfu into the story of French imperialism and, echoing the fears of Tang Jingsong, its threat to southern China. The Black Flags, it reads, went to Vietnam and won battles against "foreign devils" (*fangui*). They contributed to the strengthening of "the Chinese national spirit" (*Zhonghua minzu zhi qi*) and dealt a blow to the "tide of imperialism" (*diguozhuyi*). However, perhaps for obvious reasons, the text bears no mention of the violence involved.

Unlike southern China, there are few material traces of the Black Flags in Vietnam. The silence that overtook Vietnamese research on Liu Yongfu after the 1960s is visible in places like Bảo Thắng, Bảo Hà, and Thái Nguyên. Even in Lào Cai, designated as a city (*thành phố*) in the early twenty-first century, no ostentatious displays about the Black Flags or Liu Yongfu greet visitors. In the surrounding mountains, people still share stories, which have given us rich details about raids, resistance, and community responses to the violence of imperial bandits. Lào Cai in the twenty-first century, on the Red River below the hills, teems with new borderlands commerce, as groups of Chinese and Vietnamese day tourists, from many ethnic communities, trade places on three day passes, taking advantage of economic incentives designed to stimulate cross-border trade. The city, largely rebuilt following the Sino-Vietnamese War, has become a hub for tourism as well, a popular train stop for foreign and domestic travelers on their way to Sapa, a former French colonial *station d'altitude* and an ethnotourism destination.

FIG. 5.8. Text of the Black Flag story, Ande (author's photo).

"LOCALS"

As I approached the Lạng Sơn–Pingxiang borderline behind Friendship Pass, the renovated gate that General de Négrier had destroyed during the Sino-French War in the nineteenth century and the postrevolutionary symbol of socialist cofraternity, the guard on duty looked up. In Pingxiang, I was attending a 2004 China-ASEAN conference as an affiliated researcher with the Guangxi Social Science Academy's Office of Southeast Asia Research, so I had traveled to the border gate with a member of the delegation. Moving away from my colleague, I asked the guard if I could cross the borderline, offering him my passport (which contained a valid visa). "No," he responded flatly, taking down some information.

As I waited for the return of my passport, four people carrying large bags on their backs trudged up the hill toward the border station. One member of the group whistled. The guard, almost without looking up from his paperwork, pulled a string to raise the pole, opening the border between China and Vietnam for the group to pass.

Naively surprised, I asked the guard why he had not inspected their travel documents. Rolling his eyes, he said, "They're locals." We looked at each other in silence for a moment before he closed my passport and returned it to me. I left with my hosts for Pingxiang.

The group crossing the Pingxiang–Lạng Sơn borderline, although engaged in a mundane activity that only elicited mild interest from the guard at the gate, passively demonstrated something about the mutability of boundaries. Traversing the border did not negate it; on the contrary, the everyday act of border-crossing allowed me to see the borderline separating Lạng Sơn from Pingxiang as an easily negotiated barrier. The calm tenor of the guard, who waived the group through without even inspecting documentation, demonstrated something else. I realized that the crossing of borders, whether translocal, transnational, or cross-country, only represents bold, innovative strides against the structures of administration to a narrow perspective that takes the mythology of state projects, and state projections, as self-evident and ontologically solid. A band of locals hauling unidentified goods across an international boundary was not only a routine occurence, it harmonized with the expected norms of human activity to the extent that an official charged with policing the border permitted them to cross in an unceremonial manner. Within the space between China and Vietnam, even in the early twenty-first century, the durability of borders as barriers often yielded to the rhythms of the borderlands.

As my minder and I got back in the car and returned the way we came, the metal bar gradually faded away in the rear window. The post itself seemed like a dot firmly planted in the shifting ground.

NOTES

INTRODUCTION

1 Conversation with a resident of the Bảo Thắng District, Lào Cai Province, Vietnam, July 2005. All ethnographic work about oral traditions in this book omits proper names and names of specific villages or communes to protect the anonymity of living individuals.

2 On the Yao, see Litzinger, *Other Chinas*; Cushman, "Rebel Haunts and Lotus Huts"; and Scott, *The Art of Not Being Governed*, 117–19.

3 Jonsson, *Mien Relations*. Also Jonsson, *Slow Anthropology*.

4 For a discussion of the Yao/Dao ethnonym and its historical permutations, see Davis, "A Yao Script Project," 7–8.

5 For an overview of Wu Yazhong and his father, see Davis, "Post-Taiping Fall-out," in *On the Borders of State Power*, ed. Gainsborough, 25–34.

6 This text, the precise dating of which became a subject of debate after the fifteenth century, has been republished in its original language and in translation several times. Mai Quốc Liên, ed., *Nguyễn Trãi toàn tập tân biên, tập II*. An English translation appears in Dutton, Werner, and Whitmore, ed., *Sources of Vietnamese Tradition*, 93.

7 Anderson, *The Rebel Den of Nùng Trí Cao*, chap. 4.

8 For a recent study of ethnic classification in twentieth-century China, see Mullaney, *Coming to Terms with the Nation*.

9 NAVN. CBTN, 20:183. Nguyễn Công Hoán, the military commander (*tổng đốc*) of Sơn-Hưng-Tuyên, first suggested these incentives as a means to generate reliable tax revenue.

10 Ngô, ed., *Các nhà khoa bảng Việt Nam*, 765–66.

11 Cao, *Đại Nam chính biên liệt truyện*, 557–60.

12 An excellent study of this migration and its political dimensions is Hardy, *Red Hills*.

13 MEP. Puginier Letters (Carton 1). Puginier to Paris, 2 October 1883.

14 Braudel, *The Mediterranean*, 746. A more recent study calls attention to

banditry as a "major problem for frontier societies" in Chinese history. Shan, "Insecurity, Outlawry, and Social Order."

15 Blok, "Bandits and Boundaries," in *Honour and Violence*, 29–43.

16 Hobsbawm, *Bandits*. For a response, see Blok, *The Mafia of a Sicilian Village*; also Blok, "Social Banditry Reconsidered," in *Honour and Violence*. 14–28. Recent summaries of Hobsbawm's work and its limitations appear in Anthony, "Peasants, Heroes, and Brigands," and Bankoff, "Bandits, Banditry and Landscapes of Crime."

17 Chesneaux, *Peasant Revolt in China*.

18 Barkey, *Bandit and Bureaucrats*.

19 Blok, *The Mafia of a Sicilian Village*, 8.

20 Kuhn, *Rebellion and Its Enemies*.

21 Moertono, *State and Statecraft in Old Java*, 85–86. On Sumatra, see Colombijn, "The Volatile State in Southeast Asia."

22 Agamben, *Potentialities*, 162.

23 *The American Heritage Dictionary*, 3rd ed., 107; Love, *Collins Italian-English Dictionary*, 20.

24 The Kangxi Dictionary, compiled in the eighteenth century, does not contain a single instance of *fei* meaning "bandit"; rather, the term refers to woven bamboo baskets, a negative grammatical particle, or an adverb meaning "variegated."

25 From the *Rites of Zhou*: "*Zei* hold in high esteem harming the people, therefore they should be punished." Cited in Zhang, ed., *Kangxi zidian*.

26 For a recent study of violence as a problem in political history, see North, Wallis, and Weingast, eds., *Violence and Social Orders*. For a more nuanced perspective, see Coronil and Skurski, eds., *States of Violence*.

27 Benjamin, "Critique of Violence," in *Reflections*, 281.

28 As quoted in Weber, "Politics as Vocation," in *From Max Weber*, ed. Gerth and Mills, 77. The remark from Trotsky, according to Weber, dates to 1917.

29 Weber, *The Theory of Social and Economic Organization*, 156.

30 Massimiliano Tomba has analyzed the etymological affinity between force, violence, and power and the possible problems with translations of the terms *Gewalt* and *Macht*, particularly in English translations of Benjamin's essay. Tomba, "Another Kind of *Gewalt*."

31 Scott, *The Art of Not Being Governed*; Scott, *Seeing Like a State;* Scott, *Domination and the Arts of Resistance*.

32 Giersch, *Asian Borderlands*, 219.

33 Ibid., 96.

34 Smith, "Ch'ing Policy and the Development of Southwest China," 40–43. See also Took, *A Native Chieftaincy in Southwest* China; Faure and Ho, ed., *Chieftains into Ancestors*, especially chaps. 2 and 7. Historical studies in Chinese include Gong, *Zhongguo Tusi Zhidu* (The Chinese tusi system).

35 Smith, "Ch'ing Policy," 44–46.

36 Ibid., 47.
37 Guy, *Qing Governors and Their Provinces.*
38 Smith, "Ch'ing Policy," 74.
39 On the Miao label, see Jenks, *Insurgency and Social Disorder in Guizhou.*
40 Quoted in Smith, "Ch'ing Policy," 83.
41 Smith, "Ch'ing Policy," 269.
42 Shin, "The Last Campaigns of Wang Yangming."
43 Ibid., 119.
44 Ibid., 115.
45 Quoted in Mote, *Imperial China*, 678.
46 Shin, "Last Campaigns," 101.
47 Woodside, *Vietnam and the Chinese Model*, 141–43; Choi, *Southern Vietnam*, 45. The southern and northern regions of Vietnam, prior to the provincial system, were known as the "Gia Định Thành Tổng Trấn" and the "Bắc Thành Tổng Trấn."
48 Hoàng and Hà, ed., *Minh Mệnh chính yếu,* 1:1b. This remark is credited to Nguyễn Hữu Thận, secretary of the Ministry of Personnel in 1820.
49 In a much older discourse, Wang Fu claimed that rites (C: *li)* induced a psychological change in the people. Kinney, *The Art of the Han Essay.*
50 Trần Thị Vinh, "Thể chế chính trị thời Nguyễn dưới triều Gia Long và Minh Mệnh"; Nguyễn Sĩ Hải, "Tổ chức chính quyền trung ương thời Nguyễn-sơ," 244–45. Nguyễn Sĩ Hải's dissertation contains a flowchart of administrative paperwork after the Minh Mạng reforms.
51 Nguyễn Phan Quang, "Thêm mấy điểm về cuộc bạo động Lê Văn Khôi (1833–1835)" in *Nguyễn Phan Quang*, ed. Trần Đình Việt, 373–81. On Lê Văn Duyệt, see Võ Văn Kiệt, ed., *Lê Văn Duyệt với vùng đất Nam Bộ.*
52 Choi, *Southern Vietnam*, 66–68, 129–33.
53 Anderson, *The Rebel Den of Nùng Trí Cao*, 165; Nguyễn Phan Quang, "Khởi Nghĩa Nông Văn Vân ở Bảo Lạc" in *Nguyễn Phan Quang*, ed. Trần Đình Việt, 263–90.
54 Anderson, *The Rebel Den of Nùng Trí Cao*, 165.
55 Hobsbawm, *Bandits*, 145.
56 Ibid., xi.
57 Vansina, *Oral Tradition as History*, 196.
58 Ibid., 199.
59 Ibid., 27.
60 Amin, *Event, Metaphor, Memory*, 194.
61 Ibid., 194.
62 These include "Khởi nghĩa Nông Văn Vân ở Cao - Lạng (1833–1835)" and "Khởi nghĩa Nông Văn Vân ở huyện Chợ Ra (Bắc Thái)," both reprinted in Trần Đình Việt, ed., *Nguyễn Phan Quang*, 263–366.
63 Ngô, ed., *Các nhà khoa bảng Việt Nam*, 891; Kiều, *Bản Triều bạn nghịch liệt truyện.*

64 Kiều, *Bản Triều bạn nghịch liệt truyện*, 47A.

65 Kiều, Thiết, and Trúc, "Ai sơn hành," 1–2.

66 Ngô, ed., *Các nhà khoa bảng Việt Nam*, 919–20. Born in 1868, he came from Thạch Thất, south of Kiều Oánh Mậu's native Phúc Thọ.

67 Nguyễn, *Á-Đông luân-lý*.

68 Nguyễn, *Giặc Cờ Đen*.

69 Ibid., 7–9. Chapter entitled "17 cái đầu-lâu ở gần chùa Láng" (17 skulls near Láng Temple).

70 Ibid., 17.

71 Trần, *Lưu Vĩnh Phúc*.

72 Ibid.

73 Ibid., 75.

74 Vũ, "Những nhận định khác nhau về vai trò của Lưu Vĩnh Phúc và Quân Cờ Đen."

75 Ibid., 22.

CHAPTER 1

1 VHN 4036, "Tuyên Quang tấu tư tạp lục" (Notes on Tuyên Quang), 1885. Also A.1139 according to the EFEO system.

2 Ibid.

3 Đỗ, *Vấn đề trị thủy ở Đồng Bằng Bắc Bộ*, 113–23. Most of these requests were made in the 1850s, including proposals from Vũ Trọng Bình, Nguyễn Văn Siêu, and Nguyễn Văn Vỹ.

4 VHN 4036, "Tuyên Quang tấu tư tạp lục," 30b–32b.

5 Saint Cassia, "Better Occasional Murders than Frequent Adulterers!" in *States of Violence*, ed. Coronil and Skurski, 219–20.

6 Bế, Nguyễn Khắc Tụng, Nông, and Nguyễn Nam Tiến, *Người Dao ở Việt Nam*.

7 Lee, *The Big Smoke*, 13. Cited in Rapin and Eligh, *Ethnic Minorities*, 14.

8 Fay, *The Opium War*. See also Spence, "Opium Smoking in Ch'ing China," in *Conflict and Control in Late Imperial China*, ed. Wakeman and Grant, 8.

9 Spence, "Opium Smoking in Ch'ing China," 8. Although beyond the scope of this discussion, the notion of endemic opium use has received a recent scholarly critique. See Dikötter, "'Patient Zero.'"

10 Bello, "The Venomous Course of Southwestern Opium," 1115.

11 Tai, "Qingdai Daoguang nianjian Yunnan de jinyan wenti ji jinyan shibai zhengjie de fenxi," 59–63; also Le Failler, *Monopolie et prohibition de l'opium en Indochine*, 6–7.

12 Bello, "The Venomous Course of Southwestern Opium," 1116; Tai, "Qingdai Daoguang nianjian Yunnan de jinyan wenti," 63.

13 Woodside, *Vietnam and the Chinese Model*, 269.

14 Ibid., 280.

15 NLVN. SC M12246, Commandant Mourin, *Notice sur Lao Kay*, 1. Also NAVN. RST 1540, "Notice sur le secteur de Bao Ha (Yen Bay) 1898," Report from Lieutenant Courjon to RST, 11. The two officials in question are variously identified as Hoang Cu Nhe of Ban Lu and Nung Xa Chu of Nam Xi, and Duong Ninh of Long Bo and Nung of Hekou. Also NLVN. SC M10359, *Notice sur la province de Lao Kay*, 1919 (no author).

16 Ủy Ban Tư Liệu Văn Sử Hội Nghị Hiệp Thương Chính Trị huyện Hà Khẩu, *Tư liệu văn sử Hà Khẩu, tập* II, 179.

17 NLVN. SC M10359, *Notice sur la province de Lao Kay*, 1919.

18 VHN A.1392, Vũ Phạm Hàm, "Hưng Hóa tỉnh phú" 興化省賦 (Ode to Hưng Hóa). 7a. Bound with "Tuyên Quang tỉnh phú" 宣光省賦 (Ode to Tuyên Quang), same author, no date.

19 NAVN. CBTN, 226:121. Hưng Hóa treasurer Nguyễn Huy Trạc to Court, 4/12/TĐ13.

20 NAVN. CBTN, 226:121. Nguyễn Huy Trạc to Court, 4/12/TĐ13.

21 Ibid.

22 Ibid. 該名係是土人無知臨 (This guy is Tai, he lacks knowledge of governing).

23 NAVN. CBTN, 226:121. Rescript to Nguyễn Huy Trạc dated 4/12/TĐ13.

24 Winichakul, *Siam Mapped*, 49–50.

25 Taylor, "On Being Muonged," 30.

26 For a useful summary of work in English, see Anderson, *The Rebel Den of Nùng Trí Cao*, 72.

27 Hanks and Hanks, *Tribes of the North Thailand Frontier*, 30.

28 Viện Sử Học, ed., *Đại Nam thực lục chính biên*, 29:335; Nhóm Nghiên Cứu Sử Địa Việt Nam, ed., *Quốc Triều chánh biên*, 321.

29 In the 1850s, he helped edit a comprehensive state historiography, *Quốc Sử Tập Yếu* 國史習要. Langlet, *L'ancienne historiographie d'état au Vietnam*, 1:377–78.

30 Viện Sử Học, ed., *Đại Nam thực lục chính biên*, 29:78.

31 Ngô, ed., *Các nhà khoa bảng Việt Nam*, 776. Mark McLeod identified Nguyễn Bá Nghi as a member of the Peaceful Resolution Faction at the Huế court. The War Faction included Nguyễn Tri Phương, Hoàng Diệu, and two people who will become very important to the story of the Black Flags, Hoàng Kế Viêm (also known as Hoàng Tá Viêm) and Tôn Thất Thuyết. McLeod, *The Vietnamese Response to the French Intervention*, 52. However, Emmanuel Poisson noted that Nguyễn Bá Nghi was a serious opponent of the original French colonial project in Cochinchina. Poisson, *Mandarins et subalterns au nord du Viet Nam*, 162n30.

32 Ngô, ed., *Các nhà khoa bảng Việt Nam*, 776.

33 Cao, *Đại Nam chính biên liệt truyện*, 596.

34 Ibid.

35 Ibid., 596–97.

36 Viện Sử Học, ed., *Đại Nam thực lục chính biên*, 31:46–50.

37 Ibid., 31:71.

38 Ibid., 31:117–18.

39 Ibid., 31:125–26.

40 Đỗ, ed., *Từ điển chức quan Việt Nam*, 272-73. During the Nguyễn period, these training centers graduated people in three ranks: Tòng ngũ phẩm, Chánh lục phẩm, and Tòng lục phẩm. The term survives in contemporary Chinese as the academic title "professor" (C: 教授; V: *giáo thụ*).

41 Viện Sử Học, ed., *Đại Nam thực lục chính biên*, 31:138.

42 Yoshiharu, *L'empire Vietnamienne face à la France et à la Chine*.

43 Woodside, "The Relationship between Political Theory and Economic Growth," in *The Last Stand of Asian Autonomies*, ed. Anthony Reid, 259.

44 Woodside, *Vietnam and the Chinese Model*, 138, 277–79. Woodside cites Phan Huy Lê's study of the northern mining industry, "Tình hình khai mỏ dưới triều Nguyễn." See also Phan, Chu, Vương, and Đinh, *Lịch sử chế độ phong kiến Việt-Nam: Tập III*, 455–61.

45 Vũ, "The Politics of Frontier Mining."

46 Viện Sử Học, ed., *Khâm định Đại Nam hội điển sự lệ*, 42:229.

47 For a detailed treatment of this murder, see Davis, *States of Banditry*, chap. 1.

48 NAVN. CBTN, 271:27. Án Sát Tuyên Quang Bùi Quỹ to Ministry of Punishments, 24/7/TĐ4. Citation of report by Để Định District official Phạm Bá Điển dated 29/4/TĐ4 that includes original incident report submitted by Niêm Sơn Lý Trưởng, 20/5/TĐ4.

49 For a comprehensive study of the Panthay, see Atwill, *The Chinese Sultanate*. Also Atwill, "Blinkered Visions," and Wright, *The T'ung Chih Restoration*, 114–24. Panthay comes into English from a romanization of the Burmese word for Muslim (*pa-ti*) as transcribed by administrators in British colonial Burma.

50 NAVN. CBTN, 274:75. Tuyên Quang bố chánh sứ Bùi Duy Kỳ to Ministry of Military, 28/9/TĐ10.

Includes Ma Cửu Thản's report about the informant. During the Nguyễn period, informants or spies (*tham quân*) gathered information about military encampments in times of war. In this case, they helped the Tuyên Quang government track the Panthay Rebellion. Đỗ, ed., *Từ điển chức quan Việt Nam*, 648–49.

51 Viện Sử Học, ed., *Khâm định Đại Nam hội điển sự lệ*, 42:229. On Tụ Long, see Bonifacy, *Le canton de Tu-Long et la frontière Sino-Tonkinoise*. 5–6 [NLVN. SC, 14880]. Information in Vietnamese about the mining section can be found in Đỗ Bang, *Kinh tế thương nghiệp Việt Nam dưới Triều Nguyễn*, 31.

52 NAVN. CBTN, 190:79. Bùi Duy Kỳ to Ministry of Military, 30/10/TĐ10; NAVN-CBTN, 118:77. Định Yên thự đốc thần Nguyễn Đình Bảo to Ministry of Rites, 7/11/TĐ10.

53 NAVN. CBTN, 35:85. Hưng Hóa Lãnh bố chánh thần Nguyễn Hữu Hòa to Ministry of Military, 11/12/TĐ10.

54 Bonifacy, *Le canton de Tu-Long et la frontière Sino-Tonkinoise*, 6.

55 Viện Sử Học, ed., *Khâm định Đại Nam hội điển sự lệ*, 42:210. In the early nineteenth century, the Nguyễn government had encouraged the development of the Hương Sơn mine by refusing to demand fees for its exploitation.

56 Viện Sử Học, ed., *Đại Nam thực lục chính biên*, 30:136.

57 Ibid.

58 Viện Sử Học, ed., *Đại Nam thực lục chính biên*, 30:278. The two officers who ran away, Nguyễn Văn Thành (hiệp quân) and Phạm Mẫn Triệu (tri châu Văn Bản) received demotions.

59 Viện Sử Học, ed., *Đại Nam thực lục chính biên*, 31:25.

60 Viện Sử Học, ed., *Đại Nam thực lục chính biên*, 31:90.

61 NLVN. SC, File M.10360. *Notice sur la province de Lao Kay*, no author, no date. Another French-language source from the early twentieth century notes that He Junchang recruited a personal militia while the White Flags raided lowland settlements. NVLN. SC, M.10359 *Notice sur la Province de Lao Kay*, no author, no date (same title as M.10360).

62 Ủy Ban Tư Liệu Văn Sử Hội Nghị Hiệp Thương Chính Trị huyện Hà Khẩu, *Tư liệu văn sử Hà Khẩu, Tập II*, 179.

63 Ibid. Interview with Hoàng Bính Nam, 189; NAVN. RST, 1540 "Notice sur le secteur de Bao Ha (Yen Bay) 1898, 24. I have attempted to reconstruct the most plausible description from the available, at times contradictory, evidence about He Junchang.

64 Viện Sử Học, ed., *Đại Nam thực lục chính biên*, 30:182.

65 Viện Sử Học, ed., *Đại Nam thực lục chính biên*, 31:25.

66 Mo, ed., *Guangxi lishi renwu zhuan*, 199; Liao, *Zhong Fa zhanzheng shi*, 47.

67 Kuhn, *Rebellion and Its Enemies in late Imperial China*, 171–72; Laffey, "In the Wake of the Taipings," 65–81.

68 Mo, ed., *Guangxi lishi renwu zhuan*, 199.

69 Ibid; Liao, *Zhong Fa zhanzheng shi*, 47.

70 Liang, ed., *Zhen'an fuzhi*, 20:13b; Debao Xianzhi Bianxuan Weiyuan Hui, ed., *Debao xianzhi*, 6.

71 A few biographies of Liu Yongfu exist, mostly based on his memoirs as dictated to Huang Hai'an. In Chinese, Zhao Erxun introduced Liu Yongfu in the *Qing shi gao*, 463:12734–38. See also Li, *Liu Yongfu zhuan*; Yang, *Liu Yongfu pingzhuan*. Giles published a biography of Liu that, unfortunately, contains some inaccuracies. Giles, *A Chinese Biographical Dictionary*.

72 Huang, *Liu Yongfu lishi cao*, 171–72. This appears to be either a confusion of the "oppose the Qing, restore the Ming" slogan or possibly a deliberate intervention by Huang Hai'an to identify Liu as an anti-Manchu activist without anti-Republican sentiments.

73 Liang, ed., *Zhen'an fuzhi*, 20:14a–b.

74 Liao, *Zhong Fa zhanzheng shi*, 47.

75 Han, "Wu Yan Yun," in *Guangxi lishi renwu zhuan*, ed. Mo, 199–203. Han Shui

claims that Wu Lingyun instituted radical land reforms in areas under his rule.

76 He was either taken alive (Liang, ed., *Zhen'an Fuzhi*, 20:14a–b) or died (Debao Xianzhi Bianxuan Weiyuan Hui, ed., *Debao Xianzhi*, 7).

77 Han, "Wu Yan Yun," 202–3.

78 Interview with Huang Jinnan (83, Jingxi town resident) published in Guangxi Zhuangzu Zizhiqu Tongzhiguan, ed., *Zhong Fa zhanzheng diaocha ziliao shilu*, 3. Guishun itself had a recent history of antigovernment activism. In the 1850s, a small group of rebels broke into the government offices in town. They forced the officials to dress in women's clothes and demanded they serve them wine. Once drunk, the rebels then pushed the officials outside, which must have seemed like a rather odd turn of events for the rest of the town.

79 Guangxi Zhuangzu Zizhiqu Tongzhiguan, *Zhong Fa zhanzheng*, 3.

80 Interview with Zhuo Jinhu (65, Jingxi town resident) published in Guangxi Zhuangzu Zizhiqu Tongzhiguan, *Zhong Fa zhanzheng*, 6.

81 Ibid.

82 Guangxi Zhuangzu Zizhiqu Tongzhiguan, *Zhong Fa zhanzheng*, 13. Han Shui cites this slogan as evidence of Wu Yazhong's intentions and egalitarian spirit.

83 Huang, *Liu Yongfu lishi cao*, 186. Wong, "The Black Flags," 8–9.

84 Wong, "The Black Flags," 8–10. Based on Liu's memoirs, Wong cites the unattractiveness of Wu's sister as the reason for Liu's defection.

85 Ibid.

86 Huang, *Liu Yongfu lishi cao*, 186. Liu Yongfu claims he crossed into Vietnam at Anli, a mountain market site.

87 His power base in the area lasted at least through the 1870s. Burel, *Le contact protocolonial Franco-Vietnamien en centre et nord Vietnam*, 355; Huang, *Liu Yongfu lishi cao*, 189. Liu Yongfu called Liu Zhiping a *ba*, a term that could be rendered as "hegemon" or even "bully."

88 Huang, *Liu Yongfu lishi cao*, 189.

89 Ibid., 189–90. Lieutenants during this attack included Huang Er, Chen San, Chen Si, Xu Wan, and He Yamu.

90 Ngô, Nguyễn, and Papin, eds., *Đồng Khánh địa dư chí*, 18a.

91 NAVN. CBTN, 119:170. Ministry of Military to Court, 17/2/TĐ21. Includes report from Phan Văn Thuật to Ministry of Military, 9/2/TĐ21.

92 Huang, *Liu Yongfu lishi cao*, 191. Also known as Huang Da, Liu Yongfu identifies this bandit leader as a Qing subject who had spent a good deal of time in Vietnam.

93 Ibid., 192. In all likelihood, Liu was speaking Cantonese. Although Liu Yongfu's native language was Hakka, he spoke a few of the idioms of southern China. He did, however, remain functionally illiterate his entire life. Interview with Liu Yongfu's grandson, Qinzhou City, Guangxi, Nov. 6, 2004.

94 Huang, *Liu Yongfu lishi cao*, 192.

95 Ibid., 194; Laffey, *Relations between Chinese Provincial Officials and the Black Flag Army*, 108n45.

96 Huang, *Liu Yongfu lishi cao*, 194–95.

97 Ibid., 195. Wong Chi-Keung has cited this episode as evidence of the Black Flags' lack of humaneness toward "Miao" peoples. Wong, "The Black Flags," 16.

98 Trần, *Lưu Vĩnh Phúc*, 25.

99 Huang, *Liu Yongfu lishi cao*, 195. This was Tan Taiyuan, also known as Đàm Thái, a "người Hán" according to the historian Trần Văn Giáp.

100 Viện Sử Học, ed., *Đại Nam thực lục chính biên*, 31:191; Huang, *Liu Yongfu Lishi Cao*, 196; Peng and Fan, "Pingjia Liu Yongfu ying zunxun weiwu banzhengfa," in *Zhong Fa zhanzheng shi lunwen ji*, ed. Zhong Fa Zhanzheng Shi Yanjiu Hui, 3:224–40.

101 Huang, *Liu Yongfu lishi cao*, 196. Trần Văn Giáp claimed that the Vietnamese people (*nhân dân Việt-nam*) joyously celebrated the defeat of the White Flags. Trần, *Lưu Vĩnh Phúc*, 25.

102 NAVN. CBTN, 119:170. Phan Văn Thuật to Ministry of Military (17/2/TĐ21), cites reports from Phan Văn Thuật about the White Flags (12/1/TĐ21).

103 Viện Sử Học, ed., *Đại Nam thực lục chính biên*, 31:236, 267–70.

104 Du, ed., *Feng Congbao (Zicai) jundu jiyao*, 6:1b.

105 Laffey, *Relations*, 105.

106 Ibid., 110. Pan Lunsi remains an opaque historical figure. According to Yu Yuliang, Pan Lunsi entered Vietnam solely to steal from local communities. Interview with Yu Yuliang, Guangxi Academy of Social Sciences, Nanning, Guangxi, Nov. 5, 2004.

107 Du, ed., *Feng Congbao (Zicai) jundu jiyao*, 5:47a. Feng Zicai to Duanlin and Su Fengwen, 3/10/TZ7.

108 NAVN. CBTN, 180:170. Cao Bằng tỉnh thần Nguyễn Thịnh to Ministry of Military, 23/2/TĐ21; VHN, File A.89. "Cao Bằng Thực Tích" 高平事跡, 2b.

109 Viện Sử Học, ed., *Đại Nam thực lục chính biên*, 31:198; Cao, *Đại Nam chính biên liệt truyện*, 781. According to Cao Xuân Dục, Nguyễn Văn Vỹ refused to cooperate with Wu Yazhong, who wanted the Nguyễn official to serve as his secretary. Because he allowed himself to be captured rather than resisting, the court demoted Nguyễn Văn Vỹ upon his release.

110 NAVN. CBTN, 247:160. Cao Bằng chính bố Nguyễn Văn Vỹ to Ministry of Military, 12/4/TĐ21.

111 NAVN. CBTN, 68:172. Tuyên Quang tỉnh thần Phan Văn Thuật to Ministry of Military, 12/4/TĐ21.

112 Guangxi Zhuangzu Zizhiqu Tongzhiguan, ed., 23. Interview with Zhu Zhaoqun from Ningming. Meng Qixian, also from Ningming, claims that "Pan Lunsi" was a nickname for Huang Chongying given by Cantonese speakers, "Pan Lunsi" being the approximation of a phrase that means "very hectic."

113 NAVN. CBTN, 151:179. Tuyên Quang tỉnh thần Trương Phúc Lý and Phan Văn Thuật to Ministry of Military, 4/9/TĐ21, rescript dated 16/9/TĐ21.

114 NAVN. CBTN, 308:170. An-Tĩnh thự đốc thần Hoàng Kế Viêm to Ministry of Military, 3/3/TĐ21. Includes report from Ninh-Thái đốc thần Phạm Chi Hương, 18/2/TĐ21. Rescript dated 5/3/TĐ21.

115 Cao, *Đại Nam chính biên liệt truyện*, 643–44; NAVN. CBTN, 80:170. Ninh-Thái đốc thần Phạm Chi Hương to Ministry of Military, 26/1/TĐ21. Ministry rescript dated 10/2/TĐ21. Hai Trưởng and Ba Quý, with Hai Trưởng's wife, led this small band in Bắc Ninh. Phạm Chi Hương's investigation confirmed that several incidents of theft were directed by one organization led by Hai Trường and Ba Quý; NAVN. CBTN, 79:170. Ninh-Thái tiểu phủ sứ thần Ông Ích Khiêm to Ministry of Military, 8/2/TĐ21. Ministry rescript dated 10/2/TĐ21. Ông Ích Khiêm cites an impending case against the Hai Trưởng gang as the reason why he cannot go to Huế for an audience with the court, ostensibly to discuss his assistance to Phạm Chi Hương in northern Thái Nguyên and Lạng-Bằng. He also participated in an embassy to Beijing in the 1850s.

116 A native of Quảng Nam Province, Ông Ích Khiêm received his *cử nhân* in 1847 at the remarkably young age of sixteen. A dismissal from a district-level post preceded a career fighting "bandits." Cao, *Đại Nam chính biên liệt truyện*, 812. Ông Ích Khiêm may have been removed from a position in Hải Dương Province due to financial irregularities, or because he took on a local powerbroker. Đinh and Trương, eds., *Từ điển nhân vật lịch sử Việt Nam*, 236–37; NAVN. CBTN, 79:170. Ninh-Thái tiểu phủ sứ thần Ông Ích Khiêm to Ministry of Military, 8/2/TĐ21.

117 Viện Sử Học, ed., *Đại Nam thực lục chính biên*, 31:200–201. Estimates of the size of the raiding parties are in the thousands.

118 NAVN. CBTN, 86:172. Thái Nguyên tỉnh thần Nguyễn Hữu Điểm to Ministry of Military, 16/4/TĐ21.

119 Viện Sử Học, ed., *Đại Nam thực lục chính biên*, 31:190.

120 Ibid., 31:239–40; Cao, *Đại Nam chính biên liệt truyện*, 645. Phạm Chi Hương may have embellished the facts in an attempt to save himself from the kind of punishment that Nguyễn Văn Vỹ received.

121 Ibid. Another source glosses over this incident by saying that Phạm Chi Hương was captured and wounded by Wu in 1868. Hà, *Hoạt động của Bộ Công dưới đời Vua Tự-Đức*, 88n41B.

122 Cao, *Đại Nam chính biên liệt truyện*, 645. Phạm Chi Hương was sixty-five at the time of the Wu Yazhong incident in Cao Bằng.

123 Du, ed., *Feng Congbao (Zicai) jundu jiyao*, 5:25b–27a. Memorial of Duanlin to Grand Council, dated 23/4/TZ7, citation of Feng Zicai's report included in Su Fengwen's memorial to Duanlin, dated 30/12/TZ6. Duanlin, a blue-banner Manchu, served in Guangxi during the Taiping Rebellion. Zhao, ed., *Qing shi gao*, 388:11710.

124 Du, ed., *Feng Congbao (Zicai) jundu jiyao*, 5:27a.

125 Yunnan Sheng Lishi Yanjiu Suo, ed., *Qing shilu*. MCSL 240:32–33. Grand Council to Su Fengwen, 1868/9/9; MCSL 245:24–25. 1868/12/3.

126 Wu, "Lun Feng Zicai," in *Zhong Fa zhanzheng lunwenji I*, ed. Zhong Fa Zhanzheng Shi Yanjiu Hui, 244–56.

127 Hiromu and Fang, "Feng Tzu-ts'ai," in *Eminent Chinese of the Ch'ing Period*, ed. Arthur W. Hummel, 1:244–45; Cai, *Qing shi liezhaun*, 62:47b–50a.

128 Zhao, ed., *Qing shi gao*, 3252–57.

129 Michael, *The Taiping Rebellion*, 169–75. Feng's divisions also cooperated with the Ever-Victorious Army, which included British, French, and American soldiers.

130 Wu, "Lun Feng Zicai," 245–46.

131 Peng and Fan, "Feng Zicai de yisheng ying ruhe pingjia," in *Zhong Fa zhanzheng shi zhuanji*, ed. Guangxi Shehui Kexue Yuan, 198–205.

132 Ibid.

133 Truong Buu Lam's acknowledgment that "tributary states" functioned as defensive outposts or "as guarantees for the central government in areas where its authority was weakest" resonates with the perspective of the Qing Grand Council. "Comments and Generalities on Sino-Vietnamese Relations," in *Historical Interaction of China and Vietnam*, ed. Wickberg, 43.

134 Cao Xuân Dục recorded the date of Vũ Trọng Bình's *cử nhân* degree as 1834. Cao, *Đại Nam chính biên liệt truyện*, 685. A more recently compiled source states that he received the degree in 1836. Đinh and Trương, eds., *Từ điển nhân vật lịch sử Việt Nam*, 34–35.

135 Cao, *Đại Nam chính biên liệt truyện*, 685. On "supervisory censors," see Đỗ Văn Ninh, ed., *Từ điển chức quan Việt Nam*, 262–64. Whereas previous dynasties assigned censors to "routes" (*đạo*), the Nguyễn, perhaps based on Ming political practice, designated a censorate office for each province, increasing the level and intensity of supervision and monitoring. Lê, *Việc đào tạo và sử dụng quan lại của Triều Nguyễn*, 198–201. Censor jurisdictions were *đạo*, but their respective jurisdictions matched provinces after the Minh Mạng reforms.

136 Cao, *Đại Nam chính biên liệt truyện*, 687. The Nguyễn government would appoint Kinh Lược Sứ in times of regional crisis. Woodside, *Vietnam and the Chinese Model*, 141. I have slightly modified Woodside's translation of Kinh Lược Sứ as "commissioner in charge of patrolled border lands."

137 Cao, *Đại Nam chính biên liệt truyện*, 813. For more on this episode, see Davis, "Post-Taiping Fallout."

138 *Da Qing lichao shilu* (Veritable records of the Qing Empire), TZSL 196:7a.

139 Ibid.

140 NAVN. CBTN, 242:195. Hưng Hóa tỉnh thần Nguyễn Huy Kỷ to Ministry of Revenue, 20/5/TĐ22. rescript dated 3/6/TĐ22.

141 For instance, the collection post of Bảo Thắng saw a 73% decline in 1868. For Quán Ty, the decline was 68.8%. Source for 1868 data: NAVN. CBTN, 242:195. Hưng Hóa tỉnh thần Nguyễn Huy Kỷ to Ministry of Revenue, 20/5/TĐ22. rescript dated 3/6/TĐ22. All other years: Phan, Chu, Vương, and Đinh, *Lịch sử chế độ phong kiến Việt-Nam*, 450–51.

142 NAVN. CBTN, 43:189. Tuyên Quang tỉnh thần Phan Văn Thuật to Ministry of Revenue, 16/7/TĐ22. rescript dated 19/7/TĐ22.
143 Phan, Chu, Vương, and Đinh, *Lịch sử chế độ phong kiến Việt-Nam*, 451.
144 NAVN. CBTN, 43:189. Ministry of Revenue, Court rescript to Phan Văn Thuật, 19/7TĐ22.
145 NAVN. CBTN, 92:189. Ministry of Revenue to Vũ Trọng Bình. 23/7/TĐ22. 10,000 *tiền* (1000 *quan*) copper.
146 NAVN. CBTN, 39:189. Vũ Trọng Bình to Ministry of Revenue, 18/7/TĐ22. Rescript dated 19/7/TĐ22.
147 NAVN. CBTN, 337:189. Hưng Hóa tỉnh thần Nguyễn Huy Kỷ to Ministry of Revenue, 17/8/TĐ22. Rescript dated 21/8/TĐ22.
148 Du, ed., *Feng Congbao (Zicai) jundu jiyao*, 5:8b–10b.
149 Viện Sử Học, ed., *Đại Nam thực lục chính biên*, 31:362.
150 Ibid., 31:360–67.
151 NAVN. CBTN, 191:187. Lạng-Bằng tổng thống thần Vũ Trọng Bình to Court, 2/5/TĐ22. Rescript dated 12/5/TĐ22.
152 NAVN. CBTN, 88:205. Tuyên Quang thứ tỉnh tán tướng thần Mai Quý to Court, 26/10/TĐ22.
153 Another source notes his death, along with his entire family, at Mỏ Nhái. Kiều, *Bản Triều bàn nghịch liệt truyện*, 45B. Mo Naiqun asserts that Wu Yazhong committed suicide (Mo, ed., *Guangxi lishi renwu zhuan*, 203). Evidence from Feng Zicai's military correspondence contradicts this. (Du, ed., *Feng Congbao (Zicai) jundu jiyao*, 6:11a. Feng Zicai to Duanlin, 1/3/TZ9).
154 Viện Sử Học, ed., *Đại Nam thực lục chính biên*, 32:10. This is likely in the present day district of Đại Từ, Thái Nguyên Province.
155 Ibid.
156 Ibid.
157 Ibid., 31:370.
158 Ibid., 32:11, 20–21; Cao, *Đại Nam chính biên liệt truyện*, 598.
159 Du, ed., *Feng Congbao (Zicai) jundu jiyao*, 6:11b; Viện Sử Học, ed., *Đại Nam thực lục chính biên*, 32:11. Feng noted that Liang united with Yao people (*Yao min* 猺民), although the equivocation of this term in Feng's correspondence with the contemporary Dao ethnonym in Vietnam remains uncertain. NAVN-CBTN, 170:205. Sơn-Hưng-Tuyên thông đốc tiểu phủ quân vụ thần Đào Trí to Court, 17/11/TĐ22. Includes report from Tuyên Quang thứ tỉnh thần Mai Quý, 26/10/TĐ22. Feng noted that Liang was on the move when defeated.
160 Phạm, "Vọng Sơn niên phổ," 70. The bandit, identified only as Lực, called himself the field marshal of Bắc Kỳ.
161 NAVN. CBTN, 224:205. Lạng-Bằng quân thứ tổng thống thần Vũ Trọng Bình to Court, 17/12/TĐ22.
162 NAVN. CBTN, 226:205. Tuyên Quang quân vụ Mai Quý to Court, 18/12/TĐ22. Đặng Xuân Bảng is better known as a naturalist and historian of Tuyên

Quang Province whose work was translated by Bonifacy. EFEO-Hanoi Marr Collection, TV-3643 (Nord.prov-0035)/1.t4b-n1. Đặng Xuân Bảng, *Province de Tuyen Quang.*

163 NAVN. CBTN, 234:205. Ninh-Thái quân thứ tổng thống thần Đoàn Thọ, 14/12/TĐ22. Rescript dated 18/12/TĐ22. Suối Bốc was an upland settlement (峒, V: *động*)

164 NAVN. CBTN, 50:210. Ministry of Military to Court, 9/1/TĐ23. Includes report sent to Vũ Trọng Bình and Nguyễn Văn Tường, 6/1/TĐ23.

165 NAVN. CBTN, 29:211. Ministry of Revenue to Court, 10/1/TĐ23. Includes report by Đặng Xuân Bảng, 8/1/TĐ23.

166 NAVN. CBTN, 72:211. Ministry of Population to Court, 19/1/TĐ23. Includes report by Đặng Xuân Bảng, 17/1/TĐ23. Qing commanders received one pig, white and glutinous rice, one *phương* of salt, a jar of liquor, and one duck per month. Regular infantry divided one cow, one pig, salt, liquor, and three *phương* of rice amongst them.

167 NAVN. CBTN, 72:211. Ministry of Population to Court, 19/1/TĐ23. Includes report by Đặng Xuân Bảng, 17/1/TĐ23.

168 VHN. 4036, 25b.

169 Viện Sử Học, ed., *Đại Nam thực lục chính biên*, 31:197. Here he is identified as "Đầu Mục Đoàn Quân ở Tuyên Quang (là) Lưu Vĩnh Phúc." The term *mục* in this instance refers to Liu's status as a low-ranking military unit commander under the authority of the Tuyên Quang provincial government. During the Lý dynasty, *mục* referred to local military commanders. Đỗ, ed., *Từ điển chức quan Việt Nam*, 428–29.

170 Viện Sử Học, ed., *Khâm định Đại Nam hội điển sự lệ*, 42:226–29.

171 Viện Sử Học, ed., *Đại Nam thực lục chính biên*, 31:311.

172 Huang, *Liu Yongfu lishi cao*, 213–14.

173 Woodside, *Vietnam and the Chinese Model*, 269–70.

174 Ibid.

175 Viện Sử Học, ed., *Đại Nam thực lục chính biên*, 30:164.

176 Ibid. The officials Nguyễn Tri Phương and Hoàng Kế Viêm were also consulted.

177 Ibid.

178 Huang, *Liu Yongfu lishi cao*, 198. According to Andrew Forbes, Hui, ethnic Chinese Muslims from Yunnan, drove the beasts of burden bearing opium from Yunnan. "The 'Cin-Ho' Caravan Trade."

179 Huang, *Liu Yongfu lishi cao*, 197. The customs posts fell most directly under the authority of Bảo Thắng.

180 Ibid. Dictating these memoirs in the 1910s, Liu claimed to have acted not only in self-interest, but also in the interest of the Nguyễn court. His insistence that he helped extend Nguyễn power as well as his own deserves healthy suspicion.

181 Ibid; Trần Văn Giáp, *Lưu Vĩnh Phúc*, 26.

182 Huang, *Liu Yongfu lishi cao*, 197.

183 Ibid., 198.

184 Văn Bàn Resident E, conversation, June 2005; Văn Bàn Resident F, conversation, June 2005; Văn Bàn Resident A, conversation, June 2005. "...ống phát tiếng nổ to như tiếng mìn và phụt thuốc phía trên ống."

185 Bảo Thắng Resident A, conversation, August 2005.

186 Bảo Thắng Resident A. "Không ai dám chống lại nó vì sợ nó giết cả làng."

187 Văn Bàn Resident A; Văn Bần Resident G; Bảo Thắng Resident A.

188 Bảo Thắng Resident A.

189 Bảo Thắng Resident C, July 2005.

190 Bảo Thắng Resident G. The woman was raped to death by a gang of between six and ten men: ". . . *có khi 6–10 người hiếp chết một cô gái.*"

191 Ibid. "*Cho nên khi con gái đàn bà đi đâu cũng phải bôi nhọ nồi vào mặt hoặc làm xấu giả điên . . .*"; Văn Bàn Resident A.

192 Văn Bàn Resident A; Văn Bàn Resident G.

193 Liao, *Kang Fa mingjiang Liu Yongfu*, 20.

194 NAVN. CBTN, 324:184. Tuyên Quang tỉnh thần Trương Phúc Lý and Phan Văn Thuật to Ministry of Military, 20/2/TĐ22. Ministerial rescript dated 22/2/TĐ22. A copy of this observation about the movement of Pan Lunsi's camp was also sent to Nguyễn Bá Nghi.

195 Huang, *Liu Yongfu lishi cao*, 201. According to Liu Yongfu, Pan Lunsi paid a visit to Xu Yuanxu, offering to share the wealth of Lào Cai with the Black Flags. Xu planned a celebratory feast in Pan's honor. While preparing the meal, Xu's wife overheard a hushed conversation between Pan and his wife, detailing a plot to eliminate Liu. Xu later informed Liu that Pan Lunsi intended to use a partnership between the Black and Yellow Flags to bring all of Liu's territory under his control.

196 Huang, *Liu Yongfu lishi cao*, 203–4; Kiều, *Bản Triều bạn nghịch liệt truyện*, 46A.

197 Huang, *Liu Yongfu lishi cao*, 205–6.

198 Ibid., 206–7.

199 This is primarily from the perspective of an early twentieth-century Liu Yongfu. Although Kiều Oánh Mậu, who may not have had access to Huang Hai'an's edited text, also noted the intense hostility between Pan and Liu. Kiều, *Bản Triều bạn nghịch liệt truyện*, 46A.

200 Huang, *Liu Yongfu lishi cao*, 210.

201 Ibid.

202 Ibid., 213.

203 Ibid., 215; Peng and Fan, "Pingjia Liu Yongfu ying zunxun weiwu banzhengfa," in *Zhong Fa zhanzheng shi lunwenji,* ed. Guangxi Zhong Fa Zhanzheng Shi Yanjiu Hui, 3:224–40.

204 Huang, *Liu Yongfu lishi cao*, 216.

205 NAVN. CBTN, 180:210. Ministry of Military to Court, 25/1/TĐ23. Includes

report from Hưng Hóa tỉnh thần Nguyễn Huy Kỷ, 15/1/TĐ23. Also NAVN-CBTN, 103:216. Ministry of Military to Court, 8/2/TĐ23. Includes report from Sơn-Hưng-Tuyên thống đốc Đào Trí, 15/1/TĐ23. A copy of the proclamation honoring Liu's father rests in the Beijing Military Museum in the PRC.

206 NAVN. CBTN, 128:228. Ministry of Revenue to Court, 29/10/TĐ23. Includes report from Hưng Hóa tỉnh thần Nguyễn Duy Kỷ, 11/10/TĐ23.

207 NAVN. CBTN, 56:205. Tuyên Quang tán lý quân vụ tỉnh thần Nguyễn Đình Thọ to Court, 21/10/TĐ22; NAVN-CBTN, 170:205. Sơn-Hưng-Tuyên thống đốc tiễu phủ quân vụ Đào Trí to Court, 17/11/TĐ22.

208 NAVN. CBTN, 170:205. Rescript.

CHAPTER 2

1 Dupuis, *L'ouverture du Fleuve Rouge*, 178–79; Scott, *France and Tongking*, 8–9.

2 Võ, *La place du catholicisme*, 807–8; Dupuis, *L'ouverture du Fleuve Rouge*, 175.

3 Dutreb, "L'Amiral Dupré et la conquête du Tonkin," 196–97. Cited in Patrick J. N. Tuck, *French Catholic Missionaries*, 148–49.

4 Tuck, *French Catholic Missionaries*, 129–30; Dupuis, *L'ouverture du Fleuve Rouge*, 168; Trần Trọng Kim does not mention Lê restorationist support for Garnier. Trần, *Việt Nam sử lược*, 538–41.

5 Trần, *Việt Nam sử lược*, 530–31; Chapuis, *The Last Emperors of Vietnam*, 13. Alexander Woodside presented detailed information on Cao Bá Quát's rebellion, *Vietnam and the Chinese Model*, 234–255.

6 Trần, *Việt Nam sử lược*, 531–32; Chapuis, *The Last Emperors of Vietnam*, 13.

7 Laffey, "French Adventurers and Chinese Bandits," 38–51.

8 Viện Sử Học, ed., *Đại Nam thực lục chính biên*, 32:43.

9 Cao, *Đại Nam chính biên liệt truyện*, 868.

10 NAVN. CBTN, 50:233. Nội Các to Court, also to all offices above the rank of Tham Tri, 20/11/TĐ23.

11 NAVN. CBTN, 50:233. Rescript dated 21/11/TĐ23.

12 Viện Sử Học, ed., *Đại Nam thực lục chính biên*, 32:89; Huang, *Liu Yongfu lishi cao*, 220.

13 Huang, *Liu Yongfu lishi cao*, 220.

14 NAVN. CBTN, 93:238. Hưng Hóa lãnh phủ thần Trần Đình Túc to Ministry of Revenue, 3/5/TĐ24. Report cites incident occurring in third month of previous year.

15 NAVN. CBTN, 203:235. Hưng Hóa lãnh phủ thần Trần Đình Túc to Ministry of Revenue, 17/12/TĐ23. These were Văn Bàn, Thủy Vĩ, and Chiếu Tân.

16 Viện Sử Học, ed., *Đại Nam thực lục chính biên*, 32:106, 202.

17 NAVN. CBTN, 125:238. Tuyên Quang tỉnh thần Mai Quý to Ministry of Revenue, 7/4/TĐ24. Incident referenced as occurring two months previously.

18 NAVN. CBTN, 110:238. Sơn-Hưng-Tuyên hộ đốc thần Trần Bình to Ministry of Revenue, 6/4/TĐ24.

19 NAVN. CBTN, 125:238. Tuyên Quang tỉnh thần Mai Quý to Ministry of Revenue, 7/4/TĐ24; Ministry response dated 11/4/TĐ24.

20 Viện Sử Học, ed., *Đại Nam thực lục chính biên*, 32:143.

21 For a detailed discussion, see Davis, "Post-Taiping fallout," in *On the Borders of State Power*, ed. Gainsborough, 25–34.

22 NAVN. CBTN, 301:239. Hưng Hóa lãnh phủ Trần Đình Túc to Ministry of Revenue, 25/5/TĐ24.

23 NAVN. CBTN, 48:246. Tổng Đốc Hoàng Kế Viêm and Hưng Hóa tam lý quân thứ Trần Đình Túc to Ministry of Military, 25/11/TĐ24.

24 Viện Sử Học, ed., *Đại Nam thực lục chính biên*, 32:246.

25 Ibid., 32:202, 224.

26 Ibid.

27 Gautier, *Les français au Tonkin*, 72.

28 Ibid.

29 Ibid.

30 Jean Dupuis, *Les origins de la question du Tonkin*, xii–xxxvi; Gautier, *Les français au Tonkin*, 73.

31 Prior to 1890, the foreign-resident community in Hankou was small and tended to intermingle with Chinese residents. In 1870, the Hankou Financial Guild was founded to provide businessmen with access to finance capital. Rowe, *Hankow*, 46, 175.

32 Laffey, "French Adventurers and Chinese Bandits," 39–40; Spector, *Li Hung-chang and the Huai Army*; Mossman, ed., *General Charles Gordon's Private Diary.*

33 Gautier, *Les français au Tonkin*, 74–75; Osborne, "Francis Garnier (1839–1873) explorer of the Mekong River," in *Explorers of South-East Asia*, ed. King, 96.

34 Dupuis, *Les origins de la question du Tonkin*, 5.

35 Ibid., 5–6.

36 Ibid., 4. Gautier admitted, in the 1880s, that perhaps Dupuis did not clearly understand the difference between a tributary state and a vassal (*Les français au Tonkin,* 80). This may have been a willful misunderstanding on the part of Dupuis. Trần Trọng Kim flatly claimed that Dupuis had a poor knowledge of the political arrangement between the Qing and Nguyễn. Trần, *Việt Nam sử lược*, 541.

37 Dupuis, *Les origins de la question du Tonkin*, 13; McLeod, *The Vietnamese Response to the French Intervention*, 106.

38 Dupuis, *Les origins de la question du Tonkin*, 7.

39 Gautier, *Les français au Tonkin*, 82–84.

40 Ibid; Vũ, Phạm, Nguyễn, eds., *Lịch sử Việt Nam*, 336–37.

41 Cooke, *New French Imperialism*, 14.

42 Ibid., 15. Etiénne was born in Algeria to French-Corsican parents in 1844.

43 Gautier, *Les français au Tonkin*, 84–85. Developed by Antoine-Alphonse Chassepot in 1866, the "fusil chassepot" was a breech-loading, percussion-

cap military rifle used during the Franco-Prussian War. Dupuis seemed to be selling these, along with decommissioned Remingtons, to the Yunnanese military. At the time, repeating guns with rifled barrels that fired conical bullets represented a significant worldwide development in weapons technology. On the history of firearms, with special attention to the gun trade on the African continent during the nineteenth century, see Hendrick, "The Tools of Imperialism."

44 Gautier, *Les français au Tonkin*, 84; Trần, *Việt Nam sử lược*, 538–39; Millot, *Le Tonkin*, 1. Millot identified himself as Dupuis' second in command. More of a guide to the history of Tonkin and Asia than a biography, the cover of *Le Tonkin* describes Millot as a member of the Légion d'honneur and the former president of the administrative council for the French concession at Shanghai. On the foreign community in Shanghai during this period, see Bickers, "Shanghailanders"

45 Gautier, *Les français au Tonkin*, 82; Dupuis, *Les origins de la question du Tonkin*, 170. Sir James Scott claimed that Vlavianos served with General Gordon against the Taiping Rebellion (*France and Tongking*, 25), although Gautier noted that Vlavianos served with the Franco-Chinese forces at Zhejiang under generals Giquel and d'Aiguebelle. *Les français au Tonkin*, 84.

46 Dupuis, *L'ouverture du Fleuve Rouge*, 12–13; Vũ, Phạm, Nguyễn, eds., *Lịch Sử Việt Nam*, 337.

47 Dupuis, *L'ouverture du Fleuve Rouge*, 13.

48 Viện Sử Học, ed., *Đại Nam thực lục chính biên*, 32:207. From a Minh Hương family that traced its roots to China's Zhejiang Province, Hồ Trọng Đĩnh earned a *tiến sĩ* in 1847, serving in Ninh Bình prior to Quảng Yên. Cao, *Đại Nam chính biên liệt truyện*, 820–22.

49 Viện Sử Học, ed., *Đại Nam thực lục chính biên*, 32:209. Lê Tuấn (1818–1874), a native of Hà Tĩnh and 1853 *tiến sĩ* recipient, first became a patrol commissioner during an outbreak of sea piracy in Quảng Yên Province in the late 1860s. Ngô, ed., *Các nhà khoa bằng Việt Nam*, 844–45; Cao, *Đại Nam chính biên liệt truyện*, 858–65.

50 Viện Sử Học, ed., *Đại Nam thực lục chính biên*, 32:242.

51 Ibid., 32:253.

52 Ibid.

53 Dupuis, *L'ouverture du Fleuve Rouge*, 13.

54 Ibid., 14.

55 Viện Sử Học, ed., *Đại Nam thực lục chính biên*, 32:254; NLVN. SC, M.10352, Dillemann, "Notice de Hai-duong," 20.

56 Viện Sử Học, ed., *Đại Nam thực lục chính biên*, 32:254. In addition to expressing frustration and uncertainty, Lê Tuấn's initial reports also described the personnel of the Dupuis party. In addition to Vlavianos, the gun merchant's entourage included Chinese merchants as well as people from England, France and even the Philippines.

57 Viện Sử Học, ed., *Đại Nam thực lục chính biên*, 32:255.

58 Dupuis, *L'ouverture du Fleuve Rouge*, 15–16.

59 Ibid., 16–17.

60 Ibid., 18–19.

61 Viện Sử Học, ed., *Đại Nam thực lục chính biên*, 32:258. The two provincial officials involved, Nguyễn Đức Đạt and Tôn Thất Phiên, received demotions for failing to stop Dupuis' ships.

62 Dupuis, *L'ouverture du Fleuve Rouge*, 28. Dupuis passed through the village of Bát Trăng, a noted ceramic-producing craft village. Nguyễn sources record the cannon shot. Viện Sử Học, ed., *Đại Nam thực lục chính biên*, 32:255.

63 Viện Sử Học, ed., *Đại Nam thực lục chính biên*, 32:255.

64 Dupuis, *L'ouverture du Fleuve Rouge*, 29.

65 Ibid., 31. I have not found evidence that Feng Zicai received any such proposal.

66 Ibid.

67 Viện Sử Học, ed., *Đại Nam thực lục chính biên*, 32:276. Bùi Thức Kiên (1813–1892), a native of Hà Tĩnh Province, received a *cử nhân* in 1840 and a *tiến sĩ* in 1848. Prior to being governor-general of Hà-Ninh, he served as the governor of Hưng Yên Province and in the Ministries of Personnel, Rites, and Military in Huế. Ngô, ed., *Các nhà khoa bảng Việt Nam*, 817.

68 Viện Sử Học, ed., *Đại Nam thực lục chính biên*, 32:213.

69 Ibid., 32:228–29.

70 Ibid., 32, 255. NAVN. CBTN, 31:249. Hưng Hóa thứ phủ thần Nguyễn Huy Kỷ to Ministry of Military, 29/9/TĐ25. Includes report from Sơn-Hưng-Tuyên Tổng Đốc Hoàng Kế Viêm, 19/9/TĐ25.

71 NAVN. CBTN, 31:249. Hoàng Kế Viêm to Ministry of Military, 3/10/TĐ25. His report about the defeat of Yellow Flag units was a secret communication between the central government and Hoàng Kế Viêm.

72 Dupuis, *L'ouverture du Fleuve Rouge*, 47. Dupuis boasts that he threatened Nong Xiuye with extermination should any of his men lay a hand on his ships and crew.

73 Cao, *Đại Nam chính biên liệt truyện*, 815. Dupuis arrived after the Huế court had cashiered Ông Ích Khiêm from his position but prior to his return to Huế, finding the official, as he ascertained through his interpreter, disgraced. Dupuis, *L'ouverture du Fleuve Rouge*, 49–50.

74 Cao, *Đại Nam chính biên liệt truyện*, 815.

75 Dupuis, *L'ouverture du Fleuve Rouge*, 52. Dupuis referred to this post as Touen-hia, which, according to Shao Xunzheng, was an alternate name for Bảo Hà. Shao, *Zhong Fa Yuenan guanxi shimo*, 37. Yellow Flag control over Bảo Hà may have driven Nong Xiuye south into close contact with Nguyễn officials such as Ông Ích Khiêm.

76 Dupuis, *L'ouverture du Fleuve Rouge*, 52.

77 NAVN. CBTN, 18:252. Ngụy Khắc Đản to Privy Council, 11/1/TĐ26.

78 NAVN. CBTN, 31:252. Ngụy Khắc Đản to Privy Council, 17/1/TĐ26.
79 Ibid.
80 Dupuis, *L'ouverture du Fleuve Rouge*, 55–57.
81 Ibid., 74.
82 NAVN. CBTN, 204:250. Privy Council Edict, 21/2/TĐ26.
83 NAVN. CBTN, 181:250. Nghệ An hộ đốc thần Tôn Thất Triệt to Privy Council, 25/2/TĐ26. Tôn Thất Triệt stressed the need for secrecy.
84 NAVN. CBTN, 191:250. Court to Lạng-Bằng hộ phủ thần Lương Quý Chinh, 15/2/TĐ26.
85 NAVN. CBTN, 337:252. Nguyễn Tri Phương to Grand Secretariat, 19/4/TĐ26.
86 NAVN. CBTN, 337:252. Original report from Văn Bàn's Vũ Văn Vị, passed to Nguyễn Tri Phương by Hưng Hóa phủ thần Nguyễn Huy Kỷ.
87 NAVN. CBTN, 278:252. Nguyễn Tri Phương to Grand Secretariat, 10/4/TĐ26. Includes report from Sơn Tây đề đốc thần Trần Bình, dated 6/4/TĐ26; also 270:252. Hoàng Kế Viêm to Grand Secretariat, 9/4/TĐ26.
88 Viện Sử Học, ed., *Đại Nam thực lục chính biên*, 32:321.
89 Ibid.
90 Osborne, "Francis Garnier (1839–1873) explorer of the Mekong River," in *Explorers of the South-East Asia*, ed. King, 51–107.
91 Letter cited in ibid., 97. Garnier's sentiments found an echo in the writings of Benito Mussolini in the twentieth century.
92 Ibid., 60.
93 Vialatel, *Francis Garnier*, 67.
94 On the Mekong Expedition, see Osborne, *River Road to China*, 1–146. Garnier admired the modern weaponry used by Ma Rulong.
95 Walsh, "The Yunnan Myth," 272.
96 Võ, *La place du catholicisme*, 18.
97 Vialatel, *Francis Garnier*, 263–64.
98 Leroy-Beaulieu, *La Rénovation de l'Asie*, 439. Cited in Walsh, 284. He attended lycée with Alexandre Ribot, member of the French government who opposed Jules Ferry's colonial policy in the 1880s. Schmidt, *Alexandre Ribot*, 3. Prior to the 1880s, Leroy-Beaulieu did not receive wide attention in France for his colonialist views. Lewis, "One Hundred Million Frenchmen: the 'Assimilation' Theory in French Colonial Policy," 136.
99 Leroy-Beaulieu, *De la colonisation chez les peuples modernes*. The second edition was printed in 1886. Cited in Conklin, *A Mission to Civilize*, 12. Edward Said identified Leroy-Beaulieu as a "powerfully influential, even prophetic" writer. Said, *Culture and Imperialism*, 110.
100 Võ, *La place du catholicisme*, 62–64. Etienne Võ Đức Hạnh notes that Dupré's instructions seemed clear in written form, but that verbal instructions imparted to Garnier from Dupré most likely caused the young lieutenant to believe he had carte blanche. Osborne made a similar speculation (*River Road to China*, 198).

101 Dupuis, *L'ouverture du Fleuve Rouge*, 165.
102 Vialatel, *Francis Garnier*, 359.
103 Viện Sử Học, ed., *Đại Nam thực lục chính biên*, 32:330; Cao, *Đại Nam chính biên liệt truyện*, 698.
104 Võ, *La place du catholicisme*, 77.
105 MEP. Puginier Letters (Carton 1). Apr. 13, 1873.
106 Louvet, *Vie de Mgr Puginier*, 85.
107 Sir James Scott, *France and Tongking*, 25; Dupuis, *L'ouverture du Fleuve Rouge*, 178.
108 Dupuis, *L'ouverture du Fleuve Rouge*, 178–79; Viện Sử Học, ed., *Đại Nam thực lục chính biên*, 32:336; Thái, *Nguyễn Tri Phương*, 669, 675; Tiên, "Phò mã Nguyễn Tri Lâm," in *Tạp Chí Tri Tân*, ed. Tủ Sách Lịch Sử và Văn Hóa, 335. At his death, Nguyễn Lâm was twenty-nine.
109 Thái, *Nguyễn Tri Phương*, 675; Đào Đăng Vỹ, *Nguyễn Tri Phương*, 203. Nguyễn Tri Phương's story inspired Phan Trần Chúc, an early twentieth-century writer of historical fiction: Phan, *Nguyễn Tri Phương truyện ký*. Quoting Đào Duy Anh, Thái Hồng characterized Nguyễn Tri Phương and Hoàng Diệu as "symbols of the long-standing national spirit." Đào Duy Anh, *Nhớ nghĩ chiều hôm*, 255–56, cited in *Nguyễn Tri Phương*, Thái, 803.
110 Viện Sử Học, ed., *Đại Nam thực lục chính biên*, 32:343; MacLeod, *The Vietnamese Response to the French Intervention*.
111 Huang, *Liu Yongfu lishi cao*, 230–31.
112 Laffey, "French Adventurers and Chinese Bandits," 42; Vũ, Phạm, Nguyễn, eds., *Lịch sử Việt Nam*, 376–77; see also the detailed yet problematic account in du Caillaud, *Histoire de l'intervention française au Tonkin*.
113 Osborne, *River Road to China*, 210.
114 Huang, *Liu Yongfu lishi cao*, 231; names from CAOM. AGC, 12988. "Procès verbal d'exhumation," de Kergaradec. Nov. 3, 1875.
115 Huang, *Liu Yongfu lishi cao*, 231.
116 Viện Sử Học, ed., *Đại Nam thực lục chính biên*, 32:350–51.
117 Dupuis, *L'ouverture du Fleuve Rouge*, 237.
118 Taboulet, *La geste française en Indochine*, 738–40. Télégramme de Ministre à l'Amiral Dupré, Jan. 7, 1874; Convention du 5 janvier 1874: Évacuation de Ninh-Binh et de Nam-Dinh; Convention de 6 février 1874: Évacuation de Hanoi.
119 CAOM. AGC 12988, "Procès verbal d'exhumation." Nov. 3, 1875.
120 Bouchet, "Rapport fait au nom de la 2 Commission des Pétitions sur la Pétition du Sieur Jean Dupuis, citoyen français demeurant à Han-Kow (Chine)." Chambre des Députés, No 1519 (Session de 1879). *Annexe au procès-verbal de la séance du 14 juin 1879*.
121 CAOM. AGC12998. "Rapports du Consul de France à Hanoi, 1877." De Kergaradec to Duperré, "Liste des résidents présents à Ha Noi à la date du 27 Septembre 1876."

122 Conklin, *A Mission to Civilize*, 12. Brau's full name was François-Xavier-Joseph-Honoré Brau du Saint-Pol Lias. Hickey, *Kingdom in the Morning Mist*, 20.

123 Quoted in Hickey, *Kingdom in the Morning Mist*, 20. E. J. Tips has translated *L'ouverture du Fleuve Rouge* as *A Journey to Yunnan and the Opening of the Red River to Trade.*

124 Quoted in Hickey, 21. Hickey connects Dupuis with Brau's archetype.

125 Jean Dupuis' obituary, *The Geographical Journal* 41, no. 2 (Feb. 1913): 174.

126 Ibid.

127 Mention of the illegality of Jean Dupuis' activities did not appear in several accounts of the 1870s. For instance, Gosselin, *L'Empire d'Annam*, 162–63.

128 Cady, *The Roots of French Imperialism in Eastern Asia*, 287–88; Taboulet, *La geste française en Indochine*, 738–41; Vũ, Phạm, Nguyễn, eds., *Lịch sử Việt Nam*, 391–92; Munholland, "Admiral Jaureguiberry and the French Scramble for Tonkin," 83–84.

129 Viện Sử Học, ed., *Đại Nam thực lục chính biên*, 33:10; 12–22 includes a text of the treaty. See also Taboulet, *La geste française en Indochine*, 743–47.

130 Taboulet, *La geste française en Indochine*, 744. Article 3 stated that these items were in return for Nguyễn recognition of French primacy in commercial relations between Vietnam and other nations. See also Viện Sử Học, ed., *Đại Nam thực lục chính biên*, 33:13. "*. . . súng điểu sang mở ở bụng 1.000 cây.*" "*Fusils à tabatière*" referred to the process of converting muskets to breach loading rifles with the use of a powder box, hence *tabatière* or "snuffbox." See Ezell, Pegg, and Smith, *Small Arms of the World*, 60.

131 Lê, "Những Hệ Quả của Hòa Ước Năm 1874" in *Xã hội Việt Nam thời Pháp Thuộc*, 119–24.

132 Masson, ed., *Correspondance politique du Commandant Rivière au Tonkin*, 272n33. Full name Alexandre-Camille-Jules-Marie Le Jumeau, Comte de Kergaradec (1841–1894).

133 CAOM. AGC12985: "Rapports du Consul de France à Hanoi." de Kergaradec to Governor Duperré, 14 Octobre 1875. On Puginier, see Michaud, *"Incidental Ethnographers:" French Catholic Missions on the Tonkin-Yunnan Frontier*, 112–14.

134 CAOM. AGC12986: "Rapports du Consul de France à Hanoi a.s. de l'ouverture du Haut du Fleuve Rouge, renseignements sur les ressources minières au Tonkin." De Kergaradec to Duperré, Oct. 10, 1875.

135 Ibid; Viện Sử Học, ed., *Đại Nam thực lục chính biên*, 33:255. The Huế court moved Vũ Trọng Bình to Sơn Tây to the concurrent posts of governor and temporary military commander for Sơn-Hưng-Tuyên from which he unsuccessfully tried to excuse himself due to his advanced age. Viện Sử Học, ed., *Đại Nam thực lục chính biên*, 33: 270; Cao, *Đại Nam chính biên liệt truyện*, 690.

136 CAOM. AGC12990: "Rapports du Consul de France à Hanoi, a.s. de la pub-

lication de l'edit royal concernant des chrétiens, Puginier, voyage à Son Tay." De Kergaradec to Duperré, 5 Janvier 1876.

137 CAOM. AGC12993: "Rapports du Consul de France à Hanoi a.s. du refus d'un passeport pour voyager dans le haut du Fleuve, visite au Consulat de 2 chef des Drapeaux Noirs, etc." De Kergaradec to Duperré, Mar. 22, 1876.

138 Viện Sử Học, ed., *Đại Nam thực lục chính biên*, 34:113. Also identified as Hoàng Tài Gia. The Huế court's knowledge of this meeting came from Hoàng Kế Viêm. Trần Đình Túc, the highest-ranking official in Hanoi province, did not attend. Fearing French grievances against Liu, the Nguyễn foreign office ordered the provincial government in Hanoi to notify Liu, through Hoàng Kế Viêm, that he must act carefully to not provoke the French consulate.

139 CAOM. AGC12993. "Rapports du Consul de France à Hanoi a.s. du refus d'un passeport pour voyager dans le haut du Fleuve, visite au Consulat de 2 chef des Drapeaux Noirs, etc." De Kergaradec to Duperré, Mar. 22, 1876.

140 Ibid.

141 Ibid.

142 CAOM. AGC12997: "Rapports de Consul de France à Hanoi a.s. de voyage dans le haut de Fleuve Rouge, etc." De Kergaradec to Duperré, Nov. 17, 1876. De Kergaradec included news of Gsell's joining the expedition with his detailed description of the Nguyễn examinations taking place in Huế and Hà Nội. Émile Gsell (1838–1879), a noted photographer, worked on the Lagrée expedition along the Mekong in the 1860s and maintained a studio in Saigon until his death in 1879. Ghesquière, "Émile Gsell" in *Des photographes en Indochine*, ed. Franchini and Ghesquière, 224–25; de Kergaradec, "Rapport sur le reconnaisance du Fleuve Rouge du Tonkin," 324.

143 De Kergaradec, "Rapport sur le reconnaisance du Fleuve Rouge du Tonkin," 324.

144 Ibid., 328. He valued this at 150,000 francs.

145 Ibid., 344.

146 Ibid., 351.

147 Jennings, *Imperial Heights*, 15–17.

148 De Kergaradec, "Rapport sur le reconnaisance du Fleuve Rouge du Tonkin," 345–46.

149 Ibid.

150 Ibid., 341–42.

151 Ibid.

152 Viện Sử Học, ed., *Đại Nam thực lục chính biên*, 33:27. They each received 345 *lạng* silver and 3,000 *tiền* copper cash.

153 Ibid.

154 Ibid. 33:40–41.

155 Ibid.

156 NAVN. CBTN, 316:257. Cao Bằng tỉnh thần Lương Tuấn Tú to Grand Secretariat, 8/4/TĐ27.

157 Ibid.

158 Viện Sử Học, ed., *Đại Nam thực lục chính biên*, 33:53; NAVN-CBTN, 212:262. Tham tán quân vụ thần Tôn Thất Thuyết to Chữ Bộ Nha, 18/7/TĐ27. Tôn Thất Thuyết then insisted that the military from Nghệ An and Hà Tĩnh leave Sơn Tây.

159 Viện Sử Học, ed., *Đại Nam thực lục chính biên*, 33:81.

160 Ibid., 33:107.

161 Ibid., 33:109. Hoàng Kế Viem and Nguyễn Huy Kỷ both received a promotion of one *cấp*.

162 Ibid., 33:120.

163 Ibid., 33:126. The other *đạo* and their respective commanders were Lạng Sơn (Đinh Quán Trinh), Cao Bằng (Lương Tuấn Tú), and Tuyên Quang (Nông Hùng Phúc). The assignation of a *đạo* as an administrative division had a precedent during the 1850s when the *đạo* of Phú Yên was established. Đỗ, ed., *Từ điển chức quan Việt Nam*, 191.

164 Viện Sử Học, ed., *Đại Nam thực lục chính biên*, 33:141.

165 NAVN. CBTN 58:268. Tuyên Quang tỉnh thần Mai Quý to Ministry of Military, 15/12/TĐ27; CBTN 58:268. Ministry of Military, Court rescript, 17/12/TĐ27.

166 Zhongyang Yanjiuyuan Jindaishi Yanjiu Suo, ed., *Zhong Fa Yuenan jiaoshe dang*, document 8, 18. Grand Council, June 15, 1875; document 20, 27. Cen Yuying to Grand Council, Aug. 8, 1875.

167 NAVN. CBTN 52:271. Grand Secretariat (Bùi Văn Dị, Lê Tiến Thông, Nguyễn Thuật) to Court, 13/2/TĐ28. Nguyễn Uỷ, the previous Ninh-Thái commander, had failed to put down the Yellow Flag loyalists, who thrived due to official ineptitude and, in the estimation of the grand secretariat, storms and floods.

168 Zhongyang Yanjiuyuan Jindaishi Yanjiu Suo, ed., *Zhong Fa Yuenan jiaoshe dang*, document 29, 44a–52a. Guangxi Governor Liu Zhangyi to Guangxi-Guangdong Governor General, Oct. 29, 1875.

169 Huang, *Liu Yongfu lishi cao*, 249.

170 NAVN. CBTN, 203:271. Tôn Thất Thuyết, Lê Hưu Tạ, and Hà Văn Quân to Trần Tiễn Thành; included citation of reports to Tuyên Quang tỉnh thần Mai (Thế) Quý and Lã Xuân Oai, 9/11/TĐ28.

171 Nguyễn, *Giặc Cờ Đen*. 17.

172 NAVN. CBTN, 186:294. Hưng hóa tỉnh thần Nguyễn Huy Kỷ to Bộ Hộ, 12/12/TĐ30.

173 NAVN. CBTN, 86:298. Bùi Văn Dị to Court, 25/9/TĐ31.

174 Lê and Nguyễn, "Khảo về trị giá và tỉ giá của hệ thống tiền tệ triều Nguyễn," in *Tuyển tập những bài nghiên cứu về Triều Nguyễn*, ed. Trung Tâm Bảo Tồn Di Tích Cổ Đô Huế, 92–98.

175 NAVN. CBTN, 86:298. Bùi Văn Dị to Court, 25/9/TĐ31. Liu was identified as the phó đề đốc quân thứ Tam Tuyên. Ngô Thất Ninh, the đề đốc of Bắc Ninh, also received a *Phi Long* bonus.

176 NAVN. CBTN, 303:275. Hoàng Kế Viêm to Court, 8/3/TĐ30. The Huế court issued the directive during the tenth month of TĐ29.

177 NAVN. CBTN, 303:275. Tạ Di Đình, Hoàng Kế Viêm's assistant, noted that no one in any of these areas believed that the Black Flags intended to establish a permanent settlement.

178 NAVN. CBTN, 35:286. Tỉnh thần quân thứ Ninh-Thái Lê Hưu Tạ to Nội Các and Bộ Binh, 12/8/TĐ30.

179 NAVN. CBTN, 89:286. Thông Đốc Hoàng Kế Viêm to Bộ Binh, 18/8/TĐ30.

180 NAVN. CBTN, 115:286. Cao Bằng tỉnh thần Nguyễn Đình Nhuận to Bộ Binh, 21/8/TĐ30.

181 NAVN. CBTN, 134:286. Thông đốc Hoàng Kế Viêm to Bộ Binh, 20/8/TĐ30. Reply, 27/8/TĐ30.

182 NAVN. CBTN, 112:289. Ninh-Thái tỉnh thần Lê Hưu Tạ to Hoàng Kế Viêm, 25/8/TĐ30.

183 NAVN. CBTN, 283:328. Bộ Lễ edict, 14/12/TĐ32

184 NAVN. CBTN, 76:294, Nguyễn Huy Kỷ to Bộ Hộ, 16/1/TĐ31.

185 NAVN. CBTN, 132:296. Hoàng Kế Viêm to Court, 28/2/TĐ31. Includes citation of Cơ Mật Viện to Hoàng Kấ Viêm, 21/2/TĐ31.

186 NAVN. CBTN, 222:295. Tỉnh thần Hà Nội Trần Đình Túc to Cơ Mật Viện and Thượng Bạc, 5/3/TĐ31.

187 NAVN. CBTN, 222:295. Cơ Mật Viện to Hoàng Kế Viêm, 6/3/TĐ31.

188 CAOM. AGC 22319: "Quelques documents relatif aux correspondances officielles du huyện de Văn Chân (sic) avec les populations." Communication from Quan Đạo Tân Hóa to Văn Chấn tri huyện, dated 12/12/TĐ30.

189 Viện Sử Học, ed., *Đại Nam thực lục chính biên*, 34:121.

190 Du ed. 8:3a-4b; Yunnan sheng lishi yanjiu suo ed. DCSL 79:10–11.

191 NAVN. CBTN, 188:305. Privy Council comment on report from Ministry of Rites and Ministry of Military, 14/9/TĐ31; Viện Sử Học, ed., *Đại Nam thực lục chính biên*, 34:163.

192 NAVN. CBTN, 133:306. Bố chính sứ hộ ly quan phòng tuần phủ Lạng-Bằng Nguyễn Đình Nhuận to Court, 19/9/TĐ31. The Nội Các was later notified. These reports came from the governor of Guangxi, Yang Zhongya, and the officer in charge of the Zuojiang River area.

193 Viện Sử Học, ed., *Đại Nam thực lục chính biên*, 34:164; Yunnan Sheng Lishi Yanjiu Suo, ed., *Qing shilu*; DCSL 81:18–19. Liu Kunyi to Grand Council, 1878/12/7; Du ed. 8:13a–15a.

194 Yunnan Sheng Lishi Yanjiu Suo, ed., *Đại Nam thực lục chính biên*; DCSL 79:7–8. Yang Zhongya to Grand Council, 1878/10/31.

195 Viện Sử Học, ed., *Đại Nam thực lục chính biên*, 34:171, 181.

196 Ibid., 34:181–82.

197 NAVN. CBTN, 78:312. Chụ Bộ Nha, 23/11/TĐ31. This is an unusual piece of paperwork. The author of the submitted report knew details about Li Yangcai, including his home area, that suggest a high degree of familiarity. However,

the use of "An Nam" rather than "Việt Nam" seems to indicate a lack of rhetorical decorum that the court would not have tolerated from an official of the Qing Empire.

198 Devèria also published *La Frontière Sino-Annamite: Description géographique et ethnographique.*

199 CAOM. AGC 11932, Révolte du Kouang Si et envalissement du Nord du Tonkin par les rebelles chinois commandé par Ly-Yung-Choi, 1878 à 1879." Légation de France en Chine to Lafont, Nov. 7, 1878.

200 CAOM. AGC 11932, Governor-General of Liang-Guang to M. E. de Lagrené, Nov. 12, 1878.

201 CAOM, AGC 13006, "Rapports du Consul de France à Hanoi a.o. des bandes de Li Yung Choi." Chef Bataillon de Larson to Lafont, Dec. 11, 1878.

202 Viện Sử Học, ed., *Đại Nam thực lục chính biên*, 34:213.

203 Ibid., 34:215. This uplander, identified as Bùi Đình Tấn, was defeated by a local "Mán Mục."

204 Ibid., 34:220; Yunnan Sheng Lishi Yanjiu Suo, ed., *Qing shilu*; DCSL 95:8–9. Yang Zhongya to Grand Council, 1879/7/15.

205 NAVN. CBTN, 222:314. Thái Nguyên tỉnh thần Bùi Phác to Ministry of Military, 22/4/TĐ32. Hoàng Kế Viêm also received a copy of this report, which included a memorial about the capture of the two Lýs by Nông Đức Đàng. 30/4/TĐ32.

206 CAOM. AGC13007, "Rapports de Consul de France à Hanoi, Pilot Georges." 10 Avril 1879. Report of Vlavianos's voyage sent to Lafont in Saigon from de Kergaradec in Hanoi, Apr. 10, 1879.

207 Ibid.

208 Ibid.

209 CAOM. AGC13001, "Rapports du Consul de France à Hanoi, renseignements sur les bandes de Ly Yong Choi." May 16, 1879. De Kergaradec to Lafont, May 1, 1879. Information for reports after Vlavianos's return likely came from sources in the merchant community and in the Hanoi government.

210 CAOM. AGC13010, "Rapports du Consul de France à Hanoi, defaite de Li Yung Choi." De Kergaradec to Lafont, June 9, 1879.

211 CAOM. AGC13011, "Rapports du Consul de France à Hanoi, retrait des troupes Chinoises, etc." De Kergaradec to Lafont, July 4, 1879. De Kergaradec claimed to have secured the help of Feng Zicai in guaranteeing the orderly return of the Black Flags to Lào Cai. I have found no record of this promise in Nguyễn or Qing materials, which may indicate a certain disingenuousness in the statements by the head of the French Consulate.

212 CAOM. AGC13012, "Rapports du Consul de France à Hanoi, départ de Phong Ti Tai de Tuyen Quang." De Kergaradec to Lafont July 23, 1879, and August 7, 1879.

213 Viện Sử Học, ed., *Đại Nam thực lục chính biên*, 34:239–41.

214 For more on Nguyễn Hữu Độ, see Sogny, "Les familles illustres de l'Annam," 169–204 and Đặng, *Thăng Long-Hanoi*, 89–91.

215 Sogny, "Les familles illustres de l'Annam," 187. See also Davis, *States of Banditry*, 176 and 319.

216 Đặng, *Thăng Long-Hanoi*, 89.

217 Du, ed., *Feng Congbao (Zicai) jundu jiya*, 8:75a. Feng Zicai to Zhang Shusheng, cited in Zhang Shusheng to Grand Council, 6/10/GX4. Li was captured on 21/9/GX4 according to Feng, although Nguyễn paperwork dates the event ten days earlier. NAVN. CBTN, 38:324. Hoàng Kế Viêm to Chự Bộ Nha, 11/9/TĐ32.

218 CAOM. AGC13018, "Rapports du Consul de France à Hanoi, prise du chef rebelle Chinois Li Yung Choi." De Kergaradec to Lafont, Oct. 15, 1879.

219 CAOM. AGC13028, "Rapports du Consul de France à Hanoi, départ des derniers troupes Chinois, etc." De Kergaradec to Lafont, Feb. 15, 1880; Ouyang, ed., *Liu Zhongseng Gong Kunyi xuanji*, 15:20a–24a. Liu Kunyi to Grand Council, 24/7/GX5.

220 Yunnan Sheng Lishi Yanjiu Suo, ed., *Qing shilu*; DCSL 100: 5–7. Zhang Shusheng to Grand Council, Oct. 23, 1879, and Grand Council response to Zhang Shusheng, Nov. 19, 1879,; CBTN, 213:317. Thái Nguyên án sát Đỗ Trọng Vi to Chự Bộ Nha, 27/9/TĐ32.

221 CAOM. AGC13032, "Rapports du Consul de France à Hanoi, soulèvement de Chinois dans la province de Thai Nguyen sous le commandement de Luc chi Binh." De Kergaradec to Lafont, Apr. 14, 1880.

222 CAOM. AGC13027, "Rapports du Consul de France à Hanoi, départ de Phong Ti Tai de Tuyen Quang." De Kergaradec to Lafont, Jan. 3, 1880.

223 CAOM. AGC13037, "Rapports du Consul de France à Hanoi, a.s. d'un voyage fait dans le haut du fleuve rouge par la canonnière 'La Massue.'" De Kergaradec to Lafont, July 22, 1880; CAOM. AGC13038, "Rapports du Consul de France à Hanoi, Renseignements sur la bande Chinoise de Luc chi Binh, sur la récolte des riz, et sur le voyage de la 'Massue' au Haut Fleuve Rouge."

224 James R. Akerman, in his introduction to an edited volume inspired by the work of Brian Harley, has noted the "intimacy between empire and scientific geography, ethnography, and cartography." *The Imperial Map: Cartography and the Mastery of Empire*, 5.

225 Viện Sử Học, ed., *Đại Nam thực lục chính biên*, 33:276.

226 CAOM. AGC11788, "Voyage d'Exploration de MM Courtin et Villeroi sur le haut Fleuve Rouge, attaques dirigeés contre eux par les Pavillions Noirs, 1881–1882." De Kergaradec to de Vilers, Sep. 1, 1881.

227 CAOM. AGC11788, de Kergaradec to de Vilers, Oct. 12, 1881.

228 Ibid.; also "Nguyễn tuần phủ de Hưng Hóa à tổng đốc et tuần phủ de Hanoi," Sep. 1881.

229 CAOM. AGC11788, de Kergaradec to de Vilers, Oct. 20, 1881; Courtin and Villeroi to de Kergaradec, Oct. 7, 1881; André Masson, *Correspondance politique du Commandant Rivière au Tonkin*, 280–81n93.

230 CAOM. AGC11788, de Kergaradec to de Vilers, Oct. 20, 1881; Governor-General of Hà-Ninh to de Kergaradec, Oct. 1881; ĐNTL, 35:66.

231 CAOM. AGC11788, de Kergaradec to de Vilers, Oct. 21, 1881.

232 CAOM. AGC11788, de Kergaradec to de Vilers, Oct. 21, 1881; ĐNTL, 35:9. The court dispatched him to fight Liu Zhiping.

233 CAOM. AGC11788, de Kergaradec to de Vilers, Nov. 20, 1881; Villeroi to de Kergaradec, Nov. 25, 1881.

234 CAOM. AGC11788, de Champeaux, "Acte de décès," Jan. 3, 1882 (declared in Haiphong).

235 De Lapparenet, "Notice Mécrologique sur Edmond Fuchs, Ingénieur Chef des mines"; Pradon, "Edouard Émile Saladin (1856–1917)."

236 Fuchs and Saladin, "Mémoire sur l'exploration des gites," 185–87.

237 Viện Sử Học, ed., *Đại Nam thực lục chính biên*, 35:75; Fuchs and Saladin, "Mémoire sur l'exploration des gites," 190–92.

238 Viện Sử Học, ed., *Đại Nam thực lục chính biên*, 35:75; Fuchs and Saladin, "Mémoire sur l'exploration des gites," 195.

239 Viện Sử Học, ed., *Đại Nam thực lục chính biên*, 35:75. The Huế court recorded that security considerations caused the shortening of their trip. Similar to de Kergaradec's experiences in the 1870s, the lack of information forthcoming from the Nguyễn officialdom about mineral deposits likely represented an effort to stall or prevent exploration of a state economic sector.

240 Fuchs and Saladin, "Mémoire sur l'exploration des gites," 196–97.

241 Pradon, "Edouard Émile Saladin." Fuchs traveled to Mexico and the United States, including a stint in Colorado.

242 Fuchs and Saladin, "Mémoire sur l'exploration des gites," 190.

243 Quoted in Cooke, *New French Imperialism*, 15.

244 Leroy-Beaulieu, *De la colonisation*. Cited in Conklin, *A Mission to Civilize*, 12.

245 Conklin, *A Mission to Civilize*, 12.

246 NAVN. CBTN, 208:317. Nguyễn Hữu Độ to Cơ Mật Viện and Thượng Bạc, 16/9/TĐ32.

CHAPTER 3

1 Copies of this text exist in the Archives du Ministre des Affaires Étrangères, the Archives of the Residence du Nam Dinh, (NAVN. RND, File 2529 "Rapport (sans l'auteur) sur les exploits à Hanoi et au Tonkin de Luu Vinh Phuc, chef de Pavillons Noirs, 1899." 1a–2a); and the Centre des Archives d'Outre-Mer (CAOM. AGC13061 "Rapports du Consul de France à Hanoi, situation à Hanoi, envoi d'une traduction d'un placard de Luu vinh Phuc defiant les Francais, 10/5/1883.").

2 Võ, *La place du catholicisme, Tomes 2–4*, 941. In this instance, the colloquial Vietnamese terms *tạo* to refer to himself and *chúng bay* for the French.

3 Ibid.

4 Masson, ed., *Correspondance politique du Commandant Rivière au Tonkin*, 265–66.

5 Ibid.

6 Võ, *La place du catholicisme*, vols. 2–4:426, 430–31; Taboulet, *La geste Française en Indochine*, 769.

7 Cited in Taboulet, *La geste Française en Indochine*, 767.

8 Masson, *Correspondance politique*, 61; CAOM. AGC13059, "Rapports du Counsul de France à Hanoi, arrivée du Commandant Rivière, situation après la Prise de la Citadelle de Hanoi 15/4–31/12/1882." De Kergaradec to de Vilers, 16 April 1882. De Vilers cited the case of Fuchs and Saladin in his letter to the Tự Đức emperor that outlined Rivière's role in Tonkin. See also Taboulet, *La geste Française en Indochine*, 768.

9 Eastman, *Throne and Mandarins*, 30.

10 Ibid., 37.

11 Eastman, 38.

12 Mancall, "The Ch'ing Tribute System," in *The Chinese World Order*, ed. Fairbank, 63. Mancall also discussed "tribute" as trade, 75–79.

13 Taylor, "Surface Orientations in Vietnam," 971. ". . . dynasties and governments have through time entertained a succession of relationships that cover the full spectrum between war and amity."

14 Taylor, "Review of Liam C. Kelley, *Beyond the Bronze Pillars*."

15 Viện Sử Học, ed., *Đại Nam thực lục chính biên*, 35:98.

16 Ibid., 35:101.

17 Also known as Hoàng Kim Tích, Hoàng Diệu was a native of Quảng Nam who received a *phó bảng* appointment in 1853 at the age of twenty-two. Ngô, ed., *Các nhà khoa bằng Việt Nam*, 847.

18 Masson, *Correspondance politique*, 71–72. Rivière au Tong-Doc de Hanoi, Apr. 25, 1882.

19 Ibid.

20 Masson, *Correspondance politique*, 72–73. Rivière to de Vilers, Apr. 25, 1883.

21 CAOM. AGC13059, "Rapports du Consul de France à Hanoi, arrivée du Commandant Rivière, situation après la prise de la Citadelle de Hanoi 15/4–31/12/1882." De Kergaradec to de Vilers, Apr. 26, 1882; Viện Sử Học, *Đại Nam thực lục chính biên*, 35:108; Masson, *Correspondance politique*, 75–80; Trần, *Việt Nam sử lược*, 556–58.

22 Chu, Đặng, Nguyễn, eds., *Thơ văn yêu nước nửa sau thế kỷ XIX*, 165–69. Includes both a Quốc Ngữ and Hán-Việt translation of Hoàng Diệu's work, based on an original copy conserved by Kỳ Nam.

23 Ibid., 167.

24 Ibid., 169.

25 Hoàng Diệu's subordinates and colleagues fled as Rivière attacked. Ibid., 165.

26 Viện Sử Học, *Đại Nam thực lục chính biên*, 35:110. The other two officials were Nguyễn Chính and Bùi Văn Dị.

27 Ibid., 35:136–37.

28 Ibid. The court noted that all three had worked as counterinsurgency specialists (*tĩnh biên phó sứ*).

29 Masson, *Correspondance politique*, 74–75. Rivière aux habitants de Hanoi, Apr. 26, 1882.

30 Ibid.

31 Ibid.

32 Masson, *Correspondance politique*, 76–78. Rivière to Amiral Jauréguiberry, Apr. 27, 1882.

33 Masson, *Correspondance politique*, 81. Rivière to Amiral Jauréguiberry, Apr. 30, 1882.

34 Viện Sử Học, *Đại Nam thực lục chính biên*, 35:136; Masson, *Correspondance politique*, 82–83. Rivière to Amiral Jauréguiberry, Apr. 30, 1882.

35 Masson, *Correspondance politique*, 81. Rivière to Amiral Jauréguiberry, Apr. 30, 1882.

36 Masson, *Correspondance politique*, 85–86. Rivière to Amiral Jauréguiberry, May 13, 1882. Formerly an inspector, like Francis Garnier, in the French Cochinchina administration, Rheinart at the time served in his third appointment to the Huế court, which began August 1881. Masson, *Correspondance politique*, 269–70n19.

37 Masson, *Correspondance politique*, 86–91. Rheinart to Rivière, Apr. 27, 1882.

38 Masson, *Correspondance politique*, 134–35. De Vilers to Rivière, 7–8, Aug. 22, 1882.

39 CAOM. AGC10985, "Rapport sur la situation politique et militaire du Tonkin, bruits d'intervention Chinoise, ligne de conduite qui peut-être suivre 1882." Commandant Beaumont to de Vilers, July 25, 1882.

40 Masson, *Correspondance politique*, 140–45. Rivière to de Vilers, Aug. 22, 1882; Aug. 30, 1882;

41 Masson, Rivière to Jauréguiberry, 1 Septembre 1882.

42 CAOM. AGC13047, "Rapports du Consul de France à Hanoi, état des récoltes, voyage d'exploration de M. Aumoitte à Lang Son 25/7–21/9/1881." De Kergaradec to Saigon, Sep. 1881; Aumoitte, *De Hanoi à la frontière du Kouang-Si*.

43 NAVN. CBTN, 147:368. Kinh lược phó sứ Bùi Văn Dị to Thượng Bạc Viện, 2/9/TĐ35. A native of Hanoi also known as Bùi Ân Niên, Bùi Văn Dị received a *phó bảng* decree in 1865 and continued to work under the French protectorate, serving in the ministries of rites and personnel during the 1890s. Ngô, *Các nhà khoa bảng Việt Nam*, 860.

44 Yunnan Sheng Lishi Yanjiu Suo, ed., DCSL 138:7, Dec. 16, 1881. Zongli Yamen to Grand Council, includes citation of report by Zeng Jizhe.

45 Eastman, *Throne and Mandarins*, 13–14.

46 Yunnan Sheng Lishi Yanjiu Suo, ed., DCSL 144:9. Qingyu to Grand Council, Apr. 30, 1882.

47 Yunnan Sheng Lishi Yanjiu Suo, ed., DCSL 139:8, Dec. 29, 1881. Liu Shenyi to Grand Council.

48 Yunnan Sheng Lishi Yanjiu Suo, ed., DCSL 143:12, Apr. 4, 1882. Zhang Shusheng and Yubao to Grand Council.

49 Yunnan Sheng Lishi Yanjiu Suo, ed., DCSL 140:11–12, Feb. 1, 1882. Qingyu to Grand Council.

50 Yunnan Sheng Lishi Yanjiu Suo, ed., DCSL 144:9, Apr. 30, 1882. Qingyu to Grand Council.

51 Yunnan Sheng Lishi Yanjiu Suo, ed., DCSL 145:7–8, May 30, 1882. Zhang Shusheng to Grand Council. These were Tang Jiong and Xu Yanxu.

52 Viện Sử Học, *Đại Nam thực lục chính biên*, 35:141–42.

53 Ibid.

54 CAOM. AGC12960, "Rapports du chargé d'affaires à Hue, consideration sur la proclamation du gouverneur du Yunnan a.s. de l'entrée des troupes Chinois sur le territoire Annamite, 14/9–22/11/1882." Document from Yunnan to Thương Bạc Đại Thần Nguyễn Trọng Hiệp dated 15/5/GX8. Document from Rheinart to Cen Yuying dated 18/7/TĐ35.

55 Masson, *Correspondance politique*, 158–59. Rivière to de Vilers, Nov. 14, 1882.

56 CAOM. AGC13058. "Rapports du Consul de France à Hanoi a.s. d'un voyage du Yunnan proposé par M. Galy 22/8/1882." De Kergaradec to Saigon, Aug. 22, 1882.

57 Cao, *Đại Nam chính biên liệt truyện*, 690–91; Viện Sử Học, *Đại Nam thực lục chính biên*, 35:159–60. Vũ Trọng Bình had been previously celebrated for his work in Nghệ An. See Bùi, ed., *Tự Đức thánh chế văn (quyển mục lục, quyển I đến VIII)*, xxxviii–xxxix.

58 Masson, *Correspondance politique*, 158–59. Rivière to de Vilers, Nov. 14, 1882; Viện Sử Học, *Đại Nam thực lục chính biên*, 35:163–64.

59 Masson, *Correspondance politique*.

60 Ibid.

61 Ibid., 162–65. Rheinart to Rivière, Dec. 6, 1882.

62 Ibid.

63 Eastman, *Throne and Mandarins*, 57–59.

64 Eastman, *Throne and Mandarins*; Taboulet, *La geste française en Indochine*, 785.

65 Yunnan Sheng Lishi Yanjiu Suo, ed., Guangxi-Guangdong Governor-General Zeng Guoquan to Grand Council, Oct. 18, 1882. Tang was originally from Guanyang in the far northeast of Guangxi. Zhao, ed., *Qing shi gao*, 463:12733.

66 Zhongyang Yanjiuyuan Jindaishi Yanjiu Suo, ed., *Zhong Fa Yuenan jiaoshe dang*, 1:124, document 74. Cited in Eastman, *Throne and Mandarins*, 51. Eastman estimated that memorials destined for Beijing took twenty-four days from Nanjing, two months from Guangxi, three months from Yunnan, and five months from Qing delegates in France (53). This became a major issue during open war with the French, when Qing officials had uneven access to

the newly extended telegraph lines in southern China. On the official Qing postal system, see Pasquet, *L'évolution du système postal.*

67 Tang, *Qing ying riji*, republished in Zhong Fa Zhanzheng Shi Yanjiu Hui, ed., *Zhong Fa zhanzheng*, 2:41–229.

68 Yu Yuliang, of the Sino-French War Research Group in Nanning, Guangxi, contended that Tang's intention was to help the Nguyen government and that his criticisms resulted from frustration upon being denied a temporary stay in Vietnam. (Interview with Yu Yuliang, Nanning: Guangxi Social Science Academy, Sep. 8, 2004). Dai Kelai, on the other hand, claimed that Tang simply had no idea how the Nguyen system worked. (Interview with Dai Kelai. Beijing University, Oct. 14, 2004).

69 Tang, *Qing ying riji*, 42.

70 Ibid.

71 Tang, *Qing ying riji*, 43. Tang Jingsong identified Liu Yongfu as a fellow "Chinese person" (華人).

72 Ibid., 53–54. Tang noted that Nguyễn Văn Tường expressed surprise at his arrival, wondering what business brought a Beijing official to the Huế court.

73 Ibid., 54.

74 Ibid., 60. This is a spurious accusation with likely origins in Tang's ignorance of Nguyễn tax laws.

75 Ibid.

76 Ibid.

77 Ibid.

78 Ibid., 61–62.

79 Ibid., 62.

80 Ibid., 57–58; Viện Sử Học, *Đại Nam thực lục chính biên*, 35:190. Nguyễn Thuật came from the central province of Quảng Nam and took a *cử nhân* in 1837 and a *phó bảng* in 1868. Ngô, *Các nhà khoa bảng Việt Nam*, 866

81 Tang, *Qing ying riji*, 57–58; Viện Sử Học, *Đại Nam thực lục chính biên*, 35:190.

82 Tang, *Qing ying riji*, 60.

83 Eastman, *Throne and Mandarins*, 63.

84 Viện Sử Học, *Đại Nam thực lục chính biên*, 35:161. Nguyễn Thuật's earlier mission to China was interrupted by Rivière's attack on Hanoi in 1882 (35:121–22); Yunnan Sheng Lishi Yanjiu Suo, ed., Guangxi Governor Ni Wenwei to Grand Council, July 21, 1882.

85 Chen, ed., *Ruan Shu [Nguyễn Thuật] zhu Jin riji*, i-iii, 7–19. Nguyễn Thuật's first service as an envoy was in 1880.

86 Viện Sử Học, *Đại Nam thực lục chính biên*, 35:171.

87 Ibid.

88 Tang, *Qing ying riji*, 64.

89 Ibid., 65–66.

90 Masson, *Correspondance politique*, 176–77. Thomson to Rivière, Jan. 25, 1883.

91 Ibid., 177–85. Rheinart to Rivière, Feb. 2, 1883.

92 Ibid., 185–88. Rheinart to Rivière, Feb. 9, 1883.

93 Ibid., 185. Thomson to Rivière, Feb. 7, 1883.

94 Ageron, "Jules Ferry et la colonisation," in *Jules Ferry*, ed. Furet; Gildea, *France 1870–1914*, 17–21. For an older work on Ferry, see Power, *Jules Ferry and the Renaissance of French Imperialism.*

95 Zhongyang Yanjiuyuan Jindaishi Yanjiu Suo, ed., *Zhong Fa Yuenan jiaoshe dang*, 2:722–27, document 345.

96 Eastman, *Throne and Mandarins*, 70.

97 Masson, *Correspondance politique*, 190–92. Rivière to Rheinart, Mar. 14, 1883; 192–96. De Villers to Rivière, Mar. 14, 1883.

98 Ibid.

99 Ibid., 199–201. Rivière to Thomson, Mar. 17, 1883.

100 Viện Sử Học, *Đại Nam thực lục chính biên*, 35:177.

101 Ibid., 35:176; Masson, *Correspondance politique*, 208. Rivière to Thomson, Mar. 19, 1883; Vũ, Phạm, Nguyễn, eds., 510–12.

102 Viện Sử Học, *Đại Nam thực lục chính biên*, 35:176. The provincial military commander, Lê Văn Điếm, led a group outside the city walls to confront Rivière's troops and died during the battle.

103 Ibid., 35:174.

104 Tang, *Qing ying riji*, 66–67.

105 Ibid., 68.

106 Ibid., 69.

107 Ibid.

108 Zhou, "Lun Zhong Fa zhanzheng zhong de Tang Jingsong," in, *Zhong Fa zhanzheng lunwen ji*, ed. Zhong Fa Zhanzheng Yanjiu Hui, 1:232–43.

109 Huang, *Liu Yongfu lishi cao*, 264.

110 Zhao, ed., *Qing shi gao*, 3263.

111 Tang, *Qing ying riji*, 73.

112 Ibid.

113 Masson, *Correspondance politique*, 233–34. Rheinart to Rivière, Apr. 3, 1883; Viện Sử Học, *Đại Nam thực lục chính biên*, 35:177.

114 Ibid., 35:182; Ngô, *Các nhà khoa bảng Việt Nam*, 851; Cao, *Đại Nam chính biên liệt truyện*, 262.

115 Viện Sử Học, *Đại Nam thực lục chính biên*, 35:172, 184; Huang, *Liu Yongfu lishi cao*, 262.

116 Pierre Badens, a native of Castelsarrasin, served in Senegal and Cochinchina prior to his time with Rivière in Tonkin. He went on to positions in Cambodia (1885–86) and, again, Senegal before returning to Tonkin in the 1890s, where he drowned in a boat accident on the Clear River in 1897. Masson, *Correspondance politique*, 277n80; also 234–35, Rivière to Badens, Apr. 7, 1883.

117 Duboc, *35 mois de campagne*, 112.

118 Masson, *Correspondance politique*, 244–47, Rivière to Thomson, Apr. 21, 1883; 253–54, Thomson to Rivière, May 19, 1883.

119 Louvet, *Vie de Mgr Puginier*, 427. Letter from Landais to Puginier, July 25, 1883.

120 Ibid., 429–30.

121 CAOM. AGC13975, "Le Ministre d'Affaires d'Annam à Gouvernement Cochinchinine, communication a.s. des mésures prises au tonkin par le Ct Rivière et de la non-observation des traites, 1883." Tương Bạc to de Kergaradec, TĐ36/4/1 (May 18, 1883).

122 CAOM. AGC11023, "Renseignements sur la situation au Tonkin par le C/Amiral Meyer 1883." Meyer to Thomson, 15/Mai/1883. Meyer's assertion, while exaggerated, is correct.

123 Masson, *Correspondance politique*, 253–61. Rapport de Lieutenant de vaisseau Pissère sur le Combat du 19 Mai 1883, 20 Mai 1883.

124 Huang, *Liu Yongfu lishi cao*, 268; Võ, *La place du catholicisme*, 467; Louvet, *Vie de Mgr Puginier*, 431–33; Masson, *Correspondance politique*, 255–61. Rapport de Lieutenant de vaisseau Pissère sur le Combat de 19 Mai 1883, 20 Mai 1883.

125 Huang, *Liu Yongfu lishi cao*, 268; Masson, *Correspondance politique*, 255–61; Viện Sử Học, *Đại Nam thực lục chính biên*, 35:193.

126 Nguyễn, ed., *Bùi Văn Dị*, 143.

127 Ibid.

128 Ibid., 144n2.

129 Kiều, *Bản Triều bạn nghịch liệt truyện*, 47A. Wu refers to Wu Yazhong, Hoàng to Hoàng Sùng Anh/Pan Lunsi, and Liu to Liu Yongfu.

130 Ibid.

131 Kiều, Thiết, and Trúc, "Ai sơn hành," 1–2.

132 Tang, *Qing ying riji*, 77; 洋人非人也 (*yang ren fei ren ye*).

133 Ibid., 76. Tang stated that the forged order supposedly came from Ni Wenwei.

134 MEP. Puginier Letters (Carton 1). Puginier to Mollard, May 28, 1883.

135 Louvet, *Vie de Mgr Puginier*, 433–34.

136 MEP. Puginier Letters (Carton 1). Puginier to Paris, Oct. 2, 1883; Louvet, *Vie de Mgr Puginier*, 435.

137 Duboc, *35 mois de campagne*, 157; Trần Trọng Kim, *Việt Nam sử Lược*, 560.

138 From Barentin, Duboc served in Gabon (1873) and led the French diplomatic mission to Panama (1877) before traveling to Tonkin on board the *Surprise* in November 1882. Masson, *Correspondance politique*, 302n323.

139 Duboc, *35 mois de campagne*, 161.

140 Ibid., 179. Bouet, Courbet, Harmand, and Thomson attended.

141 Ibid., 167–71.

142 Ibid., 192.

143 Ibid.

144 "Shu Heiqijun Liu Yi xi wen hou," *Shenbao* 6/4/GX9.

145 "Lun Heiqijun Liuyi Yuenan zhi jie," *Shenbao* 5/5/GX9.

146 "France in the Far East," *New York Times*, July 1, 1883.

147 Hobsbawm, *Bandits,* 141–42.

148 Champagne, *Les Pavillons Noirs ou la Guerre du Tonkin.* Le Théâtre des Batignolles is now known as Le Théâtre Hébertot.

149 Vũ, Phạm, Nguyễn, eds., *Lịch sử Việt Nam,* 533.

150 Keith Taylor has argued that the situation at court after the death of the Tự Đức emperor "can be interpreted as a struggle between Thuận-Quảng leaders willing to accommodate French demands and Thanh-Nghệ leaders who preferred armed resistance." "Surface Orientations in Vietnam," 970. While Taylor's insight about the role of regional orientation in central decision-making helps dispense with unwieldy generalities, Hoàng Kế Viêm was a native of Quảng Bình. The issue of the Black Flags may have played a far greater role in the factional struggles over surrender to the French within the Huế court and larger Vietnamese administration.

151 Nguyễn Viết Kế, *Kể chuyện các đời Vua Nhà Nguyễn,* 47–49; Nguyễn Đắc Xuân, ed., *Chuyện ba Vua Dục Đức Thành Thái Duy Tân,* 17–26; Lê Nguyễn, "Mấy điểm cần minh xác quanh cái chết của Vua Dục Đức," in *Xã hội Việt Nam thời Pháp Thuộc,* 155–62.

152 Lê, *Xã hội Việt Nam,* 158–62; Nguyễn Đắc Xuân writes that Nguyễn Văn Tường refused to read the order enthroning Nguyễn Ưng Chân on the grounds that the new monarch understood neither the demands of the throne nor the decorum of the court, a lack illustrated by his continual giggling in the presence of Nguyễn Văn Tường and Tôn Thất Thuyết. Nguyễn Đắc Xuân, *Chuyện ba Vua Dục Đức Thành Thái Duy Tân,* 19–21.

153 Vũ, Phạm, Nguyễn, eds., *Lịch Sử Việt Nam,* 536.

154 Lê, "Về chuyện thí Vua Hiệp Hòa," in *Xã hội Việt Nam thời Pháp Thuộc,* 163–68. For a dramatized account, see Nguyễn Viết Kế, *Kể chuyện các đời Vua Nhà Nguyễn,* 49–52.

155 "Proceedings of Foreign Societies," 383–87.

156 Harmand, "De Bassac à Hué." He also, much later, published his thoughts on colonialism in *Domination et Colonisation.* See also Salkin-Laparra, *Le Triple destin de Jules Harmand.*

157 Cahu, ed., *L'Amiral Courbet en Extrême-Orient,* 10. Admiral Courbet to Minister Brun, Aug. 22, 1883. Also "Très véridique histoire de bombardement de Thuan-an," 83.

158 Cahu, *L'Amiral Courbet en Extrême-Orient,* 14–18. See also "Souvenirs d'un troupier," 237–47.

159 Also known as Nguyễn Tuyên or Nguyễn Trọng Hợp, Nguyễn Trọng Hiệp came from Hanoi Province, earning a *tiến sĩ* in 1865 and working in several provincial and central government positions throughout his career. Ngô, *Các nhà khoa bảng Việt Nam,* 857. After the Sino-French War, he traveled to Paris. His observations about the French capital were noted by Walter Benjamin. Keith, "A Vietnamese in Paris."

160 Vũ, Phạm, Nguyễn, eds., *Lịch sử Việt Nam,* 532.

161 Lê, *Xã hội Việt Nam thời Pháp Thuộc*, 165.

162 I refer to this document as a "convention" to distinguish it from a treaty, as it was never officially ratified in Paris. Eventually replaced by the 1884 Patenôtre Treaty, the Harmand Convention is often described as the *Quý Mùi* Treaty (*Hòa Ước*) in Vietnamese-language sources. For example: Lê, *Xã hội Việt Nam thời Pháp Thuộc*, 165; Lockhart and Duiker, *Historical Dictionary of Vietnam*, 152–53; Đinh and Trương, eds., *Từ điển nhân vật lịch sử Việt Nam*, 617.

163 French text of the convention in Taboulet, *La geste française en Indochine*, 807–9. Chinese text in Zhong Fa Zhanzheng Shi Yanjiu Hui, ed., *Zhong Fa zhanzheng*, 7:355–68.

164 Taboulet, *La geste française en Indochine*, 807–9.

165 Ibid. Emphasis added.

166 Lê, *Xã hội Việt Nam thời Pháp Thuộc*, 168.

167 Ibid; Tiên, "Ông Trần Tiễn Thành bị hại thế nào?" in *Tạp Chí Tri Tân*, ed. Tủ Sách Lịch Sử và Văn Hóa, 468.

168 Zhang, "Cen Yuying," in *Zhuangzu lishi renwu zhuan*, ed. Guangxi Minzu Xueyuan Minzu Yanjiu Shi, 131–39.

169 Zhao, *Qing shi gao*, 3245; Atwill, *The Chinese Sultanate*.

170 Zhong Fa Zhanzheng Shi Yanjiu Hui, ed., *Zhong Fa zhanzheng*, 1:163. Selection dated Tongzhi 24/1/TZ13.

171 Ibid.

172 Ibid., 1:164.

173 Yunnan Sheng Lishi Yanjiu Suo, ed., DCSL 162:7. Cen Yuying to Grand Council, 5/15/1883. Also Tang Jiong, *Chengshan laoren ziji nianpu*, 1:1a. Reprint of 1909 edition. Selections included in Zhong Fa Zhanzheng Shi Yanjiu Hui, ed., *Zhong Fa zhanzheng*, 2:229–48. Biographical information about Tang Jiong from Fang, "T'ang Chiung," in *Eminent Chinese of the Ch'ing Period*, ed. Hummel, 707–8; See also Jenks, *Insurgency and Social Disorder*, 155.

174 Zhao, *Qing shi gao*, 3250–52.

175 Xu, *Yuenan jiluo*, 1a–b. Also republished in an abridged version (without Xu's introduction) in Zhong Fa Zhanzheng Yanjiu Hui, ed., 1:29–53.

176 Ibid.

177 Xu, *Yuenan jiluo*, 1a.

178 Qian, ed., *Qingdai zhiguan nianbiao*, 1724 and 1942. Xu replaced Yang Zhongya, who had supervised Feng Zicai during the hunt for Li Yangcai in the previous decade. See also Eastman, *Throne and Mandarins*, 70–72; Zhao, *Qing shi gao*, 458:12681–87; Viện Sử Học, *Đại Nam thực lục chính biên*, 35:187

179 Viện Sử Học, *Đại Nam thực lục chính biên*, 35:194.

180 Ngô, Nguyễn, and Papin, eds., *Đồng Khánh địa dư chí*, 38a–39b. Located in eastern Sơn Tây, Đan Phượng hosted a merchant population as well as relatively well-educated families whom formed part of the traditional élite for historical Vietnamese states. Đan Phượng during the Nguyễn period

was roughly equivalent to the present-day district of Đan Phượng in Hà Tây Province.

181 Duboc, *35 mois de campagne en Chine*, 167–71.

182 Liao, *Kang Fa mingjiang Liu Yongfu*, 213.

183 Viện Sử Học, *Đại Nam thực lục chính biên*, 35:236–37. Lloyd Eastman noted that the Black Flags employed a combination of ambush and defensive tactics to stop the French military. Eastman, *Throne and Mandarins*, 87–88.

184 Huang, *Liu Yongfu lishi cao*, 269; Tang, *Qing yi riji*, 91.

185 Viện Sử Học, *Đại Nam thực lục chính biên*, 35:237.

186 Yunnan Sheng Lishi Yanjiu Suo, ed., DCSL 169:9–10. Guangxi Governor Ni Wenwei to Grand Council, citation of report from Xu Yanxu, Sept. 28, 1883.

187 Duboc, *35 mois de campagne en Chine*, 198.

188 Duboc, *35 mois de campagne en Chine*, 195–96; Masson, *Correspondance politique*, 261–64. "Rapport de M. Bonnal, Résident de France à Hanoi, sur la découverte de la tête et des mains du Commandant Rivière at village de Kieu-Mai," Sep. 20, 1883.

189 Duboc, *35 mois de campagne en Chine*, 195–96.

190 Ibid.

191 Ibid., 198–99. According to Duboc, this group included Jean-Thomas-Raoul Bonnal, résident de France de la province d'Hanoi; Joseph-Maire-Henri-Aime-Louis Perez de Casteras, chancelier; Louis-Roger-Gerard MM de Marolles, lieutenant de vaisseau; Duboc; Alexandre-Pierre Bouchet, capitaine adjudant-major au regiment de marche d'infanterie de marine; and Louis-Clement de Mondon, medecin de 2ème classe de la marine.

192 Ibid.

193 CAOM. AGC11040, "Demande de transport gratuit de la statue Francis Garnier de Toulon à Saigon formulée par M. H. Viénot," Governor of Cochinchina to President of the Garnier Statue Committee (Toulon), Oct. 11, 1883.

194 Huang, *Liu Yongfu lishi cao*, 271; Cen, ed., *Cen Xiangqin Gong zou gao*, 20:9a–b. Cen Yuying referred to Liu Yongfu and the Black Flags as the "Liu Militia," a term that signified their rehabilitation from anti-Qing activists to loyal allies. Cen Yuying Sơn Tây report to Grand Council, 11/2/GX9.

195 Cen, *Cen Xiangqin Gong zou gao*, 20:10a. Cen cited Zhang Shusheng's report of the Harmand Convention.

196 Cahu, *L'amiral courbet en Extrême-Orient*, 35. Courbet to Brun, Nov. 11, 1883. Liu Yongfu also overestimated Courbet, estimating that the French Admiral commanded upwards of ten thousand. Huang, *Liu Yongfu lishi cao*, 271.

197 Huang, *Liu Yongfu lishi cao*, 271.

198 Ibid; Cen, *Cen Xiangqin Gong zou gao*, 20:24a. Cen Yuying to Grand Council, 11/15/GX9. Cen noted the Algerians in particular in his report of the defeat at Sơn Tây. Cahu, *L'amiral courbet en Extrême-Orient*, 55. Courbet to Brun, Jan. 1884.

199 Huang, *Liu Yongfu lishi cao*, 271; Tang Jingsong, *Qing ying riji*, 102–3.

200 Cahu, *L'amiral courbet en Extrême-Orient*, 73. Fournier to Courbet, Jan. 1, 1884.

201 He, ed., *Zhang Jingda Gong Peilun*, 5:33b–34b. Li Hongzhang to Zhang Shusheng, 3/10/GX8; 5:18b. Zhang Shusheng to Grand Council, 10/15/GX7.

202 Qian, *Qingdai zhiguan nianbiao*, 1487–88. Zhang Shusheng later died, while in office, after a long illness in 1884.

203 Eastman, *Throne and Mandarins*, 21–23.

204 Ibid., 23–24. The Tianjin crisis of 1870, which involved a massacre and a concession to France, inspired the dissent of a small number of Qing Yi officials who clamored for war with France.

205 Ibid., 25–26.

206 Cen, *Cen Xiangqin Gong zou gao*, 20:41a–42a. Cen Yuying to Grand Council, 1/26/GX10. Originally from Từ Liêm near Hanoi, Hoàng Tướng Hiệp received a *tién sĩ* in 1865.

207 De Négrier (1839–1913) came from Belfort. Brière de l'Isle, from Martinique, suffered a wound at the Battle of Sedan in 1870. Taboulet, *La geste française en Indochine*, 822; Hardoin, *Au Tonkin*, 185.

208 Eastman, *Throne and Mandarins*, 102.

209 Hardoin, *Les Combats du Général de Négrier*, 8–15.

210 Yunnan Sheng Lishi Yanjiu Suo, ed., DCSL 177:8–10. Grand Council to Cen Yuying, including Li Hongzhang's telegraph, Feb. 12, 1884.

211 Yunnan Sheng Lishi Yanjiu Suo, ed., DCSL 178:11–12. Grand Council edict citing Li Hongzhang's telegraph, Mar. 16, 1884; 178:16. Cen Yuying to Grand Council, Mar. 21, 1884.

212 Eastman, *Throne and Mandarins*, 102.

213 *Da Qing lichao shilu*, DCSL 180:3a–b. Separate edicts, dated 3/17/GX10.

214 Liu, "Zhong Fa zhanzheng de tuoxie pai – Tang Jiong," in *Zhong Fa zhanzheng lunwen ji*, ed. Guangxi Zhong Fa Zhanzheng Shi Yanjiu Hui, 4:229–38.

215 Viện Sử Học, *Đại Nam thực lục chính biên*, 36:112.

216 Huang, *Liu Yongfu lishi cao*, 269.

217 Ngô, *Các nhà khoa bảng Việt Nam*, 857.

218 Viện Sử Học, *Đại Nam thực lục chính biên*, 36:112.; Taboulet, *La geste française en Indochine*, 844.

219 Tang Jingsong, *Qing ying riji*, 148; Huang, *Liu Yongfu lishi cao*, 275.

220 Taboulet, *La geste française en Indochine*, 825. Born in Toulouse in 1842, Fournier shot a fellow officer in a duel over the existence of the Li-Fournier Convention in October 1884. Fournier help establish the École Supérieure de Guerre in the 1890s. He passed away in Neuilly in 1934.

221 Ibid., 825–26. Text of the convention reprinted from Billot, *L'Affaire du Tonkin*, 416–17.

222 Taboulet, *La geste française en Indochine*, 827. Telegram from Fournier to Millot and Courbet, May 17, 1884.

223 Text of treaty reprinted in Vũ, Phạm, Nguyễn, eds., *Lịch sử Việt Nam*, 820–29. Also Viện Sử Học, *Đại Nam Thực Lục Chính Biên*, 36:115–20.

224 Taboulet, *La geste française en Indochine*, 828. Article 13.
225 Ibid. Article 12.
226 Ibid. Article 14.
227 Viện Sử Học, *Đại Nam thực lục chính biên*, 36:139.
228 Ibid.
229 Vũ, Phạm, Nguyễn, eds., *Lịch Sử Việt Nam*, 827. Article 9. The telegraph would have other, unforeseen applications in the case of Liang Sanqi, discussed later.
230 Baark, *Lightning Wires*, 13.
231 Ibid., 4–5. On Li's dismissiveness toward independent efforts, 87.
232 De Belval, *Au Tonkin, 1884–1885*, 210–12; Billot, *L'affaire du Tonkin*, 185–89.
233 Lecomte, *Le guet-apens de Bac-Lé*.
234 De Belval, *Au Tonkin, 1884–1885*, 185–89.
235 Liao, *Zhong Fa zhanzheng shi*, 417–64. He includes a detailed history of the military campaigns on Taiwan, 465–590. See also Taboulet, *La geste française en Indochine*, 835–37.
236 Taboulet, *La geste française en Indochine*, 837.
237 Yunnan Sheng Lishi Yanjiu Suo, ed., DCSL 200:9–10. Cen Yuying to Grand Secretariat, Feb. 8, 1885; 199:17–18. Pan Dingxin Telegraph to Grand Council, Jan. 28, 1885.
238 Armangaud, *Lang-Son*, 8–24.
239 Ibid., 34.
240 Ibid.
241 Ibid; Yunnan Sheng Lishi Yanjiu Suo, ed., DCSL 201:14–15. Pan Dingxin telegram (Longzhou relay) to Guangxi-Guangdong Governor-General Zhang Zhidong, forwarded to Grand Council from Guangzhou, Feb. 27, 1885; DCSL 201:16. Telegram from Li Hongzhang to Grand Council, Feb. 28, 1885. Pan Dingxin was injured during the explosion, an indication of the proximity of the army under his command. His telegraph most likely came through the relay station in Longzhou, northeast of Lạng Sơn in Guangxi.
242 Armangaud, *Lang-Son*, 35.
243 Yunnan Sheng Lishi Yanjiu Suo, ed., DCSL 200:9–10. Cen Yuying to Grand Secretariat, Feb. 8, 1885.
244 Yunnan Sheng Lishi Yanjiu Suo, ed., DCSL 201:8–9. Cen Yuying to Grand Council and Grand Council response, Feb. 20, 1885. The Black Flags under Liu's command received 3,000 *liang* or one *liang* each per month from the Qing government. Cen's raise put them at 33,000 per month, or eleven per person a month.
245 Ibid., DCSL 202:8. Cen Yuying telegram to Grand Council, Mar. 12, 1885.
246 Tang Jingsong, *Qing ying riji*, 148.
247 Yunnan Sheng Lishi Yanjiu Suo, ed., DCSL 199:17–18. Fan Dingxin telegram to Grand Council, Jan. 28, 1885.
248 Liao, *Zhong Fa zhenzheng*, 702.

249 Vũ, Phạm, Nguyễn, eds., *Lịch sử Việt Nam*, 590–91; Liao, *Zhong Fa zhanzheng shi*, 705–12; Vũ Ngọc Khánh, *Thị Xã Lạng Sơn Xưa và Nay*, 99; Taboulet, *La geste française en Indochine*, 850.

250 Vũ, Phạm, Nguyễn, eds., *Lịch sử Việt Nam*, 591.

251 Armangaud, *Lang-Son*, 76.

252 A very different sort of commentary emerged from writers opposed to France, although not necessarily to French colonialism. While an analysis of this discourse and rhetoric lies beyond the scope of the present study, examples of it can be found in the following: Mesney, *Tungking*; Staunton, *The War in Tong-King*. See also C. B. Norman, *Tonkin or France in the Far East*, which contains a chapter unambiguously entitled "Ignorance of Frenchman on General Matters unconnected with their own country," 329.

253 Schmidt, *Alexandre Ribot*, 34, 37.

254 Shao, *Zhong Fa Yuenan guanxi shimo*, 224–25.

255 Eastman, *Throne and Mandarins*, 121; Li Hongzhang also reminded Fournier that the Qing Empire remained a regional power despite the French presence in Vietnam. Wang and Liu, "Li Hongzhang yu Zhong Fa zhanzheng," in *Zhong Fa Zhanzheng lunwen ji*, ed. Zhong Fa Zhanzheng Yanjiu Hui, 1:257–72.

256 Yunnan Sheng Lishi Yanjiu Suo, ed., DCSL 204:8. Order to return issued by Grand Council, Apr. 6, 1885.

257 Ibid., DCSL 204:1–2. Su Yuanchun telegram to Grand Council, Apr. 1, 1885.

258 Ibid., DCSL 204:7–8. Cen Yuying to Grand Council (not sent via Longzhou telegraph station), received in Beijing, Apr. 5, 1885.

259 Huang, *Liu Yongfu lishi cao*, 285.

260 Fan, "Huang Shouzhong," in *Zhuangzu lishi renwu zhuan*, ed. Guangxi Minzu Xueyuan Minzu Yanjiu Shi, 103–9.

261 Huang, *Liu Yongfu lishi cao*, 301. Zhang Zhidong seemed particularly concerned about Liu's resettlement plans. Yunnan Sheng Lishi Yanjiu Suo, ed., DCSL 205:14–15. Zhang Zhidong telegram to Grand Council, May 5, 1885.

262 Yunnan Sheng Lishi Yanjiu Suo, ed., DCSL 205:15–16. Cen Yuying to Grand Council, May 7, 1885. Cen suggested a halt to Liu's monthly salary, which had been raised during the siege of Tuyên Quang.

263 Ibid., DCSL 206:4. Cen Yuying telegram to Grand Council, May 21, 1885.

CHAPTER 4

1 NAVN. RST76346, "Organisation des colonnes de police dans des provinces du Tonkin 1891." Vice-résident du Bay Say report from the Garde Civile Indigène.

2 Marr, *Vietnamese Anticolonialism*, 43–81.

3 Nguyễn Đắc Xuân, ed., *Chuyện ba Vua Dục Đức Thành Thái Duy Tân*, 25–26; Đào, *Phan Đình Phùng*, 43–44.

4 Nguyễn Xuân Thọ, "Vụ cướp phá hoàng cung cuộc để kháng của Vua Hàm Nghi và Triều Đồng Khánh," 14.
5 CAOM. AGC11785. "Déportation à Tahiti de Nguyen Van Tuong, Pham Van Duat [sic], Ton That Dinh, 1885." De Courcy to Governor-General in Saigon, Sep. 6, 1885.
6 CAOM. AGC11785. Capitaine de Vaisseau Réveillère to Cochinchina Governor, Feb. 19, 1886.
7 Lê, "Cái chết của phụ chánh Nguyễn Văn Tường trên Đảo Tahiti," in *Xã hội Việt Nam thời Pháp Thuộc*, 188–195. The third detainee, Tôn Thất Ninh, was Tôn Thất Thuyết's father. He died during the passage to Tahiti.
8 Nguyễn Tú, *Hoàng Kế Viêm*, 86–88.
9 Ngô, ed., *Các nhà khoa bằng Việt Nam*, 872. In an interesting assessment of Đặng Huy Xán's murder, a publication from the RVN described him as falling prey to bandits. Hà, *Hoạt động của Bộ Công dưới Đời Vua Tự-Đức*, 219n106b.
10 CAOM. AGC11782. "Renseignements et Notes de Mgr Puginier sur la Situation au Tonkin de 1884 à 1887 et en 1888." June 6, 1885.
11 Đỗ Văn Ninh, ed., *Từ điển chức quan Việt Nam*, 332–33.
12 NAVN. CBTN, 4:1. Edict (Authored by Tôn Thất Tuyết), 21/5/HN1. The edict lists French representatives as the initiators of the decision, although without naming specific individuals. 據法使懇請.
13 NAVN. CBTN, 368:2 and 370:2. Đinh Văn Cúc to Hàm Nghi emperor, 8/6/HN1.
14 Phạm, "Diễn văn kỷ niệm 100 năm mất nhà yêu nước, nhà thơ Nguyễn Quang Bích," in *Nguyễn Quang Bích*, ed. Nguyễn Huệ Chi, 17–28, 23; Đạng, "Thêm một số tài liệu về Đốc Ngữ và phong trào chống Pháp ở vùng Hạ Lưu Sông Đà cuối thế kỷ XIX," 45–46.
15 Phạm, "Triều đình Nhà Nguyễn với phong trào chống Pháp ở Tây Bắc (nửa sau thế kỷ XIX)," in *Lịch sử Nhà Nguyễn*, ed. Phan, Đỗ, Nguyễn, 410–16.
16 Marr, *Vietnamese Anticolonialism*, 69.
17 Fourniau, *Annam-Tonkin 1885–1896*, 22.
18 Ibid., 18–19. Fourniau made the connection between the hiring of "bandes irréguliers" and the participation of such bands in the struggle against French rule. See also Fourniau, *Domination coloniale et resistance nationale*, 464.
19 Đinh and Trương, ed., *Từ điển nhân vật lịch sử Việt Nam*, 178–79.
20 VHN, A.1263. 太平風物誌 (Thái Bình phong vật chí).
21 Đinh and Trương, *Từ điển nhân vật lịch sử Việt Nam*, 178–79
22 Phạm, "Diễn văn kỷ niệm 100 năm mất nhà yêu nước, nhà thơ Nguyễn Quang Bích."
23 Tang, *Qing ying riji*, 71.
24 Đinh and Trương, *Từ điển nhân vật lịch sử Việt Nam*, 154–55. Entry for Nguyễn Văn Giáp.
25 Dương, *Chính quyền thuộc địa ở Việt Nam trước Cách Mạng Tháng Tám 1945*, 103.

26 Ibid., 104–6.

27 Ibid.

28 Eckert, "Double-edged Swords of Conquest in Indochina," in *Colonial Armies in Southeast Asia*, ed. Hack and Rettig, 133–38. On Paul Bert, who served less than a year in Hanoi before his death, see Betts, *Assimilation and Association in French Colonial Theory*, 46–49; also Chailley-Bert, *Paul Bert au Tonkin*.

29 CAOM. AGC11782, "Renseignements et notes de Mgr Puginier sur la situation au Tonkin de 1884 à 1887 et en 1888." Puginier to Résident du Tonkin, 7 April 1888.

30 MEP. Puginier Letters (Carton 1). Puginier to Hanoi, Jan. 17, 1885.

31 MEP. Puginier Letters (Carton 3). "Notes explicatives. . ." Aug. 20, 1886.

32 CAOM. GGI, 22317. "Soumission de Le Dam, fils de Thuyet et partisan de Roi Ham Nghi, Septembre 1888."

33 Bibliothéque Coloniale Internationale, *Le Régime des Protectorates*, 1:205–10

34 NAVN. RST, 76319. "Listes nominatives des rebelles operant dans les provinces du Tonkin en 1890–1891."

35 Foucault, *Discipline and Punish*, 196–98.

36 NAVN. RST, 76319. "Rebelles dans Hung Hoa," "Rebelles dans Son Tay."

37 Ibid, "Rebelles dans Lao Kai," "Rebelles dans Tuyen Quang."

38 NAVN. RST, 76326–01. "Au sujet actes de piraterie commis à Tuyên Quang (November 1890 à Avril 1891)." Tuyên Quang Bố Chính Sứ "Phan" and án sát sứ "Nguyễn" to Kinh Lược (original), Nov. 17, 1890.

39 NAVN. RST, 76319. "Province de Lao Kay: Rapport sur la piraterie," Apr. 25, 1891.

40 NAVN. RST, 76319. "Lao Kai registre des pirates," July 31, 1891.

41 NAVN. RST, 76326–01. "Au sujet actes de piraterie commis à Tuyên Quang (November 1890 à Avril 1891)." Tuyên Quang bố chính sứ "Phan" and án sát sứ "Nguyễn" to Kinh Lược (original), Dec. 27, 1891.

42 Epigraph from Faulkner, "A Courtship," in *Collected Stories of William Faulkner*, 361: "Issetibbeha and General Jackson met and burned sticks and signed a paper, and now a line ran through the woods, although you could not see it. It ran straight as a bee's flight among the woods, with the Plantation on one side of it, where Issetibbeha was the Man, and America on the other side, where General Jackson was the Man. So now when something happened on one side of the line, it was bad fortune for some and a good fortune for others, depending on what the white man happened to possess, as it had always been. But merely by occurring on the other side of that line which you couldn't even see, it became what the white men called a crime punishable by death if they could just have found who did it. Which seemed foolish to us."

43 Kelley, *Beyond the Bronze Pillars*.

44 For a discussion of one such individual from the 1850s, see Davis, "Anxieties on the Frontier," in *Expanding China*, ed. Whitmore and Anderson, 322–38. *sijing*

45 Zhang and Gong, "Bianjiang—ci zai shijie zhuyao faxi zhong de jingxiang," 2–3.
46 Sahlins, *Boundaries*, 7.
47 Ministère des Affaires Étrangères, *Documents Diplomatiques: Affaires de Chine et du Tonkin, 1884–1885*, 215. Document 193: Campbell to Ferry, Mar. 25, 1885.
48 Ministère des Affaires Étrangères, 234. Document 222: Patenôtre to Freycinet, Apr. 9, 1885.
49 Ministère des Affaires Étrangères, 241. Document 241: Patenôtre to Freycinet, Apr. 11, 1885.
50 Ministère des Affaires Étrangères, 323. Document 313: Freycinet to Collin de Plancy (Shanghai), Aug. 18, 1885. Paul Neïss appears as "Neis" in most French sources, however his obituary identifies him as "Neïss."
51 Rankin, "'Public Opinion' and Political Power," 473.
52 Ibid., 466.
53 Zhao, ed., *Qing shi gao*, 442:229. "彼將自救不暇, 策之上也. 分兵為守, 敵至則戰, 敵退不追, 老師糜餉, 利害共之, 策之中也. ..不取言戰, 則其禍不勝言矣, 是謂無策."
54 Ministère des Affaires Étrangères, Document 316: Freycinet to Cogordan (Shanghai), Oct. 26, 1885.
55 Ministère des Affaires Étrangères, 326. Document 319: Cogordan to Freycinet, Nov. 16, 1885.
56 Ministère des Affaires Étrangères, 327–28. Document 320: Freycinet to Cogordan, Nov. 17, 1885.
57 Ministère des Affaires Étrangères, 329–30. Document 323: Saint-Chaffray to Freycinet, Dec. 6, 1885.
58 Salemink, *The Ethnography of Vietnam's Central Highlanders*, 59–60.
59 Neïss, *The Sino-Vietnamese Border Demarcation*, 10, 24.
60 Ibid., 30.
61 Ibid., 39.
62 Ibid., 32–33.
63 Ibid., 33–36. Benjamin ("Benedict") Balansa worked as a botanist in Morocco and Algeria prior to coming to Tonkin after the Tianjin Treaty took effect. Born in 1825 in Narbonne, he passed away in Hanoi in 1892. Gaston, *La vie de Benjamin Balansa*.
64 Neïss, *The Sino-Vietnamese Border Demarcation*, 28.
65 Ibid., 89; NLVN. SC, 12246, "Notice de Lao Kay" (1911), 3.
66 "Notice de Lao Kay," 3.
67 Neïss, *The Sino-Vietnamese Border Demarcation*, 89.
68 Ibid., 90.
69 Ibid., 92. Liu Yongfu actually retreated through Tuyên Quang, not Lào Cai. These acts of destruction may have taken place in 1885, but not by Liu Yongfu.
70 Ibid., 114.

71 "Notice de Lao Kay," 5.

72 Xiao and Huang, ed., *Zhong Yue bianjie lishi ziliao xuanbian*, 2:701–3. Bourcier's clarifications of the Lạng Sơn-Guangxi border, Dec. 24, 1885.

73 Xiao and Huang, *Zhong Yue bianjie lishi ziliao xuanbian*, 2:734. Neïss to Hanoi, May 8, 1886. These were Naliu, Nawo, Nahu, and Naxian.

74 Xiao and Huang, *Zhong Yue bianjie lishi ziliao xuanbian*, 2:734.

75 Ibid.

76 Ngô, Nguyễn, and Papin, *Đồng Khánh Địa Dư Chí*, 18b–19a.

77 Ibid., 19b–20b.

78 Zhongguo Diyi Lishi Dang'an Guan, *Guangxu chao zhupi zouzhe*, 12:592. Yunnan Governor Tan Junpei (concurrently Yun-Gui Governor-General) to Court, 29/12/GX15.

79 Xiong Chunyun, "Qing mo Gui Xi nan diqu de yimin shibian," 85–86.

80 Xiao and Huang, *Zhong Yue bianjie lishi ziliao xuanbian*, DCSL 212:54. Yun-Gui Governor-General Cen Yuying to Grand Council, July 15, 1885.

81 For more on Đèo Văn Trì, see Le Failler, *La Rivière Noire*.

82 Zhongguo Diyi Lishi Dang'an Guan, 12:592. Yunnan Governor Tan Junpei (concurrently Yun-Gui Governor-General), 29/12/GX15.

83 *Dao* is the standard Chinese reading of 刀 ("knife"). In the PRC source cited in note 84, the family is referred to with this name. However, in Qing administrative paperwork, the family in Muäng La is identified as 刁, which has the Sino-Vietnamese reading of Đèo (C: Diao). While terms such as Đèo were frequently used to approximate Tai words for proper names, they also carried a somewhat derogatory meaning. A relationship between the Dao family of Muäng La and the Đèo of Lai Châu is certainly possible, but the available evidence does not seem to suggest it. For the purpose of clarity, I use Dao for the Muäng La family, although readers should be aware of the complex administrative etymology of Tai names in China and Vietnam.

84 Gong, *Zhongguo tusi zhidu*, 514–15.

85 Zhongguo Diyi Lishi Dang'an Guan, 12:592. Tan Junpei to Court, 29/12/GX15.

86 Ibid. Cen Yuying's report is cited by Tan Junpei. Cen Yuying died in June 1889, so this report must have come before the summer of 1889.

87 Ibid.

88 Writing in 1962, two historians in the DRV claimed that Cen Yuying (Sâm Dục Ảnh) attempted to abduct several young women from uplands communities as he led the Black Flags back into China, but was prevented from doing so by Liu Yongfu. See Chương and Minh, "Lưu Vĩnh Phúc trong cuộc kháng Pháp của nhân dân Việt-Nam," 27. See also Davis, "States of Banditry," 208–86, 345–61.

89 Qian, ed., *Qingdai zhiguan nianbiao*, 1491.

90 Zhongguo Diyi Lishi Dang'an Guan, 112.594. Yun-Gui Governor-General Wang Wenzhao and Yunnan Governor Tan Junpei to Court, 2/5/GX16.

91 Ibid. 越南黑旗頭目.

92 Ibid; Yunnan Sheng Lishi Yanjiu Suo, ed., DCSL 286:9–10. Wang Wenzhao to Grand Council, July 31, 1890.

93 Zhongguo Diyi Lishi Dang'an Guan, 112:593. Wang Wenzhao and Tan Junpei to Court, 16/5/GX16.

94 Ibid.

95 Zhongguo Diyi Lishi Dang'an Guan, 112:595. Wang Wenzhao and Tan Junpei to Court, 16/5/GX16.

96 NAVN. RST, 76310. "Renseignements sur les actes de rebellions contre l'administration du protectorat dans la province de Son Tay 1884–1891." Extrait d'un rapport de Monsieur le Chef de Bataillon Fouquet, vice-résident militaire à Sơn La, Aug. 15, 1890.

97 Ibid.

98 NAVN. RST, 76310. "Renseignements sur les actes de rebellions contre l'administration du protectorat dans la province de Son Tay 1884–1891." Fouquet à Chef de Cabinet pour les Troupes de l'Indo-Chine, Sep. 2, 1890.

99 Ibid.

100 Khổng and Nguyễn, eds., *Khởi nghĩa Yên Thế*, 118, 249; Gallieni, *Gallieni au Tonkin*, 20–21.

101 Yunnan Sheng Lishi Yanjiu Suo, ed., DCSL 287:12–13. Wang Wenzhao to Grand Council, Sep. 4, 1890.

102 Barthes, "African Grammar," from *The Eiffel Tower and Other Mythologies*, 103.

103 See Marr, *Vietnamese Anticolonialism*, 122; Vinh and Wickenden, trans., *Overturned Chariot*.

104 Neïss, *The Sino-Vietnamese Border Demarcation*, 9–10.

105 Guha, *Elementary Aspects of Peasant Insurgency in India*.

106 Munier, *Le Cai Kinh*, 17.

107 Ibid; Đặng, "Cuộc kháng chiến thực dân Pháp xâm lược của nghĩa quân Hoàng Đình Kinh," 11–18.

108 Ngô, Nguyễn, and Papin, *Đồng Khánh địa dư chí*, 114b.

109 Ibid., 112a. 未經設置.

110 Neïss, *The Sino-Vietnamese Border Demarcation*, 9.

111 Xiao and Huang, *Zhong Yue bianjie lishi ziliao xuanbian*, 2:740. Neïss to Hanoi, 5/8/1886.

112 Brocheux and Hémery echo Galliéni's charge that Lưu Kỳ subsisted on illicit commerce and human trafficking. *Indochine: La colonisation ambigüe*, 59. Despite descriptions of Lưu Kỳ as the leader of a righteous uprising (*khởi nghĩa*), these allegations likely had some merit. For a more optimistic and more informative study of Lưu Kỳ, see the chapter on the Lục Ngạn Uprising in Khổng and Nguyễn, *Khởi nghĩa Yên Thế*, 97–102. Also Đặng, "Đề đốc Lưu Kỳ và những hoạt động chống Pháp của ông ở vùng Đông Bắc Bắc Kỳ cuối thế kỷ XIX."

113 Khổng and Nguyễn, *Khởi nghĩa Yên Thế*, 98.

114 Ibid., 99.
115 Munier, *Le Cai Kinh*, 20.
116 Munier, *Le Cai Kinh*, 22. Paul Chack wrote that Hoàng Đình Kinh's own followers assassinated him in February 1890. Chack, *Hoang Tham: Pirate*, 15.
117 Khổng and Nguyễn, *Khởi nghĩa Yên Thế*, 101.
118 NAVN. RST, 76319. "Listes nominatives des rebelles operant dans les provinces du Tonkin en 1890–1891." Liu Qi [Lưu Kỳ] listed as active in Hải Ninh, Hải Dương, and Lạng Sơn.
119 Khổng and Nguyễn, *Khởi nghĩa Yên Thế*, 101.
120 Ibid., 102.
121 Ibid.
122 Galliéni, *Galliéni au Tonkin*, preface.
123 Ibid., viii.
124 Ibid., 7–9.
125 Ibid., 12–17.
126 Ibid., 20–21.
127 Ibid., 21; Khổng and Nguyễn, *Khởi nghĩa Yên Thế*, 118, 249.
128 Galliéni, *Galliéni au Tonkin*, 61.
129 Ibid., 62.
130 Ibid. Galliéni seemed to have never considered the possibility that the villagers anticipated attacks from anyone else, including the French military.
131 Văn-Quang, *Hoàng-Hoa-Thám*, 60–61. For this period, historians may have exaggerated Cần Vương connections as often as French administrators, albeit for very different reasons.
132 Galliéni, *Galliéni au Tonkin*, 23–53.
133 Xiao and Cai, *Su Yuanchun pingzhuan*, 70–72.
134 The Yunnan-Guizhou governor-general noted the problem of mobile upland bandits in June 1894, while the Guangxi governor expressed his concerns to the Grand Council about the frailty of border security in December. Yunnan Sheng Lishi Yanjiu Suo, ed., DCSL 340:12. Wang Wenzhao to Grand Council, June 16, 1894; DCSL 353:14. Zhang Liangui to Grand Council, June 16, 1894.
135 Galliéni, *Galliéni au Tonkin*, 127–40.
136 Ibid., 142. These were "Sahot" (abducted) and "Hirlet" (killed).
137 Ibid., 143.
138 Ibid., 144; Taboulet, *La geste française*, 896–99. Other references to "La Méthode Galliéni" include Lyautey, *Lettres du Tonkin et de Madagascar*.
139 Fourniau, *Domination coloniale et résistance nationale*, 469.
140 Franquet, *De l'importance du Fleuve Rouge*, 53.
141 Ibid. The Cercle of Lao Kay contained 40,000 inhabitants, a low figure attributed by Franquet to the bandit groups and wars of the nineteenth century. He envisioned the role of the protectorate in Lào Cai as restorative, returning the area to its former splendor, renovating and repopulating the area. Franquet, *De l'importance du Fleuve Rouge*, 60–61.

142 Franquet, *De l'importance du Fleuve Rouge*, 53. Full figures: 1890: 5,176,859; 1891: 7,649,643; 1892: 10, 226,233; 1893: 11, 289,128; 1894: 10, 868,607; 1895: 13,089,899.

143 Ibid., 55.

144 Ibid., 33–35.

145 Ibid.

146 NAVN. RST, 1540. "Notice sur le secteur de Bao Ha (Yen Bay) 1898," 70. "Les chinois employés entre Bao Ha et Pho Lu sont anciens pirates." Bảo Hà became a *cercle* in 1896, consisting of Văn Bàn and Chiếu Tân. Franquet, *De l'importance du Fleuve Rouge*, 59.

147 For an explanation of this trope, see Duiker, *Sacred War*.

148 Hội Đồng Lịch Sử Hà Bắc, *Lịch sử Hà Bắc*, 183–86.

149 UBND tỉnh Lạng Sơn decision #41/2002/QĐUB, Oct. 2, 2002.

150 Epigraph: YNPA. 106.3.1504. Li Hongzhang to Zongli Yamen (copied to Yunnan provincial government), Dec. 1, 1888.

151 Pang, *Qinzhou shi zhi*, 19.

152 YNPA. 106.3.1504. Li Hongzhang to Zongli Yamen (copied to Yunnan provincial government), Dec. 1, 1888. 1B-5A. 北圻.

153 YNPA. 106.3.1504. Communication sent by French official identified as "法國李使" to Zongli Yamen, July 15, 1889.

154 Ibid.

155 Thévenot, *Ernest Millot*, 24–28. This audience was arranged by Nguyễn Hữu Độ.

156 Thévenot, *Ernest Millot*, 28; Duclos, "Ernest Millot," in *Des photographes en Indochine*, ed. Franchini and Ghesquière, 230.

157 Duclos, "Ernest Millot," 230.

158 Ban Chấp Hành Huyện Uỷ Định Hóa, *Lịch sử Đảng bộ huyện Định Hóa*, 18–19; Brocheux and Hémery, *Indochine*, 63.

159 Échinard, *Histoire politique et militaire*, 66–67.

160 Ibid; CAOM. RST, 56189. "Soumission de Luong Tam Ky/convention de soumission originaire 1890–1893." According to Échinard, the wounding of a French officer by Liang's followers prompted Liang to formally offer surrender in 1890. His surrender came after four years of unsuccessful French efforts to defeat Liang militarily.

161 CAOM. RST, 56189. "Soumission de Luong Tam Ky/convention de soumission originaire 1890–1893."

162 Ibid.

163 Ibid. The terms of surrender are recorded in two languages: French and Chinese. In the Chinese text of the agreement, Liang is a Qingren (清人) and a Qingke (清客), whereas in the French text he is *chinois*. Despite the requests of the Huế court representative, Liang Sanqi received a title that did not formally integrate him into the Nguyễn bureaucracy. He signed the surrender agreement with the title "Qing Militia Subcommander" (清團副領) .

164 CAOM. RST, 56221. "Actes de brigandage (11 Mars 1896)." Résident Thai Nguyen (Destenay) to Sec General.

165 NAVN. RST, 76346. "Organisation des colonnes de police dans des provinces de Tonkin (1891)." Vice-résident of Tuyen Quang to RST, affaires indigenes no. 3167, Apr. 1, 1891, 143b.

166 CAOM. RST, 56199. "Rapport de Orny, Résident de France à Thai Nguyen sur Luong Tam Ky, 1891." Orny to RST, Mar. 3, 1891, 1–4.

167 CAOM. RST, 56220. "Attaques des villages (1896)." Tri Châu Bạch Thống to Monsieur le Commandant de Cercle de Chợ Mới, Dec 8, 1895; Dec 13, 1895.

168 CAOM. RST, 56220. "Attaques des villages (1896)." Gallieni to tri châu Bạch Thống, Dec. 20, 1895.

169 NAVN. RST, 13853. "Arrestation des Chinois à Bac Giang 1904/1907." Télégramme officiel Résident Thai Nguyen à RST no. 88, Aug. 8, 1907.

170 NAVN. RST, 13853. "Arrestation des Chinois à Bac Giang 1904/1907." Résident de Thai Nguyen à RST, Aug. 21, 1907.

171 Ibid.

172 Ibid.

173 Ibid.

174 Ibid.

175 On Liang's helpfulness before the death of Đề Thám, see Maliverney, *L'homme du jour*, 159–60. On his probable role in Đề Thám's murder, historians offer a range of interpretations. Both Đinh Xuân Lâm (*Hoàng Hoa Thám và phong trào nông dân Yên-Thế*) and Nguyễn Văn Kiệm (*Phong trào nông dân Yên Thế chống thực dân Pháp xâm lược*) claim that Liang ordered his followers to kill Đề Thám. Văn-Quang, however, believed that Liang's involvement was only speculation (*Hoàng-Hoa-Thám*). Paul Chack (*Hoang-Tham: Pirate*) published an interview with Liang by a French journalist identified as Bosc (Chack, *Hoang Tham*, 252–56) that offered no clarification.

176 Échinard, *Histoire politique et militaire*, 241.

177 Pang, *Qinzhou shi zhi*, 21; Qinzhou Xianzhi Bangongshi, ed., *Qinzhou lishi mingren zhuanluo xuanbian*, 27–28. In the Qing period, "San Na" referred to three adjacent places along the area between western Guangdong and eastern Guangxi: Nali 那麗, Napeng 那彭, and Nasi 那思.

178 Qinzhou Xianzhi Bangongshi, *Qinzhou lishi*, 27.

179 Liao, ed., *Qinzhou Wenshi (4)*, 97.

180 Qinzhou Xianzhi Bangongshi, *Qinzhou lishi*, 29–30.

181 Ibid. Huang reportedly fled south to Tonkin and organized an armed group under the "Eight Brothers" moniker, although I have not been able to verify this claim.

182 Ibid.

183 Beasley, *Japanese Imperialism*, 60–61; Kerr, *Formosa*, 13–16.

184 Kerr, *Formosa*, 13–16. For an excellent discussion of the historiography of this period in Taiwan's history, see Katz, *When Valleys turned Blood Red*, 1–62.

185 Marr, *Vietnamese Anticolonialism*, 130.

186 Phan, *Chân Tướng Quân, Tái Sinh Sinh.*

187 Chương, *Phan Bội Châu*; Phan, *Chân Tướng Quân, Tái Sinh Sinh*, 20.

188 Phan Boi Chau states his lament over Viet Nam in *The Loss of Vietnam* (越南亡國史, Việt Nam Vọng Quốc Sử), a text that circulated widely among nationalist-minded intellectuals, including Liang Qichao.

189 Vinh and Wickenden, *Overturned Chariot*, 93. Also Phan, *Niên Biểu*, 5.

190 Vinh and Wickenden, *Overturned Chariot*, 104–5.

191 For more about Japanese support for Vietnamese anticolonialism in particular, see Tran, "Japan through Vietnamese Eyes." On the Đông Du, see Vinh, ed., *Phan Bội Châu and the Dông-Du Movement* and Nguyễn, ed., *Phong trào Đông Du và Phan Bội Châu.*

192 Marr, ed., *Reflections from Captivity*, 28. Phan Bội Châu was arrested in 1913 in a cooperative effort by French colonial authorities and the Guangdong officialdom to round up anticolonialists opposed to French rule in Indochina.

193 Qinzhou Xianzhi Bangongshi, 28. 廣東民團總張 (Guangdong Mintuan Congzhang).

194 Ibid. Jeffrey Barlow explored the relationship between Sun Yatsen's political ambitions and the bandit networks in the borderlands in the twentieth century. Barlow, *Sun Yat-sen and the French.*

195 三宣提督.

196 De Pouvourville, *Chasseur de Pirates!*, 52–53.

197 Ibid.

CONCLUSION

1 Trần Văn Giàu, *Chống xâm lăng*, 1:187; Nguyễn Khắc Viện, *The Long Resistance*, 27. The most recent revision of *The Long Resistance* omits any mention of the Black Flag's role in the defeat of Garnier (1873) and Rivière (1883). See Nguyễn Khắc Viện, *Việt Nam: A Long* History, 144–45; Trần Văn Giáp, *Lưu Vĩnh Phúc.*

2 Nguyễn Văn Hồng produced an unpublished manuscript in the 1960s that corrected this misconception. The historian Đặng Huy Vận described an earlier study of Liu Yongfu by Ché Thuyết (*Chiến mưu của Lưu Vĩnh Phúc*).

3 Trần Văn Giáp, *Lưu Vĩnh Phúc*, 5.

4 Ibid., 75–76.

5 Pelley, *Postcolonial Vietnam*, 26.

6 Đinh and Trương, eds., *Từ điển nhân vật lịch sử Việt Nam*, 588–89. Entry for Văn Tân, the pen name of Trần Đức Sắc (1913–1988).

7 Văn Tân, "Lưu Vĩnh Phúc Tướng Cờ Đen và các hành Động của ông ở Việt Nam," 7–8, 12.

8 Ibid., 13–14.

9 Ibid., 14.

10 Conversation with vice head of office at the Thái Nguyên Department of Cultural Information, October 2005.

11 Văn Tân, "Lưu Vĩnh Phúc Tướng Cờ Đen và các hành động của ông ở Việt Nam," 15.

12 Chương and Minh, "Lưu Vĩnh Phúc trong cuộc kháng Pháp của nhân dân Việt-Nam," 14.

13 Đặng, "Ý kiến trao đổi," 16; Đinh, "Ý kiến trao đổi đánh giá Lưu Vĩnh Phúc cần thấy mặt tích cực là chủ yếu," 52; also Tô, "Ý kiến trao đổi," 34; "Những nhận định khác nhau về vai trò của Lưu Vĩnh Phúc và Quân Cờ Đen."

14 Quoted in "Những nhận định khác nhau về vai trò của Lưu Vĩnh Phúc và Quân Cờ Đen."

15 Trương-Bá-Phát, "Bọn Cờ Đen hạ sát Francis Garnier."

16 Taylor, "Surface Orientations in Vietnam." Also Taylor, "China and Vietnam," in *The Vietnam War*, ed. Werner and Luu, 271–86.

17 Li, *Liu Yongfu zhuan*.

18 Li, "Liu Yongfu liejian Heiqi Jun," in *Qinzhou wenshi*, ed. Guangxi Qinzhou Shizheng Bian Wenshi Ziliao He Xuexi Weiyuan Hui, 10.

19 Alley, *Refugees from Viet Nam in China*; Brady, *Friend of China*.

20 Alley, *Refugees from Viet Nam in China*, 16–17.

21 Ibid.

22 Tretiak, "China's Vietnam War and Its Consequences." More recently, Young, *The Vietnam Wars*, 305–12. Maurice Meisner has written that Wei Jingsheng, one of the leaders of the Democracy Movement of the late 1970s in the PRC, was officially charged with passing on state secrets to Vietnam as punishment for his opposition to, among other things, the PRC invasion. Meisner, *The Deng Xiaoping Era*, 109–18.

23 Duiker, *Vietnam Since the Fall of Saigon*, 187–88. Duiker notes that the Chinese military maintained a reserve force of 120,000; also Tretiak, "China's Vietnam War."

24 Guangxi Shehui Kexue Yuan Indu-Zhina Yanjiu Suo, ed., *Zhong Yue guanxi shi dashi ji*.

25 Ma Honglin, "Ping Qing zhengfu dui Liu Yongfu de baoquan zheng'an," in *Zhong Fa zhanzheng lunwen ji*, ed. Zhong Fa zhanzheng shi yanjiu hui, 2:217–30.

26 Guo Weiyong, "Ye lun Heiqi Jun zai Zhong Fa zhanzheng zhong de diwei he zuoyong," in *Zhong Fa zhanzheng lunwen ji*, ed. Zhong Fa zhanzheng shi yanjiu hui, 2:231–39.

27 Yuan Shiqi, "Shilun Yuenan Lu Qunwei (La Xuân Uy) zai Zhong Fa zhenzheng zhong de gongxian," in *Zhong Fa zhanzheng lunwen ji*, ed. Zhong Fa zhanzheng shi yanjiu hui, 2:338–49; Zhang Maolin, "Liu Yongfu li Yue guiguo zhi xinli," in *Zhong Fa zhanzheng lunwen ji*, ed. Zhong Fa Zhanzheng Shi Yanjiu Hui, 4:221–28.

28 Mitter, "Behind the Scenes at the Museum;" Dirlik, "Past experience," in *Japan and the World*, ed. Miyoshi and Harootunian, 47–78.

29 Faure, "The *Tusi* That Never Was," in *Empire at the Margins*, ed. Crossley, Siu, and Sutton, 171–89.

GLOSSARY

All main entries are Vietnamese unless labeled otherwise.

ABBREVIATIONS

(C) Chinese
(H) Hakka
(Ma) Manchu
(M) Mien
(T) Tai
(V) Vietnamese
(Y) Yunnanese

An Nam Bắc Ninh Thượng Khách 安南北寧商客
An Nam Đông Kinh Thượng Khách 安南東京商客
án sát 按查
Ande (C) 安德

bá 霸
Bắc Ninh 北寧
Bàn Văn Nhị 盤文義 Pan Wenyi (C)
Bảo Hà 保河
Bảo Thắng 保勝
Beijing (C) 北京
Bùi Văn Dị 裴文禩

Cần Vương 勤王
Cao Bằng 高平
Cầu Giấy 紙橋
Cen Yuying (C) 岑毓英 Sâm Dục Anh (V)
chao (T) 主 chủ (V), zhu (C)

Chu Tường Lân 周祥麟
Chunqiu (C) 春秋 Xuân Thu (V)
cử nhân 舉人
Cứ Pháp Sứ Khẩn Thỉnh 據法使懇請
Cửa Cấm 𨷯禁

Đan Phượng 丹鳳
dân tộc 民族
Đặng Huy Xán 鄧輝燦
Đặng Xuân Bảng 鄧春榜
đạo 道
Deng Chengxiu (C) 鄧承修
Deng Wan (C) 鄧晚 Đặng Vãn (V)
Đèo Vân Trì 刁文智
Điện Biên 奠邊 Muäng Then (T)
Diguozhuyi (C) 帝国主义
Đồ Sơn 頭山
Đốc Ngữ 督語
Đồng Khánh 同慶
Dongmeng (C) 東夢
Du Wenxiu (C) 杜文秀
Duanling (C) 端麟
đức chính 德政 dezheng (C)

fangui (C) 番鬼
Feng Zicai (C) 馮子才 Phùng Tử Tài (V)
Fujian (C) 福建

gaitu guiliu (C) 改土歸流
Gia Long 嘉龍
giặc 賊 zei (C)
Giặc Ngô 賊吳
giáo thụ 教授
Giáp Tuất 甲戌
Guangdong (C) 廣東
Guangxi (C) 廣西
guanhua (C) 官話
Guishun (C) 歸順

Hà Giang or Hà Dương 河陽
Hà Nội 河內
Hải Dương 海陽
Hải Phòng 海防

Hakka (H) 客家 Kejia (C), Khách Gia or (Khách) Họ (V)
Hàm Nghi 咸宜
Hán 漢
Hankou (C) 漢口
He Junchang (C) 何均昌 Hồ Quân Xương (V)
Hekou (C) 河口 Hà Khẩu (V)
hóa 化
Hồ Trọng Đĩnh 胡仲珽
Hoàng Diệu 黃耀
Hoàng Đình Kinh 黃廷經
Hoàng Kế Viêm 黃繼炎
Hoàng Sùng Anh 黃崇英 Huang Chongying (C)
Hoàng Tướng Hiệp 黃相協
Hồi 回 Hui (C)
Hồng Lô Tự Khanh 鴻臚寺卿
Huang Shengli (C) 黃勝利 Hoàng Thắng Lợi (V)
Huang Shenglu (C) 黃勝侶 Hoàng Thắng Lữ (V)
Huang Shouzhong (C) 黃守忠
Huaren (C) 華人 Hoa nhân (V)
Hubei (C) 湖北
Huế 順化
Hưng Hóa 興化
Hưng Yên 興安

Kaihua (C) 開化
khởi nghĩa 起義 qiyi (C)
Kiều Oánh Mậu 喬瑩懋
Kinh 京
Kinh Lược Sứ 經略使

Lai Châu 萊州 Muăng Lay (T)
lặng 兩
Lạng Sơn 諒山
Lào Cai 老街 Lao Gai (Y)
Lê Hữu Thường 黎有常
Lê Tuấn 黎峻
Li Hongzhang (C) 李鴻章
Li Yangcai (C) 李揚才
Li Yuchi (C) 李玉墀
Liang Sanqi (C) 梁三岐 Lương Tam Kỳ (V)
Liang Tianxi (C) 梁天錫 Lường Thiên Tích (V)
Liu Yongfu (C) 劉永福 or 刘永富 Lưu Vĩnh Phúc (V)
Liu Zhiping (C) 陸之平 Lục Chi Bình (V)

Long Lộ 龍魯
Longzhou (C) 龍州
Lương Văn Lợi 梁文利 Liang Wenli (C)
lý trưởng 里長

Ma Rulong (C) 馬如龍
Man 蠻
Mengla (C) 猛剌 Mường La (V), Muăng La (T)
Mengzi (C) 蒙自
Miao (C) 苗 or 貓 Miêu or Mèo (V)
Minh Mạng or Minh Mệnh 明命
Minzu Yingxiong (C) 民族英雄
muăng (T) 猛or 芒 meng or mang (C), mường (V)
mục 目

Nam Định 南定
nanmin (C) 難民 nạn dân (V)
nghịch 逆 ni (C)
Ngụy Danh Cao 魏名高
Ngụy Khắc Tuần 魏克循
Ngụy Thuận Chủ 魏順主 Wei Shunzhu (C)
Nguyễn Bá Nghi 阮伯義
Nguyễn Cao 阮高
Nguyễn Đình Nhuận 阮廷潤
Nguyễn Hữu Độ 阮有度
Nguyễn Huy Trạc 阮輝濯
Nguyễn Kim Thọ 阮金壽
Nguyễn Quang Bích 阮光碧
Nguyễn Thiện Thuật 阮善述
Nguyễn Tri Phương 阮知方
Nguyễn Trọng Hiệp 阮仲協
Nguyễn Văn Bân 阮文彬
Nguyễn Văn Giáp 阮文甲
Nguyễn Văn Tường 阮文祥
Nguyễn Văn Vỹ 阮文偉
Ninh Bình 寧平
Nông Hùng Nghĩa 儂雄義
Nong Xiuye (C) 農秀業 Nông Tú Nghiệp (V)

Ông Ích Khiêm 翁益謙
Ông Thất 翁七
Ortai (Ma) 歐爾泰

Pan Lunsi (C) 盤輪四 Bàn Luận Tư (V)
Phạm Chi Hương 范芝香
Phạm Phú Thứ 范富恕
Phạm Thận Duật 范慎遹
Phan Bội Châu 番佩珠
Phan Đình Bình 潘廷評
Phan Thanh Giản 潘清簡
Phát Diệm 發艷
phỉ 匪 fei(C)
Phi Long 飛龍
phó bảng 副榜
Phó Lãnh Binh 副領兵 Fulingbing (C)
Phù Diễn 扶演
Pingxiang (C) 憑祥

Qing tuan fuling (C) 清團副領 Thanh Đoàn Phó Lãnh (V)
Qing Yi (C) 清議 Thanh Nghị (V)
Qingke (C) 清客 Thanh khách (V)
Qingren 清人 Thanh Nhân (V)
Qinzhou (C) 欽州 Khâm Châu (V)
qiyi di (C) 起義地 or 起义地
quan 貫
Quảng Yên 廣安

San Na (C) 三那
Shanghai (C) 上海
Shenbao (C) 申報
Sơn La 山喇 Muăng La (T)
Sơn Tây 山西
Su Fengwen (C) 蘇風文
Su Yuanchun (C) 蘇元春

Tai (T) 抬 Dai (C), Thái (V)
Taiping (C) 太平
Taiwan (C) 台灣
Tam Đảo 三島
Tam Tuyên Đề Đốc 三宣提督
Tân Sở 新所
Tang (C) 唐 Đường (V)
Tang Jingsong (C) 唐景崧
Tang Jiong (C) 唐炯
Tang Weibo (C) 唐微博
Thái Nguyên 太原

Thập Châu 十州 Sip Chao (T)
Thất Khê 七雞
Thổ 土
Thuận An 順安
Thực Lục 實錄 Shilu (C)
Thủy Vĩ 水尾
Tianbao (C) 天保
Tianjin (C) 天津 Thiên Tấn (V)
Tôn Thất Thuyết 尊室說
Tự Đức 嗣德
Tụ Long 聚龍
tufei (C) 土匪 thổ phỉ (V)
tusi (C) 土司 thổ ty (V)
tuyao (C) 土藥
Tuyên Quang 宣光

Việt 越
Vũ Trọng Bình 武仲平

Wang Yangming (C) 王陽明 Vương Dương Minh (V)
Wu Fengdian (C) 吳鳳典 Ngô Phương Điển (V)
Wu Lingyun (C) 吳淩雲 Ngô Lăng Vân (V)
Wu Yazhong (C) 吳亞終 Ngô Á Chung (V)
Wu Zhuyuan (C) 吳朱元 Ngô Chu Nguyên (V)

Xiao Zhangsan (C) 小張三
Xu Yanxu (C) 徐延旭

Yang Zhongya (C) 楊重雅
yangyao (C) 洋藥
Yanling (C) 延陵
Yao (C, M) 猺 or 瑤 Dao (V)
Yên Lễ or An Lễ 安禮 Anli (C)
Yên Thế 安世
Yongzheng (C) 雍正
Yunnan (C) 雲南

Zhang Shusheng (C) 張樹聲
Zhennan (C) 鎮南
Zhonghua Minzu zhi qi (C) 中华民族志气
Zhou Derun (C) 周德潤
Zhuang (C) 壯 or 獞

BIBLIOGRAPHY

ABBREVIATIONS

AGC	Amiraux et Gouverneurs de la Cochinchine
BAVH	*Bulletin des Amis de Vieux Huë*
CAOM	Centre des Archives d'Outre Mer, Aix-en-Provence, France
CBTN	Châu Bản Triều Nguyễn
DCSL	Dechong Shilu
JAS	*Journal of Asian Studies*
JSEAS	*Journal of Southeast Asian Studies*
NAVN	First National Archives, Hanoi, Vietnam
NCLS	*Nghiên Cứu Lịch Sử* (Historical Research)
NLVN. SC	Vietnam National Library Special Collection, Hanoi, Vietnam.
MEP	Archives de la Société des Missions Étrangères de Paris, France
RLK	Résident de Lao Kay
RND	Résident de Nam Dinh
RST	Résident Supérieur du Tonkin
TZSL	Tongzhi Shilu
VHN	Han-Nom Institute, Hanoi, Vietnam
YPA	Yunnan Provincial Archives, Kunming, PRC

Agamben, Giorgio. *Potentialities: Collected Essays in Philosophy*. Translated by Daniel Heller-Roazen. Stanford: Stanford University Press, 1999.

Ageron, Charles-Robert. "Jules Ferry et la colonisation." In *Jules Ferry: Fondateur de la Republique*, edited by François Furet, 191–206. Paris: École des Hautes Études en Sciences Sociales, 1985.

Akerman, James R. ed. *The Imperial Map: Cartography and the Mastery of Empire*. Chicago: University of Chicago Press, 2009.

Alley, Rewi. *Refugees from Viet Nam in China*. Beijing: New World Press, 1980.

Amin, Shahid. *Event, Metaphor, Memory: Chauri Chaura, 1922–1992*. Berkeley: University of California Press, 1995.

Anderson, James. *The Rebel Den of Nùng Trí Cao: Loyalty and Identity Along the Sino-Vietnamese Frontier.* Seattle: University of Washington Press, 2007.

Anthony, Robert J. "Peasants, Heroes, and Brigands: The Problems of Social Banditry in Early Nineteenth Century South China." *Modern China* 15, no. 2 (April 1989): 123–48.

Armangaud, Jean-Louis. *Lang-Son: Journal des opérations qui ont précédé et suivi la Prise de cette Citadelle.* Paris: Librairie Militaire R. Chapelot et Cie, 1901.

Atwill, David. "Blinkered Visions: Islamic Identity, Hui Ethnicity, and the Panthay Rebellion in Southwest China, 1856–1873." *JAS* 62, no. 4 (November 2003): 1079–108.

———. *The Chinese Sultanate: Islam, Ethnicity, and the Panthay Rebellion in Southwest China, 1856–1873*. Stanford: Stanford University Press, 2005.

Aumoitte, A. *De Hanoi à la frontière du Kouang-Si (Provinces de Bac-Ninh et Lang-Son).* Paris: Andriveau-Goujon, 1884.

Baark, Erik. *Lightning Wires: The Telegraph and China's Technological Modernization, 1860–1890.* Westport, CT: Greenwood Press, 1997.

Bankoff, Greg. "Bandits, Banditry and Landscapes of Crime in the Nineteenth-Century Philippines." *JSEAS* 29, no. 2 (September 1998): 319–39.

Barkey, Karen. *Bandit and Bureaucrats: The Ottoman Route to State Centralization.* Ithaca: Cornell University Press, 1996.

Barlow, Jeffrey. *Sun Yat-sen and the French, 1900–1908.* Berkeley: University of California Press, 1979.

Barthes, Roland. *The Eiffel Tower and Other Mythologies.* Translated by Richard Howard. Berkeley: University of California Press, 1979.

Bế Viết Đẳng, Nguyễn Khắc Tụng, Nông Trung, and Nguyễn Nam Tiến. *Người Dao ở Việt Nam* (The Yao people in Vietnam). Hà Nội: Nhà Xuất Bản Khoa Học Xã Hội, 1971.

Beasley, W. G. *Japanese Imperialism, 1894–1945.* Oxford: Oxford University Press, 1987.

Bello, David. "The Venomous Course of Southwestern Opium: Qing Prohibition in Yunnan, Sichuan, and Guizhou in the Early Nineteenth Century." *JAS* 62, no. 4 (November 2003): 1115.

Benjamin, Walter. *Reflections.* Translated by Edmund Jephcott. New York: Schocken Books, 1978.

Betts, Raymond F. *Assimilation and Association in French Colonial Theory.* Omaha: University of Nebraska Press, 2005.

Bibliothéque Coloniale Internationale. *Le régime des protectorates: Tome I.* Brussels: Adolphe Mertens, 1899.

Bickers, Robert. "Shanghailanders: The Formation and Identity of the British Settler Community in Shanghai, 1843–1937." *Past and Present* 159 (May 1998): 161–211.

Billot, Albert. *L'affaire du Tonkin: Histoire diplomatique de l'etablissement de notre protectorat sur l'Annam et de notre conflit avec la Chine, 1882–1885*. Paris: J. Hetzel, 1888.

Blok, Anton. *Honour and Violence*. Cambridge, UK: Polity Press, 2001.
———. *The Mafia of a Sicilian Village, 1860–1960: An Anthropological Study of Political Middlemen*. Amsterdam: Universiteit van Amsterdam, 1972.
Bonifacy, Auguste. *Le canton de Tu-Long et la frontière Sino-Tonkinoise*. Hanoi: Imprimerie d'Extrême-Orient. 1924.
Bouchet, Émile. "Rapport fait au nom de la 2ème Commission des Pétitions sur la Pétition du Sieur Jean Dupuis, citoyen français demeurant à Han-Kow (Chine)." Chambre des Députés, No. 1519 (Session de 1879). *Annexe au procès-verbal de la séance du 14 juin 1879*. Versailles: Imprimeurs de la Chambre des Députés, 1879.
Brady, Anne-Marie. *Friend of China: The Myth of Rewi Alley*. London: Routledge-Curzon, 2003.
Braudel, Fernand. *The Mediterranean and the Mediterranean World in the Age of Philip II, Volume 2*. Translated by Sian Reynolds. New York: Harper Colophon Books, 1976.
Brocheux, Pierre, and Daniel Hémery. *Indochine: La colonisation ambigue, 1858–1954*. Paris: Éditions la Découverte, 1995.
Bùi-Tấn-Niên, ed. *Tự Đức thánh chế văn (quyển mục lục, quyển I đến VIII)* (Celebratory verse of the Tự Đức emperor). Saigon: Phủ Quốc-Vụ-Khanh Đặc-Trách Văn-Hóa, 1971.
Burel, Laurent. *Le contact protocolonial Franco-Vietnamien en centre et nord Vietnam, 1856–1883*. Paris: Seprentrion, 2003.
Cady, John. *The Roots of French Imperialism in Eastern Asia*. Ithaca: Cornell University Press, 1954.
Cahu, Théodore, ed. *L'Amiral Courbet en Extrême-Orient: Notes et correspondence*. Paris: L. Chailley, 1896.
Cai Guanluo 蔡冠洛. *Qing shi liezhaun* 清史列傳 (Qing biographies). Taibei: Qiming Shuju, 1965.
Cao Xuân Dục. *Đại Nam chính biên liệt truyện* (Notable biographies of Đại Nam). Hà Nội: Nhà Xuất Bản Văn Học, 2004.
Cen Yuying 岑毓英, ed. *Cen Xiangqin Gong zou gao* 岑襄勤宮奏稿 (Memorials of Cen Yuying). Taibei: Chengwen Chubanshe, 1969.
Chack, Paul. *Hoang Tham: Pirate*. Paris: Les Éditions de France, 1933.
Chailley-Bert, Joseph. *Paul Bert au Tonkin*. Paris: G. Charpentier, 1887.
Champagne, G. *Les Pavillons Noirs ou la Guerre du Tonkin*. Paris: Bourges, 1884.
Chapuis, Oscar. *The Last Emperors of Vietnam: From Tu Duc to Bao Dai*. Westport, CT: Greenwood Press, 2000.
Chen Jinghe [Ch'en Ching-ho] 陳荊和, ed. *Ruan Shu [Nguyễn Thuật] zhu Jin riji* 阮術住盡日記 (Nguyễn Thuật's Tianjin diary). Hong Kong: Zhongwen Daxue Chubanshe, 1980.
Chesneaux, Jean. *Peasant Revolt in China: 1840–1949*. Translated by C. A. Curwen. London: Thames and Hudson, 1973.
Choi Byung-Wook. *Southern Vietnam under the Reign of Minh Mạng (1820–1841):*

Central Policies and Local Response. Ithaca: Cornell University Southeast Asia Program, 2004.

Chu Thiên, Đặng Huy Vận, and Nguyễn Bỉnh Khôi, eds. *Thơ văn yêu nước nửa sau thế kỷ XIX, 1858–1900* (Patriotic poets of the late nineteenth century). Hà Nội: Nhà Xuất Bản Văn Học, 1976.

Chương Thâu. *Phan Bội Châu: Nhà yếu nước, nhà văn hóa lớn* (Phan Bội Châu: Patriot, Great Man of Culture). Vinh: Nhà Xuất Bản Nghệ An, 2005.

Chương Thâu and Minh Hông. "Lưu Vĩnh Phúc trong cuộc kháng Pháp của nhân dân Việt-Nam" (Liu Yongfu during the Vietnamese people's struggle against France). *NCLS* 36 (1962): 7–14, 27.

Colombijn, Freek. "The Volatile State in Southeast Asia: Evidence from Sumatra, 1600–1800." *JAS* 62, no. 2 (May 2003): 497–529.

Conklin, Alice. *A Mission to Civilize: The Republican Idea of Empire in France and West Africa, 1895–1930*. Stanford: Stanford University Press, 1997.

Cooke, James. *New French Imperialism 1880–1910: The Third Republic and Colonial Expansion*. Hamden, CT: Archon, 1973.

Coronil, Fernando, and Julie Skurski, eds. *States of Violence*. Ann Arbor: University of Michigan Press, 2006.

Crossley, Pamela Kyle, Helen F. Siu, and Donald S. Sutton, eds. *Empire at the Margins: Culture, Ethnicity, and Frontier in Early Modern China*. Berkeley: University of California Press, 2006

Cushman, Richard. "Rebel Haunts and Lotus Huts: Problems in the Ethnohistory of the Yao." PhD diss., Cornell University, 1970.

Da Qing lichao shilu 大清歷朝實錄 (Veritable records of the Qing empire). Xinjing: Da Manguo Diguo Guomou Yuan, 1937.[[In transliterated book titles and parenthetical translations, capitalized only the first word and subsequent proper nouns.]]

Đạng Huy Vận. "Cuộc kháng chiến thực dân Pháp xâm lược của nghĩa quân Hoàng Đình Kinh" (The anticolonial resistance of Hoàng Đình Kinh's righteous army). *NCLS* 81 (1965): 11–18.

———. "Để Đốc Lưu Kỳ và những hoạt động chống Pháp của ông ở vùng Đông Bắc Bắc Kỳ cuối thế kỷ XIX" (Commander Liu Qi and his anti-French activities in the northeast at the end of the nineteenth century). *NCLS* 134 (1970): 37–44.

———. "Thêm một số tài liệu về Đốc Ngữ và phong trào chống Pháp ở Vùng Hạ Lưu Sông Đà cuối thế kỷ XIX" (Additional material on Đốc Ngữ and the resistance to France in the lower reaches of the Black River at the end of the nineteenth century). *NCLS* 96 (1967): 45–46.

———. "Ý kiến trao đổi: Góp ý kiến nhỏ về vấn đề đánh giá Lưu Vĩnh Phúc và Đội Quân Cờ Đen trong lịch sử cận đại iệt-Nam" (An exchange of views: Some modest opinions on the evaluation of Liu Yongfu and the Black Flags in the modern history of Vietnam). *NCLS* 37 (1962): 15–25.

Đặng Phong. *Thăng Long-Hanoi: The Story in a Single Street*. Hà Nội: Knowledge Publishing House, 2010.

Đặng Xuân Bảng. *Province de Tuyen Quang: Composition littéraire de Dang Xuan Bang traduit et annoté par M. Le Colonel Bonifacy*. No date.
Đào Đăng Vỹ. *Nguyễn Tri Phương*. Saigon: Nhà Văn-Hóa Bộ Văn-Hóa Giáo-Dục và Thanh-Niên, 1974.
Đào Duy Anh. *Nhớ nghĩ chiều hôm* (Evening Musings). Thành Phố Hồ Chí Minh: Nhà Xuất Bản Trẻ, 1989.
Đào Trinh Nhất. *Phan Đình Phùng: Nhà lãnh đạo 10 năm kháng chiến (1886–1895) ở Nghệ Tĩnh* (Phan Đình Phùng: Leader of a decade-long resistance in Nghệ An and Hà Tĩnh). Vinh: Nhà Xuất Bản Nghệ An, 2007.
Davis, Bradley Camp. "Black Flag Rumors and the Black River Basin: Powerbrokers and the State in the Tonkin-China Borderlands." *Journal of Vietnamese Studies* 6, no. 2 (Summer 2011): 16–41.
———. "Rebellion and Rule under Consular Optics: Changing Ways of Seeing the China-Vietnam Borderlands, 1874–1879." *Cross-Currents: East Asian History and Culture Review* 3, no. 2 (November 2014): 379–412.
———. "States of Banditry: The Nguyen Government, Bandit Rule, and the Culture of Power in the Post-Taiping China-Vietnam Borderlands." PhD diss., University of Washington, 2008.
———. "A Yao Script Project: 'Culture,' Texts, and Literacy in Contemporary Vietnam." *International Institute for Asian Studies Newsletter* 56 (Spring 2011): 7–8.
de Belval, Challan. *Au Tonkin, 1884–1885: Notes, souvenirs et impressions.* Paris: Plon-Nourrif, 1904.
de Kergaradec, le Comte. "Rapport sur le reconnaisance du Fleuve Rouge du Tonkin." *Revue Maritime et Coloniale* (October 1877): 320–52.
de Lapparenet, A. "Notice Mécrologique sur Edmond Fuchs, Ingenieur Chef des mines." *Annales des Mines* 8, no. 17 (1890).
de Pouvourville, Albert. *Chasseur de Pirates!* Paris: Aux Éditeurs Associés, 1928.
Debao Xianzhi Bianxuan Weiyuan Hui 德保县志编选委员会 (Debao District Historical Research Committee), ed. *Debao Xianzhi* 德保县志 (Gazetteer of Debao). Nanning: Guangxi Renmin Chubanshe, 1998.
Devèria, Gabriel. *La frontière Sino-Annamite: Description géographique et ethnographique.* Paris: Libraire de la Société Asiatique, 1886.
Đinh Xuân Lâm. *Hoàng Hoa Thám và phong trào nông dân Yên-Thế.* Hà Nội: Nhà Xuất Bản Văn Hóa, 1958.
———. "Ý kiến trao đổi đánh giá Lưu Vĩnh Phúc cần thấy mặt tích cực là chủ yếu" (The evaluation of Liu Yongfu must pay attention to the facts above all else). *NCLS* 38 (1962): 52.
Đinh Xuân Lâm and Trương Hữu Quýnh, eds. *Từ điển nhân vật lịch sử Việt Nam* (Dictionary of Vietnamese historical figures). Hà Nội: Nhà Xuất Bản Giáo Dục, 2004.
Dikötter, Frank. "'Patient Zero': China and the Myth of the 'Opium Plague.'" Inaugural Lecture, School of Oriental and African Studies, University of London, 2003.

Đỗ Bang. *Kinh tế thương nghiệp Việt Nam dưới triều Nguyễn* (The Vietnamese commercial economy under the Nguyễn). Huế: Nhà Xuất Bản Thuận Hóa, 1996.

Đỗ Đức Hùng. *Vấn đề trị thủy ở Đồng Bằng Bắc Bộ dưới thời Nguyễn thế kỷ XIX* (Water management in the Red River Delta during the Nguyễn). Hà Nội: Nhà Xuất Bản Khoa Học Xã Hội, 1997.

Đỗ Văn Ninh, ed. *Từ điển chức quan Việt Nam* (Dictionary of Vietnamese official titles). Hà Nội: Nhà Xuạt Bản Thanh Niên, 2002.

du Caillaud, F. Romanet. *Histoire de l'intervention française au Tonkin de 1872 à 1874*. Paris: Challamel, 1880.

Du Qimo 都欺模, ed. *Feng Congbao (Zicai) jundu jiyao* 馮宮保子材軍牘集要 (Collected military correspondence of Feng Zicai). Taibei: Wenhai Chubanshe, 1988.

Duboc, Émile. *35 mois de campagne en Chine, au Tonkin Courbet-Rivière, 1882–1885*. Paris: Charavay, Mantaux & Martin. 1886.

Duiker, William J. *Sacred War: Nationalism and Revolution in a Divided Vietnam*. New York: McGraw-Hill, 1995.

———. *Vietnam Since the Fall of Saigon*. Athens: Ohio University Center for International Studies, 1989.

Dương Đình Lập. *Căn cứ địa trong phong trào Cần Vương chống Pháp, 1885–1896* (Base areas of the Cần Vương). Hà Nội: Nhà Xuất Bản Chính Trị Quốc Gia, 2004.

Dương Kinh Quốc. *Chính quyền thuộc địa ở Việt Nam trước Cách Mạng Tháng Tám 1945* (Colonial administration in Vietnam before the August Revolution). Hà Nội: Nhà Xuất Bản Khoa Học Xã Hội, 2005.

———. *Việt Nam: Những sự kiện lịch sử, 1858–1918* (Vietnam: Historical events). Hà Nội: Nhà Xuất Bản Giáo Dục, 2003.

Dupuis, Jean. *A Journey to Yunnan and the Opening of the Red River to Trade*. Translated by E. J. Tips. Bangkok: White Lotus Press, 1998.

———. *Les origins de la question du Tonkin*. Paris: Challamel, 1896.

———. *L'ouverture du Fleuve Rouge au commerce et les événements du Tong-Kin, 1872–1873*. Paris: Challamel, 1879.

———. *Le Tonkin de 1872 à 1886: Histoire et politique*. Paris: Challamel, 1910.

Dutton, George E., Jayne S. Werner, and John K. Whitmore, eds. *Sources of Vietnamese Tradition*. New York: Columbia University Press, 2012.

Eastman, Lloyd E. *Throne and Mandarins: China's Search for a Policy during the Sino-French Controversy, 1880–1885*. Cambridge, MA: Harvard University Press, 1967.

Échinard, Afred. *Histoire politique et militaire de la province de Thai-Nguyen*. Hà Nội: Imprimerie Trung Bac Tan Van, 1934.

Ezell, Edward Clinton, Thomas M. Pegg, and W. H. B. Smith. *Small Arms of the World: A Basic Manual of Small Arms*. Harrisburg, PA: Stackpole Press, 1983.

Fairbank, John K., ed. *The Chinese World Order: Traditional China's Foreign Relations*. Cambridge, MA: Harvard University Press, 1973.

Faulkner, William. *Collected Stories of William Faulkner*. NY: Vintage, 1976.

Faure, David, and Ho Ts'ui-p'ing, eds. *Chieftains into Ancestors: Imperial Expansion and Indigenous Society in Southwest China*. Vancouver: University of British Columbia Press, 2012.

Fay, Peter Ward. *The Opium War, 1840–1842*. Chapel Hill: University of North Carolina Press, 1975.

Forbes, Andrew. "The 'Cin-Ho' Caravan Trade." *JAS* 21, no. 1 (1987): 1–47.

Foucault, Michel. *Discipline and Punish: The Birth of the Prison*. Translated by Alan Sheridan. New York: Vintage, 1977.

Fourniau, Charles. *Annam-Tonkin 1885–1896: Lettrés et paysans vietnamiens face à la conquête coloniale*. Paris: Editions L'Harmattan, 1989.

———. *Domination coloniale et résistance nationale, 1858–1914*. Paris: Les Indes Savantes, 2002.

"France in the Far East: Past Events in Tonquin and the Situation There Now." *New York Times*, July 1, 1883.

Franchini, Philippe, and Jérôme Ghesquière, eds. *Des photographes en Indochine: Tonkin, Annam, Cochinchine, Cambodge, et Laos au XIXe Siècle*. Paris: Marval, Réunion des Musées Nationaux, 2001.

Franquet, Eugène. *De l'Importance du Fleuve Rouge comme voie de pénétration en Chine suivi d'une notice sur le Cercle de Lao-Kay*. Paris: Charles-Lavauzelle, 1896.

Fuchs, Edmond, and Eduard-Emile Saladin. "Mémoire sur l'exploration des gites de combustibles et quelques-uns des métallifères de l'Indo-Chine." *Annales des Mines* 2, no. 5 (1882): 185–87.

Gainsborough, Martin, ed. *On the Borders of State Power: Frontiers in the Greater Mekong Sub-Region*. London: Routledge, 2008.

Gallieni, Joseph-Simon. *Gallieni au Tonkin (1892–1896)*. Paris: Éditions Berger-Levrault, 1941.

Gaston, Astre. *La Vie de Benjamin Balansa: Botaniste, explorateur*. Toulouse: Douladore, 1947.

Gautier, Hippolyte. *Les français au Tonkin, 1787–1883*. Paris: Challamel, 1884.

Giersch, C. Patterson. *Asian Borderlands: The Transformation of Qing China's Yunnan Frontier*. Cambridge, MA: Harvard University Press, 2006.

Gildea, Robert. *France, 1870–1914*. London: Longman Publishers, 1996.

Giles, Herbert A. *A Chinese Biographical Dictionary*. London: Bernard Quartich, 1898.

Gong Yin 龔蔭. *Zhongguo Tusi Zhidu* 中國土司制度 (The Chinese tusi system). Kunming: Yunnan Minzu Chubanshe, 1992.

Gosselin, Charles. *L'Empire d'Annam*. Paris: Libraire Académique Didier, 1904.

Guangxi Minzu Xueyuan Minzu Yanjiu Shi, ed. *Zhuangzu lishi renwu zhuan* 壮族历史人物传 (Biographies of historical Zhuang figures). Nanning: Guangxi Renmin Chubanshe, 1982.

Guangxi Qinzhou Shizheng Ban Wenshi Ziliao He Xuexi Weiyuanhui, ed. *Qin-*

zhou wenshi 10: Minzu yingxiong Liu Yongfu, jinian wenju 钦州文史10: 民族英雄刘永富纪念文具 (Works on the history of Qinzhou, vol. 10: National hero Liu Yongfu, commemorative essays). Qinzhou: Qinzhou Shi Jiangdong Yinshua, 2003.[[Capitalize all parts of transliterated proper nouns.]]

Guangxi Shehui Kexue Yuan, ed. *Zhong Fa zhanzheng shi zhuanji* 中法战争史专集 (Compiled biographies from the Sino-French War). Nanning: Guangxi Shehui Kexue Yuan Chubanshe, 1986.

Guangxi Shehui Kexue Yuan Indu-Zhina Yanjiu Suo, ed. *Zhong Yue guanxi dashiji* 中越关系大事记 (Chronicle of the Sino-Vietnamese relationship). Washington, D.C.: Center for Chinese Research Materials, Association of Research Libraries, 1981.

Guangxi Zhuangzu Zizhiqu Tongzhiguan 广西壮族自治区通志馆, ed. *Zhong Fa zhanzheng diaocha ziliao shilu* 中法战争调查资料实录 (Shilu materials related to the Sino-French War). Nanning: Guangxi Renmin Chubanshe, 1982.

Guha, Ranajit. *Elementary Aspects of Peasant Insurgency in India.* Durham: Duke University Press, 1999.

Guy, R. Kent. *Qing Governors and Their Provinces: The Evolution of Territorial Administration in China, 1644–1796.* Seattle: University of Washington Press, 2010.

Hà Mai Phương. *Hoạt động của Bộ Công dưới đời Vua Tự-Đức qua các châu bản Nhà Nguyễn* (Activities of the Board of Works under the reign of Tự Đức as see through the Nguyễn archives). Sài Gòn: Tủ Sách Sử-Học Bộ Văn Hóa Giáo-Dục và Thanh Niên, 1974.

Hack, Karl, and Tobias Rettig, eds. *Colonial Armies in Southeast Asia.* London: Routledge, 2006.

Hanks, Jane Richardson, and Lucien Mason Hanks. *Tribes of the North Thailand Frontier.* New Haven: Yale University Southeast Asian Studies, 2001.

Hardoin, Georges (Dick de Lonlay). *Au Tonkin, 1883–1885: Récits anecdotiques.* Paris: Garnier Frères, 1886.

———. *Les Combats du Général de Négrier.* Paris: Garnier Frères, 1889.

Hardy, Andrew. *Red Hills: Migrants and the State in the Highlands of Vietnam.* Copenhagen: Nordic Institute of Asian Studies Press, 2003.

Harmand, Jules. "De Bassac à Hué: Avril–août 1877." *Bulletin de la Société de Géographie* (January 1879).

———. *Domination et colonisation.* Paris: E. Flammarion, 1910.

He Sikun 何嗣焜, ed. *Zhang Jingda Gong Shusheng* 張靖達宮樹聲 (Writings of Zhang Shusheng). Taibei: Wenhai chubanshe, 1966.

Hendrick, Daniel R. "The Tools of Imperialism: Technology and the Expansion of European Colonial Empires in the Nineteenth Century." *The Journal of Modern History* 51, no. 2 (June 1979): 231–63.

Hickey, Gerald. *Kingdom in the Morning Mist: Mayrena in the Highlands of Vietnam.* Philadelphia: University of Pennsylvania Press, 1988.

Hoàng Du Đồng and Hà Ngọc Xuyền, eds. *Minh Mệnh chính yếu* 明命政要, Vol. 1 (Important administrative records of the Minh Mạng Reign). Saigon: Tủ-Sách Cổ-Văn, 1972.

Hobsbawm, Eric. *Bandits*. London: Abacus, 2000.

Hội Đồng Lịch Sử Hà Bắc. *Lịch sử Hà Bắc* (History of Hà Bắc). Hà Bắc: Xi Nghiệp In Hà Bắc, 1986.

Huang Hai'an 黃海安. *Liu Yongfu Lishicao* 劉永福歷史草 (Toward a history of Liu Yongfu). Shanghai: Zhengzhong Shuju, 1936.

Hummel, Arthur W. *Eminent Chinese of the Ch'ing Period, 1644–1911*. Washington, D.C.: United States Government Printing Office, 1943.

"Jean Dupuis obituary." *The Geographical Journal* 41, no. 2 (February 1913): 174.

Jenks, Richard D. *Insurgency and Social Disorder in Guizhou: The 'Miao' Rebellion, 1854–1873*. Honolulu: University of Hawai'i Press, 1994.

Jennings, Eric T. *Imperial Heights: Dalat and the Making and Undoing of French Indochina*. Berkeley: University of California Press, 2011.

Jonsson, Hjorleifur. *Mien Relations: Mountain People and State Control in Thailand*. Ithaca: Cornell University Press, 2005.

———. *Slow Anthropology: Negotiating Difference with the Iu Mien*. Ithaca: Cornell SEAP Publications, 2014.

Katz, Paul R. *When Valleys Turned Blood Red: The Ta-pa-ni Incident in Colonial Taiwan*. Honolulu: University of Hawai'i Press, 2005.

Keith, Charles P. "A Vietnamese in Paris: Nguyen Trong Hiep and the Capital of the Nineteenth Century." Paper presented at AAS Annual Meeting, Philadelphia, 2010.

Kelley, Liam C. *Beyond the Bronze Pillars: Envoy Poetry and the Sino-Vietnamese Relationship*. Honolulu: University of Hawai'i Press, 2005.

Kerr, George H. *Formosa: Licensed Revolution and the Home Rule Movement, 1895–1945*. Honolulu: University of Hawai'i Press, 1974.

Khổng Đức Thiêm and Nguyễn Xuân Cần, eds. *Khởi nghĩa Yên Thế* (The Yên Thế Uprising). Hà Nội: Sở Văn Hóa Thông Tin Bắc Giang / Hội Khoa Học Lịch Sử Việt Nam, 1997.

Kiều Oánh Mậu. *Bản Triều bạn nghịch liệt truyện* 本朝叛逆列傳 (Tales of the court's fight against rebellion). Saigon: Bộ Quốc-Gia Giáo-Dục, 1963.

Kiều Oánh Mậu, Thiết Chi, and Trúc Khê. "Ai Sơn Hành" (Travels in the mountain passes). *Tạp Chí Tri Tân* 195 (July 1945): 1–2.

Kinney, Ann Behnke. *The Art of the Han Essay: Wang Fu's Ch'ien-Fu Lun*. Phoenix: Arizona State University Center for Asian Research, 1990.

Kuhn, Philip. *Rebellion and Its Enemies in Late Imperial China: Militarization and Social Structure, 1796–1864*. Cambridge, MA: Harvard University Press, 1970.

Laffey, Ella S. "French Adventurers and Chinese Bandits in Tonkin: The Garnier Affair in its Local Context," *JSEAS* 6:1 (March 1975): 38–51.

———. "In the Wake of the Taipings: Some Patterns of Local Revolt in Kwangsi

Province, 1850–1875." *Modern Asian Studies* 10, no. 1 (1976): 65–81.

———. "Relations between Chinese Provincial Officials and the Black Flag Army, 1883–1885." PhD diss., Cornell University, 1971.

Langlet, Philippe. *L'ancienne historiographie d'État au Vietnam, Tome I: Raisons d'être, conditions d'élaboration et caractères au siècle des Nguyễn*. Paris: École française d'Extrême-Orient, 1990.

Le Failler, Philippe. *La Rivière Noire: L'intégration d'une marche frontière au Vietnam*. Paris, EFEO, 2014.

———. *Monopolie et prohibition de l'opium en Indochine: Le pilori des chimères*. Paris: L'Harmattan, 2001.

Lê Nguyễn. *Xã hội Việt Nam thời Pháp Thuộc: Nhân Vật & Sự Kiện Lịch Sử* (Vietnamese society under French rule: Personalities and historical events). Hà Nội: Nhà Xuất Bản Văn Hóa Thông Tin, 2005.

Lê Thị Thanh Hòa. *Việc đào tạo và sử dụng quan lại của triều Nguyễn từ năm 1802 đến năm 1884* (The training and deployment of officials by the Nguyễn Court from 1802 to 1884). Hà Nội: Nhà Xuất Bản Khoa Học Xã Hội, 1998.

Lecomte, Jean-François-Alphonse. *Le guet-apens de Bac-Lé*. Paris, Nancy: Berger-Levrault, 1890.

Lee, Peter. *The Big Smoke: The Chinese Art and Craft of Opium*. Bangkok: Lamplight Books, 1999.

Leroy-Beaulieu, Anatole. *De la colonisation chez les peuples modernes*. Paris: Librairie Guillaumin, 1874.

———. *La Rénovation de l'Asie*. Paris: Librairie Guillaumin, 1901.

Lewis, Martin Deming. "One Hundred Million Frenchmen: The 'Assimilation' Theory in French Colonial Policy." *Comparative Studies in Society and History* 4, no. 2 (January 1962): 129–53.

Li Jian'er 李建兒. *Liu Yongfu Zhuan* 劉永福傳 (A biography of Liu Yongfu). Taibei: Shangwu Shuguan, 1957.

Liang Nian 梁年, ed. *Zhen'an Fuzhi* 鎮安府志 (Gazetteer of Zhen'an). Reprint, Taibei: Chengwen Chubanshe, 1967.

Liao Zonglin 廖宗麟. *Kang Fa mingjiang Liu Yongfu* 抗法名将刘永富 (Anti-French General Liu Yongfu). Nanning: Guangxi Renmin Chubanshe, 1991.

———, ed. *Qinzhou Wenshi (4): Minzu yingxiong Liu Yongfu wenju* 钦州文史(4) 民族英雄刘永富文具 (Historical works on Qinzhou, vol. 4: National hero Liu Yongfu). Qinzhou: Qinzhou Shi Jiangdong, 1997.

———. *Zhong Fa zhanzheng shi* 中法战争史 (History of the Sino-French War). Tianjin: Tianjin Guji Chubanshe, 2000.

Litzinger, Ralph A. *Other Chinas: The Yao and the Politics of National Belonging*. Durham: Duke University Press, 2000.

Lockhart, Bruce, and William J. Duiker, eds. *Historical Dictionary of Vietnam, 3rd edition*. Lanham, MD: Scarecrow Press, 2006.

Louvet, E. *Vie de Mgr Puginier: Évêque de Mauricastre, vicaire apolistic du Tonkin Occidental*. Hanoi: F. H. Schneider, 1894.

Love, Catherine E., ed. *Collins Italian-English Dictionary*. New York: Berkley Books, 1982.

"Lun Heiqijun Liuyi Yuenan zhi jie" 論黑旗軍劉義越南之捷 (On Liu Yongfu and the Black Flag's victory in Vietnam). *Shenbao* Guangxu 9/5/5.

Lyautey, Louis Hubert Gonzalve. *Lettres du Tonkin et de Madagascar, 1894–1899*. Paris: Librarie Armand Colin, 1920.

Mai Quốc Liên, ed. *Nguyễn Trãi toàn tập tân biên, tập II* (New edition of Nguyễn Trãi's Collected Works, vol. 2). Hà Nội: Nhà Xuất Bản Văn Học, 2001.

Maliverney, E., ed. *L'homme du jour: Le De Tham*. Hanoi: Imprimerie de l'Avenir du Tonkin, 1909.

Marr, David G., ed. *Reflections from Captivity: Phan Boi Chau's Prison Notes and Ho Chi Minh's Prison Diary*. Translated by Christopher Jenkins, Tran Khanh Tuyet, and Huynh Sanh Thong. Athens: Ohio University Press, 1978.

———. *Vietnamese Anticolonialism, 1885–1925*. Berkeley: University of California Press, 1971.

Masson, André, ed. *Correspondance politique du Commandant Rivière au Tonkin, avril 1882–mai 1883*. Hà Nội: Le-Van-Tan, 1933.

McLeod, Mark. *The Vietnamese Response to the French Intervention, 1862–1874*. New York: Praeger, 1991.

Meisner, Maurice. *The Deng Xiaoping Era: An Inquiry into the Fate of Chinese Socialism, 1979–1994*. New York: Hill and Wang, 1996.

Mesney, William. *Tungking*. London: Sampson Low, Marston, Searle and Rivington, 1884.

Michael, Franz. *The Taiping Rebellion*. Seattle: University of Washington Press, 1972.

Michaud, Jean. *"Incidental Ethnographers": French Catholic Missions on the Tonkin-Yunnan Frontier, 1888–1930*. Leiden: Brill, 2007.

Millot, Ernest. *Le Tonkin: Son commerce et sa mise en exploration*. Paris: Challamel, 1888.

Ministère des Affaires Étrangères. *Documents diplomatiques: Affaires de Chine et du Tonkin, 1884–1885*. Paris: Imprimerie Nationale, 1885.

Mitter, Rana. "Behind the Scenes at the Museum: Nationalism, History and Memory in the Beijing War of Resistance Museum, 1987–1997." *China Quarterly* 161 (March 2000): 279–85.

Miyoshi, Masao, and H. D. Harootunian, eds. *Japan and the World*. Durham: Duke University Press, 1993.

Mo Naiqun 莫乃群, ed. *Guangxi lishi renwu zhuan* 广西历史人物传 (Historical biographies from Guangxi). Nanning: Guangxi difangzhi yanjiu xiebianyin, 1984.

Moertono, Soemarsaid. *State and Statecraft in Old Java: A Study of the Later Mataram Period*. Ithaca: Modern Indonesia Project/SEAP, 1963.

Mossman, Samuel, ed. *General Charles Gordon's Private Diary of his Exploits in China*. New York: Kraus Reprint Company, 1971.

Mote, Frederick W. *Imperial China: 900–1800*. Cambridge, MA: Harvard University Press, 1999.
Mourin. *Notice sur Lao Kay*. Hà Nội: 1911.
Mullaney, Thomas. *Coming to Terms with the Nation: Ethnic Classification in Modern China*. Berkeley: University of California Press, 2011.
Munholland, Kim. "Admiral Jaureguiberry and the French Scramble for Tonkin, 1879–1883." *French Historical Studies* 11, no. 1 (Spring 1979): 81–107.
Munier, Paul. *Le Cai Kinh: Homme et contrée*. Hanoi: Cahiers de la Société Géographique de Hanoi, 1934.
Neïss, P. *The Sino-Vietnamese Border Demarcation, 1885–1887*. Translated by Walter E. J. Tips. Bangkok: White Lotus Press, 1998.
Ngô Đức Thọ, ed. *Các nhà khoa bằng Việt Nam, 1075–1919* (Vietnamese degree holders, 1075–1919). Hà Nội: Nhà Xuất Bản Văn Học, 1993.
Ngô Đức Thọ, Nguyễn Văn Nguyên, and Philippe Papin, eds. *Đồng Khánh địa dư chí* 同慶地輿志 (Imperial geography of the Đồng Khánh reign). Hà Nội: Nhà Xuất Bản Thế Giới, 2003.
Nguyễn Đắc Xuân, ed. *Chuyện ba Vua Dục Đức Thành Thái Duy Tân* (A tale of three kings: Dục Đức, Thành Thái, Duy Tân). Huế: Nhà Xuất Bản Thuận Hóa, 1998.
Nguyễn Huệ Chi, ed. *Nguyễn Quang Bích: Nhà yêu nước, nhà thơ* (Nguyễn Qiang Bích: Poet, patriot). Hà Nội: Nhà Xuất Bản Khoa Học Xã Hội, 1993.
Nguyễn Khắc Viện. *The Long Resistance, 1858–1975*. Hà Nội: Foreign Languages Publishing House, 1975.
———. *Việt Nam: A Long History*. Hà Nội: Thế Giới Publishers, 2004.
Nguyễn Sĩ Hải. "Tổ chức chính quyền Trung Ương thời Nguyễn-Sơ 1802–1847" (The central administration of the Nguyễn). PhD diss., Luật Đại Học Đường Sài Gòn, 1962.
Nguyễn Thị Hồng Vân, ed. *Phong trào đông du và Phan Bội Châu* (The Đông Du Movement and Phan Bội Châu). Vinh: Nhà Xuất Bản Nghệ An, 2005.
Nguyễn Tú. *Hoàng Kế Viêm*. Đồng Hới: Sở Văn Hóa Quảng Bình, 1992.
Nguyễn Văn Bân. *Á-Đông luân-lý* 亞東倫理 (The East Asian ethos). Hà Nội: Imprimerie Francaise, 1931.
———. *Giặc Cờ Đen: Một ông cụ già 90 tuổi kể chuyện* (Black Flag bandits: Stories told by a man of ninety). Hà Nội: Trung-Bắc Thư-Xã, 1941.
Nguyễn Văn Huyền. *Bùi Văn Dị: Nhà thơ yêu nước thế kỷ XIX* (Bùi Văn Dị: Patriotic poet of the nineteenth century). Hà Nội: Hội Khoa Học Lịch Sử Việt Nam, 1995.
Nguyễn Văn Kiệm. *Phong trào nông dân Yên Thế chống thực dân Pháp xâm lược, 1884–1913*. Hà Nội: Nhà Xuất Bản Đại Học Quốc Gia, 2001.
Nguyễn Viết Kế. *Kể chuyện các đời Vua Nhà Nguyễn* (Stories of the Nguyễn rulers). Đà Nẵng: Nhà Xuất Bản Đà Nẵng, 2001.
Nguyễn Xuân Thọ. "Vụ cướp phá hoàng cung cuộc để kháng của Vua Hàm Nghi và Triều Đồng Khánh" (The theft of the imperial throne by Hàm Nghi and the Court of Đồng Khánh). *Sử Địa* 14, no. 4 (1969): 3–46.

Nhóm Nghiên Cứu Sử Địa Việt Nam, ed. *Quốc triều chánh biên* (Court history). Saigon: Tủ Sách Tài Liệu Sử, 1972.
"Những nhận định khác nhau về vai trò của Lưu Vĩnh Phúc và Quân Cờ Đen" (Some differing impressions about the role of Liu Yongfu and the Black Flag Army). *NCLS* 38 (1962): 8–22.
Norman, C. B. *Tonkin or France in the Far East.* London: Chapman and Hall, 1884.
North, Douglass, John Wallis, and Barry Weingast, eds. *Violence and Social Orders: A Conceptual Framework of Interpreting Recorded Human History.* Cambridge: Cambridge University Press, 2009.
Osborne, Milton. "Francis Garnier (1839–1873), Explorer of the Mekong River." In *Explorers of South-East Asia: Six Lives*, edited by V. T. King, 51–107. Kuala Lumpur: Oxford University Press, 1995.
———. *River Road to China: The Mekong River Expedition, 1866–1873.* NY: Atlantic Monthly Press, 1999.
Ouyang 歐陽, ed. *Liu Zhongcheng gong kunyi xuanji* 劉忠誠公坤一遺集 (Select correspondence from Liu Kunyi). Taibei: Wenhai Chubanshe, 1968.
Pang Zuichun 庞醉春. *Qinzhou shi zhi* 钦州市志 (A municipal history of Qinzhou). Nanning: Guangxi renmin chubanshe, 1994.
Pasquet, Sylvie. *'L'évolution du système postal: La province Chinoise du Yunnan à l'époque Qing: 1644–1911.* Paris: Diffusion de Boccard, 1986.
Pelley, Patricia M. *Postcolonial Vietnam: New Histories of the National Past.* Durham: Duke University Press, 2002.
Phạm Quí Trầm, trans. "Vọng Sơn niên phổ" (Vọng Sơn's biography). *Tập San Sử Đị* 2 (1969): 70.
Phan Bội Châu. *Chân tướng quân, tái sinh sinh.* Translated by Chương Thâu. Hà Nội: Nhà Xuất Bản Văn Học, 1967.
Phan Huy Lê. "Tình hình khai mỏ dưới triều Nguyễn" (Mining under the Nguyễn). *NCLS* 51 (June 1963): 40–49.
Phan Huy Lê, Chu Thiên, Vương Hoàng Tuyên, Đinh Xuân Lâm. *Lịch sử chế độ phong kiến Việt-Nam: Tập III* (History of the Vietnamese feudal system, vol. 3). Hà-Nội: Nhà Xuất Bản Giáo Dục, 1960.
Phan Ngọc Liên, Đỗ Thanh Bình, and Nguyễn Ngọc Cơ, eds. *Lịch sử Nhà Nguyễn: Một cách tiếp cận mới* (Nguyễn history: A new perspective). Hà Nội: Nhà Xuất Bản Đại Học Sư Phạm, 2005.
Phan Trần Chúc. *Nguyễn Tri Phương truyện ký* (Nguyễn Tri Phương's diary). Hà Nội: Nhà Xuất Bản Quốc Văn, 1945. Reprinted Nhà Xuất Bản Văn Hóa Thông Tin, 2001.
Poisson, Emmanuel. *Mandarins et subalterns au nord du Viet Nam: Une bureaucratie à l'épreuve, 1820–1918.* Paris: Maisonneuve & Larose, 2004.
Power, Thomas F. *Jules Ferry and the Renaissance of French Imperialism.* New York: King's Crown Press, 1944.
Pradon, Léopolde. "Edouard Émile Saladin (1856–1917)." *Bulletin de l'Association*

amicale des anciens élèves de l'École des Mines de Paris (November-December 1917).
"Proceedings of Foreign Societies." *Proceedings of the Royal Geographical Society and Monthly Record of Geography* 4, no. 6 (May 5, 1882): 383–87.
Qian Shifu 钱实甫, ed. *Qingdai zhiguan nianbiao* 清代职官年表 (An analytical table of Qing administrative appointments). Beijing: Zhonghua shuju, 1980.
Qinzhou Xianzhi Bangongshi, ed. *Qinzhou lishi mingren zhuanluo xuanbian* 钦州历史名人传落选边 (Biographical sketches of notable people in Qinzhou history). Qinzhou: Qinzhou Xianzhi Bianxie Bangongshi, 1983.
Rankin, Mart Backus. "'Public Opinion' and Political Power: Qingyi in Late 19th-Century China." *JAS* 41, no. 3 (May 1982): 453–84.
Rapin, Ami-Jacques, and Jason Eligh. *Ethnic Minorities, Drug Use, and Harm in the Highlands of Northern Vietnam: A Contextual Analysis of the Situation in Six Communes from Son La, Lai Chau, and Lao Cai.* Hà Nội: Thế Giới Publishing House, 2003.
Reid, Anthony, ed. *The Last Stand of Asian Autonomies: Responses to Modernity in the Diverse States of Southeast Asia and Korea, 1750–1900*. New York: St. Martin's, 1997.
Rowe, William. *Hankow: Commerce and Society in a Chinese City, 1796–1889*. Stanford: Stanford University Press, 1984.
Sahlins, Peter. *Boundaries: The Making of France and Spain in the Pyrenees*. Berkeley: University of California Press, 1989.
Said, Edward. *Culture and Imperialism*. New York: Vintage, 1994.
Salemink, Oscar. *The Ethnography of Vietnam's Central Highlanders: A Historical Contextualization, 1850–1900*. London: RoutledgeCurzon, 2003.
Salkin-Laparra, Geneviève. *Le triple destin de Jules Harmand: Médecin, explorateur, diplomate.* Paris: Economica, 1992.
Schmidt, Martin. *Alexandre Ribot: Odyssey of a Liberal in the Third Republic*. The Hague: Martinus Nijhoff, 1974.
Scott, James C. *The Art of Not Being Governed: An Anarchist History of Upland Southeast Asia*. New Haven: Yale University Press, 2009.
———. *Domination and the Arts of Resistance: Hidden Transcripts*. New Haven: Yale University Press, 1990.
———. *Seeing Like a State: How Certain Schemes to Improve the Human Condition Have Failed.* New Haven: Yale University Press, 1998.
Scott, Sir James. *France and Tongking: A Narrative of the Campaign of 1884 and the Occupation of Further India.* London: T. Fisher Urwin, 1885.
Shan, Patrick Fuliang. "Insecurity, Outlawry, and Social Order: Banditry in China's Heilongjiang Frontier Region, 1900–1931." *Journal of Social History* 40, no. 1 (Autumn 2006): 25–54.
Shao Xunzheng 邵循正. *Zhong Fa Yuenan guanxi shimo* 中法越南关系始末 (The beginning and end of the relationship between China, France, and Vietnam). Hubei: Hubei Jiaoyu Chubanshe, 2000.

Shin, Leo K. "The Last Campaigns of Wang Yangming," *T'oung Pao* 92, no. 1/3 (2006): 101–28.
"Shu Heiqijun Liu Yi xi wen hou" 書黑旗軍劉義檄文後 (Liu Yongfu of the Black Flags answers the call). *Shenbao* Guangxu 9/4/6.
Smith, Kent Clarke. "Ch'ing Policy and the Development of Southwest China: Aspects of Ortai's Governor-Generalship, 1726–1731." PhD diss., Yale University, 1970.
Sogny, L. "Les familles illustres de l'Annam: S.E. Nguyễn Hữu Độ." *BAVH* (1924).
"Souvenirs d'un troupier, la prise de Hué." *BAVH* (1943): 237–47.
Spector, Stanley. *Li Hung-chang and the Huai Army: A Study in Nineteenth-Century Chinese Regionalism.* Seattle: University of Washington Press, 1964.
Staunton, Sidney A. *The War in Tong-King: Why the French Are in Tong-King and What They Are Doing There.* Boston: Cupples, Upham, 1884.
Taboulet, Georges. *La geste française en Indochine: Histoire par les textes de la France en Indochine des origines à 1914: Tôme I.* Paris: Adrien-Maisonneuve, 1955.
Tai Heping 泰和平. "Qingdai Daoguang nianjian Yunnan de jinyan wenti ji jinyan shibai zhengjie de fenxi" 清代道光年间云南的禁烟失败症结的分析 (An analysis of drug prohibition and its failure in Yunnan during the Daoguang reign of the Qing dynasty). *Zhongguo bianjiang shi di yanjiu* (Historical and geographical research on China's frontiers) 4 (1996): 59–63.
Tang Jingsong 唐景崧. *Qing ying riji* 請纓日記 (A volunteer's diary). Reprinted in *Zhong Fa zhanzheng* (Documents from the Sino-French War), edited by Zhong Fa zhanzheng shi yanjiu hui, 41–229. Shanghai: Shanghai Renmin Chubanshe, 1972.
Tang Jiong 唐炯. *Chengshan laoren ziji nianpu* 成山老人自己年譜 (An old man's biography). Taibei: Wenhai Chubanshe, 1966. Reprint of 1909 posthumous edition.
Taylor, Keith W. "On Being Muonged." *Asian Ethnicity* 2, no. 1 (2001): 30.
———. "Review of Liam C. Kelley, *Beyond the Bronze Pillars: Envoy Poetry and the Sino-Vietnamese Relationship*." *JSEAS* 37, no. 2 (June 2006): 364–65.
———. "Surface Orientations in Vietnam: Beyond Histories of Nation and Region." *JAS* 57, no. 4 (November 1998): 949–78.
Thái Hồng. *Nguyễn Tri Phương (1800–1873).* Thành Phố Hồ Chí Minh: Nhà Xuất Bản Đại Học Quốc Gia TP-HCM, 2001.
Thévenot, Arsène. *Ernest Millot: Négociant, Explorateur, et Conférencier, 1836–1891.* Arcis-sur-Aube: Léon Frémont, 1892.
Tô Minh Trung. "Ý kiến trao đổi: mấy ý kiến đánh giá vai trò Lưu Vĩnh Phúc trong cuộc kháng Pháp của nhân dân Việt-Nam" (Some thoughts on evaluating Liu Yongfu's role in the Vietnamese people's resistance to France). *NCLS* 38 (1962): 31–34.
Tomba, Massimiliano. "Another Kind of *Gewalt*: Beyond Law, Re-Reading Walter Benjamin." *Historical Materialism* 17 (2009): 126–44.

Took, Jennifer. *A Native Chieftaincy in Southwest China: Franchising a Tai Chieftaincy under the Tusi System of Late Imperial China*. Leiden: Brill, 2005.

Tran, My-Van. "Japan through Vietnamese Eyes (1905–1945)." *JSEAS* 30, no. 1 (March 1999): 126–46.

Trần Đình Việt, ed. *Nguyễn Phan Quang: Theo dòng lịch sử dân tộc, sự kiện và tư liệu* (On the trail of ethnohistory: Events and materials). Thành Phố Hồ Chí Minh: Nhà Xuất Bản Tổng Hợp TP.HCM, 2004.

Trần Thị Vinh. "Thể chế chính trị thời Nguyễn dưới Triều Gia Long và Minh Mệnh" (Political institutions of the Nguyễn under the courts of Gia Long and Minh Mạng). *NCLS* 6 (2002): 8–11.

Trần Trọng Kim. *Việt Nam sử lược* (An outline of Vietnamese history). Hà Nội: Nhà Xuất Bản Văn Hóa Thông Tin, 1999.

Trần Văn Giáp. *Lưu Vĩnh Phúc: Tướng Cờ Đen (một quân nhân Thái Bình Thiên Quốc kháng Pháp trên đất Việt-Nam)* (Liu Yongfu: Black Flag general, being the story of a Taiping soldier fighting France in Vietnam). Hà-Nội: Nhà Xuất Bản Sông Lô, 1958.

Trần Văn Giàu. *Chống xâm lăng: Lịch sử Việt-Nam từ 1858 đến 1898*. (Resistance: Vietnamese history from 1858 to 1898). Hà Nội: Xây Dựng, 1956.

"Très véridique histoire de bombardement de Thuan-an et des préliminaires de paix signés le 25 auot 1883, qui en furent la suite." *La Revue Indochinoise* 1, nos. 1–2 (1921): 83.

Tretiak, Daniel. "China's Vietnam War and Its Consequences." *The China Quarterly* 80 (December 1979): 740–67.

Trung Tâm Bảo Tồn Di Tích Cổ Đô Huế, ed. *Tuyển tập những bài nghiên cứu về Triều Nguyễn* (Compilation of essays on the Nguyễn court). Huế: Sở Khoa Học Công Nghệ và Môi Trường Thừa Thiên-Huế, 2002.

Trương-Bá-Phát. "Bọn Cờ Đen hạ sát Francis Garnier" (Black Flag ruffians killed Francis Garnier). *SĐ* 25 (1973): 110–25.

Tủ Sách Lịch Sử và Văn Hóa, ed. *Tạp Chí Tri Tân, 1941–1946: Các bài Viết về lịch sử và văn hóa Việt Nam* (The Journal Tri Tân: Writings on Vietnamese history and culture). Hà Nội: Trung Tâm Unesco Thông Tin Tư Liệu Lịch Sử và Văn Hóa Việt Nam, 2000.

Tuck, Patrick J. N. *French Catholic Missionaries and the Politics of Imperialism in Vietnam, 1857–1914: A Documentary Survey*. Liverpool: Liverpool University Press, 1987.

"Ủy Ban Nhân Dân tỉnh Lạng Sơn" (Lạng Sơn provincial people's committee) decision #41/2002/QĐUB, published October 2, 2002.

"Ủy Ban Tư Liệu Văn Sử Hội Nghị Hiệp Thương Chính Trị huyện Hà Khẩu" (Historical Materials Committee of Hekou). In *Tư liệu văn sử Hà Khẩu, tập II* (Materials on the History of Hekou, vol. 2). 1993.

Văn Tân. "Lưu Vĩnh Phúc Tướng Cờ Đen và các hành động của ông ở Việt Nam" (The Black Flag general Liu Yongfu and his activities in Vietnam). *NCLS* 34 (1962): 7–15.

Văn-Quang. *Hoàng-Hoa-Thám: Bài học xương máu của 25 năm đấu-tranh* (Hoàng Hoa Thám: A visceral lesson from a 25-year struggle). Saigon: Nhà Xuất Bản Sống-Mới, 1957.

Vansina, Jan. *Oral Tradition as History*. Madison: University of Wisconsin Press, 1985.

Vialatel, Jean. *Francis Garnier (1839–1873): Sa vie d'après ses lettres et ses écrits, un théoricien et un acteur de la pénétration française en Extrême-Orient*. Metz: Etudes Orientales Olizane, 1997.

Viện Sử Học, ed. *Đại Nam thực lục chính biên* (Veritable records of Đại Nam). 37 vols. Hà Nội: Nhà Xuất Bản Khoa Học Xã Hội, 1976.

———, ed. *Khâm Định Đại Nam Hội Điển Sự Lệ* (Collected statutes of the Nguyễn dynasty). 15 vols. Huế: Nhà Xuất Bản Thuận Hóa, 1993.

Vinh Sinh, ed. *Phan Bội Châu and the Dông-Du Movement*. New Haven: Yale Center for International and Area Studies, 1988.

Vinh Sinh and Nicholas Wickenden, eds. and trans. *Overturned Chariot: The Autobiography of Phan Boi Chau*. Honolulu: University of Hawai'i Press, 1999.

Võ, Đức Hạnh Etienne. *La place du catholicisme dans les relations entre la France et le Việt-Nam de 1870 à 1886: Tome I, Texte*. Berne: Peter Lang, 1992.

Võ Văn Kiệt, ed. *Lê Văn Duyệt với vùng đất Nam Bộ* (Lê Văn Duyệt and the south). Thành Phố Hồ Chí Minh: Tạp Chí Xưa và Nay/Nhà Xuất Bản Văn Hóa Sài Gòn, 2006.

Vũ Đường Luân. "The Politics of Frontier Mining: Local Chieftains, Chinese Miners, and Upland Society in the Nông Văn Vân Uprising in the Sino-Vietnamese Border Area, 1833–1835." *Cross-Currents: East Asian History and Culture Review* 3, no. 2 (November 2014): 349–78.

Vũ Huy Phúc, Phạm Quang Trung, and Nguyễn Ngọc Cơ eds. *Lịch sử Việt Nam, 1858–1896*. Hà Nội: Nhà Xuất Bản Khoa Học Xã Hội, 2003.

Vũ Ngọc Khánh. *Thị Xã Lạng Sơn xưa và nay* (Lạng Sơn Town: Yesterday and today). Lạng Sơn: Uỷ Ban Nhân Dân Thị Xã Lạng Sơn, 1990.

Vũ Phạm Hoàng. "Những nhận định khác nhau về vai trò của Lưu Vĩnh Phúc và Quân Cờ Đen" (Some differing impressions on the role of Liu Yongfu and the Black Flag Army). *NCLS* 38 (1962): 8–22.

Wakeman, Frederic, and Carolyn Grant, eds. *Conflict and Control in Late Imperial China*. Berkeley: University of California Press, 1975.

Walsh, Warren. "The Yunnan Myth." *The Far Eastern Quarterly* 2, no. 3 (May 1943): 272–85.

Weber, Max. "Politics as Vocation." In *From Max Weber: Essays in Sociology*, edited by H. H. Gerth and C. Wright Mills. New York: Oxford University Press, 1946.

———. *The Theory of Social and Economic Organization*. New York: Free Press, 1964.

Werner, Jayne S., and Luu Doan Huynh, eds. *The Vietnam War: Vietnamese and American Perspectives*. New York: ME Sharpe, 1993.

Whitmore, John, and James Anderson, eds. *Expanding China: Two Millennia of Encounters on the South and Southwest*. Leiden: Brill, 2014.

Wickberg, Edgar, ed. *Historical Interaction of China and Vietnam: Institutional and Cultural Themes (International Studies, East Asian Series Research Publication #4)*. New York: Paragon Book Gallery, 1969.

Winichakul, Thongchai. *Siam Mapped: A History of the Geo-Body of a Nation*. Honolulu: University of Hawai'i Press, 1994.

Wong Chi Keung. "The Black Flags: A Study of Their Emergence and Their Confrontation with the France in Tonkin, 1865–1885." Master's thesis, University of Hong Kong. 1972.

Woodside, Alexander B. *Vietnam and the Chinese Model: A Comparative Study of Vietnamese and Chinese Government in the First Half of the Nineteenth Century*. Cambridge, MA: Harvard University Press, 1987.

Wright, Mary C. *The T'ung Chih Restoration: The Last Stand of Chinese Conservatism*. Stanford: Stanford University Press, 1962.

Xiao Dehao 萧德浩 and Cai Zhongwu 菜中武. *Su Yuanchun pingzhuan* 苏元春评传 (A critical biography of Su Yuanchun). Nanning: Guangxi Renmin Chubanshe, 1990.

Xiao Dehao 萧德浩 and Huang Zheng 黄铮, eds. *Zhong Yue bianjie lishi ziliao xuanbian* 中越边界历史资料选编 (Selected material on the China-Vietnam border). Beijing: Shehui Kexue Wenxian Chubanshe, 1993.

Xiong Chunyun 熊春云. "Qing mo Gui Xi nan diqu de yimin shibian" 清末貴西南地區的移民事變 (Incidents of migration into the southern areas of Guangxi and Guizhou during the late Qing.) *Zhongguo Bianjiang shi di yanjiu* 14, no. 1 (2004): 83–87.

Xu Yanxu 徐延旭 . *Yuenan jiluo* 越南輯略 (A sketch of Vietnam). Wuzhou: Mengxia Kanyu, Guangxu 2 (1876).

Yang Wanxiu 杨万秀. *Liu Yongfu Pingzhuan* 刘永福评传 (A critical biography of Liu Yongfu). Lanzhou: Henan Jiaoyu Chubanshe, 1985.

Yoshiharu Tsuboi. *L'empire Vietnamienne face à la France et à la Chine*. Paris: L'Harmattan, 1987.

Young, Marilyn B. *The Vietnam Wars, 1945–1990*. New York: Harper Collins, 1991.

Yunnan Sheng Lishi Yanjiu Suo 云南省历史研究所, ed. *Qing Shilu: Yuenan Miandian Taiguo Laowo shiliao diaocha* 清实录: 越南缅甸泰国老挝史料调查 (Veritable records of the Qing: Materials related to Vietnam, Burma, Thailand, and Laos). Kumning: Yunnan Renmin Chubanshe, 1985.

Zhang Shiming 张世明 and Gong Shengquan 龚胜泉. "Bianjiang—ci zai shijie zhuyao faxi zhong de jingxiang: Yige yuyuanxue jiaodu de kaocha" 边疆 - 词在世界主要法系中的镜像: 一个语源学角度的考察 (Frontier—A word mirrored in the main legal systems of the world: An etymological investigation). *Zhongguo Bianjiang shi di yanjiu* 14, no. 2, (2004): 1–11.

Zhang Yushu 張玉書, ed. *Kangxi zidian* 康熙字典 (Kangxi dictionary). Beijing: Zhonghua Shuju edition, 2001.

Zhao Erxun 趙爾巽, ed. *Qing shi gao* 清史稿 (Historical study of the Qing). Beijing: Zhonghua Shuju, 1998.

Zhong Fa Zhanzheng Shi Yanjiu Hui 中法战争史研究会, ed. *Zhong Fa zhanzheng lunwen ji di yi ji* 中法战争论文集第一集 (Collected essays on the Sino-French War, vol. 1). Nanning: Guangxi Renmin Chubanshe, 1986.

———. *Zhong Fa zhanzheng lunwen ji di er ji* 中法战争论文集第二集 (Collected essays on the history of the Sino-French War, vol. 2). Nanning: Guangxi Renmin Chubanshe, 1986.

———. *Zhong Fa zhanzheng shi lunwen ji di san ji* 中法战争史论文集第三集 (Collected historical essays on the Sino-French War, vol. 3). Nanning: Guangxi Renmin Chubanshe, 1988.

———. *Zhong Fa zhanzheng shi lunwen ji di si ji* 中法战争史论文集第四集 (Collected historical essays on the Sino-French War, vol. 4). Nanning: Guangxi Renmin Chubanshe, 1992.

Zhongguo Diyi Lishi Dang'an Guan 中国第一历史档案馆. *Guangxu chao zhupi zouzhe* 光緒朝硃批奏摺 (Palace memorials of the Guangxu court). Beijing: Zhonghua Publishers, 1995–1996.

Zhongyang Yanjiuyuan Jindaishi Yanjiu Suo 中央研究院近代史研究所 (Academica Sinica modern history research office). *Zhong Fa Yuenan Jiaoshe Dang* 中法越南交涉當 (Materials related to China, France, and Vietnam). Taibei: Academica Sinica, 1962.

INDEX

CRITICAL DIALOGUES IN SOUTHEAST ASIAN STUDIES

This series offers perspectives in Southeast Asian Studies that stem from reconsideration of the relationships among scholars, texts, archives, field sites, and subject matter. Volumes in the series feature inquiries into historiography, critical ethnography, colonialism and postcolonialism, nationalism and ethnicity, gender and sexuality, science and technology, politics and society, and literature, drama, and film. A common vision of the series is a belief that area studies scholarship sheds light on shifting contexts and contests over forms of knowing and modes of action that inform cultural politics and shape histories of modernity.

Imagined Ancestries of Vietnamese Communism: Ton Duc Thang and the Politics of History and Memory, by Christoph Giebel

Beginning to Remember: The Past in the Indonesian Present, edited by Mary S. Zurbuchen

Seditious Histories: Contesting Thai and Southeast Asian Pasts, by Craig J. Reynolds

Knowing Southeast Asian Subjects, edited by Laurie J. Sears

Making Fields of Merit: Buddhist Female Ascetics and Gendered Orders in Thailand, by Monica Lindberg Falk

Love, Passion and Patriotism: Sexuality and the Philippine Propaganda Movement, 1882–1892, by Raquel A. G. Reyes

Gathering Leaves and Lifting Words: Histories of Buddhist Monastic Education in Laos and Thailand, by Justin Thomas McDaniel

The Ironies of Freedom: Sex, Culture, and Neoliberal Governance in Vietnam, by Thu-hương Nguyễn-võ

Submitting to God: Women and Islam in Urban Malaysia, by Sylva Frisk

No Concessions: The Life of Yap Thiam Hien, Indonesian Human Rights Lawyer, by Daniel S. Lev

The Buddha on Mecca's Verandah: Encounters, Mobilities, and Histories along the Malaysian-Thai Border, by Irving Chan Johnson

Dreaming of Money in Ho Chi Minh City, by Allison Truitt

Mapping Chinese Rangoon: Place and Nation among the Sino-Burmese, by Jayde Lin Roberts

The New Way: Protestantism and the Hmong in Vietnam, by Tâm T. T. Ngô

Imperial Bandits: Outlaws and Rebels in the China-Vietnam Borderlands, by Bradley Camp Davis

CPSIA information can be obtained
at www.ICGtesting.com
Printed in the USA
BVOW03*1253050717
488147BV00002B/2/P

9 780295 742045